Integration of Cloud Computing with Internet of Things

Scrivener Publishing
100 Cummings Center, Suite 541J
Beverly, MA 01915-6106

Publishers at Scrivener
Martin Scrivener (martin@scrivenerpublishing.com)
Phillip Carmical (pcarmical@scrivenerpublishing.com)

Integration of Cloud Computing with Internet of Things

Foundations, Analytics, and Applications

Edited by

**Monika Mangla, Suneeta Satpathy,
Bhagirathi Nayak and Sachi Nandan Mohanty**

Scrivener
Publishing

WILEY

This edition first published 2021 by John Wiley & Sons, Inc., 111 River Street, Hoboken, NJ 07030, USA and Scrivener Publishing LLC, 100 Cummings Center, Suite 541J, Beverly, MA 01915, USA
© 2021 Scrivener Publishing LLC
For more information about Scrivener publications please visit www.scrivenerpublishing.com.

Wiley Global Headquarters
111 River Street, Hoboken, NJ 07030, USA

For details of our global editorial offices, customer services, and more information about Wiley products visit us at www. wiley.com.

Limit of Liability/Disclaimer of Warranty

Library of Congress Cataloging-in-Publication Data

ISBN 978-1-119-76887-6

Cover image: Pixabay.Com
Cover design by Russell Richardson

Set in size of 11pt and Minion Pro by Manila Typesetting Company, Makati, Philippines

Contents

Preface

Advancements in digital technology have brought about revolutionary changes to our lives. These changes are enabled by interconnected devices driven by the Internet of Things (IoT) and Cloud computing, which allow resource sharing on platforms for storage, management and further analysis. The IoT is a novel computing platform that has virtually interconnected a variety of physical objects, empowering them to interchange data and services with less human interaction. Such technology is thought to fuse the physical world with the digital world. On that note, cloud computing is promising for its off-loading storage as well as third party computing capability, which seem to grow exponentially. So, on one hand the ubiquitous smart devices and gadgets have become the foremost aspect of computing and on the other hand the integration of cloud computing with the IoT has amended the computing scheme. The assimilation of cloud computing with IoT, also known as Cloud-IoT, has proven potential for enhancement of the quality of human life and the efficient utilization of resources for smart homes, cities, education, healthcare, banking, industry and grids among others. Moreover, Cloud-IoT technology also benefits from the competence of big data and its analytical facilities.

So, its encroachment upon our lives due to the explosion of such technology and the increasing use of smart devices enabling autosensing, communication, activation and classification capabilities, have enabled the integration of the IoT with cloud computing, which in turn has increased the number of research topics in different fields. Along with these two technologies, Fog computing has also gained popularity in the field of smart cities, smart transportation, smart grids, manufacturing and healthcare, improving the availability of information storage, computation capability as well as networking services between machines and data centers.

With the above facts in mind, the main purpose of this book is to present a detailed overview of the state-of-the-art in Cloud-IoT and its foundations, analytics and applications, as well as to address various security and privacy challenges facing the use of this technology. Our key intention is to discover potential research directions and provide a reference for researchers, students and practitioners in areas relating to the IoT, cloud computing and fog computing; and smooth the way towards progress in the field by providing insight into the use of these technologies in diversified fields of science and areas of application.

The editors would like to acknowledge the assistance and contribution of all those engaged in this project, without whose support this book would not have become a reality. We would especially like to express our most sincere thanks to the contributing authors and the reviewers involved in the review process, who contributed their time and expertise to ensure the eminence, consistency and correct arrangement of the chapters. Finally, we would like to take the opportunity to express our thanks to those at Scrivener Publishing for giving this book its final form.

The Editors
January 2021

Acknowledgement

The editors would like to acknowledge the assistance of all the people engaged in this book project and especially to the contributing authors and the reviewers involved in the review process. Our sincere thankfulness goes to each one of the chapter's authors for their contributions, without their support this book would not have become a reality. Our heartfelt gratitude and acknowledgement also goes to the reviewers who contributed their time and expertise for improving the eminence, consistency, and contented arrangement of the chapters in the book.

Internet of Things: A Key to Unfasten Mundane Repetitive Tasks

Hemanta Kumar Palo* and Limali Sahoo

Department of Electronics and Communication Engineering, ITER, Siksha 'O' Anusandhan (Deemed to be University), Bhubaneswar, India

Abstract

The emergence of the Internet of Things (IoT) finds its footprints in many vivid application domains such as Cognitive Science, Artificial Intelligence, Mobile-first, Blockchain, Biomedical Engineering, Immersive Experience, Zettabyte Era, Micro-service Architecture, Robotic Process, 3D Alteration, Automation, Quantum Computing, etc. These trending technologies are likely to rule the future world in the coming years and make it a must for the industries, and academia. It will arguably change our perception of living by connecting everybody and almost everything placed anywhere in this world. It has recently found its presence in everyday human life connecting a host of home appliances such as the refrigerators, washing machines, microwaves, water taps, clocks, homewares, and even the cooking vessels or pots. It is difficult to imagine things or appliances without the IoT we use today. However, to maintain sustainability, these devices need to be economically viable, eco-friendly, and energy-efficient. This motivates the authors to coin the concept of IoT and its application domains in the current scenario and the way ahead. Some of the major areas of IoT platforms that sensitize the digitized world have been highlighted with special emphasis on the concepts of cloud, fog, edge, and virtual computing.

Keywords: Internet of things, green computing, cloud computing, fog computing, edge computing, virtual computing, semantic IoT

1.1 Introduction

The advents of green computing and green technology make the Internet of Things (IoT) an emerging field of research in recent years. Many vivid application domains such as cognitive science, Artificial Intelligence, biomedical engineering, Micro-service Architecture, Robotic Process, etc. are the outcomes of the IoT technology [1]. Any IoT domain is associated with a set of equipment, devices, machines, home appliances, agricultural or medical instruments, smart vehicles, hardware (servers, monitors, printers, sensors, actuators, etc.), software, and communication network. It is an essential commodity today that finds its footprints in smart homes or smart cities, educational institutes, smart vehicles, agriculture, wearable

Corresponding author: hemantapalo@soa.ac.in

Monika Mangla, Suneeta Satpathy, Bhagirathi Nayak and Sachi Nandan Mohanty (eds.) Integration of Cloud Computing with Internet of Things: Foundations, Analytics, and Applications, (1–24) © 2021 Scrivener Publishing LLC

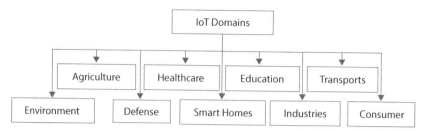

Figure 1.1 Major areas of IoT platform.

technologies such as sensors, or wearable devices using remote controls for monitoring and management [2]. The thrust areas of IoT devices are to provide efficient lighting, heating, air conditioning, security, media, and communication, e.g., the provisioning of much needed care and assistance to disabled, sick, or elderly individuals [3]. Some of the major areas of IoT platforms that occupy in the current scenario are shown in Figure 1.1.

1.2   The IoT Scenario

In recent years, the IoT domain has been extended to provide enhanced tags to monitor and control the human affective states. Such attempts can be found useful in the field of criminal investigations, lie detection, an advanced warning to in-car board systems, on-line tutoring, computer games, security, banking, human resource planning, call centers, child psychology, etc. [4–9]. The associated devices and technologies can be effectively utilized in systems such as voice control, pacemakers, advanced hearing aids, Fitbit electronic wristbands, wearable sensors for the people having sight or mobility disabilities. The use of actuators or sensors to cope with an immediate seizure or a sudden fall or similar emergency can help people or patients of all ages in the home and work environment [10]. The additional security devices mounted on the body or its part will alert nearby individuals including the health attendants or medicos at the right time hence can enhance the quality of living being.

An effective IoT framework in commercial applications requires the collection, analyzing, monitoring, and management of input data concerned with healthcare, medical, transportation, building, home automation, vehicles including agriculture. Elaborate research, control, and monitoring of these inputs can lead to new information and insights for channelizing in the desired directions. A reliable system can provide the desired freedom by linking the smart systems or devices, healthcare services, physicians, and medical resources to patients [11]. Another interesting application is to set-up smart beds in healthcare units equipped with actuators and sensors that provide patient information regularly and also to confirm whether a bed is vacated or occupied. These beds fitted with automatic sensors with appropriate supporting and pressure devices can either reduce or eliminate manual assistance to unwell individuals.

The application of IoT in the transportation system requires an efficient framework to communicate, integrate, process, and control information among many sensors and devices connected to such a system and its peripheries. The role of IoT remains vital to interact and coordinate among traffic systems, logistics and packaging systems, vehicle control, parking, toll plaza, security and safety, road assistance, etc. [12]. Similarly, IoT-based smart infrastructure systems that design and develop smart homes or apartments or campuses or a smart city must be able to manage and control the electrical/electronic/mechanical sensors, actuators, devices, and equipment as per a user demand [13]. Further, such a technology finds its place in several service-based industries, infrastructure development, product or manufacturing industries, metropolitan scale development, agriculture, energy management, living laboratories, environmental monitoring, intelligence, and security, etc.

1.3   The IoT Domains

1.3.1   The IoT Policy Domain

The policy-based IoT intends to develop, plan, and implementation of suitable rules, strategies, and policies concerned with IoT devices based on real-time data for future impact and possible environment sustainability. It helps in efficient energy management, data management, resource utilization, and user feedback that benefit the industries as well as the end-user. A few areas of policy-based IoT application are shown in Figure 1.2.

The application of policy-based IoT in smart cities helps to plan for smart healthcare, smart vehicles, smart homes, smart security, smart campuses, smart agriculture, etc. [1]. Due to scare, limited and rapid depleting of resources with an increase in global population, it demands .a smart city environment for the future generation. With the advent of industrialization and the emission of poisonous gas particles, the world becomes unhealthy and suffocated. Further, many environmental hazards such as global warming, climate change, acid rain, soil erosion, etc. tend to threaten the world ecosystem. This has compelled the government agencies, NGOs, and policymakers to find different means or ways to contain the carbon footprints that grow exponentially. To be successful, the policies and strategies must appeal and be conducive to the manufacturers, designers, service providers, as well as the end-users with energy-efficient systems. Such planning, policies, regulations, etc. facilitate the smart environment where people can utilize the air conditioners, computer labs, sensors, and networking systems with desire for economical effectiveness. The IoT application in smart cities provides the provision to many factors such as

- Smart Agriculture: Smart agriculture based on the IoT aims to integrate several heterogeneous devices, objects, equipment such as the wearable sensors, humidity sensors, temperature sensors, mobile phones, etc. with the networking system to remain successful [14].

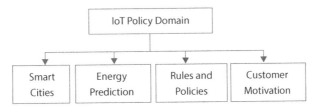

Figure 1.2 Policy-based IoT applications.

- Smart healthcare: It requires a context-aware linking system to be efficient and viable linking the agriculture, healthcare, and environment [15]. The IoT must cater to a remote health monitoring system while managing huge data by applying visualization and data mining. The linking of the IoT green computing to health industries can infuse flexibility, interoperability, and intelligence by information transmission among different modules of the healthcare system. This reduces and simplifies the administrative task.

- Smart security: The world becomes small due to the use of IoT. This makes the people, installations, equipment, etc. vulnerable to cyber-attack. The loss, theft, and exposure of private information become common today due to network interconnectivity. The IoT system must be capable to safeguard from pilferage or leakage of sensitive information by taking preventive measures. This way, it can avoid unwanted threats to national, environmental, social, and personal entities by providing smart security with efficient IoT gateways [16]. It requires the provision of password protection systems, ciphering or cryptographic or jumbling technologies, robust routing mechanism. The security clearance is a must at every level to maintain information integrity, confidentiality, authenticity.

- Smart homes: The IoT-based smart homes help the end-users to cope and deal with their busy schedules by interlinking the sensors, electronic gadgets, etc. with software set up in homes [13]. The equipment such as the computer, mobile phone, air conditioner, lighting, heating mechanism, ventilation, security systems, hardware, etc. connected through networking and sensors benefit from these ends irrespective of time and place.

- Smart vehicles: The IoT-based smart transport system equipped with smart servers can provide e-notification, traffic and weather updates, automated accident detection, etc. to drivers and vehicle owners to save up on their energy and time. It helps to restrict the vehicle speed under adverse weather condition and traffic congestion by estimating the distance traveled the driver reaction time, etc. The associated systems such as the GPRS tracking, emergency prioritization, vehicles, GSM modem, infrared proximity sensors, Xbee, embedded processor are few contributions of smart vehicle systems [12]. Similarly, smart vehicles that can handle and inform human affective states can provide a warning to a passenger or the driver for timely action by alerting the traffic management system in case of emergency [17].

- Smart campus: The resources are scarce and are rapidly depleting with an increase in the global population, hence they are limited. Further, it is not advisable to neglect the environmental effect.

- Climate change, soil erosion, global warming, acid rain, etc. in the exploration of resources on a large scale. It demands awareness among the consumers, manufacturers, designers, service providers, to develop energy-efficient IoT system for smart cities. In this regard the role of NGOs, educational institutions, think tanks, intellectuals remain vital to promoting green residences or campuses. This can be possible by providing automatic monitoring and control of IoT devices focusing on the economy, energy-efficient, reliability, etc. [18].

1.3.2   The IoT Software Domain

A few of the IoT Software domains are shown in Figure 1.3 and have been explained briefly here.

1.3.2.1   IoT in Cloud Computing (CC)

CC aims to deliver the hardware and software services across a parallel and distributed system. It has three important characteristics such as (a) virtual, (b) dynamic provision on-demand, and (c) negotiation. In this scheme, the hardware and software systems are interconnected dynamically and computerized virtually [19]. This way, the scheme reduces the carbon footprints and emissions besides decreasing the energy consumption appreciably. This can be achieved by transferring a few on-premises applications into the cloud. One of the real-life situations where CC finds its use is on-line marketing in which we procure goods and services without our presence in the shop-floor physically. Further, it reduces unnecessary expenditure on transportation and reduction in greenhouse gas emissions by each individual going to the shop-floor separately. As it is possible in CC to use the resources of the service provider rather than buying expensive equipment or systems for a business, it is economical. The reduction in the cost of using CC may be attributed to the following.

- One can include new software, hardware, and system upgrade costs in his/her contract.
- The expert data is found in the cloud, thus need to hire or pay the expert staff.
- Thus, it reduces energy consumption.
- Unnecessary time delays can be avoided.

Some of the other benefits that are offered by CC are security, flexibility, insight, quality control, increased collaboration, disaster recovery, competitive edge, loss prevention, sustainability, etc. The major advantages of CC have been shown in Figure 1.4.

The limitations of CC are briefed below.

- Privacy agreement: The user in the CC platform requires the desired privacy and service level agreement before the commencement of the services. It delegates certain responsibilities on both the service provider and the user which needs to be adhered to by both the parties.
- Security: The protection of data and the security against pilferage, theft, etc. need to be considered beforehand. While it is provided by the service

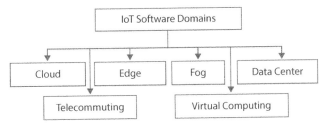

Figure 1.3 Softwarebased IoT applications.

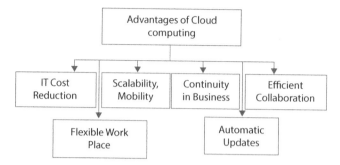

Figure 1.4 The benefits of CC.

provider in its periphery, the remote users need to weigh the security system before opting for CC.

- Vulnerability: Since each component is easily accessible via the internet, it is likely to be attacked by hackers.
- Limited flexibility and control: The uses in CC have limited control over the execution and function of the service provider as per the agreement signed by both parties.
- Platform dependencies: The vendor lock-in or implicit dependency creates deep-rooted differences between the user and the service providers. This sometimes poses difficulties for users to migrate to other service providers at will due to additional cost, security, and privacy issues.
- Cost: for small businesses or on a small scale, CC cost exceeds the cost due to staffing or hardware procurement.

Types of CC
The commonly employed CC services are briefed below.

- Infrastructure as a service (IaS): In this, an external service provider facilitates the user with computer power and disc space via the internet. The users need to have hardware such as CPU, data storage, memory, or network connectivity. Examples of IaS are the Rackspace, Amazon EC2, Windows Azure, etc.
- Software as a service (SaS): In this, the user can access the internet-hosted software by browsing. The service provider maintains and controls the software updates and the user has limited control over the configuration settings and the applications. It is mostly suitable for small businesses.
- Platform as a service (PaS): It is a crossover between SaS and Ias. In this case, the user rents the operating system, hardware, network capacity, storage, etc. to the service provider. Thus, the user has the desired control over the computing setup, technical aspects, customization, etc. as per his/her need.

1.3.2.2   IoT in Edge Computing (EC)

CC is an efficient mechanism to process the data that reduces at the network edge. New software domains have been developed that are more energy-efficient than CC are the Fog or EC [20, 21]. In EC the computation of the enabling technologies is carried out at the edge of the network. At downstream data, this function is performed using cloud services whereas, at upstream data, the IoT services are carried out.

In EC, the network resources are managed and controlled between the path of cloud data found useful in the case of a smartphone which is considered to be an edge between the body things and the cloud. Similarly, a gateway is an edge between campus things and cloud in green computing, or the cloudlet and the microdata center act as an edge between the cloud and the mobile device. While FC is oriented more towards the infrastructure side, EC is focused on the things-side. Hence, the latter remains an emerging technology at par with CC in the current scenario. The EC requires minimum use of refrigeration and maintenance as it needs a small data center for functioning. Ultimately, the technique remains energy efficient with a reduction in e-waste. The use of EC has reduced the response time to 169 ms as compared to 900 ms required by CC [22]. The hierarchy of EC is shown in Figure 1.5.

EC aims to save bandwidth and to reduce the response time by bringing the data storage and the computation closer to the desired location. It has recently been found to be applied in dealer locators, real-time data aggregators, shopping carts, and insertion engines. It is a computing technology that can deliver nearer to a request zone with low latency. As compared to CC that suits big data analysis, EC performs better in real-time processing of data generated by the users or sensors such as 'instant data'. EC moves the computation away from data centers towards the edge of the network, thus helps smart things or objects such as network gateways or mobile phones to accomplish the desired services or tasks on behalf of the cloud. On account of this shift, it becomes reliable to facilitate service delivery, content catching, IoT management, and storage with reduced response time and efficient transmission and reception of data.

The advantages of EC are as follows and are shown in Figure 1.6.

- A reduction in data volume, as the task is performed at the edge.
- It reduces the consequent traffic and traveling distance of data.
- Low latency and transmission costs.
- It provides computing offloading in real-time applications, such as facial recognition with the low response time.

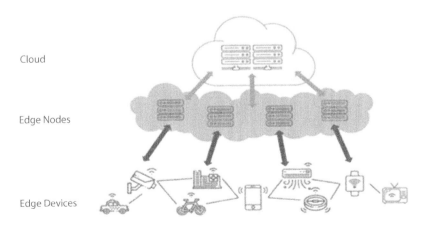

Figure 1.5 The hierarchy of EC.

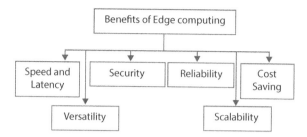

Figure 1.6 The benefits of EC.

- Instead of using the resource-rich machines such as cloudlets in the vicinity of the mobile users in the case of CC, it is better to offload a few of the tasks at the edge node to reduce the execution time.
- EC optimizes data-driven and management capabilities by efficient facilitation of data gathering, processing, reporting, etc. very nearer to the end-user as possible.

Privacy and security

The distributed paradigm of EC allows data encryption using different mechanisms, hence provide added security. This is because the data can be transferred among several distributed nodes via the internet before arriving at the cloud. This introduces flexibility in security methods to be adopted, thus Edge nodes may suit resource-constrained devices. An eventual shift from centralized top-down cloud infrastructure to a suitable decentralized Edge model helps better the functioning of the network. Further, the edge data allows the shifting ownership of gathered data from service providers to end-users. On the contrary, CC is more vulnerable since all the data is fed to the cloud analyzer and a single attack can disrupt the entire system. As against it, the EC transfers fewer amounts of data that can be accessible to hackers or interceptors. So it helps industries to tackle local compliance, privacy regulations, and data sovereignty issues.

Scalability

In CC, it is essential to forward the data to a centrally located data center. Thus, the modification or expansion of the dedicated data centers remains expensive. On the other hand, the IoT devices can be deployed at the edge with their data management and processing tools in single implantation without waiting on the coordination efforts of personnel placed at multiple sites.

Reliability

In CC, if a crucial system or component fails, it is difficult to make the service alive. As compared to this, in EC using distributed nodes, if a single node fails or unreachable, it is still workable without interruption. Further, there is every possibility of redundant data in CC that may not be useful or have the same value. Hence spending money on these data is not advisable which leads to EC. It allows the categorization of data for the perspective of management. Focusing only on relevant data reduces the bandwidth requirement, hence cost. It optimizes the data flow to maximize the operating cost. It stores the data temporarily which is sent to the cloud for storage at a later stage that causes redundant overload in clouds.

Speed
EC facilitates the availability of analytical computational resources in the vicinity of the end-users, hence can improve the speed of response. The presence of a small amount of data and its management to remote locations reduces the overall loads in the traffic. The reduction in latency can enhance the speed of communication at the user-end.

Efficiency
In EC the end-user remains at the proximity of the computing which allows the application of sophisticated Artificial Intelligence and analytical tools at the edge of a system. Such schemes improve the overall operational efficiency of the system.

Cost Saving
EC has to deal with less data that is relevant to the end-user. Removal of redundant data reduces the cost of data handling, transportation, storage, and management. Further, the bandwidth cost is also reduced as it needs to deal with large data management.

Versatility
EC remains versatile since industries can target the coveted markets with their local centers with fewer infrastructure investments. In this way, the enterprises may allow expert assistance with latency. The efficiency of EC can further increase with the involvement of advanced IoT gadgets without changing the current IT structure.

The Limitations of EC
Table 1.1 shows the limitations of EC.

Table 1.1 The limitations of EC.

Security	It is often difficult to maintain the desired security in a distributed network such as EC. The security further at risk due to the transfer of data outside the network edge. Further, the infiltration or pilferage of data when a new IoT device is introduced.
Incomplete Data	EC can analyze and process limited information and discard the rest of the data. Thus, there is a possibility of valuable information loss which compels the end-user to decide the type and amount of information before opting for such a scheme.
Investment Cost	The implementation of an EC infrastructure remains complex and costly and complex since it requires additional resources and equipment. It requires more local hardware for functioning.
Maintenance	The EC uses a distributed framework which is decentralized, thus, there are several combinations and variation in network architectures or modes. Hence the maintenance cost increases as compared to that of a centralized network such as CC.

1.3.2.3   IoT in Fog Computing (FC)

FC reduces the amount of information to be carried into the cloud and improves efficiency by extending the cloud nearer to the data generating device known as the fog nodes. These fog nodes are in the form of controllers, switches, servers, routers, cameras, etc. which provide the desired storage, network connection, and computing features is known as fog node. In general, CC is incapable of handling large data bandwidth as it is subjected to volume and latency that's leads to the advent of FC. It is found useful in compliance and data security and is a non-trivial extension of CC. It bridges several sensors appearing at the network edge to the core computing structure of the cloud [1, 23]. The system requires the processing to be carried out either on the network edge of a gateway device or router or in the data hub of the mobile device.

Although, the FC is similar to EC appear similar the key difference lies in the location or the placement of computing power and intelligence. The FC places the intelligence at the local area network to transfer the data from end-users to a gateway for further transmission. On the contrary, EC intends to place the processing power and intelligence in devices such as embedded automation controllers. The concept of cloud, Edge, and FC is shown in Figure 1.7.

Similarly, EC appears directly on the devices where the sensors or controllers are attached or it may appear at the gateway device physically nearer to the sensors. On the other hand, FC carries the edge activities to several processors connected to the LAN physically away from the sensors, controllers, and actuators.

Advantages of FC

- Since in EC the storage and processing of data to take place in LAN, the technique allows the organizations for the aggregation of information from multi-devices to regional stores.
- The data processing capability of Fog architecture is larger than that of Edge as the former allows organizations to gather data from different various devices.
- It improves and helps the real-time processing capabilities of the Edge architecture.
- It is most suitable for structures that have to handle millions of devices sharing information between them.

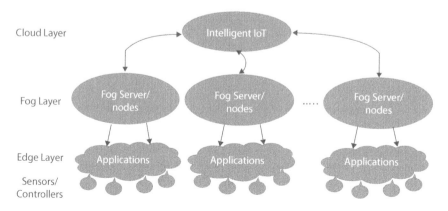

Figure 1.7 The concept of cloud, edge, and FC.

- It can provide a better quality of services, low latency, security, privacy protection, location awareness, reliability, etc. Hence, it can be efficiently employed in real-time applications than CC.

Disadvantages of FC

- A major drawback of FC is the huge data dimensions it needs to handle with millions of devices.
- It requires a large investment and consequently a large infrastructure to accommodate such volume of data and devices for reliability.

For large sensor data, it is difficult to use the cloud for transmission. Hence, it is essential to move to Fog architecture. Further, the data transmission between the sensors and the cloud or vice versa requires a large bandwidth that makes the CC inefficient. Thus, in the future, it is advisable to replace the CC with FC in the application such as a smart grid, low energy consumption, smart transportation system, smart traffic, management systems, agriculture, and health care system.

1.3.2.4   IoT in Telecommuting

In IoT software domain initiatives, it is possible to implement teleconference or telepresence applications efficiently. It can provide job satisfaction and protect the living being from the effect of greenhouse gas by limiting their traveling. Ultimately, the profit margin of an organization improves as telecommuting reduces the office overhead costs by minimizing office space, lighting, heating, etc. Evidence shows an average annual energy savings of 23 KWh per square foot amounting to 70% of total energy consumed due to air conditioning, heat, and lighting in a U.S. office building [24]. Similar expenditures can be curbed by integrating telecommuting with consulting, hoteling, field service, and sales. The framework of integrating telecommuting to IoT application domain must take care of the following few issues.

- The energy consumption
- Identification of the key energy indices for efficient utilization of different network elements
- Device and network optimization for carrier telecommunication
- Effective management of the link between the environment and the network technology.
- We need to segregate individuals or groups who can work remotely with efficiency and benefit the organization as a whole.
- We need to define the responsibilities, accountability, and expectation standard clearly.
- Describe clear rules and regulations for employees selected for telecommuting.
- Due weightage needs to be given to the career goal of the telecommuting employees.
- Move to cloud as an when required for assistance

1.3.2.5   IoT in Data-Center

Data Centers are the biggest consumer of energy and hence required to be energy efficient. These data centers require a context-aware sensing mechanism to implement selective sensing for minimizing power consumption. An effective energy management architecture can supply power uninterrupted to the dedicated sensor and switches off the idle controllers/sensors/actuators as and when required [25]. Effective data center functioning needs to tackle the following issues.

- A meticulous distribution and evaluation of workload to the dedicated servers.
- Identification and cutting-off of power supply to the ideal servers and re-distribution of the workforce and load.
- Maximizing the application of renewable energy sources.
- Efficient and economical use of power and depleted resources.

1.3.2.6   Virtualization-Based IoT (VBIoT)

The VBIoT application aims to reduce the number of hardware resources, hence it consumes less energy. It is a virtual or software-based process to represent things, such as networks, virtual applications, servers, storage, etc. It can reduce IT expenses, boosts flexibility, efficiency, scalability, and agility for many businesses. A saving of 36% energy consumption in IoT devices has been reported by using the Mixed Integer Linear Programming (MILP) in the VBIoT with four-layer architecture [25]. The benefits of VBIoT are:

- It allows managing of data or information with ease and efficiency.
- The continuity and growth in industries can be achieved.
- It is possible to access a true software-oriented data center.
- The resources and applications are made available as and when desired.
- Helps to increase responsiveness, production, efficiency, and agility.
- There is a considerable decline in operating costs and investment in capital.
- The downtime can be minimized or ideally eliminated.
- It optimizes resource allocation by providing better workload distribution, performance enhancement, and automated operations.

VBIoT emphasizes on encapsulation, isolation, partitioning, and hardware independence, thus makes the domain effective. It can be included in many levels of IoT framework such as a server, desktop, network, etc. towards creating a smart world environment.

1.4   Green Computing (GC) in IoT Framework

The benefits and limitations of the GC have been shown in Figure 1.8.

The IoT application to Green Computing (IoTGC) aims to achieve a greener and eco-friendly world. The objective is to design, develop, operate, maintain, and control the energy-efficient IoT systems that are economically viable, user friendly, and eco-sustainable.

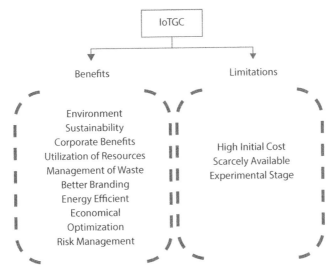

Figure 1.8 The benefits and limitations of the IoTGC.

Nevertheless, the challenges are many due to a change in global climate, depleted resources, energy crises, environmental issues, etc. [1]. Further, the hardware system must be easily disposable/recyclable and must comprise of handheld and large-scale data centers.

1.5   Semantic IoT (SIoT)

The reflection of heterogeneity on these raw data for meaningful interpretation and detection of events in real-world environments makes the IoT platform more complex. The total number of IoT domains included in 2016 is approximately 450 with an exponential rise in new IoT platforms each year [26]. By the year 2020, the number of IoT devices may reach around 50 billion with numerous heterogeneous services and applications [2]. In this accord, the SIoT concerns to a worldwide network of interconnected devices, things, heterogeneous objects, and services which can be uniquely addressable and accessible using some sort of standard communication protocols.

The steps involved in managing heterogeneous data sources for making SIoT effective are based on SEG 3.0 methodology as shown in Figure 1.9. It supports the SI from the data generation to the end-users.

Due to the involvement of a huge number of things and the services in the future IoT, it remains a challenge to represent, interconnect, store, search, address, and organize relevant information available from different IoT sources. Thus, the involvement of semantics in IoT remains crucial to provide adequate modeling, reach desired solutions for things description, and reason over IoT generated data. With an increase in demand for applications and services using semantic sensor web, the research community, and software developers are designing advanced system architecture to automatically transform data from sensors to semantic expression. The use of data somatization facilitated the end-users to understand and reason on sensor-related human's activities for effective dynamic environments. The use of SI remains vital for adequate representation and integration of huge amounts of data

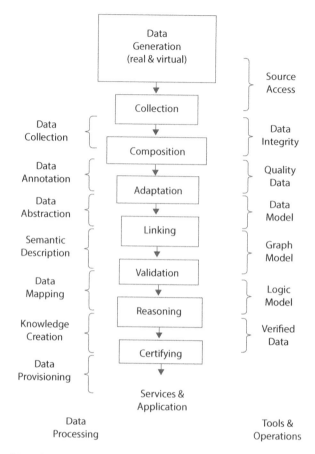

Figure 1.9 The steps of SIoT (SEG 3.0 methodology) [27].

arrived from different IoT sources for their effective utilization. The information extracted semantically from high-level abstractions or data can provide a potential solution to reduce the heterogeneity in a shared or common IoT platform. The Semantic Interoperability (SI) assisted by the SW to facilitate consolidated technologies, standards, and languages by providing data as well as IoT platform interoperability. With an ever increasing demand in applications and their developments, the use of semantic interoperability in IOT domain remains significant and essential for its success. With many different smart technologies, the SI integration costs are likely to rise and the system becomes complex. Nevertheless, with thousands of potential data sources, application areas, industries, and customers, a smart city can be smarter with the combination, cross-compilation, and re-utilization of data generated by individual applications using SI. The intersection of different IoT visions is shown in Figure 1.10.

A generalized SIoT architecture is shown in Figure 1.11.

It is not enough to gather data but requires an ability to convert or process the available data into fruitful decisions or information that can provide an edge in SI. For instance, if someone was to call an end-user on their phone and speak in London, most users would probably not be able to communicate or achieve a meaningful result. The same issue occurs in communication between things when they use implementation-specific data models.

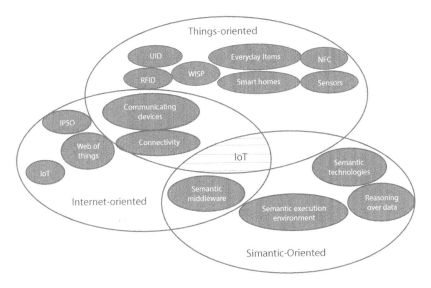

Figure 1.10 Intersection of different IoT visions [2].

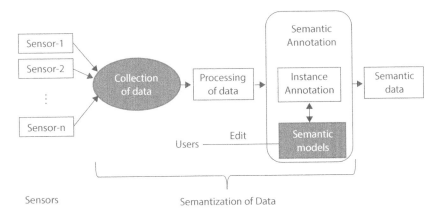

Figure 1.11 A generalized architecture of including semantics.

1.5.1 Standardization Using oneM2M

Many companies are still trying to gain a better understanding of how blending robotics, interconnected devices/systems, and convergent hybrid infrastructure, together with edge and cloud/data center compute, can improve productivity and reduce costs in the long run. Add different vendors' technology to the mix and a very complicated picture is painted.

Working to reduce this complexity is oneM2M, a global standard that hides technology complexities for IoT application developers through an abstraction layer, and a wide area network perspective. Its areas of expertise extend to the industrial sector, with several completed Technical Reports (TRs) and work in progress dedicated to this area. TR-0018 Industrial Domain Enablement, for example, maps out several use cases relating to Industry 4.0 development and the potential requirements which need to be addressed to ensure M2M communications truly enhance operations. Based on industrial domain research carried out, the document highlights the need to develop an accepted strategy to implement Industry 4.0 as a means of accelerating the update of manufacturing systems that many global organizations have started to invest in. Other completed projects dedicated to tackling the challenges of Industry 4.0 include TR-0027 Data Distribution Services usage in oneM2M and TR-0043 Modbus Interworking. Meanwhile, work is continuing on TR-0049 Industrial Domain Information Mapping & Semantics Support around proximal–distal interworking. Further support for industrial IoT applications is also expected to come when oneM2M publishes Release 3 later this year. OneM2M also collaborates on a wider scale with other industry bodies on a wide range of projects. In its TR-0018 Industrial Domain Enablement report, oneM2M referenced several organizations and industry bodies with relevant activities in the area, including the Industrial Internet Consortium (IIC) and Platform Industrie 4.0 and their respective reference architectures including IIRS and RAMI 4.0. Cooperation with the IIC is already advancing through joint workshops and a oneM2M testbed. Cooperation with Platform Industrie 4.0, the central alliance for the coordination of the digital structural transition in Germany, which includes stakeholders from businesses, associations, trade unions, and academia, is another important alignment of technologies and concepts in the industrial domain, especially as the PI4.0 concept of an Asset Administration shell and the oneM2M CSE are so complementary. OneM2M has incorporated results from Plattform Industrie 4.0's Reference Architecture Model, Industrie 4.0 (RAMI 4.0), into the TR-0018 Industrial Domain Enablement report. RAMI 4.0 provides a conceptual superstructure for organizational aspects of Industry 4.0, emphasizing collaboration infrastructures, and communication structures. It also introduces the concept of an asset administration shell that incorporates detailed questions on key topics such as semantic standards, technical integration, and security challenges. OneM2M's joint work with key transformative actors develops and delivers workshops, testbeds, and reports, along with its unique asset. The concept of a service layer on top of a connectivity layer—contributes significantly to the overall Industry 4.0 framework and industrial internet as a whole, ushering in a new wave of digitalization which will mark the beginning of Industry 4.0.

SI has been introduced in the latest specification of oneM2M standard Release 2 [Swetina]. It allows the posting, distribution, and reuse of meta-tagged data through a gateway by providing timely notifications to interested clients or entities available in semantic discovery.

OneM2M acts as a software middle layer, by interconnecting devices with their respective application–infrastructure entities (cloud-based), independently from their underlying transport networks. In effect, it creates an abstraction layer that allows application developers to create value from their business and operational applications without having to deal with the technical protocols for connecting to and managing devices. The standard solves the problem of implementation variances for common service functions. Its technical specifications provide a global standard for the basic functions, such as device management, security, registration, and so forth. The use of oneM2M specifications in field-deployed devices ensures data and vendor interoperability. Furthermore, oneM2M provides global standardized APIs on the application-infrastructure side, where customers can interact with their device and/or even their platform. On the device side, oneM2M's APIs help developers tailor applications for their specific purpose without the need to master technical details about the underlying connectivity networks. To enable end-to-end communication across different verticals, oneM2M provides the tools that enable various interworking possibilities. One approach is to map data models for shop-floor machines and sensors as oneM2M resource structures and vice versa. Since such interworking definitions are available for other verticals, such as automotive and rail, different verticals can communicate with each other relatively easily. The primary aim of oneM2M is to standardize the common services necessary to deploy and operationally support IoT applications across multiple verticals. This implies a horizontal focus, aiming for a high degree of reuse and cross-silo interoperability. Vertical sector requirements are also important to oneM2M standardization participants. In the manufacturing and industrial sectors, oneM2M established a liaison with the Industrial Internet Consortium. OneM2M is also actively involved with the Open Connectivity Foundation, targeting interworking opportunities for consumer IoT applications. OneM2M's standardization continues to address new frontiers for interoperability and interworking with the development of its latest specifications, Release 4. Release 4 will encompass industrial, vehicular, and fog/edge architectures. It also lays the groundwork for semantic interoperability and tools to help user adoption.

We all know that SIoT is taking place in modern applications for industries and is developing very fast making analytics crucial to ensure security. Since the SIoT analytics operates using the cloud and electronic instrumentation, it requires programmers to control and access IoT data. IT professionals approaching IoT analytics should capture data via packets in automated workloads, also known as flow. Flow is the sharing of packets with the for example, if you stream a video on the internet, packets are sent from the server to your device. This is flow in action. NetFlow and sFlow are both tools that monitor network traffic. IT pros are still creating methods to capture the flow of data for analysis of IoT data. The number of cloud companies has increased, and as networks continue to grow, it's very risky to carry down the large visibility gap for capturing data. Because of huge data traffic, many cloud companies have started to send information through their networks via IP Flow, sFlow, and NetFlow. When you start to capture IoT specific data, there are several advantages. The data gets standardized into industry-accepted data, and once the data is observed from the gateway, it can be correlated with traffic data coming out from the data center or cloud services in use. Every cloud environment can create flow by generating and exporting the data. For example, a few IT equipped companies such as Amazon, Google, Microsoft Azure have incorporated these attributes in different applications to facilitate the industries and consumers. Amazon is a popular platform for cloud services which takes into account both the cost and frequency response of the network. It has many features to enhance the IoT platform and can support many devices. This platform uses flow as the mechanism to communicate. The service is handled by the virtual private cloud. It comes across under certain levels such as ports, networks, traffic levels, and some other communication networks. Data gets stored using the CloudWatch logs in JavaScript Object Notation (JSON). Similarly, Google is popular in every technology. Google Cloud IoT Core is a fully managed service that allows you to handle easily and secure the connection with manages and ingests data from millions of globally dispersed devices. The data flow is run by logging the Stack driver. And the performance of the network operates with good latency. It handles large data which works still fine. Similarly, the 'Microsoft Azure' flows under a secured network system. The flow logs are work or travel in a flow and stored into Azure storage in the format of JSON. The data from the devices have been stored in a method of real-time data.

For example, the use of some sort of standards to announce each printer and its attributes is one way to elevate such an issue and there are so many such attributes.

Today, each vertical industry comes along with its protocol and specifications bodies to develop their data models. For example, in the industrial automation industry, organizations like OPC are working on data models and objects which can be used on the shop floor. In the automotive industry, ETSI's Intelligent Transport Systems technical committee is working collaboratively to define messages and data models for communication between cars. Many IoT applications also involve several partners in a distributed value chain. For instance, an intelligent application for an industrial plant might automatically order feedstock from one or more partners for its production line. Supplies are typically ordered and delivered by several partners. It is easy to see how this scenario can end up in up in an "island of things" configuration since different partners in the value chain belong to different verticals, each with their specific data models. It is thus desired to make sure the cross-availability of IoT devices, services, and data for the growth of new business and the emergence of opportunities. This can assist managing data from multiple sources, generate new avenues, and innovate suitable solutions for the existing service providers to scale new markets.

1.5.2   Semantic Interoperability (SI)

The last decade witnessed a many-fold increase in a host of heterogeneous devices, actuators, sensors, etc. with varied applications in the IoT platform. To cope up with the smart environment, an efficient distribution, monitor, support, coordination, control, and communication among these sensors remains essential that gives rise to the term interoperability. The interoperability can be achieved with the following major layers as shown in Figure 1.12.

Technical interoperability is concerned with the communicability among the things or objects in IoT domain using the software and hardware. On achieving the suitable connectivity, the syntactic interoperability deals with the data models, data formats, data encoding, communication protocols, and serialization techniques using certain specified standards. Finally, Semantic interoperability establishes the desired meaning to the content and assists to comprehend of the shared unambiguous meaning of data. The interoperability concept can be better visualized using the five major perspectives and is given in Table 1.2.

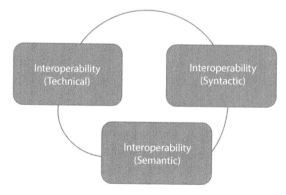

Figure 1.12 Different layers of interoperability.

Table 1.2 Taxonomy of interoperability: major perspectives.

Taxonomy of interoperability	Attributes
Device interoperability [19]	Involves both the low and high-end devices High-end devices are Raspberry Pi, smartphones, etc. with good computational abilities and resources Low-end devices are low-cost sensors, actuators, RFID tags, Arduino, OpenMote, etc. with resource-crunch, communication, low energy, and processing abilities. It aims for better integration and communication among several heterogeneous devices in advanced IoT platforms.
Network interoperability [20]	The network remains is multi-service, multi-vendor, largely distributed and, heterogeneous. It facilitates the better transfer of data among several smart systems using efficient networking systems. It can alleviate issues such as addressing, resource optimization, routing, security, QoS, mobility support, etc.
Syntactical interoperability [21]	It allows interoperation of the format and structure of the data during communication among heterogeneous IoT devices, entities, domains, systems, etc. It includes the syntactic set rules in the same or some different grammar It is significant in the case of disparities between the encode and decode rules involving the source and the end-user.
Semantic interoperability [22]	It allows the meaningful exchange of knowledge and information among agents, services, and applications. It is significant when the automatic interoperation of IoT information or data models is not materialized due to the difficulties in descriptions and understandings of operational resources or procedures.
Platform interoperability [21]	The need arises with the advancement of diverse and versatile operating systems, programming languages, data structures, IoT architectures, access mechanisms, etc. Different mechanisms are developed for efficient data management involving several IoT platforms. Similarly, cross-platform and cross-domain in different heterogeneous domains are addressed.

1.5.3   Semantic Interoperability (SI) Security

The semantic IoT is considered as a black hole in a nebulous term. It must have a security policy that is comprehensive with expansive visibility. Further, several decades-old IoT technologies require be managing or segmenting effectively along with emerging technologies. For example, the oldest IoT iteration concept is to involve multi-function printers with both copying and scanning abilities. Nevertheless, the security concerned often ignores these which pose a threat to the domain as anybody can easily route or access these from a workplace or other places. The proliferation of security corresponding to smart systems can lead to potential threats to put infrastructure, or an entire city and its traffic, lighting, and power grid systems having millions of IoT users. However, as these smart systems work in the cloud, the organization can develop several usage patterns. The integration and coordination of smart IoT devices such as wired or unwired equipment, cameras, biometric access, gesture or face identification models, keypad, etc. with interoperability, it becomes possible to place the right people at a right place. For example, the huge meshing network structure present in a smart city environment warrants a robust security traffic system, secured wired or wireless sensors, parking meters, to prevent the proliferation of the IoT system. The security system must contain visibility to maintain awareness among both users and hackers. It is thus essential to make policies about IoT security regarding the locations of cameras, conceivable devices, sensors, measuring instruments, or meters to make it effective.

1.5.4 Semantic IoT vs Machine Learning

The Machine Learners (MLs) are essential components in the field of pattern recognition, classification, and regression analysis. Over the years, several MLs have been efficiently applied in the field of power management, speech, and speaker identification, emotion recognition, etc. [28–32]. The integration and coordination of SIoT with MLs has been often discussed in the literature involving pervasive and ubiquitous computing, ambient intelligence, wireless sensor networks, artificial intelligence, human–computer interaction, cognitive science, etc. The multi-layered back-propagating Neural Networks have been effectively utilized to identify human movements such as sitting, walking, running, etc. in smart home applications. Similarly, identification ML models such as the Naive Base Classifiers, Bayesian networks, Support Vector Machines, K-Nearest Neighbor, Hidden Markov Model, etc. have been efficiently applied in the field of context-aware search systems, home automation, navigation systems, etc. in IoT domains.

The Integration and coordination of SIoT and MLs arguably increase the financial health of an industry or business. It requires the choice of specific words or vocabularies to suitably represent a set of concepts. The choice aims to bridge the semantic gap that exists among machines in IoT platform. However, many industries in the existing structure act superficially, thus unable to transform the company into a true profit-oriented entity in reality. For example, the inclusion of Artificial Intelligence in a fast-food chain allows the planning of the diet charts based on the recommendation of user habits. It helps to suggest add-on items based on the current selection, the restaurant traffic, or environmental conditions, weather, or time of a day. The integration of artificial intelligence, SIoT, machine learning, modern analytic models, etc. requires to be embedded with the lifecycle of a customer frequently and completely. For example, the satisfaction level of a customer can be enhanced by displaying his or her name, preferences, frequent visits, etc. on the menu chart makes the client feel proud and special. Efficient handling of a customer's behaviors, interests, and future intentions can provide many intelligent inputs to the food industry in real-time. Similarly, the AI-powered chat-bouts help the customers with the user-friendly experience to boost revenue due to personalization. It has been observed that most of the consumers are motivated to choose a product of a company that recognizes, remembers, and values his or her association with the product. This way, it is possible to predict a customer's next move, by upgrading and feeding SI data consistently in an IoT platform. This feedback provides the simulating engines or MLs an edge for new developments in this field with better outcomes. Ultimately, the revenue increases, productivity improves, operational expenses reduced, personalization enhanced at a large scale that leads to better customer experiences. The SI automated IoT embedded machines with intelligence assists millions of smart models functioning concurrently that benefits both the customers and service providers.

1.6   Conclusions

Internet of Things (IoT) application in smart homes or cities, workplace, agriculture, transportation, healthcare, artificial intelligence, Cognitive Science, Blockchain, Micro-service Architecture, Robotic Process, Automation, Quantum Computing are all concepts gaining attention in recent years in public, private, and corporate worlds due to media publicity and efficacy. With its growing interest on everybody and everyday applications, it helps people enjoy self-driving cars, use wearables for efficiency and timely assistance, plan taxi services or business meetings, and so on. The IoT application domains have covered all sectors, industries, and every sphere of life today, thus thrive to boost the financial health of the world. It has begun to shape the future world with a unique perspective never seen before in the history of humanity. With these intuitions, this paper elaborates several factors concerned to IoT world that rule and dominate the world today in the current scenario.

References

1. Das, S.K. and Palo, H.K., Internet of Things (IoT) Application in Green Computing: An Overview, in: *Advances in Greener Energy Technologies*, pp. 85–102, Springer, Singapore, 2020.
2. Evans, D., *The internet of things: How the next evolution of the internet is changing everything*, vol. 1, pp. 1–11, CISCO white paper, USA, 2011.
3. Philip, V., Suman, V.K., Menon, V.G., Dhanya, K.A., A review on latest internet of things based healthcare applications. *Int. J. Inf. Secur.*, 15, 1, 248, 2017.
4. Palo, H.K. and Mohanty, M.N., Wavelet-based feature combination for recognition of emotions. *Ain Shams Eng. J.*, 9, 1799–1806, 2018.
5. Palo, H.K. and Behera, D., Analysis of Speaker's Age Using Clustering Approaches with Emotionally Dependent Speech Features, in: *Critical Approaches to Information Retrieval Research*, pp. 172–197, IGI Global, USA, 2020.
6. Palo, H.K. and Sagar, S., Characterization and Classification of Speech Emotion with Spectrograms, in: *2018 IEEE 8th International Advance Computing Conference (IACC)*, IEEE, pp. 309–313, 2018.
7. Palo, H.K., Mohanty, J., Mohanty, M.N., Suresh, L.P., Comparison of similarity among subcategories of angry speech emotion, in: *2016 International Conference on Emerging Technological Trends (ICETT)*, IEEE, pp. 1–6, 2016.
8. Palo, H.K., *Spectral prosodic and hybrid features for emotion recognition*, PhD thesis, Siksha 'O' Anusandhan (Deemed to be University), Bhubaneswar, Odisha, India, 2018.
9. Palo, H.K., Pattanaik, N., Sahu, B.N., Real-Time Detection of Human Speech Emotion Using ATMEGA. *Int. J. Adv. Sci. Technol.*, 29, 12s, 1995–1301, 2020.

10. Chui, M., Löffler, M., Roberts, R., The internet of things. *McKinsey Q.*, 2, 1–9, 2010.
11. He, W., Yan, G., Da Xu, L., Developing vehicular data cloud services in the IoT environment. *IEEE Trans. Industr. Inform.*, 10, 2, 1587–1595, 2014.
12. Keerti Kumar, M., Shubham, M., Banakar, R.M., Evolution of IoT in smart vehicles: An overview, in: *IEEE International Conference on Green Computing and Internet of Things (ICGCIoT)*, pp. 804–809, 2015.
13. Galinina, O., Mikhaylov, K., Andreev, S., Turlikov, A., Koucheryavy, Y., Smart home gateway system over Bluetooth low energy with wireless energy transfer capability. *EURASIP J. Wirel. Comm.*, 178, 1–18, 2015.
14. Nandyala., C.S. and Kim., H.K., Green IoT agriculture and healthcare application (GAHA). *Int. J. Smart Home*, 10, 4, 289–300, 2016.
15. Wang, K., Wang, Y., Sun, Y., Guo, S., Wu, J., Green industrial internet of things architecture: An energy-efficient perspective. *IEEE Commun. Mag.*, 54, 12, 48–54, 2016.
16. Gou, Q., Yan, L., Liu, Y., Li, Y., Construction and Strategies in IoT Security System, in: *IEEE International Conference on Green Computing and Communications and IEEE Internet of Things and IEEE Cyber, Physical and Social Computing*, pp. 1129–1132, 2013.
17. Palo, H.K. and Sarangi, L., Overview of Machine Learners in Classifying of Speech Signals, in: *Handbook of Research on Emerging Trends and Applications of Machine Learning*, pp. 461–489, IGI Global, USA, 2020.
18. Wang, H.I., Constructing the green campus within the internet of things architecture. *Int. J. Distrib. Sens. N.*, 10, 3, 1–8, 2014.
19. Curry, E., Guyon, B., Sheridan, C., Donnellan, B., Developing a sustainable IT capability: Lessons from Intel's Journey. *MIS Q. Exec.*, 11, 2, 61–74, 2012.
20. Shi, W., Cao, J., Zhang, Q., Li, Y., Xu, L., EC: Vision and Challenges. *IEEE Internet Things J.*, 3, 5, 637–646, 2016.
21. Sun, X. and Ansari, N., Edge IoT: Mobile EC for the Internet of Things. *IEEE Commun. Mag.*, 54, 12, 22–29, 2016.
22. EPA Office Building Energy Use Profile (PDF), National Action Plan for Energy Efficiency Sector Collaborative on Energy Efficiency Office Building Energy Use Profile, http://www.epa.gov/cleanenergy/documents/sector-meeting/4bi_officebuilding.pdf, pp. 1-4, August 15, 2007, archived from the original (PDF) on 6 Mar 2009.
23. Stojmenovic, I. and Wen, S., The FC paradigm: Scenarios and security issues, in: *2014 IEEE Federated Conference on Computer Science and Information Systems*, pp. 1–8, 2014.
24. Visalakshi, P., Paul, S., Mandal, M., Green Computing, *International Journal of Modern Engineering Research (IJMER)*, in: *Proceedings of the National Conference on Architecture, Software systems and Green computing (NCASG), Paiyanoor (India)*, pp. 63–69, 2013.
25. Arshad, R., Zahoor, S., Shah, M.A., Wahid, A., Yu, H., Green IoT: An investigation on energy saving practices for 2020 and beyond. *IEEE Access*, 5, 667–681, 2017.
26. Ganzha, M., Paprzycki, M., Pawłowski, W., Szmeja, P., Wasielewska, K., Alignment-based semantic translation of geospatial data, in: *3rd IEEE International Conference on Advances in Computing, Communication & Automation (ICACCA)(Fall)*, pp. 1–8, 2017.
27. Gyrard, A. and Serrano, M., Connected smart cities: Interoperability with seg 3.0 for the internet of things, in: *30th IEEE International Conference on Advanced Information Networking and Applications Workshops (WAINA)*, pp. 796–802, 2016.
28. Palo, H.K. and Mohanty, M.N., Analysis of Speech Emotions Using Dynamics of Prosodic Parameters, in: *Cognitive Informatics and Soft Computing*, pp. 333–340, Springer, Singapore, 2020.
29. Palo, H.K., Behera, D., Rout, B.C., Comparison of Classifiers for Speech Emotion Recognition (SER) with Discriminative Spectral Features, in: *Advances in Intelligent Computing and Communication*, pp. 78–85, Springer, Singapore, 2020.

30. Palo, H.K., Chandra, M., Mohanty, M.N., Recognition of Human Speech Emotion Using Variants of Mel-Frequency Cepstral Coefficients, in: *Advances in Systems, Control and Automation, Lecture Notes in Electrical Engineering*, vol. 442, pp. 491–498, Springer Nature Singapore, 2018.

31. Palo, H.K., Kumar, P., Mohanty, M.N., Emotional Speech Recognition using Optimized Features. *Int. J. Res. Electr. Comput. Eng.*, 5, 4, 4–9, 2017.

32. Mohanty, M.N. and Palo, H.K., Child emotion recognition using probabilistic neural network with effective features. *Measurement*, Elsevier, 152, 107369, 2020.

Measures for Improving IoT Security

Richa Goel[1]*, Seema Sahai[1], Gurinder Singh[1] and Saurav Lall[2]

[1]Amity International Business School, Noida, India
[2]Azure IoT, Microsoft Seattle, Seattle, Washington, USA

Abstract

In today's world of Digital Transformation, IoT banking/online transaction is a major point of concern for the user. IoT security plays a vital role to develop the trust of end users for making frequent use of the same. There have been IoT security breaches in recent years. As a result, immoral hackers have ample opportunities to intercept and change or misuse the information. Through this paper we are going to discuss various isssue/problems faced in terms of IoT security along with the measure to be chosen to achieve higher security while going for online transactions.

Keywords: IoT security, digital transformation, breach of trust

2.1 Introduction

Through the World Wide Web, we've entered into a brand new era of connectivity. "Things have identities and virtual personalities operating in smart places using intelligent interfaces to connect and communicate inside social, environmental and user contexts [7]." More than twenty billion devices were connected with each other in 2017. This means that the potential risk of cyber-attacks is going on increasingly, equally.

Gartner's special report indicates that there is a high level of risk to all the IoT devices, whether it is the platform, their operating systems or even the other devices to which they are connected [10]. The kind of risk that exists is that ranging from physical tampering to information hacking and impersonation and many more. Organizations' functioning has completely changed with the coming in of IOT. With this change a whole range of risks have also emerged and it has become the utmost priority of organizations to manage these risks.

A variety of possible security threats are posed by IOT which could affect users: (1) Enabling unauthorized access and abuse of data and confidential information and (2) enabling attacks on linked networks and devices (3) developing security risks [22]. Scientists have proposed that privacy and online protection should not be segregated. All security policies need to be addressed with respect to IOT and its linking systems

---
*Corresponding author: rgoel@amity.edu

Monika Mangla, Suneeta Satpathy, Bhagirathi Nayak and Sachi Nandan Mohanty (eds.) Integration of Cloud Computing with Internet of Things: Foundations, Analytics, and Applications, (25–40) © 2021 Scrivener Publishing LLC

and apps. It's also true that online protection is the main problem for cloud computing. "Safety is one of the key concerns required to avoid the occurrence and use of IOT," the World Health Organization states. There are also several barriers to health at IoT. It would be necessary to explain:

   a. Expansion of the 'IoT' to the ordinary network, network controls and cell network
   b. website that links everyone
   c. exchange of objects with each other
   d. Accessible easily.

The code layer, information layer, physical layer and networking layer contain many technical obstacles to IoT security. To order to protect IoT, numerous reports discuss these security topics. Experiments that illustrate IoT's human experience are rare, though. Some of the latest works on IoT defense still consider the technical aspect. In order to achieve success in technology performance or safety management, users need to understand Dhillon and Torkzadeh's [9] expectations, values and beliefs.

We recognize that consumer expectations and values are balanced against technology to achieve positive results for information technology and the effective management of legislation. IoT Securing Science is in its infancy as it is a very active and recent research field. Further emphasis should also be placed on the confidentiality, fairness and privacy of IoT data and their credibility. Inside this article, we perform a thorough analysis to address numerous IoT security issues/problems along with the step to use the firewall for greater protection when performing online transactions.

2.2   Perceiving IoT Security

Researcher's Agarwal and Dey [4] note, "a safe and secure world allowed by IoT promises to lead to truly connected environments, where people and things cooperate to improve the overall quality of life. Truly IoT will give us operating information at our fingertips, without us having to ask for it or even recognizing that it might be required." According to some researchers, the IoT is "a dynamic global network infrastructure with self-configuring capabilities based on a standard and interoperable communication convention where physical and virtual 'things' have identities, physical attributes, and virtual personalities, use intelligent interfaces and are flawlessly united into the information network." With regards to securing IoT, some authors state that "In this context the information pump of the real world of interest is represented across billions of 'things,' many of which are updating in real-time and a transaction or data change is updated across hundreds or thousands of 'things' with differing update policies, opens up for many security challenges and security techniques across multiple policies. In order to prevent the unauthorized use of private information, research is needed in the area of vigorous trust, security and privacy management." Agarwal and Dey [4] also note that "security IoT means providing access control procedure and policies and being able to implement them, particularly in the face of the huge number of varied devices."

2.3   The IoT Safety Term

No doubt after pre-IoT days, human interaction with technology has developed as an auto-mated control and tracking (e.g. various IoT devices) to access information and utilities (e.g. e-commerce). The IoT word is sweet. This involves intelligent machines followed by various network participants. Research is in the early stages on IoT and its safety charac-teristics. It is due to creativity and the expansion of this program in different fields such as eHealth, e-commerce and e-traffic.

Several scholars have looked into the health implications of IoT; there is still a shortage of systemic comprehension. IoT technology work primarily addresses problems relevant to privacy concerns. The safety of people, the protection of company structures and the secu-rity of third parties are three main concerns for Technology. For IoT environments, there are four complex integrated devices interacting with each other.

These components are individuals, artifacts, software and equipment, which are required to oppose anonymity, protection which transparent confidence problems. Previous threats in normal networks contributing to IoT pose passive and aggressive attacks; hinders its efficiency and invalidates the benefits in utilizing the amenities.

Because IoT devices are limited by hardware tools, the usage of common safety mea-sures is troublesome, let alone user standards that would govern protection choices. At the technical point, there are three kinds of protection restrictions: equipment limitations, device limitations and network shortages. All three tell how protection can be configured for IoT apps.

Restrictions often offer a context for consumers and organizations to focus strategi-cally on the value of IoT protection. Hardware limitations on IoT protection are critical. According to the battery-driven IoT systems it is impossible to relay fully inefficient algo-rithms for encryption.

Restrictions on memory often face a major challenge. Standard protection algorithms are believed to be important RAM and hard drive space.

This will not refer to IoT devices. Thanks to the small scale and the remote location that is a security threat, IoT systems run the risk of still being compromised [3]. The smallness of the systems at the software level is the reason of some worry regarding the principle of security. To order to maintain the power and resistance characteristics safe enough, IoT systems have small network protocol batteries.

IoT systems also have issues with remote reprogramming and even reprogramming can be challenging, if not difficult. On a networking point of view, there are several questions concerning effectiveness and expandability. Because IoT systems are mobile by design, the need for the versatility of reliable protocols to ensure protection is important. It is impossi-ble for the current network access control protocol to withstand topological changes in the network.

Given the complexity of IoT and protection issues, traditional safety standards and the usage of technologies are troublesome. OWASP [27] also described many threats to harmful hazards that are unique to IoT. It provides the ability to gain usernames by communicating with authentication and raising forgotten passwords. The possibility that poor passwords mix user name information can be a security nightmare. Unencrypted networks will also raise security issues as well as the incomplete upgrade process.

2.4   Objectives

2.4.1   Enhancing Personal Data Access in Public Repositories

Conversations with our respondents showed that there was a great deal of anxiety over two key topics. The first problem is the inappropriate handling of private data in public forums. Most IoT systems and software transmit data to other apps and servers on a daily basis.

The second problem is the lack of consistency with the quality of search data. Seeing that every quest made on some of the IoT related devices and sites has been going on which increases concern among interviewees that their quest habits are not explicitly documented and are accessible. "There is a great deal of interest in the privacy literature around preserving the confidentiality of personal details in public datasets Geo-location is sensitive knowledge regarding privacy and its disclosure will seriously harm consumer privacy."

2.4.2   Develop and Sustain Ethicality

Respondents in our research described two factors relevant to the nature of ethics in the IoT world—legal principles and fair usage. Existing literature has found rational usage and ethics to be significant, in particular because of the pervasive existence of technology.

According to Abbas, Michael and Michael [1], "The four topics underpinning socio-ethical studies involve the analysis into what is the human intent, what is legal, how fairness

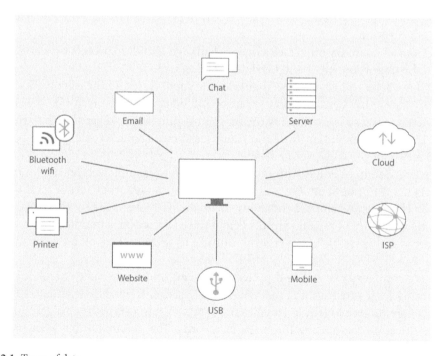

Figure 2.1 Types of data.

is served and the values that direct the usage of that methodology. Participants; their relationships with systems; people's interests and personal expectations; societal and moral beliefs; processes, laws and norms; and fairness, personal benefits and personal harms are all areas of interest in a socio-ethical approach." Figure 2.1 shows the various types of data.

2.4.3   Maximize the Power of IoT Access

Often the main objective of ensuring data confidentiality is to achieve this essential objective. Organizations may have a wealth of confidential information, but the data are not widely available to anyone. As regards IoT, there are further attack vector and hence better probability of attack, together with a large number of linked computers. Unauthorized exposure could exploit security vulnerabilities that could lead to physical security risks [28] (Figure 2.2).

2.4.4   Understanding Importance of Firewalls

The IoT is a frightening place. Criminals on the IoT have the potential to put out of sight behind their computers, or even other people's computers, while they attempt to intervene in your computer to thieve personal information or to use it for their own purposes. But how you can prevent it or safeguard? The answer is that you can protect yourself with a firewall.

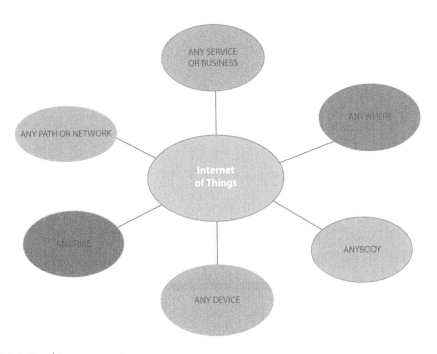

Figure 2.2 IoT and its components.

2.5 Research Methodology

We use the value-focused reasoning approach suggested by Keeney [19] to define IoT protection objectives. Keeney [20] applies this method to IoT business-associated consumer personality principles. He claims the only approach to figure out what the interest of the consumer is to question them. It is important to ask other prospective consumers since many individuals have specific beliefs and they convey various beliefs.

As values are produced, they are not automatically grouped into well-integrated classes with a good comprehension of which values are linked to the others and why. Within this analysis, the value-focused mindset methodology is used to produce IoT protection principles, goals and behavior of IT practitioners who rely on optimizing IoT protection (Figure 2.3).

According to Keeney [19], creative reasoning techniques are seen as the foundation for certain decision-making processes. In the research, the number of people to be questioned differs. Nonetheless, Hunter [16] questioned 53 people in two organisations and generated participant inceptions by performing a content review. Keeney [20] holds conversations and debates with more than 100 people about their principles for IoT transactions. In this report, we performed 40–50 min of interviews with 58 IT practitioners with different backgrounds and experience. Both participants have extensive day-to-day interaction with the IoT. Respondents covered the following sectors: transport and

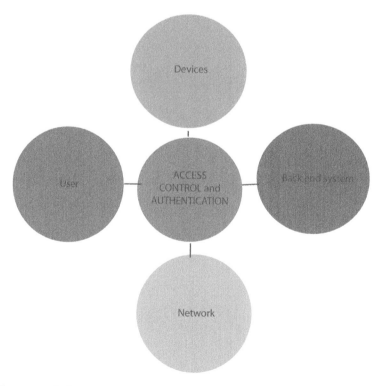

Figure 2.3 IoT access control.

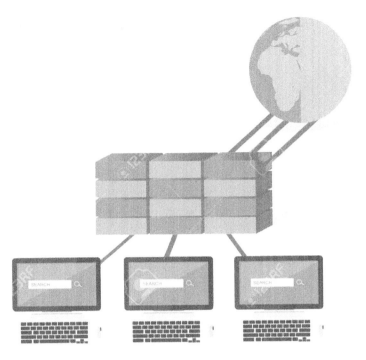

Figure 2.4 Concept of firewall.

distribution, education, hospitality, finance and banking. We used a three-step method to define and coordinate the values and protection measures that a person has in relation to IoT protection (Figure 2.4).

Includes these steps:

- Developing a value list of consumers, involving asking the people concerned what they value for IoT safety?
- Management of priorities to identify ways to accomplish end-of-life (fundamental) objectives;
- Safety mechanisms to be chosen for the firewall to ensure better protection as electronic transactions are ongoing.

2.6 Security Challenges

Security issues associated with IoT are various. Security is the only such problem. To order to ensure the security of user knowledge from IoT exposure, the Internet of Things requires special requirements to order to have a specific identity for virtually every physical or virtual person or device, which will autonomously communicate with the Web or related networks. The table below illustrates that all privacy can be impaired.

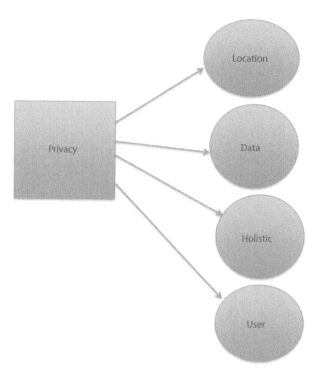

Figure 2.5 Privacy in IoT.

Challenge is of Privacy
An IoT security plan requires a holistic strategy that includes IT infrastructure, operational commands, cloud and consumer technology that function in tandem to ensure security. IoT-based threats have far too many implications to ignore. Hackers may now endanger human security and might even trigger confrontations.

Internet of Things connectivity provides versatility for remote control of devices

And in some situations, enabling the collection of data from physical sensors. There has been a huge rise in the Internet of Things, with a growing amount of physical devices connected with each other over the network. The environment created by IoT where different devices are connected through different software and operating systems, make them more vulnerable to attacks. Most IoT devices have no protection features, and even those that are there, are mostly rudimentary. Hence it is easy to attack them. IoT devices may become points of entry into smart homes and organizations Figure 2.5.

2.6.1   Challenge of Data Management

Organizations use the collected data for evaluating, preserving and enhancing operating performance. The pattern of rapid processing and use of data has contributed to a rise in data-driven business practices. Saving and sharing the collected data, however, can be a big concern for business leaders. With the issue of data privacy, businesses need to be extremely careful.

2.7   Securing IoT

2.7.1   Ensure User Authentication

This objective explores how authentication mechanisms must be established to enhance IoT security. Inherently ambiguous, yet weak verification mechanisms such as passwords. Two-factor authentication hardware tokens are usually best suited to IoT authentication. To order to enhance system security, 2FA based protection frames are now introduced. The enhanced use of biometrics often demonstrates the IoT client's identification by means of a robust and identifying tool. You can replicate your password or hardware key, but with your downward reader, you can not replicate your fingerprint. The principles and the legal responsibility for social networking sites are also assured of the authentication process Figure 2.6.

2.7.2   Increase User Autonomy

The value of the consent of the user to the processing of IoT powered data. This underlines the need for verification and preference for individual influence of sensitive data and hence for increased privacy. Not all data has to be selected. If the usage of data is incompatible with the meaning of experiences, a simple and easy-to-read alternative will be given to individuals. Similar claims have been made in the literature. As regards the freedom of individuals, in particular with regard to IoT privacy security (Kounelis *et al.* [21]), it is argued that only if a mixture of person and artifact retains the ability to make deliberate choices and decisions in architecture, and awareness and vigilance in the field of freedom and security, can the overall interactions maintain confidence and trust Figure 2.7.

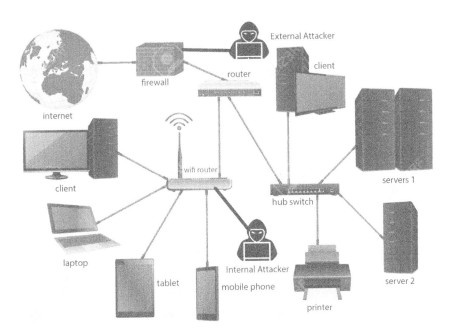

Figure 2.6 Internal and external attacker on IoT Infrastructure.

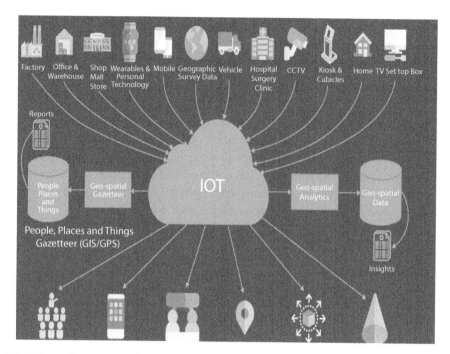

Figure 2.7 Different data sources of IoT.

2.7.3 Use of Firewalls

Earlier firewalls were high-ticket items of hardware that solely corporations would make use. The general public weren't on the web, and if they were they were connected via a dial up that isn't quick enough for many hacker's functions. Consequently, hackers primarily attack United Nations organizations which with wider repositories of information available. At present, almost everyone has the ability to link to the website, and many hackers tend to concentrate on the house user since they are additionally capable of not securing their computers properly, which transform them into an unimpressive target. This in mind, yet strong home firewall technologies were built by developers to protect themselves. The house users' firewalls are either a hardware or a cable.

Hardware firewall: A hardware firewall may be a bridge between your network association and the other blocked computers. In addition, these firewalls have an interconnected gateway that allows you to connect several devices to them so that anyone can join a network association. Such firewalls secure any single device linked to the Network Address Translation or NAT using a technology. Both secure computers, such as 192.168.1.X, that can not be reached via the network are secure by victimization and non-public data abuse. These internal data processors are then combined into one by the firewall. This allows the hardware firewall to accept all incoming requests you received and forward them to the internal PC received. This system, beyond machines, cannot be linked to the computers by the victimization of this technique.

Personal firewall: Any computer to be covered will be a Private Firewall kit that is installed into it. This kit then filters all input and generally outgoing traffic and makes only required or specifically allowed information. Computer firewalls are typically abundant in additional functionality than hardware models, but they have little capacity to connect the site connection with other network computers.

The decision on which form of firewall is based on what you want to use. Unless you want to just protect 1 pc, then mainly personal firewall kit is more than sufficient. When you want to protect many machines, a hardware-based solution is also of great benefit. Many people also say you can use a hardware firewall to save your network and a virtual firewall to secure your device. While sometimes this is not a good program, for other consumers it will be a prevention feature. When cash isn't paired in nursing, instead through victimization will provide a degree of protection, as the bigger practicality found in personal firewalls.

2.7.4   Firewall Features

Filtering is carried out once a firewall examines the passage of information and determines whether that information is permitted to be transmitted and received or if supported rules and filters that are created must be discarded. It is the firewall's usually first operation, and the protection demands extremely the way it performs these functions. The general public believes that the firewall is the most significant firewall operation, specifically, the transfer of inward knowledge to the computers. However, the departing filtering also plays a key role in protecting your machine. You may have malware inserted on your PC while your data was not, and you will suddenly see that the PC package tries to transmit information to a foreign host someplace on the web after you install a firewall with departing filtering. Now, you don't just understand this package, but the filtering stopped distributing non-public information.

These filters can be modified so that all PCs on the network can effectively transfer information into your device or probably apps on your computer. Nevertheless, your desires will be guided by these laws. You would need to open port for remote desktop-related communications protocol (port 3389) to allow the traffic to move through your firewall, for example if you want remote users to connect to the remote victimization device remotely. The following example of this can be found in the nursing when permission to access the computer behind the firewall is granted to a particular remote PC Figure 2.8.

2.7.5   Mode of Camouflage

It's critical that your firewall doesn't actually obstruct attempts to access your laptop, but it doesn't even appear like your laptop exists on the network. You are in what is known as concealment mode after square measuring connected to the web and your laptop can not be detected by samples on the laptop. Hackers will see how the computer is scanned with special expertise and the findings on the site. If you calculate in a cover-up mode, the firewall does not return this information, but appears to be connected. This information is not really connected. Thanks to this hacker your laptop does not continue to hit, because they believe that you are not online.

2.7.6   Protection of Data

There are actually a great number of firewalls with the ability to dam spyware, hijackers and adware. It helps you to shield your machine from interference of code which is marvelous to

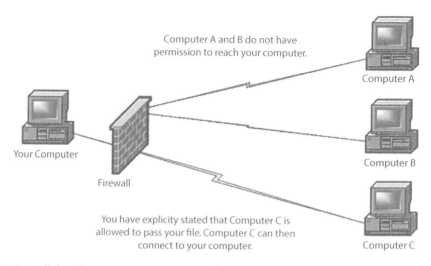

Computer A and B do not have
permission to reach your computer.

Computer A

Your Computer

Computer B

Firewall

You have explicity stated that Computer C is
allowed to pass your file. Computer C can then
connect to your computer.

Computer C

Figure 2.8 Firewall that allows remote user access to a firewall device.

expose sensitive knowledge about what you do on the net or other programming activities. Ses square solutions are also packaged into firewall kit business versions.

2.7.7   Integrity in Service

Integrity of operation is where the firewall controls the computer's files to change them or how they are released. If such an alteration is detected, the user will be informed and the application will not be able to execute or transmit IoT information. Sometimes those improvements could have been used in an update, but now you will be told of it, if, it is changed by the malicious software.

2.7.8   Sensing of Infringement

Intruders use various techniques to breach the computer's protection. Intrusion detection checks incoming system signature data and notifies you when these attempts are detected. With intrusion detection, you can see what a hacker wants to do to hack your computer.

Notifications help you to see what's going on your firewall and to warn you of potential intrusion attempts on your device in different ways.

2.8   Monitoring of Firewalls and Good Management

2.8.1   Surveillance

Whatever firewall you use, it is a smart thing to obey and occasionally show firewall logs. You will improve your protection automatically through careful observance of your logs. Most hacks can theoretically be avoided if people track their logs because most hackers will check a laptop before hacking them. When a participant in the PC nursing supervisor detects these tests, they will check that their machines are sensitive to what they were checking. You'll be shocked by the amount of people WHO tries to access your laptop, but not your results, until you start installing your firewall and reviewing logs.

The reasons behind tracking the log files are three: There are three key reasons:

Preventative Measures: You can see what harbors and services hackers are able to manipulate by tracking the firewall logs. Such knowledge will then be used to guarantee that the machine is safe against such exploits. For starters, when you see on your logs that other people are checking and investigating your machine for port 3127, you will discover that people and viruses will check for the backdoors on your machine which are left behind by the early version of the My Doom virus. You will then ensure that this new attack doesn't damage the computers.

2.8.2   Forensics

If your machine is hit by a long distance virus, then you can check the date and time it was installed on your device by the hacker. Forensics: You will be able to search your log files for maltreatment of this data through all of this point of time, however the hacker has infiltrated your computer. This information is then used to encrypt your computer.

Officials reporting: With the data stored in the log files, you are able to supply officials with the details whether a hack or attempt is a success. The logs send you the IP address, system and time and date of the offending device.

2.8.3   Secure Firewalls for Private

- A Free online armor of Emsisoft
- The Firewall Outpost
- Zone Free Alarm

2.8.4   Business Firewalls for Personal

- The McAfee Human Firewall
- The Firewall Outpost Pro
- Zone Pro/Plus Alarm

2.8.5   IoT Security Weaknesses

There's no single IoT security vendor that can provide a full end-to-end security solution. However, some organizations provide more than others and some may provide a full end-to-end IoT security solution in tandem with their partner ecosystem.

Authentication/authorization is one of the biggest issues to tackle in IoT security, followed by access control and data encryption. IoT security respondents didn't consider firewall, passwords, server security and privacy as a major weakness.

2.9   Conclusion

This chapter uses a value-driven reasoning method to establish goals for securing IoT. Some studies [9] have used Keeney's meaning-focused approach in order to explain the

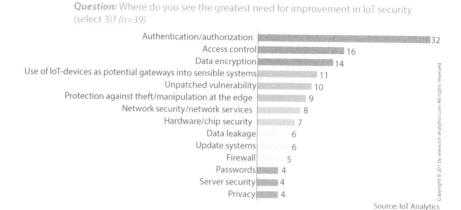

Question: Where do you see the greatest need for improvement in IoT security (select 3)? *(n=39)*

Figure 2.9 Where is security in IoT needed.

goals and their relationships dependent on people's interest, according to Keeney [20] values of knowledge. and their relationships based on people values and learning the importance of firewalls Figure 2.9.

The value-focused thought methodology has not been used to describe the protection goals of IoT from the consumer viewpoint. Extracting IoT security relevance from consumer expectations will enable administrators and professionals optimize IoT protection based on a detailed set of objectives.

This research adds to the scope of the literature by incorporating basic goals and strategies for protecting IoT. This research explores the largely unexplored field of IoT protection. We perform a systematic analysis utilizing value-focused reasoning that has helped to identify goals and protection steps clustered into four simple and medium-sized priorities, which are important for protecting IoT from the individual perspective. We see why the device's firewall is a must to defend the device from unethical hackers or viruses. We should be able to use the applications on the IoT with sufficient supervision and rules to further improve the protection of our device. We lock our doors to deter stolen robes when we leave our building, why not use a firewall to protect your computer?

References

1. Abbas, R., Michael, K., Michael, M.G., Using a Social-Ethical Framework to Evaluate Location-Based Services in an IoT of Things World. *Int. Rev. Inf. Ethics*, 22, 12, 2015.
2. Abie, H. and Balasingham, I., Risk-based adaptive security for smart IoT in eHealth, in: *Proceedings of the 7th International Conference on Body Area Networks*, February, ICST (Institute for Computer Sciences, Social-Informatics and Telecommunications Engineering), pp. 269–275, 2012.
3. Agarwal, Y. and Dey, A.K., Toward Building a Safe, Secure, and Easy-to-Use IoT of Things Infrastructure. *Computer*, 49, 4, 88–91, 2016.
4. Bassi, A. and Horn, G., IoT of Things in 2020 A ROADMAP FOR THE FUTURE, *European Commission: Information Society and Media*, 22, 97–114, 2008.

5. Dhillon, G. and Torkzadeh, G., Value-focused assessment of information system security in organizations. *Inf. Syst. J.*, 16, 3, 293–314, 2006.

6. Gartner, (n.d.), IoT of Things: The Gartner Perspective, Retrieved May 2, 2020, from https://www.gartner.com/en/information-technology/insights/IoT-of-things.

7. Hunter, M.G., The use of RepGrids to gather interview data about information systems analysts. *Inf. Syst. J.*, 7, 1, 67–81, 1997.

8. Keeney, R.L. and McDaniels, T.L., Value-focused thinking about strategic decisions at BC Hydro. *Interfaces*, 22, 6, 94–109, 1992.

9. Keeney, R.L., The value of IoT commerce to the customer. *Manage. Sci.*, 45, 4, 533–542, 1999.

10. Kounelis, I., Baldini, G., Neisse, R., Steri, G., Tallacchini, M., Pereira, A.G., Building trust in the human? IoT of things relationship. *IEEE Technol. Soc. Mag.*, 33, 4, 73–80, 2014.

11. Rakic-Skokovic, M., *Guidelines for Overcoming some IoT Security Issues*, XVII International Scientific Conference on Industrial Systems, 1–6, 2017, Retrieved from http://www.iim.ftn.uns.ac.rs/is17.

12. OWASP Application Security – Building and Breaking Applications, OWASP, https://owasp.org/www-community/OWASP_Application_Security_FAQ

13. FTC. (2017). Privacy & Data Security Update, | Federal Trade Commission, 2016. Retrieved from https://www.ftc.gov/reports/privacy-data-security-update-2016.

## 3

An Efficient Fog-Based Model for Secured Data Communication

V. Lakshman Narayana[1]* and R. S. M. Lakshmi Patibandla[2]†

[1]Department of IT, Vignan's Nirula Institute of Technology & Science for Women. Peda Palakaluru, Guntur, Andhra Pradesh, India
[2]Department of IT, Vignan's Foundation for Science, Technology and Research, Guntur, Andhra Pradesh, India

Abstract

Fog Computing is an effective computing model that expands Cloud Computing administrations to the edge of the system to provide security for the data. The new features offered by Fog Computing if effectively applied for time-sensitive applications that can possibly quicken the revelation of early crisis circumstances to help smart dynamic applications. While promising, how to plan and grow certifiable fog registering based information checking frameworks is as yet an open issue. As an initial step to address this issue, in the proposed work, a fog based model for Secured data communication is developed and shows the functional relevance and centrality of such a framework. In this work, a unique Fog Based elevated level programming model for sensitive applications that are geospatially circulated, enormous scope is designed. The fog registering system gives the model to oversee IoT benefits in the fog prospect by methods for a certifiable proving position. Moreover, the system encourages the communication between the gadgets, fog gadget arrangements, IoT administration and dynamic asset provisioning in a secured way. The proposed model overcomes communication issues in IoT gadgets to build up a powerful programming condition with fog computing method in performing resource handling, validations and IoT device arrangements. The proposed Fog Computing model effectively establishes communication among IoT devices and provides security to the data during communication.

Keywords: Secure data transmission, data empowerment, communication, security, IoT device security, resource handling

3.1 Introduction

Fog computing is a service initiated framework by a systems administration. It might be extremely hard to illustrate fog computing exclusive of primary illustrating cloud computing as Fog Computing is actually an expansion of the cloud. Cloud computing is that the modes to in turn ICT activities and benefits and put away PC resources beyond the web. This make

---

*Corresponding author: lakshmanv58@gmail.com
†Corresponding author: patibandla.lakshmi@gmail.com

Monika Mangla, Suneeta Satpathy, Bhagirathi Nayak and Sachi Nandan Mohanty (eds.) Integration of Cloud Computing with Internet of Things: Foundations, Analytics, and Applications, (41–56) © 2021 Scrivener Publishing LLC

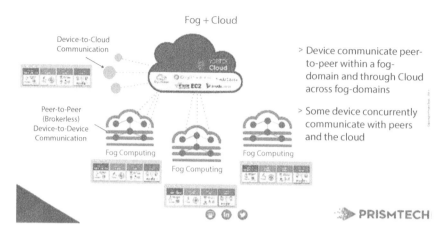

Figure 3.1 Cloud computing vs fog computing.

it realistic for people and organizations to utilize outsider equipment and program facilitate on online [1]. Figure 3.1 depicts the cloud computing vs fog computing model. Cloud computing make it especially effortless to urge to data and PC resources as of everywhere thus extreme as an internet association is available. Among them, within and out convenience of shared/collective compute resources, cloud computing offer preferences more conventional on position facilitate administrations as far as speed, cost, and productivity. In spite of the very certainty that cloud computing facility very well and excellent eventually, it depends extremely on the info transmission through available, which relies in the lead and the edge of the system experts. As a result of billions of consumers handling, conveyance, and accepting information during the cloud, the framework seems to be gradually cogged up [2].

Fog computing is also termed as fogging, but, is that the expansion or bring of cloud computing capacity along with the edge of the system and so on grant closer ICT administrations to the less clients. Along these lines, what identify Fog Computing from cloud computing is it's more rapidly proximity to modest end-clients, its further pervasive customer attainment, and better portability [3]. As against expectant gadgets to expertise the scheme of main framework, Fog Computing grants gadgets to edge straightforwardly and permits them to affect their associations and errands any way they esteem fit. Accordingly, Fog Computing improves the character of supervision, diminishes attacks, and provides a gradually agreeable consumer practice [4].

Fog computing simply sustains the expanding internet of things (IoT)—properties (vehicles, home machines, and even outfits) that are inserted with sensors to allow them to retrieve information [5]. Fog Computing can be actualized utilizing a fundamental association structure instead of being executed utilizing an awesome spike organizes [6]. Accordingly, it has a denser inclusion. This bit of flexibility makes it simpler to run an ongoing, large information activity with the capacity to help millions of hubs in profoundly unique, different conditions.

3.1.1   Fog Computing Model

Fog Computing is a layered model for empowering pervasive access to a common variety of versatile computing assets. The model encourages the arrangement of conveyed, dormancy mindful applications and administrations, and comprises of fog nodes (physical or virtual), living between keen end-gadgets and unified (cloud) administrations [7]. The fog hubs are setting attentive and support typical information with the executives and correspondence framework. They can be composed in bunches - either vertically (to help separation), on a level plane (to help association), or comparative with fog hubs' security separation to the sharp end-gadgets. Fog computing limits the solicitation reaction time from/to supported applications, and gives, for the end-gadgets, neighborhood computing assets and, when required, arrange availability to incorporated administrations [8]. Fog computing isn't seen as an obligatory layer for such environments nor is then brought together (cloud) administration saw as being required for a fog computing layer to help the usefulness of perception end-gadgets [8]. Distinctive use case situations may have various structures dependent on the ideal way to deal with supporting end-gadgets usefulness.

The fog hub is the center segment of the fog computing engineering. Fog hubs are either physical segments (for example passages, switches, switches, servers, and so forth.) or virtual parts (for example virtualized switches, virtual machines, cloudlets, and so on.) that are firmly combined with the confidence end-gadgets or access arranges, and give computing assets to these gadgets. A fog hub knows about its topographical dissemination and legitimate area inside the setting of its cluster [9]. Also, fog hubs give some type of information the board and correspondence administrations between the system's edge layer where end-gadgets reside, and the fog computing administration or the brought together (cloud computing) assets, when required. To convey a given fog computing ability, fog hubs work in a brought together or decentralized way and can be arranged as independent fog hubs that impart among them to convey the administration or can be united to frame groups that give level adaptability over scatter geo areas, through reflecting or augmentation components.

3.1.2   Correspondence in IoT Devices

The Internet of Things is answerable for gathering certifiable information, from a wide range of gadgets including sensors, actuators, doors, and that's only the tip of the security. Sensors, specifically, have been for quite a long time utilized in different ventures. Figure 3.2 clearly represents the basic fog computing model which represents different layers in the model. The Internet of Things is answerable for gathering genuine information, from a

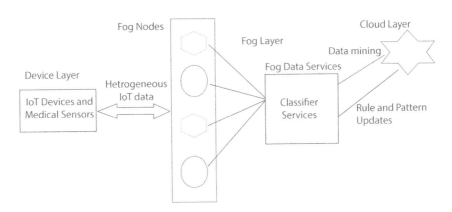

Figure 3.2 Basic fog computing model.

wide range of gadgets including sensors, actuators, passages, and the sky is the limit from there. Sensors, specifically, have been for quite a long time utilized in different businesses. Typically, they're not unreasonably costly and obviously, they are extremely little, so they can be appended to any gadget. For instance, most present-day cell phones are furnished with light sensors, accelerometers, magnetometers, spinners, closeness sensors, temperature sensors, and even dampness sensors or gauges.

There are additionally numerous sensors utilized in watches, wrist groups, contact focal points, and so forth [10]. A significant component of the Internet of Things arranges is layer transport, which guarantees information preparing from sensors, neighborhood stockpiling, and sending. It very well may be acknowledged through norms made explicitly for information transport needs, for example, TCP, or progressively modern conventions that incorporate numerous layers in their innovation stack including a vehicle layer, for example, LwM2M [11]. The guideline, notwithstanding, continues as before — to share sensor information, the Internet of Things for the most part requires a web association. Such availability can be given by wired systems or remote advances. The process of communication in IoT devices are represented in Figure 3.3. By far most of Internet of Things systems utilize an assortment of advancements (a large portion of them being remote), and the most well-known are:

- Cellular systems which necessitate retrofitting in the SIM card and continue inside the scope of a given system cell
- WiFi — a short-extend remote system. Most current telephones, tablets, PCs, and different gadgets are furnished by a WiFi element. To guarantee the Internet get to we additionally require a switch or WiFi passage

Figure 3.3 Communication in IoT devices.

- Bluetooth, a convention which permits the association of gadgets prepared in the Bluetooth module, devoted for the trade of a limited quantity of information, gives a generally fast transmission
- ZigBee, a convention devoted to working systems and applications that require low transmission capacity, gives vitality effectiveness to battery gadgets and is intended for systems in which information trade happens irregularly or in which gadgets furnished with sensors or info gadgets transmit information to the outlet.

3.2   Attacks in IoT

Numerous ways of attacks have been roughly for moderately a whilst. What's happening is the extent and virtual sincerity of attacks in the Internet of Things (IoT) – a huge amount of gadgets that are an expected object to customary manner digital attacks yet on a lot higher scope and habitually with controlled, if any security [12]. At its core, IoT is coupled with associating and systems admin gadgets that as of recently have not truly been related. This implies those gadgets; despite of whether it is your bright out of the box latest associated cooler or your associated vehicle, are building an extra passage peak to the system and accordingly growing security and protection chance.

While the sort of assaults regularly follows a similar methodology as already, the achieve of every attack can fluctuate severely, reliant upon the biological system, the widget and provision, the reachable assertion intensity [13].

In the course of the most recent couple of weeks, we ran a little arrangement of the 5 most regular digital assaults and how their danger ascends to an uncommon level with the potential outcomes of the IoT [14]. In this blog, you will locate a synopsis of all the potential assaults, however follow the connections for inside and out inclusion on each assault – every one of them have been shrouded on our blog in earlier weeks!

3.2.1   Botnets

Botnets while thing bots include a legitimate scope of contraptions, all related with each other – from PCs, workstations, phones, and tablets to now in like manner those "insightful" devices. these things shares two essential traits in every way that really matters: they're web enabled which they will move data normally by methods for a framework. Unfriendly to spam advancement can spot pretty reliably inside the occasion that one machine sends countless practically identical messages, yet it's essentially harder to spot if those messages are being sent from various devices that are a dash of a botnet [15]. Every one of them have one target: sending an enormous number of email requesting to a goal with the anticipation that the stage crashes while engaging to adjust to the monstrous proportion of sales.

3.2.2   Man-In-The-Middle Concept

The man-in-the-inside thought is that the spot an aggressor or developer is wanting to prevent and break correspondences between two separate structures. It okay could even be a perilous ambush since it's one where the aggressor inconspicuously squares and transmits messages between two get-togethers once they're under the conviction that they are examining really with each other. Since the attacker has the principal correspondence, they're going to trick the recipient into instinct they're hitherto getting a genuine message. Various cases have recently been represented inside this zone, occurrences of hacked vehicles, and hacked "sharp coolers" [16].

These attacks are frequently extremely unsafe inside the IoT, as a result of the idea of the "things" being hacked. for instance, these contraptions are regularly anything from mechanical instruments, device, or vehicles to innocuous related "things, for instance, sharp TVs or parking space door openers [17].

3.2.3   Data and Misrepresentation

While the news is stacked with terrifying and whimsical software engineers getting to data and money with a legitimate scope of incredible hacks, we are consistently also our own most noteworthy security foe. Foolish insurance of web related contraptions (for instance phone, iPad, Kindle, savvy, at that point forward.) is making ready for the plans of pernicious crooks and guileful pioneers.

The essential approach of discount extortion is to accumulate data – and with a touch of resilience, there's bounty to ask. General data available on the web, got together with web based systems administration information, moreover to data from shrewd watches, wellbeing trackers and, if open, splendid meters, clever coolers, and tons more gives an awesome all-round idea of your own character [18]. The more nuances are frequently discovered a few customer, the more straightforward and in this manner the further developed a concentrated on ambush concentrated on information extortion are regularly [19].

3.2.4   Social Engineering

The social structure is that the showing of controlling people so as that they give up characterized information. such information that hoodlums attempt to search out can change, in any case, when individuals are centered around, the criminals are by and large endeavoring to trick the customer into giving them passwords or bank information. Or then again, they could be endeavoring to desire to a PC so on stealthily present malevolent programming which can by then give them access to singular information, while providing them order over the PC. Ordinarily, social structure hacks are done through phishing messages, which intend to have you ever unveil your information, or diverts destinations like banking or shopping districts that look legitimate, tricking you to enter your nuances [20].

3.2.5   Denial of Service

A Denial of Service (DoS) ambush happens when help which may for the principal part work is distant. There are frequently various clarifications behind unavailability; in any case, it by and large suggests structure that can't adjust because of breaking point over-trouble. During a Distributed Denial of Service (DDoS) attack, endless systems malignantly ambush one goal. This is regularly normally done through a botnet, where various contraptions are changed (as often as possible unbeknownst to the owner) to request help at the same time.

Interestingly with hacking attacks like phishing or creature influence ambushes, DoS doesn't for the chief part choose to take information or prompts security mishap, yet the loss of reputation for the impacted association can, regardless, cost an eminent arrangement of some time and money. Much of the time customers in like manner like better to change to a competitor, as they fear security issues or essentially can't stand to have blocked off help. As often as possible a Dos assault fits activists and blackmailers.

3.2.6   Concerns

A significant worry in the IoT is the affirmation of protection. By what means will buyer information be utilized and by whom? A situation where your home, office, vehicles, apparatuses, office gear, and numerous different gadgets are associated with the web raises new worries for the two shoppers and organizations about where their information will go and how, obviously, it will be utilized. Organizations should assess the arrangements for protection and information security to up their game and guarantee gathered information is defended and kept hidden. Just when organizations begin doing this, there will be affirmations of protection.

While your business is probably going to be confronted with various kinds of assaults after some time, the primary objective isn't to get occupied by the endeavor of the week.

Put your time and cash in a strong security structure, center around the most widely recognized assaults, and offer normal preparing to your staff to guarantee they can spot assaults when they occur. Concentrate on the dangers that are well on the way to influence your business and are destined to have a serious result. The responses to security concerns are out there: as expanded security, verification, and the board of information. The different types of attacks in IoT devices are represented in Figure 3.4.

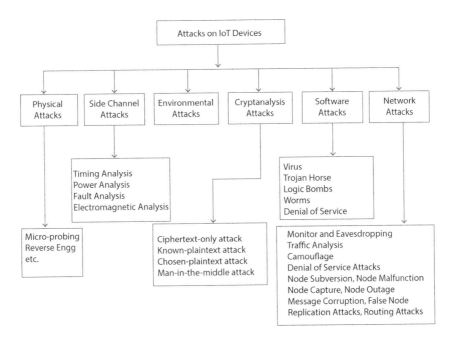

Figure 3.4 Attacks in IoT.

3.3   Literature Survey

Fog computing is seen on the grounds that the most sensible edge computing stage for IoT frameworks and applications. Since it had been first pronounced by Cisco as a sort of edge computing and an extension of the cell edge computing, investigates and mulls over are made to take a gander at, portray, improve and consolidate Fog computing. Various works that consider Fog computing for IoT are driven; either without the course of action of SDN advancement or with SDN.

The more prominent a piece of these works are composing studies; inside the going with section(s), we anticipate a couple of segment of those undertakings. In Reference, the makers developed a structure for an IoT interface with Fog computing association. This work was for the principal part made for considering IoT applications from a Fog computing viewpoint. The makers introduced a circled data stream instrument, insinuated as DDF, which is programmable [11]. The dataflow programming model was used for building differing IoT applications and organizations. The information estimation was endorsed over the open-source stream-based run time and visual programming gadget, Node-RED. The testing was familiar just favorably that the arranging and count are sensible. In any case, no introduction estimations were thought of. In Reference, the makers developed a dynamic computing structure for clinical applications over IoT frameworks.

The dynamic structure includes a concentrated cloud and appropriated Fog units. The proposed perspectives knew about section and oblige the AI methodologies used for human administrations applications over IoT frameworks. The estimation tasks and clinical data are scattered among two computing levels during a dividing that assembles the system availability. In addition, a shut circle the administrators system was developed that is basically dependent upon the customer's condition (e.g., clinical limits). The system was endorsed the extent that reaction time and openness. Our proposed work shares the similarity of using Fog perspective with this work, while this work in a general sense thinks about clinical applications over the IoT frameworks and moreover just cares openness as a display metric.

Fog computing and SDN gauges. The work for the principal part minds a particular issue, which is that the SDN controller circumstance. The SDN organize includes two degrees of controllers; the fundamental controller and discretionary controller. The fundamental controller might be a united one that takes the control and in this manner the officials undertaking of the general system. The discretionary controller might be a scattered controller resolved to differed locale of the made sure about zone. the 2 controllers are really related. A smoothing out issue was understood to strengthen the geographic game plan of the coursed controllers [12]. The work shares the resemblance of sending Fog computing and SDN with an IoT associate with our proposed framework, while it considers only the IoV, which might be a high convenience application. One standard issue of this computation is that it's not been evaluated which the show wasn't checked.

The makers just introduced a system structure. In Reference, the makers developed a secured IoT structure that passes on Fog computing, SDN and blockchain to upgrade the well being of IoT frameworks. The system uses SDN and blockchain to shape sure about and control the scattered Fog structure. Fog organizations are allowed at the sting of the entryway mastermind by the appropriated Fog centers. The structure achieves higher torpidity and security viability since bringing computing resources at the sting of the IoT framework could affirm about the center framework traffic and breaking point the start to finish inactivity between IoT devices and subsequently the computing unit. The system presents a totally remarkable security methodology that permits the structure to control to the risk scene therefore. This permits structure administrators to run a proportional number of propositions at the framework edge shifting.

In one paper the creators center around task planning calculations for the minimization of the vitality in reconfigurable server farms that serve static customers. They proposed a ravenous methodology based booking calculation for planning assignments to VMs and afterward to reasonable servers. In spite of the fact that the accomplished vitality execution is calculable yet their utilization case doesn't think about portable customers, which are inescapable in SG. To present a programming model including a basic asset provisioning technique, which depends on outstanding task at hand limits, i.e., if the use of a specific fog cell surpasses a predefined esteem, another fog cell is rented. Aside from fog-explicit asset provisioning arrangements, asset designation and administration booking are significant exploration challenges in the general field of cloud computing.

Despite the fact that such strategies offer propelling bits of knowledge, there are key contrasts between fog administrations and cloud administrations. In this manner it forestalls an immediate adjustment for the utilization in the current work. In the first place, the size and kind of fog assets are altogether different from its cloud computing partners. While cloud assets are normally dealt with fair and square of physical machines, virtual machines (VMs), or compartments, fog assets are generally not as ground-breaking and broad. While cloud assets are generally positioned in incorporated server farms, the FCNs might be conveyed in a fairly more extensive territory having heterogeneous system geography, making it increasingly essential to consider information move times and cost in FC. This is particularly significant since one specific motivation to utilize FC in IoT situations is the higher postponement affectability of fog-based calculation. Subsequently, asset provisioning approaches for the fog need to ensure that this advantage isn't thwarted by broad information move times and cost [13].

3.4 Proposed Model for Attack Identification Using Fog Computing

The proposed design for IoT Applications introduced in this paper is based on certain ideas and models examined out of sight area. The design is seen as comprising of two basic layers: the oversaw component and overseeing component. The accompanying subsections are committed to present the structure and engineering of these two layers just as any supports and clarifications about any plan choices made in this proposed design. A. Demonstrating of Managed System the oversaw framework as pointed before speaks to the application rationale of the framework to be created. Here are a few ideas and a lot of wording we utilize when displaying the framework being referred to. Space: The area here is the framework in question which includes a lot of assignments. Instances of area incorporate the medicinal services, home mechanization, brilliant metering, and savvy building. Assignment: An undertaking is a significant level objective that is tended to so as to understand the general framework necessities. Each errand, thusly, includes a lot of administrations liable for accomplishing that task.

An assignment in a social insurance framework is, for instance, screen remotely glucose level for a diabetic patient. Administration: Assistance is a deliberation of a programming (virtual substance) or equipment element (physical element or gadget) that assumes a job intending to the undertaking objective. These administrations, later at the code age stage, are spoken to as programming segments, for example, RESTful web administrations. A temperature sensor is a case of administration. In our methodology, every gadget or thing engaged with IoT applications is treated as a help. Composite: The administrations of a specific task interface and arrange with one another to address the reason for that task. Such coordination is exemplified in a substance called composite.

The overseeing framework speaks to the control circle that controls and directs the usefulness of the oversaw framework. The four parts, notwithstanding the information base segment, of the control circle which are liable for the observing, investigation, design and execute exercises are displayed and facilitated on a lot of haze hubs found proximate to the physical gadgets or things that offer the types of assistance of the framework being referred to (oversaw framework). We here examine the format and plan of the control circle segments over the mist figuring stage just as the cloud. The proposed design for the control circle is driven by the accompanying prerequisites: The control and guideline of the functionality of IoT applications must be directed on an opportune way. Ground-breaking registering, examination and storage capacities ought to be given to meet the prerequisites of huge scope and complex IoT applications. The help for the separating of the local control circle into a lot of littler control circles with every one answerable for controlling and directing a specific zone in a similar application in a wide arrangement region. The help and arrangement of the coordination between the nearby control circles to direct the usefulness of the oversaw framework in a decentralized mode.

The assignment of at least one exercises of the control circle to at least one neighborhood control circles and direct the oversaw framework in an incorporated mode. To meet the above expressed necessities, we have conveyed a neighborhood control circle on haze hubs close by the gadget layer where the administrations of the oversaw framework are given. We offer this control work as a MAPE a Service in the fog presuming stage. We likewise offer a similar help on the cloud stage to provide food for the need of ground-breaking calculation and capacity abilities when growing huge and huge information producing applications. The control circle at the cloud contains just, notwithstanding the information segment, the examination and arranging exercises. Subsequently, we allude to this administration as an A PaaService. We offer two methods of control: unified and decentralized. In the concentrated mode, a focal control circle is conveyed either on the mist figuring or cloud stage (relies upon the application scale) to direct the working of the diverse control circles that dwell at a similar level. We draw the connection between the focal and nearby control circles utilizing the ace slave model. The neighborhood control circle is responsible for controlling the usefulness of a sub framework, where observing and keeping benefits of fascinating boundaries identified with this sub framework is occurred.

Adding appropriated Fog to an IoT organize gives an offloading way to the gathered information and along these lines, diminishes the information traffic at the center system. Moreover, Fog hubs give the processing capacities close to IoT gadgets and in this manner, diminish the start to finish inertness. Moreover, the presentation of Fog registering builds the general system adaptability and accessibility. The top layer is the cloud layer that is spoken to by the remote cloud unit. The IoT cloud underpins distinctive IoT administrations and conventions. The fog layered model is depicted in Figure 3.5. The IoT nodes are in the basic layer and fog nodes are in upper layer to IoT nodes and the top most layer is the cloud layer.

The proposed design for IoT Applications introduced in this paper is based on certain ideas and models examined out of sight area. The design is seen as comprising of two basic layers: the oversaw component and overseeing component. The proposed design for the control circle is driven by the accompanying prerequisites: The control and guideline of the functionality of IoT applications must be directed on an opportune way. Ground-breaking registering, examination and storage capacities ought to be given to meet the prerequisites of huge scope and complex IoT applications. The help for the separating of the local control circle into a lot of littler control circles with every one answerable for controlling and directing a specific zone in a similar application in a wide arrangement region. The help and arrangement of the coordination between the nearby control circles to direct the usefulness of the oversaw framework in a decentralized mode.

We offer this control work as a MAPEaaService in the mist figuring stage. We likewise offer a similar help on the cloud stage to provide food for the need of ground-breaking calculation and capacity abilities when growing huge and huge information producing applications. The control circle at the cloud contains just, notwithstanding the information segment, the examination and arranging exercises. Subsequently, we allude to this administration as an A PaaService. We offer two methods of control: unified and decentralized. In the concentrated mode, a focal control circle is conveyed either on the mist figuring or cloud stage (relies upon the application scale) to direct the working of the diverse control circles that dwell at a similar level. Adding appropriated Fog to an IoT organize gives an off-loading way to the gathered information and along these lines, diminishes the information traffic at the center system. Moreover, Fog hubs give the processing capacities close to IoT gadgets and in this manner, diminish the start to finish inertness. Moreover, the presentation of Fog registering builds the general system adaptability and accessibility. The top layer is the cloud layer that is spoken to by the remote cloud unit. The IoT cloud underpins distinctive IoT administrations and conventions.

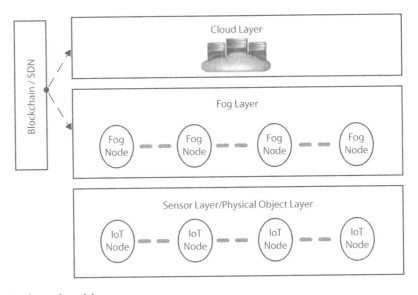

Figure 3.5 Fog layered model.

3.5 Performance Analysis

The proposed FBELPM model for handling IoT devices is implemented in JAVA. The proposed model utilizes strong security mechanisms for successful data transmission. The proposed model is compared with the traditional Trust Based Detection (TBD) method and the results exhibit that the proposed model exhibits better performance in terms of security and data transmission. The time levels for grouping IoT devices are depicted in Figure.

The computational time levels for data processing in Fog model is less when compared to the traditional Secured Data Aggregation (SDA) model. The time levels for IoT group establishment in proposed and traditional models are depicted in Figure 3.6. The time for processing

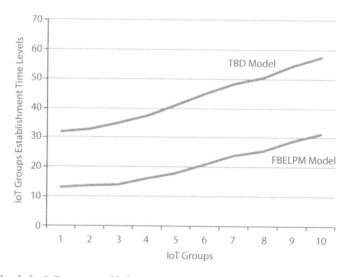

Figure 3.6 Time levels for IoT group establishment.

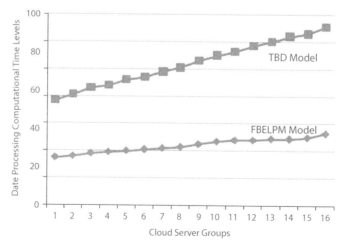

Figure 3.7 Computational time levels for data processing.

the data shared among the group is less as the authorization method verifies the users sharing the data are genuine or not. The computational time levels are depicted in Figure 3.7.

The process of identification of malicious activities among the IoT devices is a challenging task. Because of malicious actions, the data in the group will be lost or modified to cause ambiguity in the group. The detection rate of malicious nodes in the proposed model is high when compared to the traditional methods. The malicious node detection rate is depicted in Figure 3.8.

The Fog computational Secured data storage levels are depicted that indicates that the proposed model takes less time to store the data after computational process. The data storage in cloud should undergo a strong verification process to avoid data loss and also to complete the computational process. The fog computational security levels for data storage is depicted in Figure 3.9

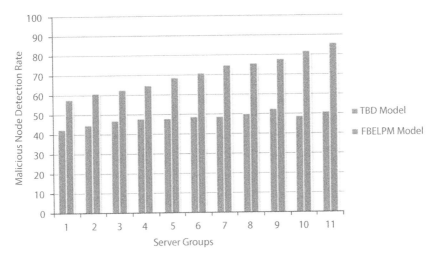

Figure 3.8 Malicious node detection rate.

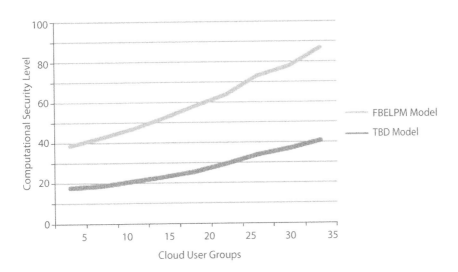

Figure 3.9 Fog computational security levels for data storage.

3.6   Conclusion

Fog computing is viewed because the most reasonable edge computing stage for IoT systems and applications. As it had been primary declared by Cisco as a kind of edge computing and an expansion of the cell edge computing, explores and examines are created to interrupt down, characterize, improve and incorporate Fog computing. Numerous works that consider Fog computing for IoT are directed; either without the arrangement of SDN innovation or with SDN. Joining the online of things and fog computing, this paper proposed an IoT-based fog computing model and depicted the model in layers. We talked about the elevated level engineering of Fog computing and its advantages for the plan and advancement of IoT applications. Since IoT applications are profoundly powerful in nature and include a lot of observing and investigation exercises, we have thought that it was useful to design these applications by utilizing a few ideas and models from the self-versatile and autonomic frameworks. As an underlying advance to address this issue, in the proposed work, a fog based model for Secured applications and shows the useful importance and centrality of such a structure. The relentless association of convenient and sensor devices is making another condition specifically the Internet of Things (IoT), which engages a wide extent of future Internet applications. In this work, an exceptional Fog Based raised level programming model for delicate applications that are geospatially flowed, colossal degree. The fog enlisting framework gives the model to administer IoT benefits in the fog prospect by techniques for an authentic demonstrating position.

References

1. Liu, J., Liu, F., Ansari, N., Monitoring and analyzing big traffic data of a large-scale cellular network with Hadoop. *IEEE Netw.*, 28, 4, 32–39, 2014.
2. Chiang, M. and Zhang, T., Fog and IoT: an overview of research opportunities. *IEEE Internet Things J.*, 3, 60, 854–864, 2016.
3. Lakshmi Patibandla, R.S.M., Kurra, S.S., Kim, H.-J., Electronic resource management using cloud computing for libraries. *Int. J. Appl. Eng. Res.*, 9, 18141–18147, 2014.
4. Bagula, A., Mandava, M., Bagula, H., A Framework for Supporting Healthcare in Rural and Isolated Areas. *J. Netw. Commun. Appl.*, 120, 17–29, 2018. https://doi.org/10.1016/j.jnca.2018.06.010
5. Patibandla, R.S.M.L., Kurra, S.S., Mundukur, N.B., A Study on Scalability of Services and Privacy Issues in Cloud Computing, in: *Cloud computing and Internet Technology, ICDCIT 2012. Lecture Notes in Computer Science*, vol. 7154, R. Ramanujam and S. Ramaswamy (Eds.), Springer, Berlin, Heidelberg, 2012.
6. Tarakeswara Rao, B., Patibandla, R.S.M.L., Murty, M.R., A Comparative Study on Effective Approaches for Unsupervised Statistical Machine Translation, in: *Embedded Systems and Artificial Intelligence. Advances in Intelligent Systems and Computing*, vol. 1076, V. Bhateja, S. Satapathy, H. Satori (Eds.), Springer, Singapore, 2020.
7. Hosseinian-Far, A., Ramachandran, M., Slack, C.L., Emerging Trends in Cloud Computing, Big Data, Fog Computing, IoT and Smart Living, in: *Technology for Smart Futures*, pp. 29–40, Springer International Publishing, Cham, Switzerland, 2018.
8. Cui, L., Yu, F.R., Yan, Q., When big data meets software-defined networking: SDN for big data and big data for SDN. *IEEE Netw.*, 30, 58–65, 2016.

9. Ateya, A.A., Muthanna, A., Gudkova, I., Abuarqoub, A., Vybornova, A., Koucheryavy, A., Development of Intelligent Core Network for Tactile Internet and Future Smart Systems. *J. Sens. Actuator Netw.*, 7, 1, 2018.

10. Panarello, A., Tapas, N., Merlino, G., Longo, F., Puliafito, A., Blockchain and IoT Integration: A Systematic Survey. *Sensors*, 18, 2575, 2018.

11. Banafa, A., IoT and Blockchain Convergence: Benefits and Challenges, in: *IEEE Internet of Things*, IEEE, Piscataway, NJ, USA, 2017.

12. Peter, H. and Moser, A., Blockchain-Applications in Banking & Payment Transactions: Results of a Survey. *Eur. Financial Syst.*, 2017, 141, 2017.

13. Uddin, M., Mukherjee, S., Chang, H., Lakshman, T.V., SDN-based Multi-Protocol Edge Switching for IoT Service Automation. *IEEE J. Sel. Areas Commun.*, 36, 2775–2786, 2018.

14. Alliance, N.G.M.N. 5G White Paper; Next Generation Mobile Networks: Frankfurt, Germany, 2017.

15. Ateya, A.A., Muthanna, A., Koucheryavy, A., 5G framework based on multi-level edge computing with D2D enabled communication, in: *Proceedings of the 2018 IEEE 20th International Conference on Advanced Communication Technology (ICACT)*, Chuncheon-si Gangwon-do, Korea, 11–14 February 2018, pp. 507–512.

16. Azimi, I., Anzanpour, A., Rahmani, A.M., Pahikkala, T., Levorato, M., Liljeberg, P., Dutt, N., HiCH: Hierarchical Fog-assisted computing architecture for healthcare IoT. *ACM Trans. Embed. Comput. Syst.*, 16, 174, 2017.

17. Borcoci, E., Ambarus, T., Vochin, M., Distributed Control Plane Optimization in SDN-Fog VANET. *ICN*, 2017, 135, 2017.

18. Sharma, P.K., Chen, M.Y., Park, J.H., A software defined Fog node based distributed blockchain cloud architecture for IoT. *IEEE Access*, 6, 115–124, 2018.

19. Khakimov, A., Muthanna, A., Muthanna, M.S.A., Study of Fog computing structure, in: *Proceedings of the 2018 IEEE Conference of Russian Young Researchers in Electrical and Electronic Engineering (EIConRus)*, Moscow, Russia, 29 January–1 February 2018, pp. 51–54.

20. Rofie, S.A., Ramli, I., Redzwan, K.N., Hassan, S.M., Ibrahim, M.S., OpenFlow Based Load Balancing for Software-Defined Network Applications. *Adv. Sci. Lett.*, 24, 1210–1213, 2018.

## 4

An Expert System to Implement Symptom Analysis in Healthcare

Subhasish Mohapatra[1]* and Kunal Anand[2]

[1]*Department of CSE, ADAMAS University, Kolkata, India*
[2]*School of Computer Engineering, KIIT University, Bhubaneswar, India*

Abstract

An expert model can highlight the clinical decision for patients that need accurate, timely, and up-to-date healthcare information, effectively. In this paper, the authors try to construct a use case that collects information from a variety of sources. It showcases objects, situations, in semantic use case domain. Unified Modeling Language (UML) emphasizes on software construction and OWL (web ontology language) formalizes knowledge representation about any system before development. The promotion of an expert model needs the digital competencies of a healthcare professional at a remote hospital. Recent reviews regarding healthcare show that in remote areas people are still dying because of the lack of timely health care facilities. The mortality rate is still high among infants and pregnant women. Because of lack of human expert in a remote area, paramedical workers run certain hospitals. They cannot predict symptoms of some disease because of lack of sufficient knowledge and proper training. An expert system assists the patient at the point of contact. The knowledge base for symptoms, collected from patient end, continues to be observed regularly. UML is a powerful technique to explore the syntactic behaviour of any decision logic framework. For a significant expert model design in healthcare, it needs integration of a colossal amount of heterogeneous data from multiple sources such as symptom data, image data, disease information. For a major health-care project, the semantic web delivers a recurrent infrastructure an expert system can segregate and rephrase which. Here in this paper, the authors make a good attempt by analyzing the UML use case model and ontology-based use case model for an expert system in healthcare.

Keywords: Expert model, supervised learning, symptom-disease, knowledge base, decision logic

4.1 Introduction

The expert system provides an adequate treatment of information and attention without delay. We should not treat the patient as a specimen by a healthcare professional if adequate human expert is not available. The patient does not like delayed information because the delaying of information may deteriorate the health condition of the patient.

*Corresponding author: mohapatra.subhasish@gmail.com

Monika Mangla, Suneeta Satpathy, Bhagirathi Nayak and Sachi Nandan Mohanty (eds.) Integration of Cloud Computing with Internet of Things: Foundations, Analytics, and Applications, (57–70) © 2021 Scrivener Publishing LLC

Again, some issue lies with the patient side also as some patients face difficulty in communicating their health issues to the doctor properly. Some people dislike going to the hospital as they have certain allergic reactions to the smell of drugs [1–3]. So, an expert system based preliminary diagnosis can be a solution for the above-discussed scenario [4–6]. It is a discouraging sign for any developing nation like India if it does not check mortality rates because of minor ailments and lack of in-time treatment [10–12]. It only happens for the delay in information. For countries like India, one of the major issues is depicted as follows for predominant rural communities a few medical experts available because most of them like to serve the urban hospital [18]. There is a widening quality of service gap between urban and rural areas. So, an expert model described in this paper presents a novel medical diagnostic approach that can check on the mortality rate. Here, we have focused on a robust mechanism, i.e. CNN-Fuzzy inference mechanism. Expert systems (ES) arise from artificial intelligence (AI) which learn, understand, and solve problems based on decision logic & inference mechanism. An Expert system is an essential requirement for every organization as it provides sound and in-time advice to the patients, which is an essential requirement to set up a multidisciplinary and value-based healthcare infrastructure [13–15]. Ontology entails correct information dissemination by integrating controlled use case models and class models. Ontology use case analysis is a powerful technique to further analyze a decision support system in health care. In a health context, it will improve decision making in healthcare. UML Class profile ontology provides an actionable knowledge sequence. It can showcase medical inconsistencies after analyzing the semantic gap between Class and ontology use cases. Expert model analysis through ontology can diversify concepts as per the growth of information. Nowadays, an expert system is considered as one of the effective, accessible, and resilient techniques to bridge the communication gap between a patient and the doctor. It is tremendously improving healthcare sustainability and provides access to the patient in remote areas. It can avoid over diagnosis treatment by mining symptoms i.e. collected from the patient. The expert model is in utmost demand to build a sustainable healthcare ecosystem. As per some reports, 74% of doctors are in the urban area and they are only serving 28% of the population. So, the universal health coverage to all people of India by 2022 remains a bliss. The crucial variation in healthcare service still lies in remote areas. Considering all these issues, an expert system hopes to provide significant healthcare solutions in remote areas. The decision support service expert system makes it an autonomous agent [15]. The proposed expert model effectively coordinates the patient request [16–18]. It is a supervised adaptive form of learning that can manage symptom data from the patient to detect disease patterns. This research is studied upon UML (Unified Modelling Language) service model [19]. UML analysis is necessary for providing fast and efficient service implementation in real-world scenarios. It can capture the correct diagnosis path and immediate monitoring before it's implementation. UML is a corrective technique for any successful project implementation. Various approaches to UML are used to improve the healthcare expert model. This research paper projects upon class interaction technique, Flow chart, Use case analysis, Activity diagram [5]. An expert system provides correct and immediate responses that can serve the people in remote areas. Decision logic explained in this paper is used to classify symptoms based on disease, subsequently the CNN-Fuzzy inference mechanism is considered as an effective data mining tool for adaptive expert learning.

4.2   Related Work

In healthcare services, the expert system is used to manage autonomy in disease diagnosis and client request processing. The proposed expert agent model can detect disease pattern, and it provides an advance treatment plan to save lives. For real-time analysis, UML adaptive technique is used to diagnose its accuracy and efficiency. It implements UML for object-oriented ontological modelling. It formalizes knowledge interaction format in ontology. Further, it establishes linking knowledge base from class to class. UML defines ontological sets to class, activity and use case. Expert system is an autonomous control agent. It can solve complex problems. It focuses the core idea behind expert system learning on data acquisition, learning, perception, and communication. We consider an expert system a boon for society as it can find an expert solution technique where constraints lie for human expert i.e. unavailability of hospital, doctor, etc. We give the abstract expert model for health care in Figure 4.1. The control flow of this model was presented in ESDA-2019, International conference, Kolkata. We give the detail flow of this model in section-3. We give the detailed analytical processing of this model in section-4. In section–5, we focus upon real-time scenario analysis that delivers extensive analysis of UML behavioral diagram, class interaction diagram, etc. We invoke the fundamental aspect behind this expert model design to consult service remotely. Subsequently, semantic operation, control flow detection, of expert module design is given by UML static, and behavioral diagram. UML need and demand for expert model design before its implementation is adopted widely as it bridges the gap between client need and demand. Subsequently, it provides financial and technical protection to the research group. We consider UML as first arm strategy to provide value-based healthcare infrastructure can improve the quality and safety of the model by analyzing explicitly choice from the outside environment and client. It optimally chooses resources to illustrate the right health care program. This is a new paradigm for quality-based healthcare, though it finds a wonderful balance between individual patient needs and remotely assisted clinical services [21]. It enshrines the UML concept in the object-oriented analysis where each diagram contributes specific action of the expert module from cradle to grave. The concept of

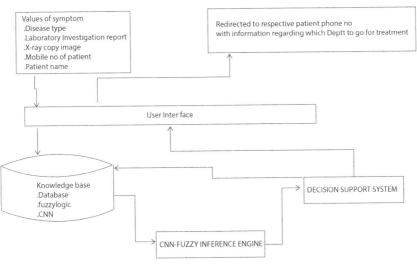

Figure 4.1 Expert model in the healthcare domain for capturing patient symptoms.

UML analysis in the healthcare expert model provides re-emergence of an adaptive supervised learning scheme. Seeking in-time healthcare service is the social right of every citizen. It should be the primary focus of every hospital to provide curative healthcare help to every citizen. The expert system can only ensure social health care cohesion within the nation [20].

4.3   Proposed Model Description and Flow Chart

4.3.1   Flowchart of the Model

The model described above has its benefits and future scope for smaller symptoms based on applications in the complex research-based domain in healthcare. Following are the components that make up this healthcare model:

4.3.1.1   Value of Symptoms

This phase collects the Disease type and its corresponding symptoms tabular. Patient name and their contact number, is collected using an interactive user interface terminal for further information dissemination. If the patient has an X-ray report or any such report, then they are kept in a separate database using a graphical end-user specific interface.

4.3.1.2   User Interaction Web Module

The user specific interactive page is a web-based application to collect information from the patient, and it acts as a sensor in this expert system-based model.

4.3.1.3   Knowledge-Base

The knowledge-base (KB) comprises symptoms database, convolution neural network and used for image analysis and prediction for a set of diseases like (blood cancer, bone cancer, flaws in the ligament, etc.). The fuzzy logic establishes a fuzzification of symptoms data and emerges with certain rules. If certain symptoms match with specific disease or disease set, then the output is moved forward to the decision support system [22]. We show this in Figure 4.4. The fundamental paradigm of KB emerges within this expert model as three synergistic approaches, like symptoms collection database from patient, CNN algorithm for analyzing, and predicting various set of disease, and fuzzy rule to analyze the set of symptoms and to generate one crisp set of disease for these symptoms that the expert system collects from the patient [23].

4.3.1.4   Convolution Neural Network

CNN provides the architectural idea for the detection of disease. It is a further enhancement of learning for feature extraction based on symptoms data. CNN, otherwise known as conv net. It is exhibiting a linear computation. It is nothing but a combination of multiplication with a set of weight and input parameter, same as a conventional neural network. It takes a two-dimensional feature pattern which is nothing but an array of linear input and weight based on RELU at inner layer and Softmax at the outer layer [27–29].

4.3.1.5   CNN-Fuzzy Inference Engine

It is a novel approach in which a fuzzy specific convolution neural network (F-CNN) method is suggested to foretell the disease from symptoms data more accurately. Here, a precise fuzzy method has been implemented to showcase symptoms of features when instigating unsure disease-based symptom details. They then feed it into the CNN at a specific interval of time. This is used to pull out the place of occurrence and time of initiation of characteristics to the symptoms database, CNN and fuzzy-based inference mechanism that can give the desired information to the patient that he is seeking for his treatment [24–26].

Decision support for a patient is a highly heterogeneous task because of the structural symptom complexity of the disease, so this paper introduces a new cooperative task tracking in the expert model as shown in the Figure 4.2. This paper focuses on the idiosyncrasy of CNN-FUZZY based event-driven model for a patient. A huge disparity in access to doctors and the distribution of healthcare experts in India makes this model patient-friendly.

Diagnosis of disease in Decision support systems logic (DSS) formally establish a precise framework of clinical knowledge management technologies through their capacity to support the clinical process and to extraction of knowledge, from prognosis and scrutiny through treatment and long-term care. The Fuzzy-CNN based conceptual model can serve the patient efficiently while handling and tracking their symptoms and give proper guidance to further service consultation where a human expert does not give precise information to the patient [30–32].

Finally, the model redirects the person for consultation, at which place of the hospital is given to a person either displaying the information on-screen of the user interface or through their sufficient contact number.

The flowchart, as shown in Figure 4.6, represents the initial stage of understanding. It discusses the integration logic of each module. Each subsystem schedules activity of information from patient login, symptom data analysis, and decision logic. The flow chart emphasizes the static and dynamic aspects of design. It captures the client in the initial phase of design. Along with the flowchart description, the authors give a wide scope of narration by using UML analysis.

The flow chart description is:

- First, users register themselves through the user interface.
- In this step, we collect all symptom data and store them in knowledgebase (KB).
- The CNN-FUZZY inference interacts with KB for classification of disease and it provides high-end decision logic for prediction [7].

Expert module interaction flowchart has a well-documented process. It can customize the module to show the steps of the process. The conceptual approach of the flowchart has contributed significantly in module design. It delivers a systematic service framework to enhance the performance of the model during the implementation phase. It proposes a feasibility set of actions by evaluating different constituents. New artifacts, from the flow chart visualization, are added and deleted to improve the service. It captures the operational perspective of the module by visual orientation.

4.4 UML Analysis of Expert Model

The use case diagram, UCD, is a tremendous application to a sustainable expert system. It is an innovative approach to save energy, resource, and infrastructure cost. It concentrates upon the standardization of expert module interaction. It also highlights the major points for expert module interaction. It highlights a certain point for expert module development. The use case-based utility checking of method interaction ensures the success rate of the expert system. We study the abstraction phase of an expert module through an incremental approach, which is an innovative scheme supported by use case analysis as it provides a visual modelling framework to the expert system. This paper concentrates upon building online service components of the expert system. The use case analysis is needed to automate and to enhance the performance of the expert system. It integrates services through the external environment. A vital goal of use case analysis is to schedule events integrate with external environment, knowledgebase (KB), user interface (UI). In Figure 4.2, the researchers provide tracking of interaction among patient and expert modules. It provides a detailed insight into effective action control mechanisms under the natural environment. It focuses on the monitoring of the event. Here, in this paper use case does the fundamental management of patient interaction with the expert module [33, 34].

In this context, the use case diagram given in Figure 4.3 provides a trace-ability tool that accomplishes connectivity, authentication, and presentation layout of an expert model. The Use Case Analysis (UCA) approach, in this subsection, provides a precise understanding of the communication pattern between the patient and expert module. This use case analysis leads to several advantages as it ensures a clear graphical representation of the vital components in the expert module. It assists the module specific requirement for a new software unit and its nascent stage of development. It is an effective technique to specify extern user behaviour. As said, the use case analysis maximizes the relationship between the patient, expert module, and a core communication. It can capture system validation by developing test cases.

It gives the UCA conventional notation:

- An actor replica is given by a stick man symbol.
- A use case is illustrated by an ellipse.
- Communication between actors with use cases are established by arrows.

In this paper, the patient and expert module are the actors as depicted in Figure 4.3. The granularity of use case tells how the information is organized to achieve the right level of specification.

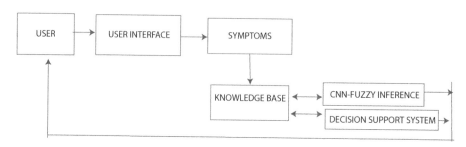

Figure 4.2 Expert module interaction process.

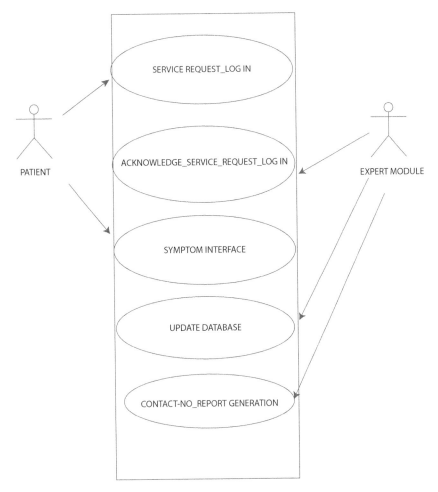

Figure 4.3 Use case diagram of patient and expert module.

4.4.1 Expert Module Activity Diagram

The expert module activity diagram is one of vital aspects of UML that narrates the dynamic behavior of the system. It is a flowchart like representation that shows the flow from one activity to another [5]. The operating system controls it. It is a visual representation of the preceding and succeeding task and hence, gives a pictorial view of model operation is given by authors in Figure 4.4.

The activity diagram exhibits sequential or concurrent message flow using a graphical representation. It conceptualizes the dynamic flow of the model and subsequently; it concentrates on forward and reverse mapping of the model. Figure 4.4 gives a clear understanding of the model. It captures the graphical modelling simulation to a model, though the high-level view of activity diagram investigates the operational requirement of the model in later development stage. In Figure 4.4, we give the conventional notation used for the activity diagram. The dark filled circle symbol represents the start and end of the activity. The rounded cornered rectangle symbol represents activity, the diamond symbol shows the decision condition, the arrow represents control flow from one activity

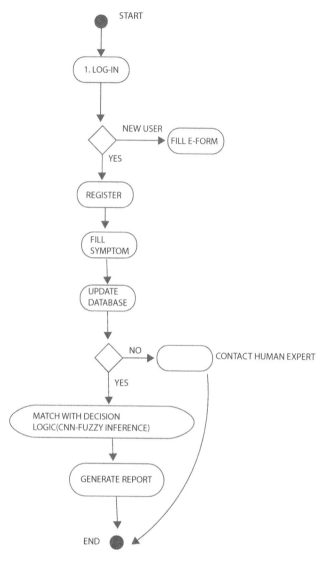

Figure 4.4 Expert module activity diagram for decision logic.

to another, and it maintains concurrent activity in the same layer. The high-level view of this model investigates the operational requirement in a later stage. In Figure 4.4 authors provide a high-level view of an activity diagram. As the knowledge layout of authors is sharpened by activity analysis, so we transform a good activity analysis into a suitable model [12]. This pictorial representation works as a software blueprint, as an activity diagram describes the real-time dynamic flow of a system. Each activity flow gives the developers a piece of precise information regarding the model. Each activity collaborates with the responsibility that will provide access and equity during the developmental stage of the model. The Figure 4.4 shows the validation of patient information, symptom collection, availability of the report, and exception handling for the external events. It provides a computer interpretative structure ontology from end-user login to the report generation by an expert module. This is a unified ontology plan to synchronize intuitive model flow and explore a workable diagnosis plan [35, 36].

4.4.2   Ontology Class Collaboration Diagram

The collaboration diagram, as shown in Figure 4.5, depicts the structural framework of a model. It is another flavour of the ontological linking of knowledge interaction diagram. The impetus of the collaboration diagram is to show the flow of messages between the classes. Classes are the building blocks of any model. In Figure 4.5, the authors have shown several classes that are involved in offering services. It shows the service request transfer, and service request send between the classes.

In this service class ontology model, request transfer and sending of service responses are added between sub-classes i.e. user interface, knowledgebase, login, decision support system, and external contact for remote patients. It can facilitate platform-specific ontology function establishment between nodal class and subclass. It is a prototype framework for ontology integration between clusters of specific classes.

- User Interface Class: It provides a graphical user interface for patients. The patients can fill their credentials as per the expert system data capture form.
- Knowledge base class: It acts as a repository for collecting patient information (patient data, symptom data, etc).
- Login class: This class checks and validates the patient credential by providing a user-id and password that the patients can use to access the expert module remotely.
- Decision Support Class: This class can efficiently interact with knowledge base class to classify disease patterns based on adaptive learning techniques. Here, in this expert module, the authors have focused on the CNN-FUZZY inference mechanism.

The message flow among classes depicts relevance, and authenticity of the model class relationship is given by arrow signs in Figure 4.5. It is the preparatory phase to establish an outline of the expert model. We will analyse the detail class attribute, method interaction, and external cloud connectivity module class as a future direction of this paper.

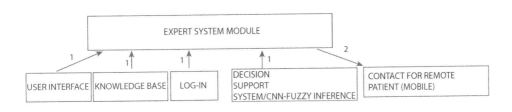

Figure 4.5 Class collaboration diagram.

4.5   Ontology Model of Expert Systems

The ontological use case model retrieves the extensive knowledge for real-life scenario analysis. It provides an easy conceptualization domain for IoT healthcare stakeholders. It automates the model for test case generation. Hence, in this section, the authors introduced the use case model analysis for an expert system that delivers action semantic information between the user and the expert system. The Figure 4.6 graphically shows an abstract level of standardization that UML provides.

The use case model makes an informal analysis of any model [36]. So, to automate the analysis of an expert system, the authors introduced ontology-based use case analysis in Figure 4.6 for the model shown in Figure 4.1. In this paper, ontology highlights the use case driven architecture and ontology-driven development. The rationale idea behind this paper is not only to overview their extensive relationship but also to compare their core features to the wholesale integration to a model. Many industries adopt both UML and OWL because of their rich infrastructure [18]. In this paper, the authors precisely embedded these two techniques that provide a meta-model facility to real-world applications. We consider UML

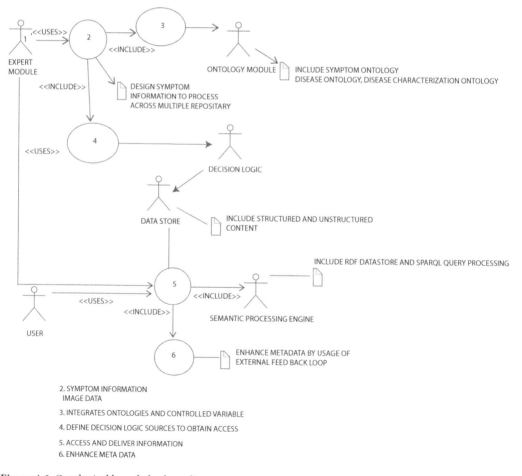

Figure 4.6 Ontological knowledge base diagram.

as an object constrained language but OWL provides a resource description framework to specialize in each activity of use case model. In this section, the authors clarify the aim of the expert model given in Figure 4.6, by semantic use case mapping. It gives the discrete semantic representation of an expert model in this section. The ontology module gives the semantic repository of disease symptoms and relevant precautionary measures. It collects information for the disease meta-data repository. The theoretic semantic model explicitly defines how to construct a semantic domain for the symptom. In this paper, the authors integrate the underlying goal of both UML and OWL for an expert model in healthcare. It represents an object centric intention to knowledge representation [20]. Object centric representation provides a logical cut insight to analyse object behaviour in a system and OWL analysis for any model differentiates the role of empirical knowledge and coherent knowledge. Ontology provides the terminological information about a system. In Figure 4.6, we depict these as symptom data, feedback for enhancement, and ontology module. Because of the limited scope of this paper, the authors have only given the behaviour analysis of the model in UML and Ontological use cases for model interpretation given in Figure 4.1. It centers both UML and OWL on the objects which are the backbone of extensional knowledge representation. The Ontology framework is best suited for a heterogeneous environment that enhances automatic inter-operability and deployment. It reduces the shift of complexity of operation. Here, in Figure 4.6, the ontological work flow analysis is an enhanced form of the UML use case model which has been elaborated in Section 4.4.

4.6   Conclusion and Future Scope

In this research finding, we conceptualized end user interactive patterns by taking the logic of the UML diagram. For documenting this healthcare based expert system authors focused upon several principles i.e. effectiveness, solidarity, and trustworthiness analysis shows the technical aspect of implementation modelling of the system gives a quick understanding as developers can map and change system requirements in a dynamic environment. UML infrastructure analysis can detect flaws in scenario analysis in use cases. AI-based expert system is still under research as it needs continuous UML based simulation before its implementation. UML captures intelligently the flow of algorithm that enhances the learning automation. The authors are taking it sincerely as a point to integrate expert module decision logic over cloud-connected architecture. The OWL supports distributed and interoperable properties. Therefore, it grants the existence of any model. The ontological aspect shows the class- and set-based operation between them. It offers flexibility and remote help to a patient for any unknown pattern of symptoms. The ontological processing and UML processing can provide autonomy to the expert system that can transform the entire healthcare pathway by linking expert module and patient that may include the not so digitally literate and old people who face difficulty in communication. Providing rational service is an essential feature of the expert system. Migrating symptom database to cloud is a challenging task that needs deliberate planning. Researchers must map the significant obstacle of cloud computing with the expert module. Cloud assisted decision making is the key feature to enhance trustworthiness in the expert system. Cloud migration for the expert system needs large data centers to store, process, and analyze symptoms information as they may include images, X-ray reports, data sheets, etc. CNN model needs a high-end GPU to analyze an image. We must develop a use case for cloud functionality module before its implementation. This scientific paper expands the logic of cloud activity, planning, messaging, and decision-logic in compliance with existing technologies. Last, the ontology facilitates system driven use case classification i.e. concentrated upon terminological information. The Ontology model further describes the service of decomposition for a conceptual model.

References

1. Organization for Economic Co-operation and Development (OECD), Tackling Wasteful Spending on Health, Available from: https://www.oecdilibrary.org/content/publication/9789264266414-en, 2017.
2. Berwick, D.M. and Hackbarth, A.D., Eliminating waste in US health care. *JAMA*, 307, 14, 1513–1516, 2012.
3. Expert Panel on effective ways of investing in Health (EXPH), Benchmarking access to healthcare in the EU, 2018.
4. Organisation for Economic Co-operation and Development (OECD), *Spending on Health: Latest trends*, OECD Focus, 2018 June.
5. O'Sullivan, J.W., Stevens, S., Hobbs, F.R., Salisbury, C., Little, P., Goldacre, B., Bankhead, C., Aronson, J.K., Perera, R., Heneghan, C., Temporal trends in use of tests in UK primary care, 2000-15: Retrospective analysis of 250 million tests. *BMJ*, 363, 2018.
6. Lallemand, N.C., Reducing waste in health care. *Health Aff.*, 13, 1–5, 2012.
7. Donahedian, A., *Explorations in quality assessment and monitoring: The definition of quality approaches to its assessment*, vol. 1, Health Administration Press, Ann Arbor, MI, 1980.
8. McKee, M., Solidarity in a unified Europe. *Eur. J. Public Health*, 18, 1, 2–4, 2008.
9. European Convention, Charter of Fundamental Rights of the European Union, 2000.
10. Rawls, J., *A Theory of Justice*, Belknap Press, United States, 1973.
11. Alesina, A., Glaeser, E., Sacerdote, B., *Why doesn't the US have a European-style welfare system?*, No. w8524, National Bureau of Economic Research, 2001.
12. Mau, S. and Burkhardt, C., Migration and welfare state solidarity in Western Europe. *J. Eur. Soc. Policy*, 19, 3, 213–229, 2009.
13. European Commission (EC), The European Pillar of Social Rights in 20 principles, 2017 Feb 7th, 2019, Availablefrom:https://ec.europa.eu/commission/priorities/deeper-and-fairer-economic-andmonetary-union/european-pillar-social-rights_en.
14. Prainsack, B., Centre for the Study of Contemporary Solidarity (CeSCoS), Available from: https://politikwissenschaft.univie.ac.at/en/research/main-areasof-research/centre-for-the-study-of-contemporary-solidarity-cescos/, 2018.
15. Opriş, V.N. and Opriş, M.E., The expert system development technologies in cloud. *Scientific Bull. "Mircea cel Batran" Naval Academy*, 20, 1, 557, 2017.
16. Saufi, N.A.A., Daud, S., Hassan, H., Green growth and corporate sustainability performance. *Procedia Econ. Financ.*, 35, 1, 374–378, 2016.
17. Abatal, A., Khallouki, H., Bahaj, M., A semantic smart interconnected healthcare system using ontology and cloud computing, in: *2018 4th International Conference on Optimization and Applications (ICOA)*, 2018, April, IEEE, p. 1–5.
18. Sondes, T.I.T.I., Elhadj, H.B., Chaari, L., An ontology-based healthcare monitoring system in the Internet of Things, in: *2019 15th International Wireless Communications & Mobile Computing Conference (IWCMC)*, 2019, June, IEEE, p. 319–324.

19. Azimi, I., Rahmani, A.M., Liljeberg, P., Tenhunen, H., Internet of things for remote elderly monitoring: A study from user-centered perspective. *J. Ambient Intell. Humaniz. Comput.*, 8, 2, 273–289, 2017.

20. Coulter, A. and Cleary, P.D., Patients' experiences with hospital care in five countries. *Health Aff.*, 20, 3, 244–252, 2001.

21. Frost, L.J. and Reich, M.R., Creating access to health technologies in poor countries. *Health Aff.*, 28, 4, 962–973, 2009.

22. Russell, S.J. and Norvig, P., *Artificial Intelligence: A Modern Approach*, Prentice Hall Series, 2003.

23. Negnevitsky, M., *Artificial intelligence: A guide to intelligent systems*, Pearson Education, UK, 2005.

24. Malaria Site [Internet], Clinical features of Malaria, c2011-13 [cited 2012 Sep 20]. Available from: http://www.malariasite.com/.

25. Ryan, K.J. and Ray, C.G., *Medical microbiology*, vol. 4, p. 370, McGraw Hill, New York, 2004.

26. GIDEON: The world's premier global infectious diseases database, c1994–2012, Available from: http://www.gideononline.com/.

27. Sliwa, J., Scientist study bacterial communities inside us to better understand health and disease, 2008 June 3, Available from: http://www.eurekalert.org/pub_releases/2008-06/asfm-ssb052908.php.

28. McGuinness, D.L. and van Harmelen, F., OWL web ontology language overview: World Wide Web Consortium (W3C) recommendation, 2004.

29. Hart, L., Emery, P., Colomb, B., Raymond, K., Taraporewalla, S., Chang, D., Ye, Y., Kendall, E., Dutra, M., OWL full and UML 2.0 compared, OMG TFC Report, 2004.

30. Borgida, A. and Brachman, R.J., 2 Conceptual modeling with description logics, *ACM Digital Library*, 0003, 349–372, 2003.

31. Atkinson, C. and Kühne, T., Rearchitecting the UML infrastructure. *ACM Trans. Model. Comput. Simul. (TOMACS)*, 12, 4, 290–321, 2002.

32. Álvarez, J.M., Evans, A., Sammut, P., Mapping between levels in the metamodel architecture, in: *International conference on the unified modeling language*, 2001, October, Springer, Berlin, Heidelberg, p. 34–46.

33. Atkinson, C. and Kuhne, T., Model-driven development: A metamodeling foundation. *IEEE Software*, 20, 5, 36–41, 2003.

34. Chen, D., Jin, D., Goh, T.T., Li, N., Wei, L., Context-awareness based personalized recommendation of anti-hypertension drugs. *J. Med. Syst.*, 40, 9, 202, 2016.

35. Zhang, Y., Qiu, M., Tsai, C.W., Hassan, M.M., Alamri, A., Health-CPS: Healthcare cyber-physical system assisted by cloud and big data. *IEEE Syst. J.*, 11, 1, 88–95, 2015.

## 5

An IoT-Based Gadget for Visually Impaired People

Prakash, N.[1]*, Udayakumar, E.[1], Kumareshan, N.[2], Srihari, K.[3] and Sachi Nandan Mohanty[4]

[1]Dept. of ECE, KIT—Kalaignarkarunanidhi Institute of Technology, Coimbatore, India
[2]Dept. of ECE, Sri Shakthi Institute of Engineering and Technology, Coimbatore, India
[3]Dept. of CSE, SNS College of Engineering, Coimbatore, India
[4]Dept. of CSE, ICFAI foundation of Higher Education, Hyderabad, India

Abstract

The proposed system is based on the camera-based product and person identification for blind persons. The main aim of this chapter is to help the blind users, so we have proposed a camera-based method to detect the object of interest, while the blind user simple capture the object for a couple of seconds. To identify the product first the images are saved in the data base and the images are detected by using the MATLAB software. In MATLAB, the image processing is done by using image acquisition tool box, and the output of the MATLAB is transmitted to processor. The IoT-based Raspberry pi is used for interfacing with mat lab software. It verifies the image with the data base images which were saved before and particular product or person is identified. Image is captured by using web camera and it will process image such that name of the person or product is produced through an earphone as a voice output to blind users. The complete details of the product are announced, so the visually impaired people can easily identify his friends or product.

Keywords: Registration, IoT, Raspberry Pi, Zigbee, LCD

5.1 Introduction

There are numerous issues for outwardly debilitated and dazzle individuals in the public eye; they face many kind of obstacles in playing out each day's schedule of works, including the limitations of low vision that does not let them to turn out to be a part of this general public. They likewise feel humiliation commonly while playing out these errands when they are fruitless in performing or finishing them, as a result of their visual weakness and insufficiency. It is an incredible gift of God; in the event that anybody has superbly 6/6 visual perceptions, one ought to be grateful to God for this. The outwardly disabled client resembles that individual whom we can say has lost his/her way on venture and doesn't have the foggiest idea where and how to pass a simple life. The people are a sharp disapproval of creation on the planet; for this, an innovation would contribute a great deal to fill this hole

---

Corresponding author: prakash1591@gmail.com

Monika Mangla, Suneeta Satpathy, Bhagirathi Nayak and Sachi Nandan Mohanty (eds.) Integration of Cloud Computing with Internet of Things: Foundations, Analytics, and Applications, (71–86) © 2021 Scrivener Publishing LLC

in [5] society and for outwardly impeded individuals. Step by step headway in the field of science presents new innovations for advantages of ordinary and debilitated people to make their existence simple and agreeable.

The designers ought to likewise remember this thing that the individuals with visual debilitation and other sort of inabilities ought to likewise be encouraged, on the grounds that they are additionally part of society and not disregarded as persons. Utilitarian restrictions of individuals with visual debilitations incorporate poor night vision, decreased shading differentiation capacity or a general right of passage of all vision. The individuals who are lawfully [6] visually impaired may even now hold some view of shape and differentiate light versus dark (the capacity to find a light source), or they might be thoroughly visually impaired (having no attention to natural light). To conquer the above issues experienced by these outwardly weakened individuals, a proposed technique is useful for them.

The pictures are gained from an outside camera associated with the PC through a USB port. This is finished by utilizing picture procurement tool stash in tangle lab. These gained pictures are prepared to acquire maximally happened dim levels in the event of shading and coordinating removed highlights in the event of individual distinguishing proof. The item to be distinguished is introduced before the webcam. The image is brought into the tangle lab content through a picture obtaining tool stash. At that point the particular item is recognized from the maximally happening dim level obtained from the histogram [2]. The face to be perceived is acquainted with the web camera. A comparative camera is used to take the face picture that are taken care of, and recuperated for feature organizing. The picked up picture is adjusted first using histogram leveling, and shortly after the edge is recognized for the balanced picture. The corner features of this edge perceived picture are removed and a short time later the isolated features are facilitated with the evacuated features of the set apart from the picture.

Here headband is associated with a different [1] smartphone-sized unit lodging the processor and battery by means of a 1-meter (3.3 ft) link. Clients can alter the volume and change settings with a coordinating arrangement of catches on both the processor unit and the headband. Inside, a 'tegra' design handling unit controls the profound learning calculations, permitting the gadget to perceive who and what, is confronting it.

At the press of a catch the gadget can portray the scene before it in detail, down to the furnishings and individuals present. It observes, comprehends and portrays nature to the individual, giving valuable data (content perusing, acknowledgment of countenances, and items) in a cautious path and with the correct planning [4]. Utilizing bone conduction, the becoming awareness of the individual is not the slightest bit influenced (rather than utilizing headphones) and it will be conceivable to hear the gadget even in loud circumstances. It is made out of two sections: the RST, containing the visual and equalization sensors that can be worn like a head amplifier. The second can, without much of a stretch, be worn or conveyed in a sack and contains the battery and the processor of the gadget involves a band that folds over the rear of the head, with earpieces, and two next to each other cameras toward one side. The cameras watch out for what's before the wearer, and can direct what it sees through the earpiece, which uses bone conduction innovation to sidestep the ear trench and animate the minor ear bones legitimately. That way, the client can in any case hear what's going on around them, and the gadget's portrayal won't upset any other person.

The fundamental target proposed framework helps client with identifying the item and their companions and relatives. With over 285 million individuals being evaluated to be outwardly weakened around the world, most battle with distinguishing items and individuals [8], so it will be a useful device for them. It is practical so that all sorts of individuals can utilize and profit from it.

5.2   Related Work

Visual weakness and visual deficiency brought about by different maladies have been tremendously decreased. However, there are numerous individuals who are in danger of age-related visual debilitation. The IoT-based visual data is the reason for most navigational errands, so outwardly weakened individuals are at a disservice since important data about the general condition isn't accessible. With the ongoing advances in comprehensive innovation it is conceivable to stretch out the help IoT has given to individuals with visual impedance during their portability. In this setting we propose a framework, named Smart Vision, whose goal is to assist the [12] visually impaired. This is centered basically in the improvement of the PC vision module of the Smart Vision framework.

The disadvantages of these checking gadgets are comprised of leads and links so that they normally limit the portability of patients alongside the skin disturbances or diseases, and so forth caused during implantation into persistent body. To stay away from such circumstances, non-intrusive techniques which are comprised of wearable sensors that touch the patient's body yet don't require any activity for their connections [17]. This strategy included non-reaching sensors and associating wires which creates a few issues for dazzle people.

We propose a camera-based assistive substance examining structure to assist shock when peopling read content names and item packaging from hand-held articles. To keep the thing from muddled establishments or incorporating other articles in the camera vision, we propose from the start a profitable and practical development based procedure to portray an area of interest (ROI) in the video by mentioning that the customer trembles while reading the article. This arrangement isolates moving thing zone by a mix-of-Gaussian-based establishment reasoning methodology. In the isolated ROI, content constrainment and affirmation are directed to make sure about substance nuances. To subsequently focus the substance locale [20] from the item ROI, we offer a novel book limitation figuring by learning slant features of stroke bearings and spreads of edge pixels in an Ad help model. Content characters in the limited substance areas are then combined and seen by ready to move optical character conspicuous verification programming. The esteemed substance codes are changed over into sound respect for the outwardly hindered customers. Execution of the proposed content limitation estimation is quantitatively surveyed on ICDAR-2003 and ICDAR-2011 Robust Reading Datasets. Test outcomes show that our computation achieves the most raised degree of upgrades at present time. The affirmation of thought model is also evaluated on a dataset accumulated using ten outwardly debilitated individuals to survey the practicality of the arrangement. We research the UI issues and power of the computation in removing and scrutinizing content from different articles with complex establishments [21].

A downside of this framework is it is just for content perusing and it can't distinguish the individual so it is single reason framework with PC. The IoT based visually impaired individual may not be ready to convey the PC. The advancement in the innovation today has made our way of life a lot simpler and creative. This venture means to help individuals who are visually impaired identify certain ways effectively and therefore help them explore through structures, utilizing the up and coming innovations that exist in the market today. This undertaking has social and monetary future for itself. The most recent development in advances, for example, radio recurrence IDs gadgets, has provoked me to think about an application which would be useful to the individuals who will require it and guarantee to have an open future to a changing in its structure and utilization [25].

Another downside of this framework is it is dependent on the RFID framework so visually impaired client can't be ready to convey the standardized identification of the considerable number of things and they don't know about web and GPS so it isn't valuable for all the visually impaired clients. Daze individuals need some guide to have a sense of security while moving. Astute stick comes as a proposed answer to improve [23] the adaptability of both outwardly disabled and apparently obstructed people. Stick game plan uses different head-ways like ultrasonic, infrared and laser yet in spite of everything they have drawbacks. In this we propose, light weight, unobtrusive, simple to utilize, snappy response and low power use, sharp stick subject to infrared advancement. Two or three infrared sensors can recognize step cases and different impediments near the client's way, in a scope of 2 m. The exploratory outcomes accomplish great precision and the stick can recognize the entirety of deterrents.

A downsides of this framework is it is a stick with sensor so it will consistently insinuate the client, they can't walk openly in nature then it has numerous challenges to utilize. It is significant expense which typical people can't be ready to purchase. The IoT advances have developed to a point where energizing applications are getting feasible for visual replace-ment. Actually, the industry has made an assortment of PC vision items and administra-tions by growing new electronic guides for the visually impaired so as to beat the challenges that the pooch and stick don't react [20]. This gives an outline of different visual replace-ment frameworks to be created. This strategy depends on video examination and trans-lation. In this manner, our commitment is to introduce a visual replacement framework dependent on assessing quick and powerful calculations to perceive and find protests in pictures. Downsides of this framework are, it is a significant expense and if client knows about the extraction strategies [24]. It has complex calculations so we need a few methods to take care of the issues. It depends on Image preparing strategy as it has perplexing coding and methods.

5.3 System Design

The proposed IoT framework depends on the camera based item recognizable proof for dazzle people. To tackle the basic pointing issue for dazzle clients, they proposed a camera created strategy to identify the thing or item. This will likewise be helpful for the outwardly weakened to recognize their companions and adversaries utilizing face distinguishing proof programming which is actualized in here. In the proposed framework the recognition of interlopers in the safeguard can be made simple [22]. As the term 'Synergistic' signifies the joining of two parameters with the goal that effectiveness is improved. So in the proposed framework MATLAB and implant are joined to execute [26]. The proposed diagram is shown in **Figure 5.1**. The perceived pictures are put away in a database. The camera records

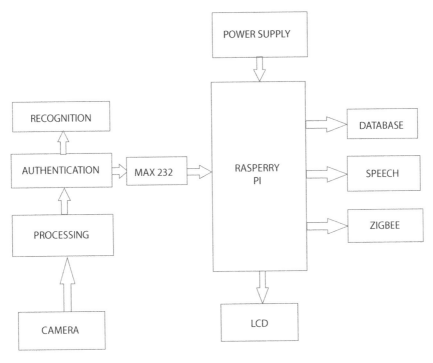

Figure 5.1 Proposed system.

the pictures progressively and are perceived by utilizing acknowledgment area and given to controller. It transmits the data through Zigbee. At whatever point the strange development is distinguished, it initiates the caution and sends data through Zigbee.

An outside camera is tailored with specs for gaining pictures. The procured picture was handled to get the necessary highlights, for example, hues on account of sound hues or facial highlights on account of individual recognizable proof [2]. The acquired highlight is encoded utilizing MATLAB, which at that point takes care of what goes into through which speakers are associated with the resulting individual sound signs. The shading introduced to the camera is changed over to comparing sound.

This is finished utilizing picture procurement tool compartment in tangle lab. These procured pictures are prepared to acquire maximally happened dim levels in the event of shading and coordinating extricated includes if there should arise an occurrence of individual recognizable proof [3]. The item to be distinguished is introduced before the webcam. The image is brought into the tangle lab content through a picture securing tool compartment. At that point the separate item is recognized from the maximally happening dark level obtained from the histogram. The IoT-based face to be perceived is acquainted with the web camera. A comparable camera is used to take the face picture that is taken care of, and recuperated for feature planning. The obtained picture is balanced first using histogram leveling, and a short time later the edge is recognized for the reasonable picture, where the corner features of this edge perceived picture are isolated and a while later the evacuated features are facilitated with the removed features of the set aside picture.

Here headband is associated with a different smartphone-sized unit lodging the processor and battery by means of a 1-meter (3.3 ft) link. Clients can alter the volume and change settings with a coordinating arrangement of catches on both the processor unit and the headband. Inside, a 'tegra' design handling unit controls the profound learning calculations, permitting the gadget to perceive who and what, is confronting it. At the press of a catch the gadget can depict the scene before it in detail, down to the furnishings and individuals present. It observes, comprehends and [9] depicts the earth to the individual, giving helpful data (content perusing, acknowledgment of appearances, and articles) in a tactful path and with the correct planning. Utilizing bone conduction, the becoming awareness of the individual is not the slightest bit influenced (rather than utilizing headphones) and it will be conceivable to hear the gadget even in boisterous circumstances. It is made out of two sections: the RST, containing the visual and equalization sensors that can be worn like a head amplifier.

The second can, without much of a stretch, be worn or conveyed in a sack and contains the battery and the processor the gadget involves a band that folds over the rear of the head; with earpieces, and two one next to the other cameras toward one side. The cameras watch out for what's before the wearer, and can direct what it sees through the earpiece, which uses bone conduction innovation to sidestep the ear waterway and invigorate the minor ear bones legitimately. That way, the client can in any case hear what's going on around them, and the gadget's portrayal won't upset any other person.

The pictures are obtained from an outer camera associated with the PC through a USB port. This is finished utilizing picture obtaining tool kit in MATLAB. These procured pictures are handled to get maximally happened dark levels if there should be an occurrence of shading and coordinating removed highlights if there should be [10] an occurrence of individual distinguishing proof. The item to be distinguished is introduced before the webcam. The image is brought into the tangle lab content through a picture procurement tool compartment. At that point the separate item is recognized from the maximally happening dim level got from the histogram. The face to be distinguished is introduced to the web camera. A similar camera is utilized to take the face picture that are put away, and recovered for highlight coordinating. The procured picture is evened out first utilizing histogram balance, and afterward is IoT-recognized for the adjusted picture, distinguished picture highlights are removed and afterward the separated highlights are coordinated [11] extricated highlights of the put away picture. The correlation procedure is done in Raspberry pi area.

The Raspberry is utilized for interfacing with MATLAB. Here, the picture preparing is done and the yield is sent to speaker as a voice yield. Highlight coordinating is actualized by ROBUST MATCH POINT Algorithm, which covers the most extreme coordinating focuses and back ground brilliance in the image so that the [7] outwardly debilitated individuals can without much of a stretch distinguish the individual and item at whatever point the shading and back ground changes. The flow graph is exposed in **Figure 5.2**.

This proposes a novel and vigorous way to deal with the point set enrollment issue within the sight of a lot of clamor and anomalies. Every one of the point sets is spoken to by a blend of Gaussians and the point set enrollment is treated as an issue of adjusting the two blends. We determine a shut structure articulation for the L2 separation between two Gaussian blends, which thus prompts a computationally effective enrollment calculation. This new calculation has an instinctive translation and is easy to actualize and displays intrinsic measurable vigor. Exploratory outcomes demonstrate that our calculation accomplishes generally excellent execution regarding both vigor and precision.

The primary thought of our procedure is, to quantify the comparability between two limited focuses sets by thinking about their persistent estimate in this specific circumstance,

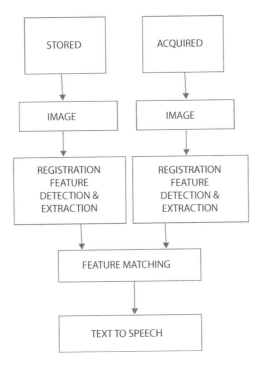

Figure 5.2 Flow graph of over all process.

one can relate a point set to likelihood thickness work. Considering the point set as an assortment of Dirac delta work, it is normal to think about a limited blend model as portrayal of point set [15].

The pictures are obtained from an outer camera associated with the PC through a USB port. This is finished utilizing picture securing tool stash in MATLAB. These gained pictures are handled to acquire maximally happened dim levels if there should arise an occurrence of shading and coordinating removed highlights in the event of individual distinguishing proof. The item to be distinguished is introduced before the webcam. The image is brought into the tangle lab content through a picture obtaining tool compartment. At that point the individual item is recognized from the maximally happening dark level got from the histogram [16]. The face to be distinguished is introduced to the web camera. A similar camera is utilized to take the face picture that are put away, and recovered for include coordinating. The procured picture is adjusted first utilizing histogram evening out, and afterward the edge is distinguished for the leveled picture, with this edge recognized picture the corner highlights are separated and afterward the removed highlights are coordinated with the extricated highlights of the put away picture. The examination procedure is done in Raspberry pi segment.

The Raspberry is utilized for interfacing with MATLAB, here the picture handling is done and the yield is send to speaker as a voice yield. Highlight coordinating is actualized by ROBUST MATCH POINT Algorithm, which covers the most extreme coordinating focuses and back ground splendor in the image so the outwardly impeded individuals can undoubtedly distinguishes the individual and item at whatever point the shading and back ground changes.

Along these lines for helping blind individuals, a few new compact and wearable advancements have been built up that help them to manage them in their manner. Wearable frameworks help individuals by limiting the utilization of hands and furthermore decline the work by them. This likewise diminishes the multifaceted nature they experience and likewise causes them in free agreeable development in human territory. Building up a wearable deterrent identification framework can do snag evasion. Framework includes the innovation and structure of the voice order in which the outwardly impeded individuals see with the assistance of sound waves. The strolling stick is likewise joined with the GPS to identify the area [26]. The Bluetooth headset is worn by the individuals. The principle qualities of the framework incorporate limiting the remaining task at hand among the client, OK with versatility, simple development with world. As the bat recognizes its prey with the assistance of reflections from ultrasonic waves discharged by them, the equivalent strategy has been utilized to identify the obstructions. If the distinguished obstruction is at a range closer to the stick the quality of the hindrance is bigger and if the identified obstruction is at a scope of longer separation then the quality of the vibration is littler. The item to be planned is displayed as a unit to be client separable, which is battery-powered, with the assistance of lithium particle battery, for example, those normally found in versatile telephones and advanced cameras.

The location of obstructions utilizing ultrasonic sensors is constrained by the microcontroller. This venture depend on building up a device that is, a mobile stick and a Bluetooth headset (wearable), for them that causes them to discover their way in this world. This device encourages them to reach their goal by telling them through voice acknowledgment framework. This device gets the goal address through voice order. The present area of the visually impaired individuals is discovered utilizing GPS in the strolling stick. The headset furthermore, the strolling stick are combined utilizing Bluetooth Stick. The GPS-GR 87 distinguishes the present area and recognizes the route to the location got through Bluetooth. Way to their goal is passed on to them through voice acknowledgment framework accessible in route framework, which is transmitted to them through headset. The "keen stick" is a thing, which is typically done by the outwardly hindered individuals to recognize deterrents. Its employments include ultrasonic sensors to distinguish deterrents and educate the client with assistance of vibration.

The vibration delivered relies upon the separation between the client and the article as deterrent. The framework is removable and appendable. The stick is mounted on the highest point of the ordinary stick and it goes about as a savvy stick to recognize obstructions. This gadget doesn't hurt people and is easy to understand. In any case, the significant drawback of this is it is not completely created and is not known to basic visually impaired individuals [27]. The most acknowledged innovation among daze individuals is the RFID-based mapping framework which causes individuals to pass without any problem also, openly in open areas utilizing the RFID tag and RFID stick Reader which is interfaced with Bluetooth innovation as well as that in Personal advanced help. This innovation has significant detriment in that it gets meddled with the recurrence of traffic light and furthermore, very high cost is required to manufacture such framework. The proposed framework is intended to generally give gauges (i.e.) object location and ongoing help through GPS. This work concentrated on building up a contraption that is, a mobile stick and furthermore a Bluetooth headset (wearable), for them to discover their way in this world. This contraption causes them to arrive at their goal by managing them through voice [27].

The test as seen by dazzle people is confronting impediments. To tackle this issue, our framework gives the usefulness by utilizing ultrasonic sensor to maintain a strategic distance from the approaching impediments. The ultrasonic sensor is utilized to quantify the separation of target object. It utilizes electrical–mechanical vitality change to quantify the separation. The ultrasonic sensor comprises of transmitter and beneficiary which are installed all together single unit. Ultrasonic Sensor is fixed at the focal point of Belt. It is utilized to recognize the snags. The ultrasonic sensor go was programming restricted to 30. This assistive gadget comprises of two sections, one which makes a difference the outwardly debilitated to maintain a strategic distance from hindrances with the assistance of ultrasonic sensor and the other which is utilized for route reason utilizing google map. The proposed framework employments [13]. Arduino Mega which is modified to distinguish the hindrance inside separation. The ultrasonic sensor utilizes the reverberation signal for the impediment to recognize the separation and this is prepared utilizing arduino, at that point haptic input is acquired through little engine. The gadget is fueled utilizing lithium particle battery pack which is answerable for estimations preparing, input and client interface collaboration. So as to begin the estimation techniques, the HCSR04 needs a trigger contribution of 10 μs.

Once the trigger transmitting a pattern of 8 blasts at 40 kHz and trusts that the reflected sign will come back to its accepting terminal. The gadget can give both acoustic and material input to illuminate the client if there is an obstruction in his strolling way. The MCU yields a Pulse Width Modulated (PWM) signal at one of its I/O pins and the obligation cycle is legitimately dependable for the power of the input signal. The gadget is fueled by a lithium-particle battery that can give a yield voltage of 9 V. Sound and Touch based Smart Cane: Better Walking Experience for Visually Challenged [25]. Moving with the assistance of a white stick is a subtle undertaking for the outwardly tested except if they make a psychological course map with conspicuous reference components. The keen stick is expected to give the outwardly tested a superior strolling experience. The configuration is fused with Bluetooth empowered Obstacle discovery module, upheld with heat identification and haptic modules [14].

The ultrasonic range discoverers help in distinguishing obstructions. The separation between the hindrance and the client is sent to an Android gadget by means of Bluetooth. The client gets voice cautions about the separation through Bluetooth headset. Haptics module is incorporated to caution the client of moving obstructions with the assistance of vibratory engines. This examination work clarifies about the arrangement we utilized for the usage, configuration subtleties and test aftereffects of the deliberate parameters. Voice-Controlled Smart Assistive Device for Visually hindered individuals [25]: This paper presents the demonstrating, usage and testing of an exploratory microcontroller (MCU)-based savvy assistive framework which can be utilized by the outwardly disabled or visually impaired individuals [18]. This gadget incorporates haptic and sound input choices from which the client can choose. A smart phone can be utilized to control the gadget utilizing predefined voice orders and Bluetooth network. The gadget is convenient and the motivation behind its use is to caution the client when items are present on the strolling way so crash can be dodged.

Separation estimations, between the client and conceivable hindrances, are performed utilizing ultrasonic echolocation and the information given by the ultrasonic sensor is handled by a microcontroller, which additionally handles the input part. Numerous difficulties can be performed through IOT gadgets. What's more, IOT is the ongoing quickly developing innovation which expands the limit and endeavors each figuring gadgets. Genuine time checking, restriction and breaking down methodology can be performed through application program in IOT. There are some logical data which play key jobs like physical condition, client action about speed and direction, just as time of day, week or temperature and regardless of weather conditions. Regularly GPS beneficiary takes an area, thinks about it and educates the client, as it ordinarily contrasts and computerizes map. As there are various sorts of visual weaknesses like fringe vision misfortune, focal vision misfortune and furthermore, absolutely visually impaired. IOT-based stage is progressively appropriate and critical for definite human interest necessity.

Here we pick IOT stage since it is more powerful, adaptability, functionality and accommodating for fathoming in any conditions. So through application doors one can interface any gadget to IOT stage. There has been move in inquiry about work like for future correspondence and registering through coordination of ideas to web of things. For this solitary three things are required, one as productively and determining the actualizing gadget appropriately next as taking care of and in conclusion dealing with the information. Also IOT stage approach is currently simply like encompassing insight framework. In the earth environment, signals are obtained and passed through cell phone to change over longitude and even more, scope to topographical area by utilizing an advanced guide. This GPS kind of innovation gives indoor and outside, for example, relevant data about the client [19]. For this android application Fing and MQTT ought to be downloaded by the client. Enormous number of remote sensors can be controlled through MQTT light weight convention. Python can be without any problem executed in MQTT. Fing portable application finds the gadget associated with the system or not. To empower the usefulness conveyed by Fing, one should initially get API key and approve it. Fing is a free system scanner.

For family unit and business apparatuses can be constrained by individual system these days. Fing can naturally perceive the best coordinating sort, brand and model of each device. Ear telephone will be utilized by the visually impaired individuals for the motivation behind tune in to the sound originating from the GPS and ringer alert because of route in bearing. The proposed framework can be utilized for loaded with wellbeing and route, when older and daze individuals are attempting to any natural or new region [28]. Strolling stick is the key specialized apparatus for route in a few angle and it is extremely useful to dazzle also, mature age individuals. By one way or another the proposed framework lets them be in better wellbeing while at the same time moving. It likewise builds the self-assurance and gives essential assistance to the client for their development by securing him/her from hitting object/hindrances. The purposed framework alarms the visually impaired about obstructions through sound. So visually impaired individuals build up their sense to limit them by hearing the sound. The general framework is an IOT-based idea of a brilliant electronic guide for the visually impaired individuals.

One can likewise say as it is an ongoing help of the outside natural situation by giving data about items around them. Of late, quantities of individuals experiencing visual deficiency have expanded quickly. The essential explanations for these are the consistently developing mishaps occurring in everyday life. To keep away from such setbacks we have planned a framework which will certainly push the incognizant in regards to a safe and better life. Being visually debilitated consistently gives a feeling of inadequacy to the individual because of he feels totally needy and depressed [1]. This framework will likewise assist the individual with being free and carry on with a standard life. Over the globe and in India, the quick development of outwardly impeded has prompted a wonderful advancement in this innovation sector. Devices which are as of now accessible in the market might be cumbersome and expensive which may not be moderate for a typical man. Thinking about the above viewpoint, the framework is made minimal by not mounting many segments on a solitary board making it less massive and cost-effective. The framework would then be able to be bought by individuals who are monetarily feeble. Assistive gadgets region key angle in wearable frameworks for biomedical applications, as they speak to potential guides for individuals with physical and tangible incapacities that may prompt upgrades in the personal satisfaction.

This venture is contains Obstacle recognition, Live following, Scene discovery, Fall Detection. Innovation is a beam of trust in handicaps to carry on with an autonomous life. This innovation is only an Assistive Technology [29]. This innovation is typically high in cost. Guide stick is one existing framework which when contrasted with the typical white stick normally utilized by the blinds is heavier [5]. A servo engine and a joystick are mounted on the highest point of the framework which helps in the route. 10 ultrasonic sensors made it progressively massive and it additionally couldn't recognize an article at the line of sight [27]. Absolutely, it could recognize the deterrents inside a predetermined outskirt every which way making the end to be vaguer. Thus, a shrewd stick was likewise imagined. Four catches printed with various bearings are available on the stick. To recognize the heading of a visually impaired individual RFID labels are given. Already, the framework comprising fake vision, object identification and area data utilizing GPS was proposed [29]. It gives the Static and Dynamic data of the encompassing around daze individual. Arduino board has been interfaced with the variety of ultrasonic sensors and independent GPS beneficiary with magnetometer was additionally utilized. A light on the best, a horn for traffic, vibrating sensors, high power LEDs were prepared on the stick. Ultrasonic sensors utilized here were having a scope of 20–350 cm. On the opposite side infrared sensors to recognize little hindrances are additionally utilized which help them having the scope of 2–10 cm.

Tap on/give discourse contribution to walkthrough hindrance at that point turning the framework on as the gadget prepares to distinguish the impediments. Here the IR sensors on the equipment gadget put on its left, right and front side discharges the radiation ceaselessly. At the point when any obstruction appears near the gadget the beams discharged by the IR will be thought about back the IR collector and the sign is then transmitted to the ADC. ADC changes over the simple sign into advanced signs that are required for the further calculation. Atmega32 microcontroller acknowledges these computerized signals and performs calculation which will contrast these qualities and the edge esteem. On the off chance that the worth is not exactly the edge esteem the impediment is recognized and an alarm message is given by the advanced cell as discourse yield. All the while the status of the deterrent distinguished is refreshed on the server figure and contrast [30] present facilitate values and the edge esteem. In the event that the worth is not exactly the edge esteem the fall is identified and an alarm message is given by the advanced mobile phone as discourse yield just as the ringer actuates for a particular timeframe to educate the individuals around. An alarm message is sent to the enrolled number about the fall detected along with its area.

At the same time the status of the fall recognized is refreshed on the server. For scene recognition, number of items and scenes should be put away and prepared. This is finished utilizing train information button on that application which verifiably turns on the camera. Presently the articles and scenes are caught and are enrolled. The preparation is performed on this data set with the assistance of RGB-HSV calculation and put away in the database. At the point when a disabled individual needs to perceive the scene/object he needsto give a voice input/press perceive button which open the camera. Presently he needs to catch the scene/object that will be perceived. These caught scene/objects are then contrasted and the prepared informational index [31]. In the event that the match is discovered the voice yield is created about the enrolled data spared while preparing, else it gives yield as null. For following the area of a hindered individual, GPS in the advanced cell is of course turned on which gathers the scope and longitude esteems and maps this area with the Google map. The latitude–longitude values are refreshed as the individual ventures more than a kilometer than his real area. This area is then put away on the server.

5.4   Results and Discussion

Monitoring Section
This is an overall circuit diagram which consists of IoT-based Raspberry pi and LCD. The camera is fitted with goggles and MATLAB coding is dumped into Raspberry, the system is monitored and speaker is connected with system to user as shown in **Figure 5.3**.

Product Identification
This diagram is used to show the output for product identification. Here the text and background color are captured and compared with stored images and corresponding image's name is identified and voice output is send to blind user through the speaker as shown in Figure 5.4.

Person Identification
This diagram is used to show the output for person identification. Here the image of the person and background color are captured and compared with stored images and corresponding image's name is identified and voice output is sent to blind user through the speaker as shown in **Figure 5.5**.

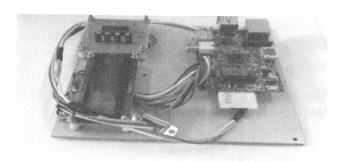

Figure 5.3 Hardware in monitoring system.

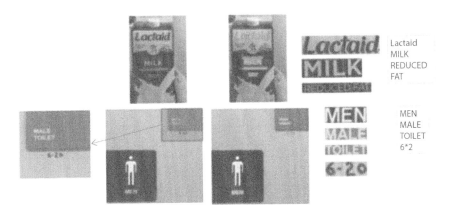

Figure 5.4 Product identification.

Figure 5.5 Person identification.

Figure 5.6 Comparison process in MATLAB.

Simulation of MATLAB Output
This is a diagram of MATLAB software, the image processing is done and comparison process is carried over with Figures 5.3 and 5.4, the name of the figure is identified from the database and voice output is passed to blind user as shown in **Figure 5.6.**

5.5   Conclusion

Finally, in this proposed system, MATLAB and embedded are combined to implement the innovative gadget for blind user to identify the obstacles and their friends. Previously the recognized images are stored in database. The camera records the images in real time and are recognized by using recognition section & given to processor. It transmits the information through max 232. The IoT-based face detection is obtained through image processing via camera. The person's face is matched with the database where the authentication occurs. The person's name is exposed with the speaker to blind user. In this system we can enroll the products and person directly to the database. It is a self-self-sufficient gadget and it offers inventive arrangements so as to supplant the customary techniques for controlling outwardly weakened individual. This gadget is one bit nearer to the objective of a protected and free direction to diminish the reliance with others.

5.6   Future Work

In future work, the system is connected to internet and the product is identified with and without database. All the images are detected and the entire people are identified by their enrollment identification (Adhaar number, voter id number). They can easily overcome their problems by using this device with advanced manner.

References

1. Fernandez, A., Carus, J.L., Usamentiaga, R., Casado, R., Face Recognition and Spoofing Detection System Adapted To Visually-Impaired People, in: *IEEE Latin America Transaction*, vol. 14, no. 2, pp. 913–921, 2016.
2. Ahonen, T. *et al.*, Face description with local binary patterns: App to face recognition. *IEEE Trans. Pattern Anal. Mach. Intell.*, 28, 12, 2037–2041, 2006.
3. Nada, A.A., Fakhr, M.A., Seddik, A.F., Assistive infrared sensor based smart stick for blind people. *Science and Information Conference (SAI)*, 2015.
4. Balduzzi, L., Fusco, G., Odone, F., Dini, S., Mesiti, M., Destrero, A., Lovato, A., Low-cost face biometry for visually impaired users, in: *Biometric Measurements and Systems for Security and Medical Applications (BIOMS), 2010 IEEE Workshop on*, 2010, September, IEEE, pp. 45–52.
5. Kramer, C., Hedin, K.M., D.S., Rolkosky, D.J., Smartphone based face recognition tool for the blind, in: *Engineering in Medicine and Biology Society (EMBC), 2010 Annual International Conference of the IEEE*, 2010, August, pp. 4538–4541.
6. Jabnoun, H., Benzarti, F., Amiri, H., Object recognition for blind people based on features extraction. *Image Processing, App. and Systems Conference (IPAS), 2014 First International*.

7. Maidenbaum, S., Hanassy, S. *et al.*, The "EyeCane", a new electronic travel aid for the blind: Technology, behavior & swift learning. *Restor. Neurol. Neurosci.*, 32, 6, 813–824, 2014.

8. Bhambare, R.R., Koul, A., Moh, S., Bilal, S.P., Smart vision system for blind. *Int. J. Eng. Comput. Sci.*, 3, 5, 579, 2014.

9. Anand, Rajkumar, N., Barathiraja, M.G.N., Portable Camera-Based Product Label Reading For Blind People. *Int. J. Eng. Trends Technol. (IJETT)*. 10, 11, 521–524, 2014.

10. Srikanthan, P. *et al.*, Contrive and effectuation of active distance sensor using MATLAB and GUIDE package. *IOSR J. Electr. Electron. Eng.*, 2, 4, 29–33, 2012 Sep–Oct.

11. Tan, X. and Triggs, B., Enhanced local texture feature sets for face recognition under difficult lighting conditions, in: *IEEE Transactions on Image Processing*, vol. 19, no. 6, pp. 1635–1650, USA, 2010.

12. Santhi, S. *et al.*, SoS Emergency Ad-Hoc Wireless Network. Computational Intelligence and Sustainable Systems (CISS), in: *EAI/Springer Innovations in Communications and Computing*, pp. 227–234, 2019.

13. Vetrivelan, P. *et al.*, *A Neural Network-Based Automatic Crop Monitoring based Robot for Agriculture. The IoT and the Next Revolutions Automating the World*. D. Goyal *et al.*, (eds.) pp. 203–212, IGI Global, United States, 2019.

14. Tamilselvan, *et al.*, A Smart Industrial Pollution Detection and Monitoring using Internet of Things (IoT), in: *Communication in Computer and Information Science (CCIS) series. Futuristic Trends in Network and Communication Technologies (FTNCT 2019)*. Singh, P., Sood, S., Kumar, Y., Paprzycki, M., Pljonkin, A., Hong, W.C., (eds.), vol. 1206, Issue 1, pp. 233–242, Springer, Singapore, 2020.

15. Arun Pradeep, B. *et al.*, Automatic Battery Replacement of Robot. *Adv. Nat. Appl. Sci., AENSI Publications*, 9, 7, pp. 33–38, June 2015.

16. Kanagaraj, T. *et al.*, Foot Pressure Measurement by using ATMEGA 164 Microcontroller. *Adv. Nat. Appl. Sci., AENSI Journals*, 10, 13, pp. 224–228, September 2016.

17. Srihari, K. *et al.*, Automatic Battery Replacement of Robot. *Adv. Nat. Appl. Sci.*, 9, 7, 33–38, June 2015.

18. Vetrivelan, P. *et al.*, Design of Smart Surveillance Security System based on Wireless Sensor Network. *Int. J. Res. Stud. Sci. Eng. Technol.*, 4, 5, 23–26, August 2017.

19. Prakash, N. *et al.*, Arduino based traffic congestion control with automatic signal clearance for emergency vehicles and stolen vehicle detection. *Proceedings of IEEE International Conference on Computing, Communication and Informatics (ICCCI-2020)*, Coimbatore, 2020.

20. Srihari, K. *et al.*, Implementation of Alexa Based Intelligent Voice Response System for Smart Campus, in: *Innovations in Electrical and Electronics Engineering, Lecture Notes in Electrical Engineering*. Saini, H., Srinivas, T., Vinod Kumar, D., Chandragupta Mauryan, K. (eds.), vol. 626, Issue 1, pp. 849–855, Springer, Singapore, 2020.

21. Jabnoun, H., Benzarti, F., Amiri, H., Object recognition for blind people based on features extraction. *International Image Processing, Applications and Systems Conference*, 2014.

22. Prakash, N. *et al.*, GSM based design and implementation of women safety device using Internet of Things. *Proceedings of International Conference on Big Data and Cloud Computing (ICBDCC-2019), Advances in Big Data and Cloud Computing, Springer-Advances in Intelligent Systems and Computing (AISC) series*, 2019.

23. Kanagaraj, T. *et al.*, Control of Home appliances and projector by smart application using SEAP Protocol, in: *Progress in Computing, Analytics and Networking, Advances in Intelligent Systems and Computing (AISC)*. Das, H., Pattnaik, P., Rautaray, S., Li, K.C. (eds), vol. 1119, pp. 603–610, Springer, Singapore, 2020.

24. Ramesh, C. *et al.*, An Enhanced Face and Iris Recognition based New Generation Security System, in: *Proceedings of First International Conference on Computing, Communications, and*

Cyber-Security (IC4S 2019). Lecture Notes in Networks and Systems. Singh, P., Pawłowski, W., Tanwar, S., Kumar, N., Rodrigues, J., Obaidat, M. (eds), vol. 121, pp. 845–855, Springer, Singapore, 2020.

25. Ashiq, H., Kurian, M., Roshin, M., Sooraj, S.B., Perumprath, A.S., Smart Assistive Device for Visually Impaired. *Int. Res. J. Eng. Technol.*, 6, 05, 5884–5887, May 2019.

26. Nada, A.A., Fakhr, M.A., Seddik, A.F., Assistive infrared sensor based smart stick for blind people. *2015 Science and Information Conference (SAI)*, 2015.

27. Mala, N.S., Thushara, S.S., Subbiah, S., Navigation gadget for visually impaired based on IoT. *2017 2nd International Conference on Computing and Communications Technologies (ICCCT)*, Chennai, pp. 334–338, 2017.

28. Mohapatra, B.N., Mohapatra, R.K., Panda, P., Path Guidance System For Blind People. *Int. J. Open Inf. Technol.*, 7, 5, 29–32, 2019.

29. Srihari, K. *et al.*, An Innovative Approach for Face Recognition Using Raspberry Pi. *Artificial Intelligence Evolution, Universal Wiser publisher*, 1, 2, 103–108, August 2020.

30. Padade, S., Mali, S., Mote, S., Omkar, R., An EYE for a Blind: Assistive Technology. *IRJET*, 04, 04, 532–534, 2017.

31. Takizawa, H. and Aoyagi, M., *Assistive Systems for the Visually Impaired Based on Image Processing, Causes and Coping with Visual Impairment and Blindness*, S. Rumelt (Ed.), IntechOpen, United Kingdom, 2017.

## 6

IoT Protocol for Inferno Calamity in Public Transport

Ravi Babu Devareddi*, R. Shiva Shankar and Gadiraju Mahesh

Computer Science and Engineering Department, S.R.K.R. Engineering College, Bhimavaram, India

Abstract

In this work, safety of passengers in any Journey, especially at the railway's passengers air-condition coaches or air-condition buses transportation is considered. It is one of the most important aspects to be considered by public transporters. This is of top level priority for passenger safety in Journeys where running conditions are harsh in night time where passengers will be sleeping in that time and unable to observe while train or bus is running. With the passenger's numbers were reaching hundreds in a single transport vehicle, it necessitates measure of safety for the passengers from any possible inferno calamity situations. In order to solve problems in this scenario, a monitoring system to be installed in railway coaches or buses could be initiated. By using this system, coach environment as temperature, smoke and fire critical safety parameters in these cabins could be instantaneously monitored. So that automatically fire prevention actions take place by releasing the fire prevention material on that spot and alert the passengers and respective authorities to avoid the cases of occurrence of such type of calamity. For the structure of this framework, an ESP32 Wi-Fi and Bluetooth low energy chip based microcontroller is used. To this, three sensors are connected i.e. one auto valve to release carbon dioxide, one to monitor temperature (DHT11 sensor), flame sensor and a MQ2-sensor used for smoke. These sensors keep an eye in the passenger cabins and bottom of the coaches and engine cabins and these parameters values are published to the cloud platforms as topics by utilizing Message queuing telemetry transport (MQTT) protocol. MQTT protocol is a significant remarkable cloud platform that helps to focus information by various aspects and alerts the passengers along with necessary actions to take place automatically.

Keywords: MQTT, wireless sensor network, transmitted power, MQ2-sensor

6.1 Introduction

With the advancement of transportation systems in air, road and water, the passenger's fire safety is the primary concern for journeys. Inferno calamity might be lethal and defame for factories and domestic home protection and sensitive for life of humans. Most of the reports furnished the inquiry results as accidents that occurred by the fire and by the oral interview of experts from the fire department confirmed that the fire could occur by electrical short

Corresponding author: ravibabu.devareddi@gmail.com

Monika Mangla, Suneeta Satpathy, Bhagirathi Nayak and Sachi Nandan Mohanty (eds.) Integration of Cloud Computing with Internet of Things: Foundations, Analytics, and Applications, (87–110) © 2021 Scrivener Publishing LLC

circuits or fault and passengers stayed in the concealed air condition cabins which lead to major part of passenger life jeopardy. The human response time is not sufficient to control the situation thus leads to inferno calamity, so that there is a need to find the best way to respond as early as possible. By this way there is necessity for standby automatic fire mishap identification detection and fire risk regulation systems. It is used to restore and strive for expeditious identification, indication as notifications by alarm, and around the clock fire action. The systems were installed for containing smoke, temperature, flame sensors that detect unwanted problems caused by fire and by the utilization of a processing mechanism of unit that alerts instantaneously for warning measures. Sensors play the key role in measuring certain dynamic and static variables like humidity, kind of fuel variance, by considering the slope of the land, the direction of wind, and wind speed, smoke, to name just a few. In such dangerous circumstances early identification and faster warning can result in lowering property and life losses.

Life and property safety concerns call for considering an energetic and reliable system of fire stability. It has seen an increased use as an emerging technology in the terrain of fire. A fire prevention system may be controlled locally at the premises, or if needed, remotely at a distant location. Remote alarm system allows the property owner for the perk to keep an eye on from a remote district and catch prompt action upon receiving an emergency call, unlike a manual device. That means it can be very useful for these sensor-based systems to detect a fire and to take decisions to eradicate it. Remote control systems can be configured to use Wi-Fi, image processing, Ethernet and remaining technologies related in communication digital era in many different ways. Despite being robust and providing a broad boundaries of ruler, the systems are followed by burden around convoluted, uncompact, cost, non-standalone, and providing superfluous apparatus. By this way, a system that would be decisive and sensitive, easy to implement and price-impressive is required.

Even if a range of progressive methods are used in realistic situations, dependable, simple to implement, and price impressive mechanized fire based alarm system in developing countries is non-feasible. Accordingly, an analysis of reality of fire identification equipment is depleted in this examination. By this way an optimized cost and rapid-response fire based identification prevention mechanism was developed and implemented using one of those detectors. Through the message exchange protocol developed by IBM [1], the device is able to send data to IoT via MQTT using Wi-Fi communication technology and warning messages through the topics PUBLISH/SUBSCRIBE mechanism.

MQTT protocol framework acted as a networking protocol that can be helpful in saving power along with network bandwidth [2]. MQTT is a protocol [3] which takes less time for execution that offers messages tiny as stature. MQTT structure is based on Publish and Subscribe is more effective for implementing IoT applications compared with remaining protocols using Request and Response since the MQTT client is not required to deliver an upgrade request which leads to impressive bandwidth as pool as long losses in system life of battery [4] in this system. These properties reveal the perfection for multiple ways, considering restricted environments such as Machine to Machine (M2M) communication and Internet of Things (IoT) communication as well known. This MQTT protocol [5] is used on social media.

Cloud MQTT provides a lodging of services of related computations for cloud which make up a computing platform on insistence. Here this process we show is a particular

MQTT along with cloud MQTT [6] which are acceptable specialized aspirants for applications for small IoT businesses. In order to apply for railway air conditioning or bus coaches, we developed a wise model to control fire; we are creating a Cloud MQTT broker. The MQTT broker was used as a forum for the provision of IoT services that can be used to track and regulate temperature and sensibility alarms for fire suppression via the carbon dioxide gas pipeline network in coaches. Arduino type boards were utilized for the IoT end system joining to the distributed network using Wi-Fi channel with a temperature reading device in a fire sensor and fire alarm, aerosol actuator and air conditioner. We've used the Web API based on Gluon for mobile application creation. This application facilitates indoor area temperature supervisor system that controls setting of desired temperature, reception of alarm based on fire and preventive functions.

Here we used the availability of half-sized single-board credit card computers such as the ESP32 that made it possible to build multiple automated and control systems with optimized power consumption, less response time for processing capabilities at small amount of price. The proposed fire control program combines the use of inexpensive devices, networking, and wireless communication. Here ESP32 called as microcontroller is used to interface with the flame sensor, gas sensor and temperature sensor and actuator. Whenever the connected sensor devices sends the signal to controller as collectively or independently then the controller will publish this messages to the cloud with the help MQTT protocol mechanism. If the required parameters are acquired to identify the fire incident by subscriber messages then actuator will activated to enable the carbon dioxide cylinder valve to release the fire suppression gaseous elements.

6.2   Literature Survey

Different types of research lead to diverse models of self-working security video camera system abide developed with the help of different platforms. With the latest advances in technology like Web server, GSM and Microcontroller called as embedded microprocessors, these extend the platform to design the various productions of various fire alarm indication systems.

Fang *et al.* [7] proposed a smart fire alarm system with the help of the fuzzy neural network concept using Single Chip Microcontroller (SCM) AT89C51 and voice chip IS1420.

Shunxia *et al.* [8] introduced a smart home fire accident alarm system consisting of anti-theft feature with the help of wireless technology, fire proof feature and anti-harmful leakage feature from gas. Wireless communication and couple of SCMs were utilized to show the concentration of gas and hosting the warning signals given by the alarm. When smoke is detected by the sensor, a voice appended message is delivered to the correspondent department. Here there is some problem like if any error occurs at the time of detection then it leads to issue a false alarm by the lack of no user authentication in this system.

Jun *et al.* [9] introduced a protection device for home with intelligent behavior, using a surveillance camera to track important positions within a home using Zigbee. If any penetration has activated the device, the user is notified via SMS and also Multimedia Message Service (MMS). Using Zigbee modules, the temperature reading device and the gaseous level reading device were attached to the control board general purpose input output pins and also enables an umbrella of Wireless Sensor Network (WSN). While this might be used as accounting widely used advanced systems, the WSN management control board utilization is too costly.

With the help of Beagle board, Rakesh *et al.* [10] introduced FTP Web server and Zigbee which can be utilized to observe the significant locations within the home by installing a camera and identifying smoke presence and this system they called as real-time home surveillance security system. Here, whenever any smoke or some other persons entered the house environment, it can detect those incidents and immediately delivers the messages to mobile phones and also start recording the video camera for specific timing boundaries and raising the indicator as alarm. A drawback is that this system only delivers the SMS to set right the owner of the home and instead of transferring the streaming of the live video record, the recording of video is stored in internal memory of the system. The single board microcontroller covers the economic burden and it contains fewer technological requirements compared to the Raspberry Pi.

Luo Ren and Kuo Su [11] introduced the multisensory fire detection algorithm which handles significant current problems in the group of detection of fire systems used in smart homes via an adaptive-fusion algorithm. It works on fire and detection of fire and with the help of a sensor to measure smoke content, fire identification with a sensor and measuring temperature with a sensor. It is helpful to identify the origin of fire. To make a more accurate decision they considered the algorithm called as adaptive-fusion algorithm. It is very high complex in real world situations. Here the modified Taylor expression is compared with results of 1st, 2nd and 3rd order expressions by the simulation of adaptive-fusion. The updated adaptive-fusion technique might yield sufficient reliable computer simulation for fire detection using fusion to enhance the accuracy and adequacy of the adaptive fusion algorithm.

Qingying *et al.* [12] proposed a flexible rapid-reaction fire control system that would orient number of targets, set its system structure and analyze the mechanism of cooperative targets. A network environment is built that integrates physical media, wireless communication and data base maintained for the fire control with a structure of five layers, which leads to critically solve the problem of flexible control in the control system for fire. The machine should easily make a joint decision and efficiently harmonize all resources so that the working environment is balanced and the mission of fire control is accomplished with the lowest damage in the shortest time. Building a cooperative rapid-response fire control system is designed to efficiently enhance work efficiency, reduce losses and ensure on-site fire fighters' health.

Muller *et al.* [13] developed a multi-sensor technology for tile enhancement of fire detective systems in the desired direction. The key point is the assessment and interpretation of tile signals provided by the monitored phenomena. This signal processing (detection algorithm) mainly defines the capabilities of lie detectors. Modern signal processing techniques (neural networks, fumy logic) could be used due to the availability of microcontrollers specific to fire detector technology with its extreme technological limitations (i.e., power consumption). This paper introduces an MSb FD Algorithm, which is based on the input as temperature and optical density of smoke for fire. These two input devices being selected as ionization systems lead extremely challenging to deploy due to the regulations for environment applied. This sensor signals estimation and analysis is performed using Fuzzy Reasoning.

Hu *et al.* [14] proposed to use nRF2401 applied for wireless communications within short range as well as GPRS utilized for long-range. Similarly, ARM9 dedicated to point soothe connectionless Multi-sensor utilized to identify as knob, BP algorithm to determine the likelihood of a fire. It consists of sensors called as electrochemical carbon monoxide sensors which consume less power, a smoke detector based on photoelectric and a temperature sensor depending on semiconductor mechanism. The BP algorithm software is implemented in the ARM S3C2440A. Samples of BP algorithm were obtained in accordance with the regular identification of fire within room of China's State Main Fire Science Laboratory. Point console utilizes Embedded GIS to specify the state of fire location and use GPRS to send message to the fire control center as SMS.

Peinl *et al.* [15] introduced early detection of fires in the forests by using the Aspires an advanced system for the fire prevention. They collecting al the related data by using cameras, drones and sensors and stored to cloud. They provided the entire data freely accessible to everyone in cloud. By using this technology they allowed to minimise the observation of incidents.

Kodali and Valdas [16] proposed a network of IoT devices that work around the clock to monitor the incidents about fire and its location and send a message as alert to central hub by the chance of fire occurrence. This system might send data to the respective persons or corresponding authorities leads to take the necessary actions. They introduced a MQTT network with the help of Raspberry Pi microcontroller worked as MQTT Broker and Node MCU's are distributed and interfaced with Pi. If any fire accidents happen in that location then that respective senior node issues the fire accident warning for that place.

Molla Shahadat, Tahia *et al.* [17] introduced smoke identification device by using wireless technology. They installed smoke detector devices within the range of Wi-Fi signal area. They used hard equipment as Microcontroller board, temperature reading sensor, smoke identifier, receiver and optimized power consumed transmitter along with receiver. Here drawback is arbitrary extraneous noise added from the different types of sources from electromagnetic radiation.

Luzuriaga *et al.* [18] introduced a technique to boost MQTT flexible to mobile users. They did not focus more on the network penetrated protocols as LISP or Mobile IP. Also, information loss was minimized due to the mobility of mobile devices through node to node transition. But it needs large number of buffers concerning nodes for mobile.

Kodali and Yerroju [19] proposed an emergency response system useful to fire accidents that is developed with the help of Internet of things system framework. For the implementation, they proposed a low cost scheme as Express if Wi-Fi module ESP-32 with Flame detection sensor, Smoke identification sensor MQ5, Flammable gaseous elements identification detection sensor and also with one GPS module are considered. The electronic devices are called sensors that monitor hazard and pass the information like location and incidents to the nearby team or group of people who are involved to control fire like fire department or police department and local emergency rescue organizations like fire departments. Here they used the protocol which consumes less data oriented publish–subscribe messages model based protocol MQTT for dependable and believable communication channel. Thus, they designed with the help of IoT but here human intervention is involved.

Kodali and Valdas [20], proposed a system which based on the IoT which can always monitor for fire mishaps and pass information to the central point by the occurrence of any fire, where there is a fire situation and place of where it happened. Thus the information is forwarded to the respective sources of the concerned responsible persons and in that way suppressive methods are applied. MQTT protocol based network with the help of a Raspberry Pi were utilized as the MQTT Broker and a distributed Node MCUs as group attached with smoke, temperature sensors behave as a sensor network to pass information to the Raspberry Pi. In this way, when there is a fire in some location, the appropriate sensor node passes a message as well as generated an email which tells about the incident to the respective authorities.

Kang *et al.* [21] made a MQTT operator on Amazon Web Service (AWS). The MQTT middle person has been helpful as a phase to give the Internet of Things (IoT) organizations the ability to screen and control room temperatures, and sense, alert, and cover fire. Arduino was used as the IoT end device interfacing sensors and actuators to the phase by methods for Wi-Fi channel. They made keen home circumstance and organized IoT rubs satisfying the circumstance need. They moreover executed some splendid structure in gear and programming, and checked the system action. They revealed that MQTT and AWS are adequate specific competitors for little IoT business applications.

Mahgoub *et al.* [22] introduced fire alert frameworks that are imperative to warn individuals before a fire incident is going to happen to their local places like their homes. By this way, today's alarm systems should outfitted which require a mass of electrical links and labor. This demoralizes clients from introducing them in their homes. By the manner in which they proposed an IoT based remote alarm framework it should be anything but difficult to introduce. The proposed framework is a specially appointed system that is comprised of a few hubs dispersed over the house. Every one of these hubs comprises of a microcontroller (ESP8266 node MCU) associated with smoke, temperature, stickiness, fire, Methane and Carbon Monoxide (CO) sensors that ceaselessly sense the general condition to identify the nearness of fire. The hubs make their own Wi-Fi arrange. These hubs speak with an incorporated hub executed with a Raspberry Pi microcontroller coordinated with a 4G module. When fire is recognized by a hub, it imparts a sign to be brought together by the hub which is activated to send a SMS to the local group of fire-fighters and the client, by considering the client and caution about the house by delivering a neighborhood alert. The client can likewise get data about the status of his home through sending a SMS to the framework. The detecting hubs make a work system and they are connected to the focal hub by means of a scaffold hub. Correspondence between the extension hub and the detecting hub is through MQTT convention. A model was created for the proposed framework and it completed the ideal functionalities effectively with a normal postponement of fewer than 30 s.

Kodali and Mahesh [23] proposed that technology is phenomenal growling engine of change and Internet of Things (IoT) is the establishment of such dynamic engines. Basically, as a general rule the things having sensor limit, satisfactory power deftly and accessibility to web makes field like Internet of Things (IoT) possible. For such fast creating development, it needs to be amazingly light, affordable and have the least information transmission show like MQTT Protocol. By virtue of such non-set up show it is straightforward for the clients to convey or/and purchase in the aching subject through the host going about as server of the framework also known to be the expert. In this paper, it is demonstrated that correspondence between the low power ESP8266 Wi-Fi as client with the clients on PDAs and PC using a MQTT show gets less difficult and progressively reliable. The Wi-Fi enabled

ESP8266 board interfaces with DHT11 sensor and LDR sensor to screen the encompassing condition and as shown by the light force level the splendor level of $8 * 8$ Neo-pixel network is controlled. The adafruit.io is the MQTT server, and that operator which furthermore gives the workplace a watching structure through the dashboard. The client on wireless and PC purchases into the subjects of temperature, moistness and light force level gets the different updates. The key objective of the paper is to realize the idea for the android to home machines, street light structure for the clever urban regions and fire prepared systems.

Kang *et al.* [21] presented component with the assistance of manufacturer a MQTT intermediary on Amazon Web Service (AWS). The MQTT merchant has used a stage to give the Internet of Things (IoT) administrations which screen and control room temperatures, and sense, caution, and smother fire. Arduino was utilized as the IoT end gadget associating sensors and actuators to the stage by means of Wi-Fi channel. They made savvy home situation and structured IoT rubs fulfilling the requirement. Kurniawan *et al.* [24] used the preceding technique to develop an application to control server room environment.

Cheng *et al.* [25] stressed that the regular fire mishaps of open vehicle have brought about the rejecting of vehicles, disastrous property misfortunes and setbacks, which had drawn across the board the worry of individuals and society for open security. The traveler lodge space of transport is generally little. When a fire happens, high temperature, warm radiation and smoke created by burning will cause incredible troubles for staff departure. Focusing on the prerequisites of Chinese GA1264-2015, this paper did full-scale fire-dousing tests in the transport lodge. The boundaries of temperature dispersion, smoke focus and putting out fires time in the traveler lodge of the transport are broken down, in order to confirm the putting out fires execution of oneself created water-based fire quenching operator and the fixed fire-stifling framework in the traveler lodge. The framework can extinguish fire rapidly and productively. Additionally, it can adequately diminish temperature and convergence of poisonous and destructive gases in the lodge after the fire. It could clearly improve the fire insurance limit.

Jun *et al.* [26] presented that IOT is viewed as another data industry wave following PC, Internet and versatile correspondence arrange, and has gotten one of key predominant places of new monetary and innovative advancement everywhere throughout the world. The general public putting out fires for the wellbeing of the executives is a significant application field of Internet of Things (IOT) innovation. Here we mainly focus on an IoT innovation which as indicated puts out fires, business prerequisite to talk about the putting out fires with IoT orderly edge and the proposed necessity of improvement purposes of society putting out fires securing the executives as IoT innovation.

Vijayalakshmi and Muruganand [27] presented that Internet of Things (IoT) gives a decent opportunity to assemble ground-breaking framework in fire industry. The growing demand of radio frequency identification (RFID) technology, mobile and wireless sensor network give fire region related applications with high utilization level. This paper is about the ebb and flow exploration, advances and uses of IoT in file related businesses and distinguishing research patterns and difficulties in fire enterprises. The fire IoT intends to associate various things over the systems related with fire. Administration Oriented Architecture is applied to help fire IoT in that layers communicate each other for checking fire and items. This paper practically understands a portion of the layer required for fire observing and industry. Detecting layer is practically acknowledged with WSN hub with sensors, RFID labeled gadget and Video hub for fire and item checking. Everything, for example, sensor arrange, versatile system are associated together in the system layer. Administration layer and interface layer are utilized to acknowledge Mobile hub information, WSN hub information and diagrams show the fire related boundaries.

Li and Hou [28] proposed NB-IoT alludes to a cell based narrowband Internet of Things, which has become a significant piece of the Internet of Things. NB-IoT is another innovation developing in the field of Internet of Things as of late. It has clear focal points in innovation and application. Moreover, the use of narrowband Internet of Things (NB-IoT) innovation in the field of fire assurance can on a very basic level improve the battle capacity of putting out fires powers, maintain a strategic distance from fire and lessen the death toll and property of the individuals. This theory investigates and presents a clever putting out fires framework dependent on the new business standard, and a smoke-fire identification and alert gadget dependent on the Internet of Things (IoT) stage and Nb-IoT innovation. It additionally advances relating answers for the issue of savvy smoke, for example, the worth, focal points and future desires for the arrangement.

Prabha [29] explained that the business' dynamic nature presents uncommon difficulties to the government. High amount of dangerous material stock has expanded fire dangers with enormous misfortunes. Web of Things (IoT) is a structure of numerous simultaneous gadgets that are implanted and ready to work for information transmission over the Internet. It comprises of all internets empowered gadgets answerable for social occasion, transmitting and working on data extricated by encompassing environment using sensors, locators and processing equipment. In mechanical security and control, IoT assumes a significant job. This exploration work presents another gadget equipped for distinguishing fire and giving an admonition to clients. To screen the incorporated gadgets with a few sensors and cameras, the Raspberry Pi 3 has been utilized. The sensor ceaselessly sense and really starts to communicate esteems over a Wi-Fi relationship to the online advanced server. At whatever point fire is detected, the camera begins to record the picture just as the gadget begins to send the message with the influenced spot pictures. When the blast is detected by the fire transmitter, this will animate the smoke caution and initiate a sprinkler engine. For sensor data the database could be designed by the executive and checked at anyplace.

As mentioned above, the solution to the problems from the earlier introduced work is to create a new fire identification mechanism that warns respective authorities immediately if any incidents happened and then the user can take preventive action. The goal of this investigation is to fabricate a blaze identification and warning system with the help of an Arduino Uno processor based on a microcontroller in combination with other components that is a reliable and cost-effective system and is simple to implement.

6.3 Methodology

The main use of the MQTT protocol as message publish–subscribe mechanism is applied to monitoring the environment as fire alarm and prevention management. This is used to distantly notify fire and smoke events that occur inside or outer the cabins within the locations quickly by conveying short alert message through Wi-Fi to IOT cloud platform. The range of the fire notification arrangements is to make great use of contemporary communications in dealing with emergencies. The purpose of this system is to direct alert notification to a group of mobile numbers or even one (if desired) when fire happens in a specific locality and spontaneously activate the actuator to discharge the fire avoiding material such as carbon dioxide to destroy the fire. The intentions of this fire monitoring and avoidance by MQTT base protocol with ESP32 microcontroller board is to sense the environments for happening of fire with help of flame sensor, monitor temperature, humidity with DHT11 sensor and gaseous level by MQ2 sensor after distributing these characteristics as topics to the IOT cloud platform with the help of PUB/SUB messages based protocol. This system examines the data with the IOT cloud platform and distributes topics to the matching subscriber to trigger the actuator and distributing alerts to particular person's mobile number.

Present fire panels use the Wireless Alarm Communicator (DACT) transmitter [30] to convey the significant commands as data to the station where it is central point. Here, DACT accompanies just few panels, while the majority of the panels required an external DACT device to transmit the data to that station. The use of DACT is old, since it needs additional hardware components and interface. The distribution unit is produced to resolve the oldness of the DACT that is used to build the cost effective product. Function block diagram could be seen in Figure 6.1.

During this job, the machine manufactured has a device that mechanically prevents fire and distributes any incident on premise fire to the corresponding authority. If the fire detector detects any fire-related incident, the data will be sent to the central station after handling the situation in the fire panel dialler. The built framework has smaller peripherals of hardware supporting parts and hence less the circuit connections with the control board. It eradicates the price and provides flexibility to reuse the programming part.

The MQTT is well-defined as protocol for PUBLISH/SUBSCRIBE messages to the cloud. It is a protocol which consumes less amount processor time for execution and embedded port no: 1883 for TCP/IP. It is also a protocol with free available for usage by open source mechanism by the OASIS Technical forum that finds out how the broker is used to transfer the messages among the clients and developed a tool for implementation and grant Quality of Services (QoS) that facilitates interfacing channel or web with the fine source of internet bandwidth, excels the reliability and to some extent the transfer on guarantee [32]. Either device to device interfaces or device to gateway interfacing will be instituted in this work. A device to gateway interfacing using hardware system displayed in Figure 6.2 is created. The experimentation could be completed with the support of device, gateway and applications. To work with MQTT, user can configure devices or use open software tools (Mqtt lens for MQTT) in place of several devices.

Eclipse Mosquitto is a freely available software tool used as message a broker to deliver the messages that defines variations 3.1 and 3.1.1 of the MQTT protocol. Mosquitto is trivial and ideal for use with complete servers on several devices within boundary of tiny power single board type computers.

It offers a low processing time for messaging conveyance technique using publish/subscribe methodology. This means it is ideally suited for communicating on the Internet of Things with optimized power consumption sensors or devices like mobiles, tablets, inbuilt computers or embedded microprocessors. The Mosquitto platform also facilitate "C-language" library helpful to clients of MQTT and it is most prevalent publish by mosquito and subscribe by mosquito command line.

This para describes about "topic". The term topic is described as an UTF8 string, which is used by the broker to filter the messages delivered to every connected client in this system.

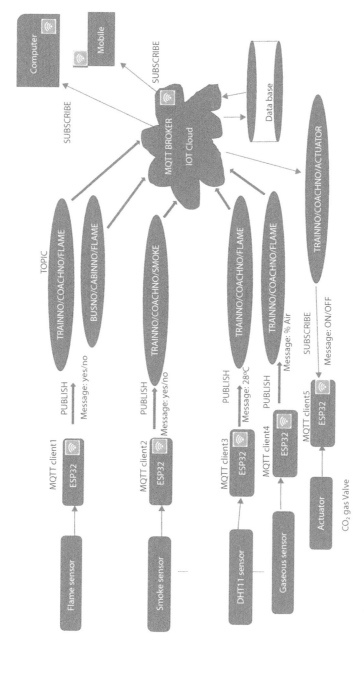

Figure 6.1 System architecture as shown as functional block diagram.

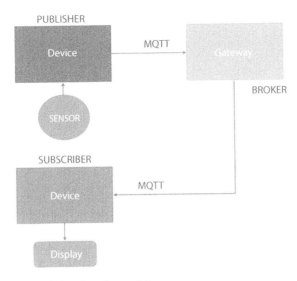

Figure 6.2 MQTT protocol: publish–subscribe model.

Topics contains one or more topic levels, each is divided by forward-slash. Topics should contain minimum of length one character along with case sensitive and are lightweight. The topics are accepted by the broker without any initialization. Here the topics levels used are as shown in the Table 6.1.

In this work the sensor data parameters across several numbers of trains and buses are stored to the cloud platform with the unique id of TRAINO and BUSNO as top level

Table 6.1 Topic descriptions.

Topic Id	Topic	Topic description
T1	TRAINNO/COACHNO/FLAME	The top level topic TRAINO, sublevel topic COACHNO and topic name FLAME
T2	BUSNO/CABINNO/FLAME	FLAME related to Bus
T3	TRAINNO/COACHNO/SMOKE	SMOKE related to Train
T4	BUSNO/CABINNO/SMOKE	SMOKE related to Bus
T5	TRAINNO/COACH NO/TEMP	TEMP related to Train
T6	BUSNO/CABINNO/TEMP	TEMP related to Bus
T7	TRAINNO/COACHNO/FLAME	FLAME related to Train
T8	BUSNO/CABINNO/FLAME	FLAME related to Bus
T9	TRAINNO/COACHNO/ACTUATOR	ACTUATOR related to Train
T10	BUSNO/CABINNO/ACTUATOR	ACTUATOR related to Bus

Topic published to the cloud, further identifies the respective coach number or cabin number using sublevel topic COACHNO and CABINNO and finally topic values as FLAME, SMOKE and TEMP. Whenever these parameters reached threshold values then the subscribers topics from the clients enabled the topic ACTUATOR respective to the coach or cabin and released the carbon dioxide to suppress the fire immediately without intervention of human being.

6.3.1   IoT Message Exchange With Cloud MQTT Broker Based on MQTT Protocol

In this division we designate IoT messages interchange within MQTT clients and cloud MQTT broker proposal using MQTT protocol that allows appropriating for the establishment of the above atmosphere observing in train coaches or bus. Figure 6.3 demonstrates the MQTT protocol publish/subscribe message exchanges between MQTT broker and client devices. The IoT messages are for the management of room humidity, the detection or suppression of fire and the monitoring of system status. The name of the MQTT subject has been given for each message, who will deliver and subscribe in has been established, and the behaviour of the recipient after receiving the message has also been well defined.

MQTT protocol for coach cabin or outer cabin fire and monitoring temperature or controlling fire sensing or notifying or destruction and system status checking is done.

6.3.2   Hardware Requirement

- ESP32
- DHT 11 sensor
- Flame sensor
- MQ2 sensor
- Connecting wires.

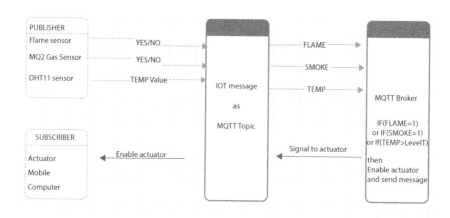

Figure 6.3 MQTT protocol message exchanges.

ESP32 Microcontroller Board

ESP32 is a sequence of financially lower priced with finest use of low power supply on micro-controllers with embedded Wi-Fi and dual-mode Bluetooth that is displayed in Figure 6.4.

Flame Sensor

Sensor is an electrical machine that works as input device. Not all the inputs are collected from sensors, but majority inputs make use of sensors. The output data depends on the measurement. There are several varieties of sensors. Fire sensor used in the section is illustrated below in Figure 6.5.

The flame sensor identifies the fire within its range. The range of flame sensor is

i.   3-feet distance.
ii. 60° angle.

Figure 6.4 ESP 32 board.

Figure 6.5 Flame sensor.

MQ2

MQ2 sensor is used to read the gaseous level and is used mainly to track the attentiveness of airborne LPG gas particles in air, propane, methane, propane, alcohol, carbon monoxide and smoke. The chemiresistor is best known or called as the MQ2 gas sensor. This contains a sensing substance whose resistance in contact with the gas varies. This variability in the resistance measurement is used to classify a gas. This sensor operates at voltage +5 V DC. This device can detect gasses within 200 to 10,000 ppm range as displayed below in Figure 6.6.

DHT11 Sensor

DHT11 device is a low priced, humidity and temperature sensor. It is not the wildest sensor nearby but it is less costly in price. This sensor requires tri-interfaces pins as positive 3 V, earth pin as Ground finally General purpose input/output (GP-I/O) pin. This device is equipped with Quadra pins out of which only three are used and 4th is not used. The DHT11 sensor is displayed in Figure 6.7. The components have three pins, and are easy to attach to the GPIO header of the microcontroller. It measures Humidity as 20 to 80 percentile with accuracy of only 5 percentile Temperature as 0 to 50 °C with accuracy of only 2 °C.

Figure 6.6 MQ2 gas sensor.

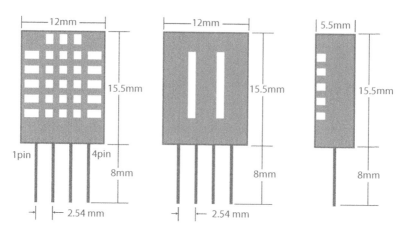

Figure 6.7 DHT11 sensor.

Actuator

It is a part of a device which is responsible for providing control and move mechanism e.g. by triggering a valve. This is a "mover" in common terms. It should require signal for control purpose with sources of energy. Here optimized power is enough for all operations like pneumatic or hydraulic or even human strength. The central source of energy may be electric current, pneumatic strain, hydraulic fluid. By receiving the signal for controlling, it enables by energy of the source converting as some motion automatically, as shown in Figure 6.8.

Software Requirement

Arduino IDE: Arduino facilitates a Computer, "C" type programming language compiled for Arduino type boards and contains the server name such as adafruit.com and port no: 1883 used by server, which appears to use the MQTT protocol, Adafruit account username, as allocated to the TCP/IP address. Arduino IDE [31] are used to write and upload code onto an ESP32 board. The newest version of Arduino IDE is installed. The installation process of Arduino IDE on the computer is furnished below in Figure 6.9.

Arduino IDE split as quadruple.

1. Tool-Bar
2. Status Window
3. Serial Monitor Window.

Figure 6.8 Actuator valve.

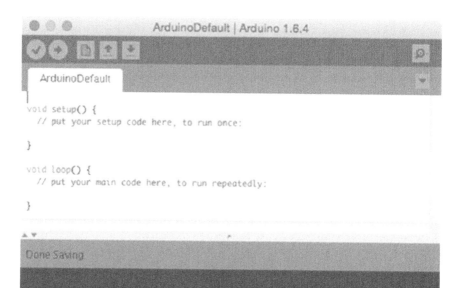

Figure 6.9 Initial window of Arduino IDE.

Figure 6.10 Sample Arduino IDE toolbar.

Table 6.2 Toolbar options.

Options	Description
Option for Code Verify/code Compile	This is the first left-hand press. To prove the exactness of the code, press this button to compile. We can see the consequences at the bottom of the Status pane.
Code Uploaded to the Board	This is left-hand click 2. By connecting Arduino type board to the computer and selecting the usb port in the IDE, then the code will be transferred to the Arduino board. By using Status Window in the downside we will see the deployment progress.
New File/Open File/ Save File	As their names indicate, the next three buttons allow you to trigger a new blank sheet for writing the code named as code window or open an already created file. Arduino application files have as extension (.ino) e.g. filename.ino.
To view output Serial-Monitor	The final right button let us open the Serial Monitor window.

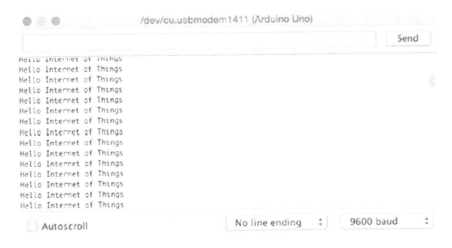

Done compiling.

Sketch uses 2,006 bytes (6%) of program storage space. Maximum is 32,256 bytes.
Global variables use 208 bytes (10%) of dynamic memory, leaving 1,840 bytes for local variables. Maximum is
2,048 bytes.

Figure 6.11 Sample compiling arduino IDE status window.

/dev/cu.usbmodem1411 (Arduino Uno)

Send

Hello Internet of Things
Hello Internet of Things
Hello Internet of Things
Hello Internet of Things
Hello Internet of Things
Hello Internet of Things
Hello Internet of Things
Hello Internet of Things
Hello Internet of Things
Hello Internet of Things
Hello Internet of Things
Hello Internet of Things
Hello Internet of Things
Hello Internet of Things
Hello Internet of Things

Autoscroll   No line ending :   9600 baud :

Figure 6.12 Logs file messages on the serial monitor window.

Toolbar
On the IDE, toolbar is placed on Upper side as displayed in Figure 6.10. It offers simple access to regularly used alternatives. The whole toolbar choices are displayed in Table 6.2.

Status Window
The Status window furnished in Figure 6.11 lists all results when you substantiate the code or upload it to a server. Any faults that occur during the validation or upload of code may appear in the Status window.

Serial Monitor Window
The Serial Monitor window as shown in Figure 6.12 prints all messages generated in login file and the code by the functions "Serial.print" and "Serial.println". To print any message on the Serial Monitor window, initializing the message in the code is needed first.

6.4   Implementation

Figure 6.13 displays the MQTT Broker design assembled on Amazon Web Services (AWS) [33]. The execution process is as follows. At first, build a cloud MQTT account. Next, build a server by utilizing EC2 an Elastic-Compute-Cloud that can be called as best elementary and extremely wide spacey utilized setup in cloud MQTT that offers a virtual server associated to the Internet. Cloud MQTT spontaneously allocates internet Protocol address within Public domain to procured server. If consumers' wants IP address in public domain to be permanent, they need to bear the cost of buying address of Internet Protocol. Else, every

Public domain: IoTwarrior.mynimbus.abc

Figure 6.13 MQTT broker architecture built on cloud MQTT.

time while starting the server, new IP address in public domain will be generated and allocated to the respective server.

Figure 6.14 displays the hardware networks regarding the sensors (Flame.MQ2, DHT11) and actuators communicating with the microcontroller ESP32. Connect ESP32 to Arduino IDE by using USB cable and select the appropriate ESP32 board and upload the program to board. Once button is reset on micro controller ESP32 the MQTT client is linked to cloud MQTT by making use of wireless sensor network, sensors and actuators together initiates functioning and generates the original values. At this point flame sensor sends flame logic value as 1 if it predicts any flame, if it doesn't not predict flame then will send flag logic value as 0, then message is circulated as the subject name FLAME to cloud MQTT broker. Likewise DHT11, MQ2 gas sensors reading initial values are also circulated as the subject name TEMP, SMOKE to cloud MQTT broker. At end the MQTT broker verifies the sensors values and functioning as described in the below flow chart illustrated in Figure 6.15.

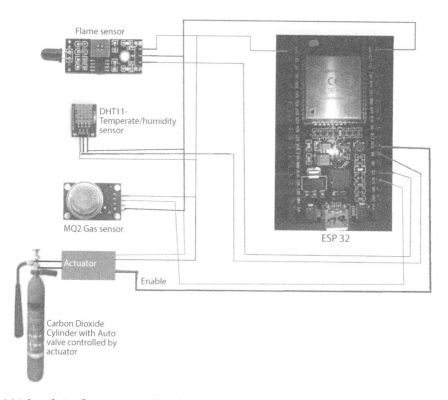

Figure 6.14 Interfacing flame sensor with Arduino.

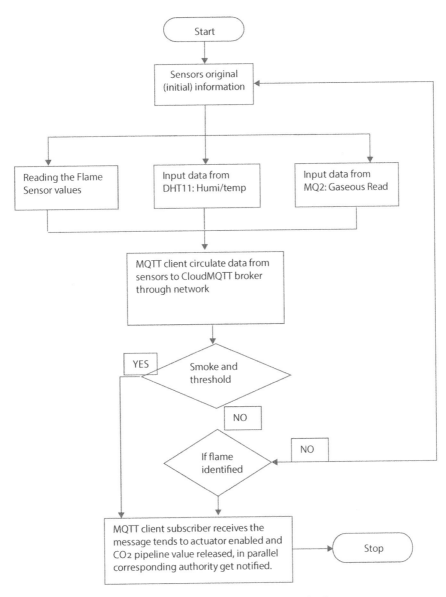

Figure 6.15 IoT system data flow for PUBLISH/SUBSCRIBE in MQTT broker.

6.4.1   Interfacing Diagram

Interfacing sensors and actuator with ESP32 are described in Figure 6.14.
   The interfacing hardware connections are below:

1. G2 of ESP32 microcontroller is linked to flame sensor D_0 input line and GND of flame sensor is linked with GND of microcontroller ESP32. VCC of flame sensor is associated to 5v of ESP32 microcontroller.

2. G4 of ESP32 microcontroller is linked to DHT11 sensor data line and GND of DHT11 sensor is linked with GND of microcontroller ESP32. VCC of DHT11 is associated to 3V of microcontroller ESP32.
3. G15 of ESP32 microcontroller is linked to MQ2 gas sensor out line and GND of MQ2 gas sensor is linked with GND of microcontroller ESP32. VCC of MQ2 gas sensor is connected to 3V of ESP32 controller.
4. G16 of ESP32 microcontroller is linked to Actuator EN line and GND of actuator is linked with GND of microcontroller ESP32. VCC of Actuator is linked to 3V of microcontroller ESP32.

Languages Used

The main motive for C language used here for this project due to the comfort and easily control, the Computer "C" language friendly to any program learner's as starting language in computer programming and connected to circuit for input/output components. "C" type language is flexible and best fit with the system based coding to instance a level of intermediate coding terminology to maintain remembrance, Input/Output with marginal components. User interface part is developed in Android for smart phones and tablets.

Algorithm

Step 1: Download and install Arduino IDE software in your personal computer machine.
Step 2: Arrange flame sensor, MQ2 gas sensor and DHT11 temperature sensor to ESP32 microcontroller.
Step 3: Arrange carbon dioxide pipeline by enabling the Actuator valve.
Step4: Find whether the flame present in cabin or outside the cabin by utilizing Trios (Flame, MQ2 & DHT11sensors).
    If fire presents, then jump to the step-5 else jump to step-4.
Step 5: Permit the actuator to discharge the CO_2 pipeline tap and send alert notification to respective authority.

Platform Used

Operating system Windows 7 or upper released version to be used for designing for the Embedded C for simulation based on Open AT platform.

6.5 Results

The testing of environment monitoring fire prediction and avoidance based fire notification used in this work is shown in Figure 6.16. The system has selected range boundaries. Flame sensor identifies the fire in a range of 3 feet expanse and inside the angle of 60°. In outcomes, there are four scenarios as displayed in Figures 6.17, 6.18, 6.19 and 6.20.

In two cases flame sensor successfully identifies the fire and in rest two cases it fails to predict the flame.

Case 1: In this scenario keep the fire in the range of distance <3 feet from fire sensor, so it detects the flame and sends the alert notification.

Case 2: In this scenario fire is placed outside the range of sensor, i.e. above the 3 feet distance. Then fire sensor is unable to predict the fire, and then no alert notification is sent.

Case 3: In this scenario fire is placed within the angle of 60° within the range of flame sensor. Then sensor identifies the flame and sends alert notification.

Case 4: In this scenario fire is placed outside the 60-degree range of flame sensor. Then flame sensor is unable to identify, no alert message is sent.

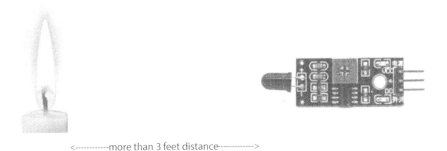

Figure 6.16 Testing of fire detection.

<------------less than 3 feet distance------------>

Figure 6.17 Flame placed within the range of flame sensor.

<-----------more than 3 feet distance------------>

Figure 6.18 Flame placing outside the range of flame sensor.

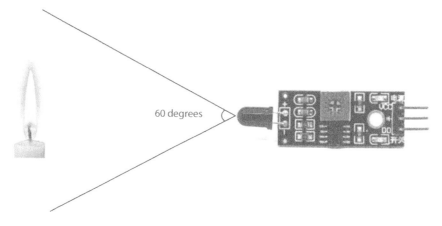

Figure 6.19 Flame is placed within 60° range of flame sensor.

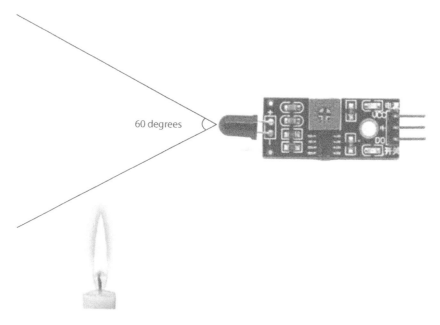

Figure 6.20 Flame is placed outside the 60-degree range of flame sensor.

6.6   Conclusion and Future Work

The designed fire identification and avoidance system for railway coaches or bus coaches could efficiently save lives of passengers during fire calamities. This system has its wide usage in airplanes, ships, households, shopping malls, film theaters and safety industries, particularly in growing countries such as India. By using the designed system, fast and consistent alert is likely to originate precautionary actions to avoid consequences of fire.

The designed system requires less costly environment monitoring system that acts consistently to safeguard against fire. It leads to easily equip this system in the domestic or commercial houses, industries, offices and warehouses, etc. The small scale industries where cost to rent internet is the main problem could easily use this system. Big scale industrial areas or dwelling spaces could be observed via the designed system by establishing many modules, one for each unit or floor. The system could be also promoted with additional characteristics such as forecasting the fire situation depending on the constraints like smoke, temperature and fire area tracing and then effective fire defeat resources could be deployed early.

References

1. The HiveMQ Team, Introducing the MQTT Protocol - MQTT Essentials: Part 1, https://www.hivemq.com/blog/mqtt-essentials-part-1-introducing-mqtt/, 2015.
2. Grgić, K., Špeh, I., Heđi, I., A web-based IoT solution for monitoring data using MQTT protocol. *2016 International Conference on Smart Systems and Technologies (SST)*, IEEE, pp. 249–253. 2016.
3. The HiveMQ Team, Quality of Service 0, 1 & 2 - MQTT Essentials: Part 6, https://www.hivemq.com/blog/mqtt-essentials-part-6-mqtt-quality-of-service-levels/, 2015.
4. Karagiannis, V., Chatzimisios, P., Vazquez-Gallego, F. and Alonso-Zarate, A survey on application layer protocols for the internet of things. *Trans. IoT Cloud Comput.*, 3, 1, pp. 11–17, 2015.
5. Lee, S., Kim, H., Hong, D.K. and Ju, H., Correlation analysis of MQTT loss and delay according to QoS level. *The International Conference on Information Networking 2013 (ICOIN)*, pp. 714–717. IEEE, 2013.
6. Hou, L., Zhao, S., Xiong, X., Zheng, K., Chatzimisios, P., Hossain, M. S., Xiang. W., Internet of things cloud: Architecture and implementation. *IEEE Commun. Mag.*, 54, 12, pp. 32–39, 2016.
7. Yu, Q., Zheng, D., Fu, Y. and Dong, Intelligent fire alarm system based on fuzzy neural network. *2009 International Workshop on Intelligent Systems and Applications*, pp. 1–4, IEEE, 2009.
8. Shunxia, C. and Yanda, C., Design of wireless intelligent home alarm system. *2012 International Conference on Industrial Control and Electronics Engineering*, pp. 1511–1513, IEEE, 2012.
9. Hou, J., Wu, C., Yuan, Z., Tan, J., Wang, Q. and Zhou, Y., Research of intelligent home security surveillance system based on Zigbee. *2008 International Symposium on Intelligent Information Technology Application Workshops*, pp. 554–557, IEEE, 2008.
10. Rakesh, V.S., Sreesh, P.R., George, S.N., An improved real-time surveillance system for home security system using BeagleBoard SBC, Zigbee and FTP web server. *2012 Annual IEEE India Conference (INDICON)*, pp. 1240–1244, IEEE, 2012.
11. Luo, R.C. and Su, K.L., Autonomous fire-detection system using adaptive sensory fusion for intelligent security robot. *IEEE/Asme Trans. Mechatron.*, 12, 3, pp. 274–281, 2007.
12. Li, C., Zhang, Q., Ma, F., Research on the cooperative quick-response fire control system. *2008 3rd International Conference on Innovative Computing Information and Control*, pp. 516–516, IEEE, 2008.
13. Muller, H.C. and Fischer, A., A robust fire detection algorithm for temperature and optical smoke density using fuzzy logic. *Proceedings the Institute of Electrical and Electronics Engineers. 29th Annual 1995 International Carnahan Conference on Security Technology*, pp. 197–204, IEEE, 1995.
14. Hu, H., Wang, G., Zhang, Q., Wang, J., Fang, J. and Zhang, Y., Design wireless multi-sensor fire detection and alarm system based on ARM. *2009, 9th International Conference on Electronic Measurement & Instruments*, pp. 197–204, IEEE, 2009.
15. Peinl, P., Goleva, R., Ackoski, J., Advanced system for the prevention and early detection of forest fires (ASPires). *Proceedings of the 35th Annual ACM Symposium on Applied Computing*, pp. 1200–1203, 2020.
16. Kodali, R. K. and Valdas, A., MQTT Based Monitoring System for Urban Farmers Using ESP32 and Raspberry Pi. In *2018 Second International Conference on Green Computing and Internet of Things (ICGCIoT)*, pp. 395–398, IEEE, 2018.

17. Lipu, Molla Shahadat Hossain, Tahia Fahrin Karim, Md Lushanur Rahman, and Sultana, F., Wireless security control system & sensor network for smoke & fire detection. In *2010 IEEE International Conference on Advanced Management Science*, IEEE, 3, pp. 153–157, 2010.

18. Luzuriaga, J.E., Cano, J.C., Calafate, C., Manzoni, P., Perez, M. and Boronat, P., Handling mobility in IoT applications using the MQTT protocol. *2015 Internet Technologies and Applications (ITA)*, pp. 245–250, IEEE, 2015.

19. Kodali, R.K. and Yerroju, S., IoT based smart emergency response system for fire hazards. *2017 3rd International Conference on Applied and Theoretical Computing and Communication Technology (iCATccT)*, Tumkur, pp. 194–199, 2017.

20. Kodali, R.K. and Valdas, A., MQTT Implementation of IoT based Fire Alarm Network. *2018 International Conference on Communication, Computing and Internet of Things (IC3IoT)*, Chennai, India, pp. 143–146, 2018.

21. Kang, D.H., Park, M.S., Kim, H.S., Kim, D.Y., Kim, S.H., Son, H.J. and Lee, S.G., Room Temperature Control and Fire Alarm/Suppression IoT Service Using MQTT on AWS. *2017 International Conference on Platform Technology and Service (PlatCon)*, Busan, pp. 1–5, 2017.

22. Mahgoub, Tarrad, N., Elsherif, R., Al-Ali, A., Ismail, L., IoT-Based Fire Alarm System. *2019 Third World Conference on Smart Trends in Systems Security and Sustainablity (WorldS4)*, London, United Kingdom, pp. 162–166, 2019.

23. Kodali, R.K. and Mahesh, K.S., A low cost implementation of MQTT using ESP8266. *2016 2nd International Conference on Contemporary Computing and Informatics (IC3I)*, Noida, pp. 404–408, 2016.

24. Kurniawan, D.E., Iqbal, M., Friadi, J., Borman, R.I. and Rinaldi, R., Smart Monitoring Temperature and Humidity of the Room Server Using Raspberry Pi and Whatsapp Notifications. In *Journal of Physics: Conference Series*, IOP Publishing, 1351, 1, 2019.

25. Cheng, Y., Mou, C., Chen, K., Bai, H., Liu, Y., Zhang, Y., Experimental Study on Fire Extinguishing Effect of Water-based Fixed Fire Extinguishing System in full-Scale Bus Cabin. *2019 9th International Conference on Fire Science and Fire Protection Engineering (ICFSFPE)*, Chengdu, China, pp. 1–6, 2019.

26. Jun, W., Di, Z., Meng, L., Fang, X., Hu-Lin, S., Shu-Feng, Y., Discussion of Society Fire-Fighting Safety Management Internet of Things Technology System. *2014 Fifth International Conference on Intelligent Systems Design and Engineering Applications*, Hunan, pp. 422–425, 2014.

27. Vijayalakshmi, S.R. and Muruganand, S., A survey of Internet of Things in fire detection and fire industries. *2017 International Conference on I-SMAC (IoT in Social, Mobile, Analytics and Cloud) (I-SMAC)*, Palladam, pp. 703–707, 2017.

28. Li, T. and Hou, P., Application of NB-IoT in Intelligent Fire Protection System. *2019 International Conference on Virtual Reality and Intelligent Systems (ICVRIS)*, Jishou, China, pp. 203–206, 2019.

29. Prabha, B., An IoT Based Efficient Fire Supervision Monitoring and Alerting System. *2019 Third International Conference on I-SMAC (IoT in Social, Mobile, Analytics and Cloud) (I-SMAC)*, Palladam, India, pp. 414–419, 2019.

30. Jesus Zepeda, Digital Alarm Communicator/Transmitter DACT-UD2, https://www.academia.edu/36459184/Digital_Alarm_Communicator_Transmitter_DACT_UD2, 2008.

31. Arduino Team, Control your Internet of Things projects from anywhere with the new Arduino IoT Cloud Remote app, https://blog.arduino.cc/2020/07/22/control-your-internet-of-things-projects-from-anywhere-with-the-new-arduino-iot-cloud-remote-app/,2020.

32. Upadhyay, Y., Borole, A., Dileepan, D., MQTT based secured home automation system. *Symposium on Colossal Data Analysis and Networking (CDAN)*, pp. 1–4, IEEE, 2016.

33. Michael Garcia, MQTT Broker design assembled on Amazon Web Services (AWS), https://aws.amazon.com/blogs/iot/how-to-bridge-mosquitto-mqtt-broker-to-aws-iot/, 2020.

## 7

Traffic Prediction Using Machine Learning and IoT

Daksh Pratap Singh and Dolly Sharma*

Department of Computer Science and Engineering, Amity School of Engineering and Technology, Amity University, Noida, India

Abstract

Real-time traffic information uses advanced APIs and IOT-based mobile phone sensors to send information required like speed, average road density and differentiation using colors and graphs from low, moderate, and high traffic with a traffic simulator for creating customized routes to predict certain traffic scenarios manually. Google maps was very able to predict the traffic but was dependent only on GPS sensors to predict the traffic whereas this application stands out to be more precise by using a vehicle's speed to predict the traffic. The objective of this work is to develop an android application by targeting user's need to see real-time traffic using IOT, Machine Learning and GPS-based advance APIs. APIs are collecting data using crowdsourcing and real-time user's location accumulation on server by microservices. This application consists of industry-ready MVVM architecture, JSON parsing, real-time data rendering, data manipulation, and IOT-based cloud computing. The application predicts traffic with utmost precision and is capable of taking a vehicle's speed into consideration to predict vehicular traffic and is also capable of simulating the traffic on one's own terms.

Keywords: APIs, GPS, machine learning, IOT, simulation

7.1 Introduction

The application is constructed and divided into two parts. The first section is used for predicting traffic on two ideas accelerometer and Google APIs, the second section is based on rust programming to construct a traffic simulator.

7.1.1 Real Time Traffic

Android Application is based on Real-time traffic data engine using advanced cloud APIs, IOT, Machine learning, and cloud computing [1–5]. It includes crowdsourcing data concept also to collect the user's location to enhance the information accuracy from time to

*Corresponding author: dolly.azure@gmail.com

Monika Mangla, Suneeta Satpathy, Bhagirathi Nayak and Sachi Nandan Mohanty (eds.) *Integration of Cloud Computing with Internet of Things: Foundations, Analytics, and Applications*, (111–130) © 2021 Scrivener Publishing LLC time. In backend APIs we have used TensorFlow advance methods to train our model for giving results effectively.

It consists of all updated technology on android environment because this is really flexible for users.

7.1.2   Traffic Simulation

Traffic diversion or the reenactment of transportation structures is the logical showing of transportation systems (e.g., interstate convergences, vein courses, roundabouts, downtown grid structures, etc.) through the usage of program to all the more probable help plan, structure, and work transportation frameworks. Reproduction of transportation structures started indeed forty years prior, and is a critical locale of request in busy time gridlock building and transportation masterminding today. Distinctive national and close by transportation workplaces, insightful associations and directing firms use reenactment to help in their organization of transportation frameworks [5].

This chapter explains the android application project based on real-time traffic information engine. It is based on IoT, ML, MVVM, cloud computing, microservices, and JSON parsing. It will explain the whole workflow, architecture, and model of android application. Real life use cases and scenarios where it can help users to get the real time information and how they are contributing to make this better are also discussed thoroughly in this chapter.

The backend workflow of machine learning and how it will improve real-time data rendering engine from time to time is also explained briefly.

Here a combination of different new technologies is used to tackle the problem of real time traffic information. To understand the whole working model, one should first understand how traffic is being calculated.

7.2   Literature Review

In previously written research papers, it was very well discussed that, adaptability to bigger systems, steady information assortment at different areas all the while and guaranteeing the unwavering quality are issues which are tended to. Travel time information obtained from Google Distance Matrix API, which is a prepared data discharged dependent on publicly supported cell phone information, is utilized in this investigation to distinguish utilization of publicly support travel time information and transport arranging exercises [6]. In simple words, it is very well written that, The Distance Matrix API can be utilized to play out various errands, for example, mentioning the separation information for various travel modes, mentioning separation information in various units (for instance, in kilometers or miles), and assessing travel time in rush hour gridlock. The API is planned for designers who wish to figure travel separation and time between various focuses inside maps that are given by one of the Google Maps APIs. As discussed in various smart city models that, the objective is build up a coordinated administration framework that would combine forecasts for vehicular and other urban traffic streams, for example, person on foot or bicycle. This new age of brilliant city the board frameworks could uncover significant level relationships between vehicles, passerby and bicycle streams inside cities [6].

The most important job is to make it possible for vehicles to communicate with the internet and it was very well described by Zachary W. Lamb that, Vehicular ad-hoc Networks (VANETs) are a basic piece of Intelligent Transportation Systems (ITS) that encourage interchanges among vehicles and the web [7]. As discussed by Mr. Sun Ye that it is necessary to use public transportation to get rid of traffic congestion, he proposed a model called traffic congestion charge which says, traffic congestion charge will elevate resident to utilize open transportation. In this way it must take full advancement of open transportation as the reason. Right off the bat, the system of open transportation must have the option to fulfil individuals' solicitation for transportation openness, accommodations and solace. Also, open transportation ought to be depended with some administration need, for example, liberated from blockage charging, foundation open transportation selective path, traveling some portion of charge reserve to open transportation put, etc. so as to draw in more individuals to take open transportation rather than vehicle excursion to diminish traffic clog. The base for the application remains strong because of tensor flow because it gives an assortment of work processes to create and prepare models utilizing Python, JavaScript, or Swift, and to effectively send in the cloud, on-prem, in the program, or on-gadget regardless of what language you use [7].

7.3   Methodology

This application is constructed with the help of various sensors present in a smartphone and also uses some various mapping features.

GPS—Global Positioning System—There is a set of twenty-four satellites to provide locations and other information. It supplies information of locations like what we are seeing on Google Maps but in case of traffic, the problem is there are not many satellites to track each vehicle that's in this API. We are using Crowdsourcing in which we are taking real-time location from user's phone and speed from phone sensors using IOT and ML and sending it to API to store in DB [8]. Like this all users are sending the data to API and accordingly with **FLY-CROW** algorithm we are calculating average traffic in different locations. It's not accurate because we are getting data from different mobiles who have only installed the application that's why we are using ML to make our model always learn.

FLY-CROW

```
INPUT ACC_INPUT, LONGITUDE, LATITUDE
API_PLANK(ACC_INPUT, LONGITUDE, LATITUDE)
INITIALIZE RES
SET RES = API_PLANK(ACC_INPUT, LONGITUDE, LATITUDE)
RETURN RES
```

In API_PLANK POST request call we are sending all the required parameters and doing calculations in backend using cloud computing.

TensorFlow—TensorFlow plans to give world class on-contraption selection for any TensorFlow model. In any case, the TensorFlow mediator before long supports an obliged subset of TensorFlow managers that have been streamlined for on-contraceptive use. This induces two or three models to require extra strides to work with TensorFlow [9].

Location Manager—Before my application can start suffering region reestablishes, it is required to play out sensible walks around set up get to. In this activity, we'll grasp what these procedures entail. The terminating advance of setting up zone update get to will be to verbalize real supports in the show. In case assents are feeling the loss of, the application will get a Security Exception at runtime.

Machine Learning—We have used cognitive learning APIs to make self-learning model. Machine learning is one the best technologies which we are using in our application to make it more accurate from time to time.

PC-based understanding (ML) is a depiction of figuring that draws in programming applications to wind up being dependably exact in anticipating results without being unequivocally adjusted. The key clarification for AI is to make tallies that can get input information and utilize quantifiable assessment to imagine a yield while fortifying yields as new information gets open.

Maps JavaScript API—The Maps JavaScript API enables us to show people in general travel system of a city on our guide utilizing the Transit Layer object. At the point when the Transit Layer is empowered, and the guide is focused on a city that supports travel data, the guide will show significant travel lines as thick, shaded lines. The shade of the line is set dependent on data from the travel line administrator [10]. Empowering the Transit Layer will modify the style of the base guide to all the more likely accentuate travel courses. Travel data is just accessible in select areas. To see a rundown of urban communities where open travel data is as of now accessible, if it's not too much trouble counsel this rundown. In case we're an open organization that directs open transportation for our city and might want our information to be incorporated, it would be ideal to visit the Google Transit Partner Program site to find out additional.

Data.Polygon—The Data.Polygon class handles polygon twisting for us. We can pass it a variety of at least one straight rings, characterized as scope/longitude organizes. The principal direct ring characterizes the external limit of the polygon. On the off chance that we pass more than one straight ring, the second and ensuing direct rings are utilized to characterize inward ways (gaps) in the polygon.

GeoJSON—GeoJSON is a typical standard for sharing geospatial information on the web. It is lightweight and effectively intelligible, making it perfect for sharing and teaming up. With the Data layer, we can add GeoJSON information to a Google map in only one line of code [10].

Layers—Layers are questions on the guide that comprise of at least one separate things, yet are controlled as a solitary unit. Layers for the most part reflect assortments of articles that we add over the guide to assign a typical affiliation. The Maps JavaScript API deals with the introduction of articles inside layers by rendering their constituent things into one item (commonly a tile overlay) and showing them as the guide's viewport changes [10]. Layers may likewise adjust the introduction layer of the guide itself, somewhat changing the base tiles in a manner predictable with the layer. Note that most layers, by configuration, may not be acquired by means of their individual articles, however may just be controlled as a unit.

Distance Matrix—Getting to the Distance Matrix organization is nonconcurrent, since the Google Maps API needs to make a call to an outside server. Thusly, we need to pass a callback method to perpetual stock of the requesting, to process the results.

We get to the Distance Matrix organization inside your code through the google.maps. DistanceMatrixServiceconstructorobject [11]. This system begins a sale to the Distance Matrix organization, passing it a Distance Matrix Request object demanding containing the causes, objectives, and travel mode, similarly as a callback method to perpetual stockpile of the response.

Heatmap—A heatmap is a perception used to delineate the power of information at land focuses. At the point when the Heatmap Layer is empowered, a shaded overlay will show up over the guide. As a matter of course, territories of higher force will be shaded red, and zones of lower power will seem green [11]. It is a bit of the google.maps.visualization library, and isn't stacked as per usual. The Visualization classes are a free library, separate from the essential Maps JavaScript API code. To use the value contained inside this library, we ought to at first stack it using the libraries parameter in the Maps JavaScript API bootstrap URL.

Point by point and Realistic Simulation—PTV Vissim is shown to be the world's standard for traffic and transport masterminding and for a substantial avocation: It gives we a down to earth and point by point outline about the situation of the traffic stream and impacts, with the possible results to describe various think about how conceivable it is that circumstances [12]. With our associations and connectors thought in PTV Vissim, we can depict framework in detail and model different geometries—from a standard center to complex assemblies.

Speedy and Simple Set-Up—Our traffic diversion writing computer programs is definitely not hard to use, and certainly no scripting required. PTV Vissim is the most incredible programming for infinitesimal, mesoscopic, or even a blend of both in a crossbreed reenactment. If we are starting at now using transport mechanical assemblies, chances are we can rely upon PTV Vissim without acquiring new capacities.

Adaptable and Seamless Integration—As a significant part of the PTV Traffic Suite, we can perfectly interface the traffic multiplication programming to other PTV programming game plans. That, yet the nonexclusive COM interface licenses we to similarly help out external applications. PTV Vissim is a versatile programming that broadens our microscopic orchestrating entertainment into a consistent test condition paying little mind to how we choose to utilize the traffic generation programming [12].

Solid Network and Support—Within excess of 16,500 customers, PTV Vissim is an option that is other than a traffic and transport programming; it is a system that is reliably creating. PTV has over 40 years of contribution with the vehicle strategy and traffic game plans industry so we can misuse our sweeping documentation, wide getting ready projects, customer bundle get-togethers similarly as our master customer help and support gathering, all day every day.

TransModeler is an earth shattering and versatile traffic amusement pack proper to a wide bunch of traffic masterminding and showing assignments as shown in Figure 7.1. TransModeler can reenact a wide scope of road frameworks, from streets to downtown districts, and can stall wide zone multimodal arranges in amazing point of interest and with high unwaveringness. We can exhibit and picture the lead of complex traffic structures in a 2-dimensional or 3-dimensional GIS condition to depict and evaluate traffic

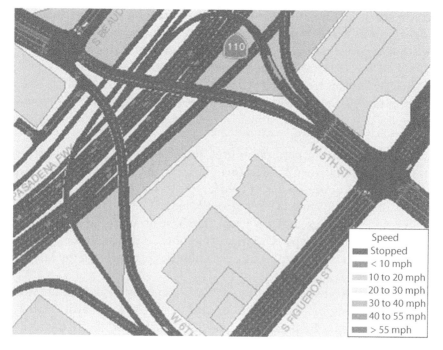

Figure 7.1 Transmodeler.

stream components, traffic sign and ITS exercises, and for the most part organize execution [13].

Endorsement—It is the strategy to choose if the reenactment model is an exact depiction of the structure under scrutiny. This sets up that the model direct exactly and constantly addresses this present reality system being reenacted, over the extent of conditions predicted and it incorporates the going with critical advances.

1. Picking up and orchestrating genuine data.
2. Setting up the endorsement criteria—Hypotheses, Statistical tests, etc.
3. Test plan for endorsement including a grouping of circumstances.
4. Perform endorsement study.
5. Perceive the purposes behind dissatisfaction expecting any and fix the model in like way.
6. Street transportation, that is, convincing progression of individuals and things through physical street and road systems is an enrapturing issue.

7.4 Architecture

The root of an application is basically the proper division of its modules that is constructing a prefect road map to the desired application and in this application division of workflow in APIs was most important.

7.4.1   API Architecture

We are using cloud computing and google traffic channeling API for getting data and using FLY-CROW to make more accurate with cognitive learning models as shown in Figure 7.2.

As per the architecture or request we are using SSL offloading to make it more secure and routing for service resources. We are using logger to log all the operations whatever is happening. It will help to debug the issue at the time of emergency.

Response caching helps to make application more fast at the time of giving response of same request data [14].

7.4.2   File Structure

It is important to divide basic file structure to access the correct file at appropriate executable time as shown in Figure 7.3.

GPS Enabled Architecture—As we all know crowdsourcing data process in which we are getting data from many users and tell results on the basis of the data but in traffic analysis case we are using data from user's device and GPS satellites both. Here the accuracy depends on the number of active satellites on specific location.

We can understand this by taking one example:

Let's say we are going from Location A to Location B with surrounding of n no. of users having GPS enabled in their device so the data what we will get as a traffic on our devices it depends on number of users, their vehicle speeds, and GPS data given by number of active satellites on specific location. One more important thing is required, the latitude and longitude of specific location because without this API can't able to give specific outputs for different locations.

ML plays an important role in this process because with each operation it is getting smarter to provide more accurate output for users [14].

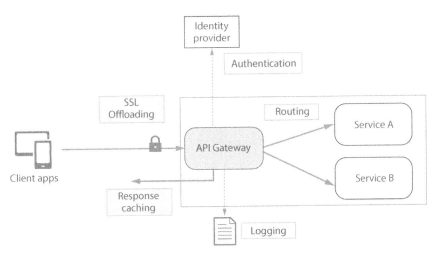

Figure 7.2 API Gateway. Image Source- https://docs.microsoft.com/en-us/azure/architecture/microservices/design/gateway.

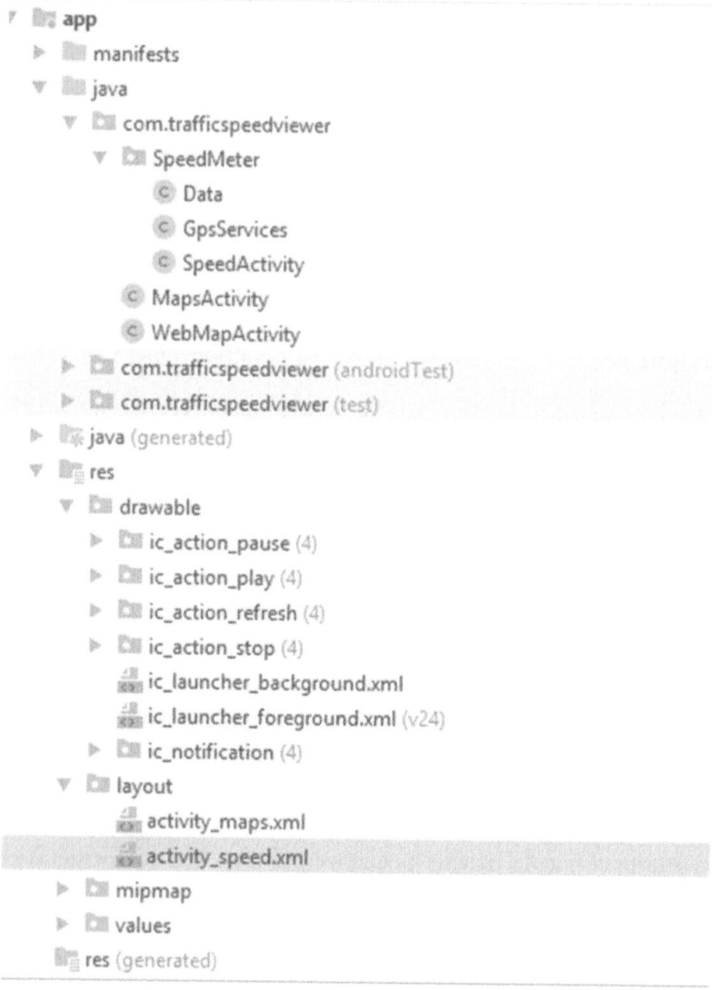

Figure 7.3 Application file structure.

Why AWS IoT—There are such a large number of administrations expansive and profound, multi-layered security, unrivaled AI incorporation, and demonstrated at scale. There are some different things which API has based on AWS IoT center, AWS IoT Device Defender, AWS IoT Device Management, AWS IoT Things Graph, AWS IoT Analytics, AWS IoT Events, and AWS IoT Sitewise [15].

7.4.3   Simulator Architecture

Parameterized Turning Speed—The speed at which turns are made ought to be tunable by the client or variable subject to turning range, number of ways, and so on. It is possible that the turning-speed model could influence computation of surrogate measures. SIMTRAFFIC claims a parameterized turning-speed model and VISSIM and Texas licenses going rate to be subject to vehicle type and turning range [16].

Response to Yellow—Appearing of a driver's response to yellow is major to quantify issue zone execution. It could be colossal for computation of surrogate measures if the response model is variable by driver type, vehicle type, and so forth. Most models explored have response "by driver type." Paramics records its showing limits "by driver." This assembles a steady size of parameters, as opposed to a lot of fixed parameters (one for each sort) [16]. VISSIM has response models with unequivocal driver-type parameter settings for both sign groupings with and without blasting completions administrative work (for both European and North American signalization moves close).

Variable Driver Reaction Time—Mirrors the model's capacity to address the concede experienced between the driver's particular confirmation of a potential mishap and the utilization of control measures (slowing down, accelerating, or route change) to stay away from influence. When in doubt, drivers' response times fluctuate by getting, age, and so on. HUTSIM is planning coordination of nanoscopic appearing of driver responses and Paramics models driver care.

Intersection point Box Movements- For assessment of surrogate flourishing measures, it is colossal for the reenactment to show headway of the vehicles in the convergence point with fundamental commitment. For instance, for left turns, Texas models get together progressions as blends of properly evaluated round parts from the purpose of intermingling of the starting route to the point of assembly of the getting way

Variable Acceleration (and Deceleration) Rate—Diversions should join displaying of various vehicle constrains by vehicle type. Unbelievable DRs (and most remarkable DR distributions) may deride the genuine encounters of surrogate measures. This is related with all models that were watched out for.

Sight-Distance Limits—Models that limit the "look-ahead" parcel of drivers when picking (or model the look-ahead separation by driver or driver type) can much more precisely model the shared trait with drivers in surrogate measure encounters. Additionally, sight-separation cutoff centers can mirror the displaying of roadway counteractions, for example, turns, tops, trees, structures, and so forth. This may also apply to appearing of in-vehicle sight imperatives, for example, those that happen when following a huge truck. A gigantic piece of the models outlined need refined sight-segment hindrance showing. VISSIM makes them model of both the measure of vehicles to look forward and a division ahead to consider before making moves (as do different models as recorded in the table), yet no block impacts are appeared [16]. CORSIM has a sight-division limit for vehicles at the stop bar to examine ahead for vehicles clashing with their improvement in the crossing point.

Moving Yield—Cautious displaying of posted notification and zones will be basic for precise gathering of surrogate measures. It is guessed that the SSAM will be utilized for flourishing assessments of yield assignments versus stop or signalized works out [16]. A "moving" yield displays that the yield development can happen with a moved back vehicle that doesn't appear at a stop before returning the traffic stream.

Vehicles Interact With Pedestrians—Individual by strolling success is of over the top centrality to traffic engineers. Redirections that model vehicle correspondences with walkers may have the choice to review the person by strolling security impacts of different various decisions. VISSIM and Paramics expressly model walker enhancements in crosswalks during individual by strolling timings.

All around masterminded Merging—Suggests the marvel where certain driver types moderate or stop to permit vehicles to blend (more) securely, which happens when in doubt, instead of just demonstrating moving back or halting from a responsive perspective. Neighborly joining shows that the going with vehicle can make a hole for a joining vehicle. CORSIM and VISSIM join such lead and AIMSUN unites such direct for incline assemblies.

Appearing of Multilane Merging Behavior—In different locales, it is run of the mill for vehicles entering the mainline stream to cross the strategy for an advancing toward vehicle going a practically identical course as the masterminded bearing of advancement of the entering vehicle and begin charging in the circumscribing way. As of now, advancing toward vehicle can proceed at its current speed without breaking for the turning vehicle (the move is viewed as obliging conduct). Expansion models that consider such practices to happen will considerably more unequivocally address the debate direct of territories that experience high volumes of such practices with wide multilane arterials [17]. VISSIM can show such direct with upheld passages for unequivocal driver types, yet it isn't reliant on the way that the pushing toward vehicle is in.

Appearing of Right-of-Way in Intersection—A fundamental issue for demonstrating trouble occasions is that some turning practices must make slowing down occasions by the traffic that has the decision to proceed (i.e., making a left turn before advancing toward traffic) to be viewed as risky occasions. On the off chance that an amusement model doesn't address this direct, the surrogates can't be sensibly evaluated [17]. For instance, AIMSUN registers the TTC around the start of a left-go move to pick whether an opening can be perceived with sensible slowing down by the choice to proceed with vehicle. Along these lines, some initial attestation moves will, by definition, produce strife occasions.

Representing/Recording of Maneuver Failures—Certification of an opening is one occasion that can cause struggle occasions. Then again, the "dismissal of hole" occasions may also have a surrogate security proposal. Models that can record the removal or "disappointment" of the initial assertion technique could pass on another surrogate degree of the dispersing and number of dismissed holes. Models that can trade hole insistence occasion subtleties could in like way reasonably pass on hole dissatisfaction occasion subtleties. For instance, Texas can trade a table of contention "check" (normally an ejection if not followed by a certification occasion) and confirmation occasions.

Halting Maneuvers—On-road ending (proportional and twofold stopping) makes struggle conditions, way changes, and so on when in doubt and has a basic success impact. Reenactments that model on-road ending moves are delighted in. CORSIM models leaving as "emotionally happening on-road scenes of variable term," rather than unequivocally indicating genuine vehicles halting to stop and a brief timeframe later restarting their excursion later. The mean term of ending occasions must be under 100 s, and there must be in excess of 14 occasions for consistently.

Displaying of Turn Signaling—One essential bit of back fight occasions is the utilization of signs by drivers. How flags (i.e., nonattendance of hailing) sway the vehicle following and way changing strategies for thinking is fundamental to investigating the rehash and truth of back fight occasions. Turn hailing is strikingly a badly arranged indicating wonder. AIMSUN, for instance, models the "crisis" of a vehicle changing to another way ahead of schedule of a go to pick how solid the vehicle will be in cutting off decision to proceed with vehicles to make its turn, which could be viewed as a sort of evident appearing of turn hailing. VISSIM models signals for way changes (i.e., signals are constantly utilized and two or three drivers will open holes to permit hardening), in any case doesn't show the nearness or nonappearance of a sign at an advantage or left turn at an intersection point. Also, the vicinity of a sign on a vehicle in a circumscribing way impacts driver lead.

U-Turns—U-turns some of the time cause fight conditions and a few regions experience sufficiently high volumes of U-turn traffic that their effect on success ought to be tended to (e.g., including U-goes to relationship at the mix corner or to locate a decent pace entrance.

Minute vehicle lead and correspondence with the close to vehicles pick generally speaking traffic direct at the typically indisputable level subject to the going with segments: most unmistakable accelerating/deceleration and driver practices, for example, upheld headway and reaction time, hole confirmation edge for way changing, and shrewdness advance timespan or parcel for way creating [17]. Those parameters genuinely sway thickness and postponements in the engendering, and subsequently the general traffic structure. Underneath, we talk about the two elective models and feature the rule highlights.

State Route (SR) 99 northbound was picked for model change. This zone of interstate scopes from the Elk Grove Blvd. trade to the US-50 interstate exchange south of downtown Sacramento, CA. There are 9 exchanges with near to vein boulevards; 4 divided cloverleaf trades, 3 full cloverleaf exchanges, and 2 important stone exchanges with the region arterials. The entrance ramp hardening and weaving districts orchestrated at the Sheldon Rd. exchange, the Florin Rd. trade, likewise as the exit ramp at the US-50 road exchange, add to the morning top unpredictable postpone saw right now. This summit period usually starts at 6:30 AM and finishes around 10:00 AM, and the morning blockage arrangement shows the normal top time allotment when there is notoriety for suburb to downtown excursions during the morning hours [17].

As shown in Figure 7.4 is the carpool way information was amassed with those of the broadly significant routes considering the way that the carpool way is nearly plugged up and shows directly around a relative blockage design (bottleneck an area and length) as the for the most part accommodating ways. It may be seen that taking everything into account, the reproduced streams fulfilled the alteration measures. In any case, the AIMSUN model can't actually reenact the development of the downstream weaving bottleneck at US-50, under the GEH, MAPE, and RMSE measures. This could be credited to the restriction that model's way changing defense doesn't mirror the curiously solid and visit way change direct. Indicating such zone may require better cleared a path changing opening certification standards that unequivocally fit such an exit ramp bottleneck [17].

Traffic reenactment models can give a financially savvy and adaptable choice to assess the different roadway plans and traffic the executive's choices. To do as such, we first need to guarantee that the models are suitably aligned to mirror the current conditions. The utilization of unmanned elevated vehicle (UAV) has increased specific consideration in the transportation framework industry. On an across the country scale, there has been a pattern to join UAV in rush hour gridlock tasks, for example, traffic observing and framework the board exercises which incorporate extension and roadway assessments. The objective of this examination is to assess the viability of using UAV to approve traffic recreation model yields. Keeping that in mind, two reproduction models of a convergence in Auburn.

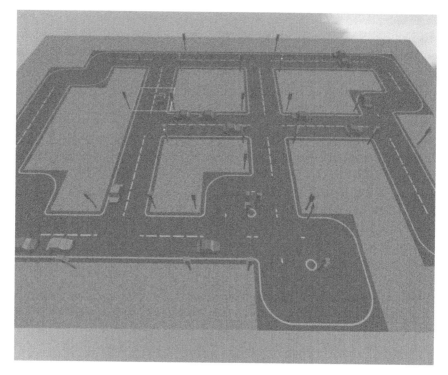

Figure 7.4 Road transplant simulation board with extra road patch.

7.4.4   Workflow in Application

The activity diagram as shown in Figure 7.5 depicts the workflow in the application, when a user installs the application, GPS is enabled and then traffic data from Google server is requested map API is invoked and that particular response is received by the device and after rendering the data is received by the application.

7.4.5   Workflow of Google APIs in the Application

The pictorial representation of the workflow of APIs in the application and only depiction of the relation between the Google APIs in the application as shown in Figure 7.6.

7.5   Results

The application displays three features i.e. it shows traffic scenarios, it shows vehicle moving speed and it also shows the traffic scenario simulator.

7.5.1   Traffic Scenario

The traffic scenario is presented in the conventional traffic display methods i.e. using heatmaps.

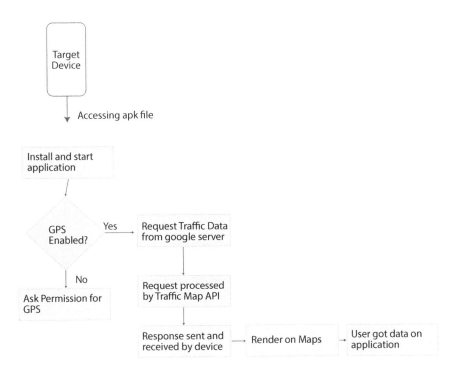

Figure 7.5 Workflow in application.

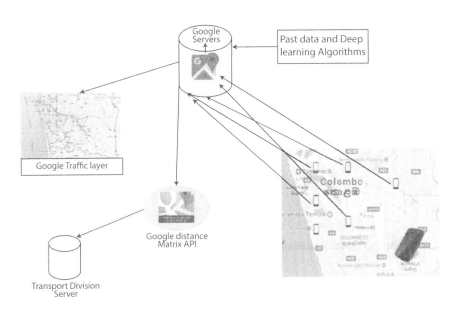

Figure 7.6 Workflow of Google API in the application.

7.5.1.1   Low Traffic

As shown in Figure 7.7 this is the main screen for traffic status of your current location by which users can get to know how much traffic he or she can face during the driving.

As shown in Figure 7.7, the green color on the route predicts lowest traffic.

The heatmap is responsible for showing colors on the basis of traffic. For example—The green color on the image shows low traffic. The Google maps feature provide a very well visualized and accurate display that is why this is used in this application.

7.5.1.2   Moderate Traffic

The moderate traffic scenario is the yellow color of the route predicts that there is moderate traffic on that route as shown in Figure 7.8.

Layers provides a good number of layering factors on the map structure to differentiate between the roads, highways and other concrete structures. The best thing the color effects are precise and are sequentially connecting themselves. The moderate traffic is always considered as the most less accurate traffic scenario but in this application usage of accelerometer makes it much more precise.

Figure 7.7 Low traffic.

Figure 7.8 Moderate traffic.

7.5.1.3 *High Traffic*

As shown in Figure 7.9 there is only red color on the route, this predicts that there is high traffic on that particular route. The main reason for choosing Google Maps API was to display the map in a much more attractive manner rather than just displaying text for traffic scenario. Lesser the vehicles speed lesser the average of the speeds and larger the vehicular traffic hence technically the average of speed of vehicles is indirectly proportional to the traffic scenario.

7.5.2 **Speed Viewer**

As shown in Figure 7.10 it shows speed screen with max speed, average speed, distance, time, and accuracy. The use of chronometer provides much more accurate speed detection

Figure 7.9 High traffic.

and hence provide concrete data for traffic prediction. The speed is also considered as a proof for showing the applications accuracy for finding the speed and using it at the back end for finding the traffic scenarios.

7.5.3 Traffic Simulator

The simulator provided the flexibility to construct own passages and add/delete vehicles.

7.5.3.1 1st View

The simulator shows the traffic into 3 structural views, as shown in Figure 7.11 it shows the 1st view with edit mode turned on to add or remove cars. This could help the administration with various traffic scenarios.

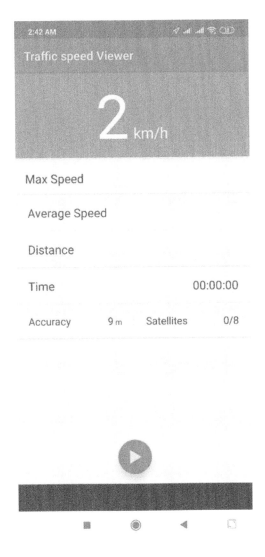

Figure 7.10 Speed status screen.

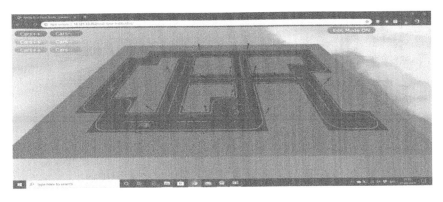

Figure 7.11 Traffic simulator 1st view.

Figure 7.12 Traffic simulator 2nd view.

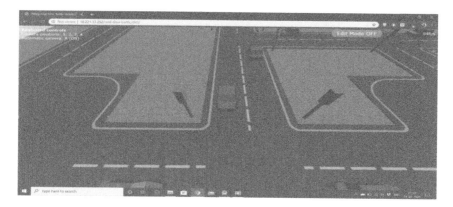

Figure 7.13 Traffic simulator 3rd view.

7.5.3.2   2nd View

As shown in Figure 7.12 the simulator shows the traffic into 3 structural views, this image shows the 2nd view. The image shows the cars on road with traffic lights working hence predicting the proper movement.

7.5.3.3   3rd View

As shown in Figure 7.13 the simulator shows the traffic into 3 structural views. Road can be edited using the "edit option" hence creating our own routes and scenarios to help and create the necesarry environment.

7.6   Conclusion and Future Scope

We will enhance the model what we are using to calculate traffic in different locations and make required updates in FLY-CROW. In our case we are totally dependent on mobile phone sensors to implement IoT and cloud computing operations for better results. In the future we will include information like under construction, road break-down and other required features for user's accessibility.

For example—There are certain scenarios when we select a particular path to travel and even the map shows no traffic on that route because there are no vehicles on that road but a blocked road maybe because of construction could sometimes become misleading while planning to reach our destination through that specific road. So as to know the road blockages due to construction, accidents or any other emergency need to be displayed on the map as well. This feature needs human involvement because when a certain amount of user reports on the application about the emergency then only this thing gets published on the internet hence making it authentic and trustworthy.

Recently due to the spread of covid-19, borders of states are sealed and a few people unknowingly were trying to pass through them so this feature could help in such cases letting people know that the route you are trying to travel through is blocked due to certain condition.

So, the app with user feedback may help in achieving the feature but needs manpower and a big database support.

References

1. Sharma, D., Singh, S., and Mittal, M., Models in Grid Computing: A Review. *Recent Pat. Eng.*, 13, 2, 94–100, 2019.
2. Sharma, D., Singh, S., Mudgil, S., An Approach to find Trustworthiness among Different Domains in a Grid Environment. *Int. J. Adv. Res. Comput. Sci.*, 1, 4, 474–482, 2010.
3. Mudgil, S., Singh, S., Sharma, D., An Access Control Framework for Grid Environment. *Indian J. Comput. Sci. Eng. (IJCSE)*, 2, 6, 937–948, 2010.
4. Garg, R., Mittal, M., Son, L.H., Reliability and Energy Efficient Workflow Scheduling in Cloud Environment. *Cluster Comput.*, 22, 1283–1297, 2019.
5. https://cloud.google.com/docs/tutorials.
6. Kumarage, S., *Use of Crowdsourced Travel Time Data in Traffic Engineering Applications*, University of Moratuwa, Sri Lanka, 2018. 10.13140/RG.2.2.16856.75521
7. https://www.sciencedirect.com/science/article/pii/S187538921200274X.
8. https://www.researchgate.net/figure/Collecting-traffic-data-from-Google-Maps_fig2_327644181.
9. https://www.tensorflow.org/learn.
10. Nagy, A.M. and Simon, V., Survey on traffic prediction in smart cities. *Pervasive Mob. Comput.*, 50, pp. 148–163, 2018.
11. Lamb, Z.W. and Agrawal, D.P., Analysis of Mobile Edge Computing for Vehicular Networks. *Sensors*, 19, 6, 1303, 2019. https://doi.org/10.3390/s19061303
12. https://www.ptvgroup.com/en/solutions/products/ptv-vissim/.
13. https://www.caliper.com/transmodeler/default.htm.
14. https://developer.rackspace.com/blog/introduction-to-the-google-distance-matrix-api/.
15. https://www.javatpoint.com/aws-tutorial.
16. https://en.wikipedia.org/wiki/Aimsun_Live.
17. https://www.w3schools.com/graphics/google_maps_intro.asp.

## 8

Application of Machine Learning in Precision Agriculture

Ravi Sharma* and Nonita Sharma

Department of Computer Science and Engineering, Dr. B.R. Ambedkar National Institute of Technology Jalandhar, Punjab, India

Abstract

Agriculture is one of the most prominent sectors that add a significant contribution to the economy of any nation. The whole cycle of crop processing from soil mapping to harvesting is time-consuming and does not yield an acceptable outcome due to lack of experience and time. Precision Agriculture (PA) involves the application of Machine Learning (ML) methods to produce strong outcomes and forecasts for the development and well identification of disease and cannabis well in advance. Further, Machine Learning is applied in agriculture to help monitor the usage of agro-chemicals and to generate more benefit from the prospective of farmers and environment. A different machine learning technique being applied in agriculture is discussed in this chapter. The chapter attempts to correlate the numerous Machine Learning applications in the field of precision farming primarily in soil mapping, seed selection, irrigation, crop quality, disease detection, weed detection and yield prediction. Various Machine Learning models, Support Vector Machine (SVM), K-mean, Convolution Neural Network (CNN), Artificial Neural Network (ANN) are studied and use of these models is demonstrated in smart farming.

Keywords: Artificial neural network, machine learning, support vector machine, deep learning, convolution neural network, precision agriculture

8.1 Introduction

Machine learning is a belief that generalizes algorithms and will tell you something important about a collection of data without needing to compose some particular custom code for the problem. Instead of writing code, you feed the generic algorithm with info, and it constructs its own evidence-based logic. One form of algorithm, for example, is a classification algorithm. It will split the data into different categories. The same classification algorithm used to identify handwritten numbers may also be used without modifying a line of code to distinguish emails into spam and non-spam. Agriculture is not only important because it provides food but it also helps to produce raw material for many industries such as jute, fabric and sugar, etc. So, agriculture plays a very important role in any nation's economic

*Corresponding author: ravis.cs.19@nitj.ac.in

Monika Mangla, Suneeta Satpathy, Bhagirathi Nayak and Sachi Nandan Mohanty (eds.) Integration of Cloud Computing with Internet of Things: Foundations, Analytics, and Applications, (131–152) © 2021 Scrivener Publishing LLC

growth. Use of sensors and IoT devices in agriculture is increasing day by day to get maximum crop production from the field. Data collected from these devices is processed by Machine learning algorithms. Machine learning plays a very important role to predict the future yield production and any disease well in advance.

In this chapter upcoming sections are a) Machine Learning, where basics of machine learning and its types are discussed, b) Basics of Precision Agriculture and c) Different fields of agriculture, where various techniques of machine learning are discussed based upon the recent studies.

8.2 Machine Learning

ML may also be defined as automating and enhancing computers' learning process based on their interactions without any human support. Machine learning is about training robots to do what appeals to human beings naturally: knowing from practice. Machine learning algorithms use mathematical techniques to "gain: facts from data directly, without depending as a standard on a predetermined equation. The performance of the algorithm boosts, when there is a hike in the number of available research samples.

Some of the most commonly used forms of ML are unsupervised and supervised learning; other types of machine learning techniques are also available. Figure 8.1 provides a preview of machine learning techniques.

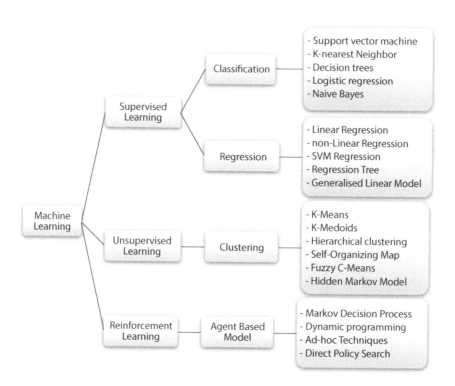

Figure 8.1 Machine learning techniques with commonly adopted algorithms.

8.2.1   Supervised Learning

In Supervised Learning, a "teacher" trains the machine by using example inputs and its expected output, and aims to develop a general mapping law for inputs to output. The training cycle proceeds until a satisfactory degree of precision is achieved on the training results. The goal is to construct a model in the presence of uncertainty which makes predictions based on proof.

By using the classification and regression techniques, supervised learning forms the predictive models

Classification techniques used to classify data into different classes based on their feature, for example, if a tumor is benign or cancerous, whether an email is spam or legitimate. Medical screening, voice recognition, and credit assessment are common technologies. Figure 8.2(a) is an example of classification technique. In this example two different types of tree are classified based on their features

- *Regression techniques* are used to find out patterns in continuous data—for instance, changes in temperature or weather forecasting. Figure 8.2(b) shows the representation of regression problem. For electricity load forecasting regression techniques is used. Problem may be a classification or regression depends upon the nature of a problem. For instance, in weather forecasting, to predict will tomorrow be a sunny day or cloudy? Then the problem is classification type because we divided the prediction into two different categories. To predict the precipitation for upcoming days then the value may vary in range and then the problem become regression type.

8.2.2   Unsupervised Learning

Unsupervised learning is a type of ML, where no labels are given to input dataset that leaves the learning algorithm alone to find out a hidden pattern in its input. This type of learning is able to identify hidden pattern in results. It detects secret trends or underlying data structures and creates a cluster dependent on the related data characteristics. This technique is very useful to identify a cluster in input data without label responses.

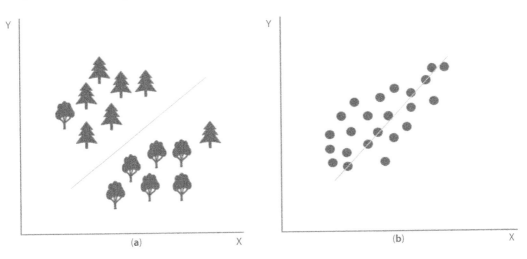

Figure 8.2 (a) Classification technique, (b) Regression technique.

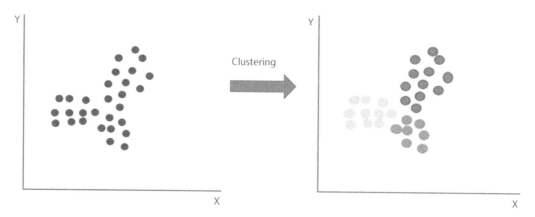

Figure 8.3 Clustering technique.

- *Clustering* is a popular method of unsupervised learning. For data analysis, it is used to identify hidden trends or clusters in the data. Applications of clustering include market research, gene sequence analysis and object recognition.

Clustering is a type of unsupervised technique because no label has given to training dataset. Figure 8.3 shows the representation of clustering technique, in left the figure data is represented without any label and in right, clustering technique is applied on this data that divided it into different cluster based on features.

8.2.3   Reinforcement Learning

This is a type of ML where an agent operates in an environment, and can learn from feedback how to work. "Reinforcement learning means learning what to do—how to link conditions to actions—to optimize a numerical reward signal. The learner is not told what actions to perform, but must figure out which actions are most rewarded by attempting to do so." [1].

The three main components of this method include: the agent (the learner or decision maker), the world (everything the agent communicates with) and behavior (what the agent will do). The goal is for the agent to take behaviors that optimize the incentive received over a specified period of time. By adopting a sound strategy, the agent can hit the target even sooner.

Traffic light control, robotics and resources management in computer clusters are some of the applications where reinforcement learning is used.

In Figure 8.4, agent (robot) learns from the environment and improves its performance. Based on the action that agent performs in environment will be given reward and improves his performance based on this reward.

8.3   Agriculture

Agriculture is a critical component of the world's economy. Pressure would intensify on the agriculture system as the human population continues to develop. Precision agriculture, now

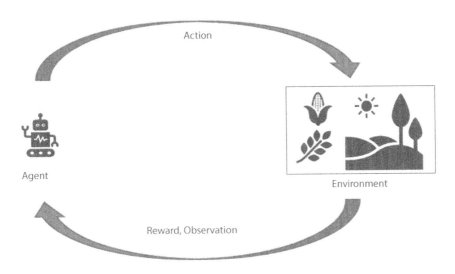

Action

Agent

Environment

Reward, Observation

Figure 8.4 Reinforcement learning.

also recognized as digital agriculture, have arisen as emerging fields of study utilizing data-intensive methods to improve agricultural efficiency while rising its environmental impacts. Data produced in modern agricultural operations are endowed by a variant sensor providing an improved understanding of the operating environment and the activity itself (machine data), resulting more accuracy and rapid decision-making. Machine Learning has developed new ways for unraveling, quantifying and evaluating data-intensive processes in agricultural operating environments with high-performance computing and Big Data technology.

8.4   ML Techniques Used in Agriculture

PA involves the application of Machine Learning methods to produce strong outcomes. A different machine learning technique being applied in agriculture is discussed in following sections.

8.4.1   Soil Mapping

Soil mapping is a tedious task due to heterogeneity that is present in soil, the structure of soil may not be same within the confined area that makes a soil mapping task very complicated. In his research, Jenny [2] concludes that "this is tough to formulate a single definition for soil." In another research that took place five decades after the previous research, Davies *et al.* [3] gave definition of soil as "a varying mixture of minerals, gases, organic matter and living organisms." Soil map is a spatial depiction that displays soil pH, shapes, organic matter, heights of horizons, etc. It's usually the end product of an array of soil surveys. Soil maps are more widely used for soil assessment, strategic planning, agrarian expansion, climate Standard soil maps usually display only general soil distribution, followed by soil survey research. The automated soil analysis technologies are used to extract several modern soil charts. These maps are usually more contextually rich and display greater spatial clarity than standard soil maps. Soil maps developed using (geo)statistical techniques provide a model uncertainty estimation as well.

Applications of ML techniques in Digital Soil Mapping (DSM) [4] are being widely used for various soil mapping purposes. It is necessary to know their output in relation to the soil data and environmental variables involved in soil mapping, taking into consideration the range of models available. ML techniques were most commonly utilized in soil science for the creation of predictive or automated soil maps in the pedometric subfield [5].

Tree-Based Learners

Decision Tree Analysis is a type of divisive assortment. In this analysis data is partitioned until there is a same type of data in subset and these subsets are called terminal nodes [6]. These types of subsets are made in recursive manner, so it forms a tree like structure. Splitting of data is done by information statistics that define how impurity is decreased in datasets. This statistic is applied from the root node in iterative manner till terminal node. When the tree construction is being completed, decision rules are made that tells about the data partition process. Testing data can be classified and predicted based on these rules. Pruning is the technique used to reduce the overfitting and complexity of the tree. Figure 8.5 shows a graphical representation of the Decision Tree.

There are two types of decision tree analysis classes:

1. Homogenous Decision Tree—In this type of decision tree class same algorithm is used on all the levels of tree.
2. Hybrid Decision Tree—In hybrid decision tree different algorithm is used at different level of tree.

Tree-based algorithm can be used in assortment problem and in regression problem. In classification analysis data is divided into different classes based on their features whereas

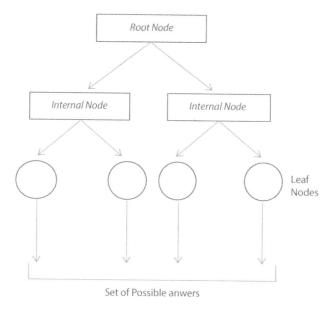

Figure 8.5 Decision tree.

regression technique is used where there is continuous data. Boosting is used in regression tree because it reduces the problem of overfitting and increases the prediction accuracy that is a problem in simple regression tree.

In different study researchers use tree-based learning for digital soil mapping. Jafari *et al.* [7] use Boosted Regression Tree (BRT) for soil mapping in arid region of Iran. They have used two approaches: Logistic-BRT as an indirect approach, and Multiclass-BRT as a direct approach to digital soil mapping. In the indirect approach, first of all specific diagnostic horizons were mapped and then separate pixel-wise classification maps were merged. This classification is done to find the diagnostic horizon in great group soil. In direct prediction great group soil is itself a dependent variable so that probability of soil group was directly predicted. This study shows that geomorphology map plays a very important role in prediction of soil mapping, because accuracy decreased rapidly when geomorphology map was removed, and it affect the prediction accuracy of both direct and indirect approach. The authors conclude that prediction accuracy decreased where sample size was very small and direct approach provides better result.

Artificial Neural Networks
ANNs are one of the key methods used in machine learning. As the "neural" portion of their name implies, they are brain-inspired structures which are intended to mimic the way we humans learn. Figure 8.6 shows the basic structure of ANNs that comprises of input layers, hidden layers and output layers. Hidden layer of neural networks extract features from data that the output layer can use. This networks help to locate patterns that are too complicated or too complex for a human programmer to isolate and teach machine to recognize these patterns.

An ANN's structure is a series of interconnected units or 'neurons' measuring the non-linear interactions between the variables. The input neurons are attached to one or more neurons of hidden layers that connected to the output neurons. Output layer represent the soil vector classes. In the ANN, developer sets the number of number of neurons and layers in each section. During training phase, neuronal relationships are formed by giving weights

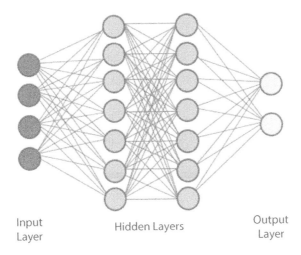

Input Layer   Hidden Layers   Output Layer

Figure 8.6 Structure of ANN.

based on an inherent learning mechanism that iteratively modifies the weights to suit the results of the training data set [8].

In Ref. [9] researchers use ANN technique to produce good quality maps of soil property. They used ANN to predict soil organic content and soil texture in land with minimum cost and high accuracy. For this they have used average soil drainange, sand clay, solt content and DEM-derived topo hydrological data as input and soil properties as a predicted output. They have made three ANN model for soil properties for soil texture, SOC and soil drainage and set the structure of ANN layers in such a manner that will give good accuracy. ANN model has built for soil texture in which they predict clay type and sand type of soil by giving six input. They trained this model with different number of layers and different epochs and they get maximum overall accuracy 86 and 81% for clay and sand types respectively.

In Ref. [10], [11] authors have used ANN to predict continuous soil variables such as a fraction of particle size, and [12] has used neural networks to predict soil loss.

Support Vector Machines

SVM is supervised algorithm that can be used for classification and regression problems. It is mostly used for classification. The main objective of this technique is to find hyperplane in multidimensional space. In Figure 8.7 hyperplane is used to distinguish different classes. There may be many hyperplanes to classify different classes, but the ultimate goal is to find a hyperplane with a maximum margin. Maximum margin is the maximum distance between the data points of different classes and these points are called support vectors.

It is very beneficial to find optimal hyperplane that provides model more ability to classify new data points more accurately. Hyperplane works as a decision boundary between the data points that classify the data points into different classes. Hyperplane can be of any dimension depending upon the features. If we have two features then classes can be identified by a line. For three features we require two-dimensional plane. So that we require n − 1 dimensional plane for n features. In SVM value ranges from [−1, 1]. If function output is one or greater than one then it will classify with one class, if it is −1 then it is classified with other class.

In Ref. [13] author uses SVM to process the soil image to classify it into different soil classes. The study was conducted in West Guwahati, Assam, India. To collect the sample, they used an android device with 13 MP camera. They specifically used this device so that

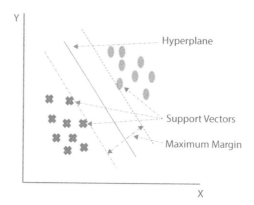

Figure 8.7 Classification using Support Vector Machine (SVM).

rural farmer can easily use this model in real life. For this study fifty soil samples were collected. Samples were collected from different region with five samples from the same field with 200-meter distance between each sample. Out of 50 samples, 29 images had been used for training and 21 for testing. Before model training, they have done image pre-processing, segmentation and feature extraction to obtain feature vectors from the image. After this they proposed two multiSVM models with linear kernel to classify soil class. First model was used for 3 soil classification and second model was used for 12 soil classification. 3 class soil classification has average percentage accuracy of 95.72% and 12 class soil classification has average percentage accuracy of 91.37%. Main reason for less accuracy in 12 class soil classification was small sample size. Overall, this model has good accuracy and require less time as compared to traditional hydrometer testing. Details of other researches has been provided in Table 8.1, where SVM is used for soil classification.

Distance-Based Learners

It is a method of learning based on instance. The classifiers based on instances are also known as lazy learners. The lazy learners store all the training samples and do not build a classifier until the classification of a new unlabeled sample is required. They require less calculation time during training than the eager-learning algorithms [17].

KNN is based on the principle that objects within the same dataset normally exist near other objects having similar properties [18]. It categorizes the artifacts in the dataset dependent on the groups of their closest neighbors.

Let us take an example, if you don't know how to tag a Bluetooth-headset on an online listing, you can find 5 similar headsets, and, if 4 of them are labeled as "accessories" and only the remaining 1 as "Technology", then you will also label it under "accessories".

Working of algorithm: To classify the data point from the test set, one needs to perform the following operations:

1. First, calculate the distance to each of the samples in the training set
2. Now, select k samples from the training set with the minimal distance to them
3. The class of the test data point will be the most frequent class among those k nearest neighbors.

In this research [19], soil mapping of forest land in Canada has been done using KNN method. Forest land plays a very important role for any country or in the world environment. They have selected 538 ground plots from the national forest inventory across Canada and use KNN method to produce digital soil map. 18 environmental predictors variable have been selected to predict the soil mapping. To measure the distance

Table 8.1 Other researches where SVM used for soil classification.

Reference	Proposed methodology	Accuracy
[14]	Soil Classification Analysis using SVM	71.18%
[15]	Rock and soil classification using SVM	96.67%
[16]	SVM, ANN and Decision Tree algorithm were used for soil classification	90.7%

of weights Euclidean distance has been used, and to compare the predicted soil value to observed value, Cross validation method is used. First method that was used is Root Mean Square Error to provide standard deviation of error against the values predicted; second one was bias:

$$RMSE\%_m = \frac{\sqrt{\frac{1}{n}\sum_{i=1}^{n}(y_i - \tilde{y}_i)^2}}{\bar{y}} \times 100 \tag{8.1}$$

$$Bias\%_m = \frac{\frac{1}{n}\sum_{i=1}^{n}(y_i - \tilde{y}_i)}{\bar{y}} \times 100 \tag{8.2}$$

In Equations (8.1) and (8.2), m contains n pixels indexed i, $\tilde{y}_i$ is predicted values of KNN and $\bar{y}$ and are the observed values. Differences between observed and predicted values are less, if RMSE% and Bias% are lower

To select the best k nearest neighbor for inputting multiple attributes many KNN analysis were done with these 12 attributes using Euclidean distance K = 10 would be find as the optimal value for k nearest neighbor. This study gives good prediction accuracy for identifying the soil characterization in the mineral layer.

8.4.2 Seed Selection

The roots of a healthy crop are healthy and good-quality seeds. The seeds used to cultivate new crops must be picked with considerable caution and should be of good quality. The seeds of good quality may either be imported from various suppliers or the farmers may grow them on their own. Seed selection is utilized to improve yield quality. Several diseases are spread through the seeds. When the harvested seeds come from the polluted fields otherwise seed-borne diseases can cause serious agriculture process problems.

Using machine learning, researchers on a single farm will forecast yields and risks associated with various crops, and pick a mixture of varieties that reflects the optimum trade-off.

In this research [20], seed classification of wheat done with the help of weka tool. Dataset for this study is taken from UCI website. The method used for this study was Multi-Layer-Perceptron (simple feed forward ANN), Logistics, SMO (Used in support vector machine for optimization), Naïve Bayes (type of supervised learning, the main features of this method is that it treats every pair of features independently) and multi-classifier. 10-fold, 5-fold and 2-fold cross validations are used and training set method is used to check the performance of each classification.

The result shows that in cross validation 10-fold multi-layer perception and logistic gave the best accuracy of 95.2% as compare to rest and accuracy decreased for most of the classes the fold value decreases to 5 and 2 only. Multilayer perception accuracy increased to 97.6% when training set method used. Multilayer perception gave the highest accuracy of 99.5%. 210 samples of wheat seeds collected from site and seven geomorphological features were considered to be classified into three classes of wheat seed i.e. Kama, Rosa and Canadian.

8.4.3   Irrigation/Water Management

One of the most precious resources of our planet is water, and it is the fundamental reason for the existence of life on our planet. Presence of water is one of the key factors that distinguish our planet from other planets of our solar system. Earth is called blue planet because majority of the area of the planet is covered with water. Approximately 71% of the Earth's surface is occupied by water, and about 96.5% of all Earth's total water is hold by the oceans. The water present in oceans is saline and hence, non-drinkable. The freshwater resource accounts for 2.5% of the total water capacity. Thus, it is very important to preserve this precious resource. For the preservation of water, it is very important to manage it properly so as to have equity in its distribution.

Water management is an umbrella term used to represent all the activities including planning, managing, distributing the water resource. The distribution should have to be optimum and in accordance with the needs of the people. Water management is a multi-level approach so as to achieve optimization of water resources. Water management is a multilevel approach at national, state and local level. Water management. Water patronage enables us to recharge ground water by reducing consumption and using alternative source of water. Rainwater harvesting, groundwater recharge, reuse of graywater and recycling wastewater are some of the examples of water patronage. Water management also includes behavioral modification of people towards water consumption in such a way that an overall equity in the use of water can be achieved.

From ages, agricultural water has been used for the purpose of supporting livestock and growing fresh produce i.e. fruits and vegetables, which is a major part of our diet. It is also used as an important medium for the purpose of irrigation, natural chemical & nutrient applications External, field refrigeration (e.g. light irrigation), and freeze prevention. It has a very positive impact on the productivity and crop yield when used safely and effectively but in case of deceased water, it may lead to decrease in the output and yield. Managerial techniques are very fruitful for maximizing the usage of farm resources and maintaining output and yield maximum. The aim is to incorporate management techniques that increase productivity of water usage without reducing yield. Such definitions include enhanced irrigation timing and the control of irrigation unique to crops. These techniques require water and energy conservation, and raising the costs of growers. Poor patterning of industrial sites, livestock fields, and barnyards and feedlots may impact water quality. Previously, the type of water supply has been representative of the possible risks of pollution. Undesirable quality of the water may influence the overall quality of food crops and trigger disease among the consumer of these crops. For instance, germ containing water is more likely to cause human disease. Irrigation of crops with polluted water may lead to polluted food products which, when consumed, lead to disease. Soil water, for example, was known to be one of the best water supplies. However, the location of the field and the area size are some of the factors may influence the use of water from these sources for irrigation. For making a smart irrigation system, it is important to have a look on factors like Soil moisture, perception and evaporation, etc.

In Ref. [21] authors had used a hybrid algorithm that is combination of supervised and un supervised machine learning technique to make a smart irrigation system. Support vector Regression (SVR) and K mean clustering algorithm were used to predict the soil moisture for upcoming days. For this, they have deployed one IoT device in which there is Ultraviolet (UV) sensors, soil temperature, soil moisture, air temperature, relay switch Arduino board and raspberry P1 attached on this device. In Figure 8.8 a picture of the device is shown.

SVR model is trained based on soil moisture difference that is collected from this device. The SVR predicted value was given as input to K-mean clustering to more accurate to predict the soil moisture difference. SVR is the extended version of SVM in which the dependent variable is numerical. After collecting the soil moisture, data was also collected from some open online weather forecasting website. So, if there is any chance of perception in upcoming days then system would not turn on the motor. Data was collected from the sensor mode after every hour and 21 days data is collected out of which 70% data is used for training and 30% for testing. This model shows good prediction with 96% of accuracy and very less mean square error.

Ref. [22] proposed an ML model based on sensor data to make an irrigation management in Israel. This study was conducted in Jojoba, Israel that produce Jojoba product. This agriculture land was covered with sensor to collect soil moisture data. This data was combined with metrological data that was collected from the nearby metrological station to make a data base for irrigation management. Three different ML models were tested to check the accuracy of the best model and these are linear regression, gradient boosted regression Tree (GBRT) and boosted tree classifier (BTC). GBRT is regression technique in which prediction is made based on sequence of regression tree. Boosted tree classifier is same as GBRT but in this output is Categorical so it is a classification technique. The data set for these models was collected for 98 weeks and 695 observations were recorded. Then

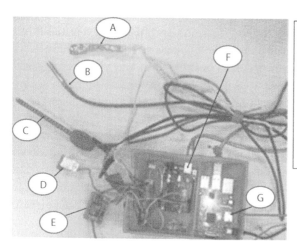

Component list: -

A – UV Sensor

B – Soil Temperature Sensor

C – Soil Moisture Sensor

D – Air temperature & Humidity Sensor

E – Relay Switch

F – Arduino Board

G – Raspberry Pi

Figure 8.8 IoT device used for field data collection. Reprinted with permission [21].

Table 8.2 Other research where ML techniques used in Water Management.

Reference	Proposed methodology	Accuracy
[23]	Irrigation System Automation using KNN	97.35%
[24]	Irrigation Mapping with Convolutional Neural Networks	93%
[25]	Evapotranspiration Estimation using Neural Network Models	83%

this data is divided into 70:30 ratio for training and testing respectively. Each of these three models was tested on 8 sets of data set. Therefore, there are 8 models for each ML method. Final result shows that linear regression has the least accuracy 66% whereas GBRT and BTC have 93 and 95% accuracy respectively. In this study BTC gave the best accuracy but GBRT also gave good result. In BTC the output is categorical whereas in GBRT predict actual value so that GBRT has little less accuracy as compare to BTC. Table 8.2 provides the major study with the proposed methodology and accuracy for water management.

8.4.4   Crop Quality

Several considerations go into crop production, fitness, and yield. The important features to constantly check include firmness, size and increased yield of fruit or vegetables. While such visual signs can suggest a quality or yield issue in your area, a proper diagnosis is essential for effective issue correction. For most people, a natural response will be to put out more nitrogen, because it is a main component of growing plant or crop cell. Nitrogen is also found in plants, which results in instant plant quality which yield tests. However, when an additional quantity of nitrogen is added to the soil increases the amount of nutrients a plant or crop will consume. While high quantities of nitrogen added to the soil of the crops are not inherently detrimental, a good balancing of the carbon to nitrogen ratio allows plants consume nutrients more effectively, ultimately resulting in a decreased fertilizer application pace.

Ref. [26] presents in this paper a ML model that can classify the region of rice based on their chemical component. The samples were collected from Goias and Rio Grande do Sul of Brazil. Three ML techniques SVM, multilayer perceptron (MLP) and random forest (RF) methods were used to predict the rice region based on chemical component. They have collected 31 samples of rice for this study from both regions. The sample size was quite limited such that the data could not be used specifically for training and testing in order to use K-fold cross validation. In k-fold dataset M is randomly distributed in k subsets. The classifier is trained and tested k times and, each time, M/M_t is trained and tested on M_t. where t = 1, 2,…..k.

Accuracy for these models is calculated based on confusion matrix i.e.

$$Accuracy(\%) = \frac{TP + TN}{TP + FP + TN + FN} \tag{8.3}$$

In Equation (8.3), TP represents the number of true positive sample and TN is the number of true negative sample, FP is false positive sample FP are those misclassified sample which are wrongly classified as positive sample. FN is the positive sample that is classified as negative.

There are 20 chemical components on the basis of which rice region were classified. F scores were calculated for each component to check the composition of each component in rice. It means component that has high composition can manipulate the prediction result so that 20 subsets were made in which, first subset contained only one chemical component that has highest %. Second subset contained the first two highest % component and so on. And all the ML techniques have been applied on all 20 subsets. MLP gave best accuracy of 90% on second subset and SVM and RF gave highest accuracy of 93.66 and 93.83% respectively in 18 subsets.

8.4.5 Disease Detection

Agriculture is considered as the backbone of Indian economy and any factor that affects agriculture has serious consequences on our economy. This is one of the reasons that disease detection is considered as one of the major domains in the agriculture sector. Disease detection plays a crucial role in overall quality, quantity and productivity of the crop and thus affects the overall agricultural output. Thus, this domain needs to be properly taken care not only for the betterment of agricultural sector but also for the betterment of Indian economy as a whole

There are various methods in regard to disease detection and they vary from naked eye detection from a scientist to systematic scientific processes of disease detection. To achieve valid and reliable disease detection, a comprehensive and continuous observation is necessary. Traditionally plant disease detection is an expensive task because it uses huge amount of manpower, time and energy. Thus, it was considered as a non-economical task but with rapid progress in computation and data analysis, automatic detection of plant disease is a growing branch which is less laborious and takes less time and energy for completion. This has transformed the agriculture sector drastically. These practices have played a fundamental role in making agriculture a viable option for masses.

Accurate assessments of the occurrence of disease, extent of disease, and its harmful impacts on the qualitative and quantitative characters of agricultural produce are essential for crops in the agricultural field, horticulture, plant breeding, and for the sake of improving the effectiveness of fungicides as well as basic and applied science [27]. Valid and timely assessments of the frequency and spread of plant diseases are the basic foundation for preparing defense programs for the targeted plant in field or greenhouse development and for predicting the spread of temporal and spatial diseases in different rising regions. Popular approaches for the detection of plant diseases include estimation of human raters for visual plant disease, microscopic evaluation of morphological characteristics to detect pathogens, and molecular, serological and microbiological diagnostic techniques. Such time-consuming methods involve skilled people with well-developed diagnostic and disease detection abilities, and therefore may leads to human biasness. Infection with disease in agricultural goods, such as grains, fruits and vegetables, contributes to depletion of the consistency and quantity of agricultural products. It has a strong impact on farmers' financial base and on public wellbeing. Thus, early developmental disease detection in crops of plants, fruits and vegetables leads to a reduction in yield loss and quality.

Ref. [28] did a research on classifying 5 grained cassava leaf disease using CNN. For this study they used the data set that was available on Kaggle. In which there are 10,000 labeled images of cassava leaves. To get the best prediction result one of the main factors is balanced data set but in real life it is not possible to always get a balanced data set. In this study the data set is also imbalanced and small in size. That makes prediction task more complexed because imbalanced data can manipulate the result and can give wrong prediction. CNN is a combination of a convolutional layer and a fully connected layer. Convolutional layer is used for feature extraction from the data base whereas, fully connected layer is same as ANN architecture where there is an input layer hidden layer and output layers. In this study researchers use 512 neurons in first layer, in second and third layers 1,024 neurons were used and 256 neurons in 4th and 5 neurons in output layers to predict each class of a leaf. The data set is also divided in 5 categories out of which one category is for healthy leaves

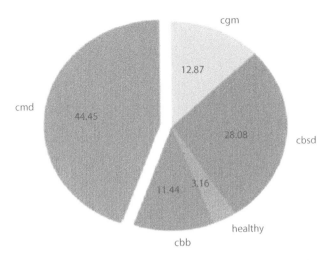

Figure 8.9 Pie chart showing the distribution of data. Reprinted with permission [28].

and other four categories for leaf diseases that are Cassava brown streak disease (CBSD), cassava green mite (CGM), Cassava mosaic disease (CMD) and cassava bacterial blight (CBB). Figure 8.9 shows his data set was highly imbalanced the % of CMD and CBSD images were 44.45 and 28.08% respectively.

Due to the biasness it is very hard to predict the result. To make the unbiased data set image flipping, center zooming, random scaling and random crop techniques were used to artificially increased the data set size. After that CNN model was applied to the data set with K-fold cross validation that use k = 3. Precision, recall and accuracy were measured to test the efficiency of the model.

$$Precision = \frac{TP}{TP + FP} \tag{8.4}$$

Precision is used to check the correct prediction of the true positive sample from total number of the positive sample.

$$Recall = \frac{TP}{TP + FN} \tag{8.5}$$

Recall is used to check the number of predicted true positive class against true positive and false negative.

Train and test accuracy of the cassava disease detection model has been shown in Figure 8.10. This model had achieved average accuracy of 93% using CNN model. This is a good accuracy with such an imbalanced and small size data. Other important researches using machine learning for the identification of diseases are listed in Table 8.3.

8.4.6   Weed Detection

A weed can be described as any plant or vegetation that interferes with farming or forestry objectives, such as growing crops, grazing animals, or forest plantations. Also, a weed can be described as any plant which grows where it is not needed. For e.g. in a greenhouse, or on

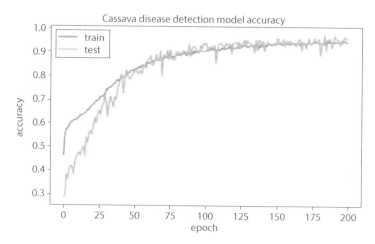

Figure 8.10 Cassava disease detection model accuracy. Reprinted with permission [28].

Table 8.3 Other researches where ML techniques used in disease detection.

Reference	Proposed methodology	Accuracy
[29]	Identification of apple leaf disease by regression, focus loss function and multi-label classification	93.71%
[30]	Plant disease recognition using CNN	97.33%
[31]	Plant disease identification with the help of leaf image using KNN	99%

a farm or plantation, a plant can be desirable or beneficial—but if the same plant develops where it decreases the value of agricultural production or spoils aesthetic or environmental standards, it is called a weed. Some trees, however, are weeds irrespective of their position of growth.

Since the first human effort to farm seeds, humans have had to combat the invasion of weeds into areas selected for crops. It has been recognized that certain plants are unacceptable and not necessary, and have therefore been withdrawn from the field under cultivation. Different cultivated plants escaped cultivation when transplanted into new climates, and became weeds or invasive species. The weeds group is a complex and constant term, because it varies from time to time.

Weed detection is a group of systems that gives settlement to one of the current agricultural problems-unmechanized control of weeds. Weed detection able us to minimize or eliminate over-use of herbicides, mitigate environmental and health impacts on agriculture and improve crop sustainability.

Ref. [32] conducted a study to identify weeds as a broadleaf and grass in soybean crop images using CNN. The site that had chosen for this research was Campo Grande in Brazil. DJI 3 unmanned aerial vehicle was used to take the snapshot of the research land. 15,336 images were taken from December 2015 to March 2016. All images were taken in normal mode. After collection of the data, image segmentation process was done with Simple Linear Iterative Clustering (SLIC) superpixel. This algorithm makes grouping of pixel based

Table 8.4 Other researches where ML techniques used in weed detection.

Reference	Proposed methodology	Accuracy
[33]	Automatic weed classification using Deep Learning	98.23%
[34]	Image based weed detection with Deep CNN	99%

on spatial proximity and color similarity. In this it combines pixel that is called superpixel. This algorithm constructs a cluster of pixels using K-mean algorithm. Value of K is defined in such a manner that cluster will contain multiple weeds and leaf of soybean in one segment. Segment size should not be either very small or very large so different value of K is checked between 100 and 1,200 range. K = 300 has the satisfactory result so this value is used for segmentation purpose. With superpixel, dimension of images was also reduced to 200 ∗ 200 pixels. Total images in dataset were 15,336 out of which 3,249 images of soil, 3,520 images of grass, 1,191 of broadleaf and 7,376 images of soybean. To compare the prediction accuracy some other ML algorithm were also tested with this model. There are total four algorithm Adaboost-C4.5 (This algorithm uses Decision Tree approach), Random Forest (Combination of multiple Decision Tree) Support Vector Machine and Convnet (CNN technique). Performance of first three algorithms were compared with Convnet. In the prediction test Convnet gave the best precision result with 99.1% with balanced dataset. In balanced dataset only 4,500 images were selected from the dataset and out of these 4,000 images, 3,000, 500 and 1,000 images were used for training, validation and for testing respectively. Second prediction test were performed without restriction in which 15,000 images were used out of which 70% is used for training and 10, 20% were used for validation and testing respectively. In this test ConvNet again gave the highest precision with 99.5%. One drawback with ConvNet is that it has very high training time as compared to another algorithm.

Table 8.4 depicts important researches that used ML techniques in weed detection. With the aid of new models and increasing computational and data analysis different traditional machine learning techniques are being replaced by deep-learning techniques for detecting weeds. More forms of hybrid machine learning are growing, utilizing the benefits of various techniques. Both large scale crop and weed picture databases are now accessible online and this offers researchers and engineers both evidence and resources to participate and contribute to weed detection.

8.4.7 Yield Prediction

Crop yield prediction plays a crucial role in global food production and supply chain. Various organizations responsible for sustainable and optimum agricultural output rely on yield prediction mechanisms. Policy makers also rely on the data of yield production to ensure food security for all. Thus, yield prediction plays a crucial role in agro-economic sector.

Agricultural production depends primarily on temperature, pests, and harvest process preparation. Accurate knowledge regarding crop yield background is an essential aspect for making agricultural risk management decisions. In agriculture the estimation of yield is a very important problem. Any farmer is eager to learn how much yield he is going to make. In the past, yield prediction was accomplished by considering the experience of farmers on

Table 8.5 Other researches where ML techniques used for yield prediction.

Reference	Proposed methodology	Accuracy
[36]	Soybean yield prediction using deep learning	R^2—0.72
[37]	Prediction of potato yield using machine learning	R^2—0.93
[38]	Prediction of Wheat yield using machine learning	R^2—0.75

a particular field and crop. The yield estimation is a big problem yet to be addressed on the basis of available evidence.

Ref. [35] conducted a study for wheat yield prediction using ML techniques. This study was conducted at 22 ha Horn End Field, Bedfordshire, UK. Physicochemical parameters were collected with spectroscopy sensor and satellite imagery used to measure crop growth. These physicochemical parameters were used as an input parameter. There are 8,798 total feature vectors. Prediction of wheat yield was tested by three ML algorithms. These three algorithms are Supervised Kohonen Network (SKN), XY-Fused network (XY-F) and Counter Propagation Artificial Neural Network (CP-ANN).

CP-ANN can be used as unsupervised learning and supervised technique. CP-ANN is used as a Classification algorithm. There are two layers in this model, that is, Kohonen and output layer. The weights of every neuron in each layer are equal to the modeled class. There are l rows and m columns in class vector, where l and m are the number of samples and total number of classes respectively. XY-F is a supervised classification technique. In this network, winning neuron is selected based on Euclidean distance. SKN is also a Supervised classification technique. In this model, Kohonen layer and output layer are combined. Every sample and class vector is used for classification.

The test for prediction was done on two different approaches. First test was conducted with Cross Validation in which 25% sample were used for testing and 75% were used for training. In second approach independent validation were used where 1,000 samples used for testing and remaining 7,798 for training. These two different approaches were used because in cross validation training and testing set were not fixed but this model could not be used for future prediction whereas independent validation can used. There are three output classes Low, Medium and High Yield. And all three ML techniques predicted class values compared with actual class values. SKN model provides highest overall accuracy with 81.65% in cross validation and 79.03% accuracy in independent validation. In individual class, highest accuracy was achieved in low yield class in both approaches. In cross validation XY-F has highest accuracy with 92.15%, whereas in independent validation SKN has the highest accuracy of 91.3%. Table 8.5 enlists important researches with proposed methodology and accuracy in weed detection.

8.5   Conclusion

In this chapter use of machine learning techniques in different areas of agriculture is discussed. Weather it is soil mapping or yield prediction machine learning is used everywhere. Supervised learning techniques are used more frequently as compared to unsupervised learning techniques. One of the main reasons for using supervised machine learning technique is it require less data and time to train. Use of deep learning in agriculture is also on the increase. It is a subfield of machine learning. Soil Mapping, Irrigation, weed detection, Disease Detection and yield prediction are area where lots of work has done in precision agriculture.

References

1. Sutton, R.S. and Barto, A.G., *Introduction to Reinforcement Learning*, MIT press, Cambridge, 1998.
2. Jenny, H., *Factors of soil formation*, McGraw-Hill Book Company, Inc., New York and London, 1941.
3. Davies, D.B., Eangle, D.J., Finney, J.B., *Soil Management*, Farming Press Ltd, Ipswich, England, 1993.
4. McBratney, A.B., Mendonça Santos, M.L., Minasny, B., On digital soil mapping. *Geoderma*, 117, 1–2, 3–52, 2003.
5. Scull, P., Franklin, J., Chadwick, O.A., McArthur, D., Predictive soil mapping: A review. *Prog. Phys. Geogr.*, 27, 2, 171–197, 2003.
6. Lees, B.G. and Ritman, K., Decision-tree and rule-induction approach to integration of remotely sensed and GIS data in mapping vegetation in disturbed or hilly environments. *Environ. Manage.*, 15, 6, 823–831, 1991.
7. Jafari, A., Khademi, H., Finke, P.A., Van de Wauw, J., Ayoubi, S., Spatial prediction of soil great groups by boosted regression trees using a limited point dataset in an arid region, southeastern Iran. *Geoderma*, 232–234, 148–163, 2014.
8. Behrens, T., Förster, H., Scholten, T., Steinrücken, U., Spies, E.D., Goldschmitt, M., Digital soil mapping using artificial neural networks. *J. Plant Nutr. Soil Sci.*, 168, 1, 21–33, 2005.
9. Zhao, Z., Meng, F.-R., Yang, Q., and Zhu, H. Using Artificial Neural Networks to Produce High-Resolution Soil Property Maps, in *Advanced Applications for Artificial Neural Networks* (eds. El-Shahat, A.), IntechOpen, Rijeka, pp. 51–75, 2018.
10. Priori, S., Bianconi, N., Costantini, E.A.C., Can γ-radiometrics predict soil textural data and stoniness in different parent materials? A comparison of two machine-learning methods. *Geoderma*, 226–227, 1, 354–364, 2014.
11. Silveira, C.T., Oka-Fiori, C., Santos, L.J.C., Sirtoli, A.E., Silva, C.R., Botelho, M.F., Soil prediction using artificial neural networks and topographic attributes. *Geoderma*, 195–196, 165–172, 2013.
12. Licznar, P. and Nearing, M.A., Artificial neural networks of soil erosion and runoff prediction at the plot scale. *Catena*, 51, 2, 89–114, 2003.
13. Barman, U. and Choudhury, R.D., Soil texture classification using multi class support vector machine. *Inf. Process. Agric.*, 7, 2, 318–332, 2019.
14. Vibhute, A.D., Kale, K.V., Dhumal, R.K., Mehrotra, S.C., Soil type classification and mapping using hyperspectral remote sensing data. *Proc.—2015 Int. Conf. Man Mach. Interfacing, MAMI 2015*, 2016.
15. Yang, G., Qiao, S., Chen, P., Ding, Y., Tian, D., Rock and Soil Classification Using PLS-DA and SVM Combined with a Laser-Induced Breakdown Spectroscopy Library. *Plasma Sci. Technol.*, 17, 8, 656, 2015.
16. Bhattacharya, B. and Solomatine, D.P., Machine learning in soil classification. *Neural Networks*, 19, 2, 186–195, 2006.
17. Bhavsar, H. and Ganatra, A., A Comparative Study of Training Algorithms for Supervised Machine Learning. *Int. J. Soft Comput. Eng.*, 2, 4, 2231–2307, 2012.

18. Kotsiantis, S.B., Supervised Machine Learning: A Review of Classification Techniques. *Informatica*, 31, 3, 249–268, 2007.
19. Mansuy, N., Thiffault, E., Paré, D., Bernier, P., Guindon, L., Villemaire, P., Poirier, V., Beaudoin, A., Digital mapping of soil properties in Canadian managed forests at 250 m of resolution using the k-nearest neighbor method. *Geoderma*, 235–236, 59–73, 2014.
20. Hussain, L. and Haroon Ajaz, R., Seed Classification using Machine Learning Techniques. *J. Multidiscip. Eng. Sci. Technol.*, 2, 5, 1098–1102, 2015.
21. Goap, A., Sharma, D., Shukla, A.K., Rama Krishna, C., An IoT based smart irrigation management system using Machine learning and open source technologies. *Comput. Electron. Agric.*, 155, 41–49, 2018.
22. Goldstein, A., Fink, L., Meitin, A., Bohadana, S., Lutenberg, O., Ravid, G., Applying machine learning on sensor data for irrigation recommendations: Revealing the agronomist's tacit knowledge. *Precis. Agric.*, 19, 3, 421–444, 2018.
23. Pradeep, H.K., Jagadeesh, P., Sheshshayee, M.S., Sujeet, D., Irrigation System Automation Using Finite State Machine Model and Machine Learning Techniques. *Adv. Intell. Syst. Comput.*, 1034, 495–501, 2020.
24. Colligan, T., Brinkerhoff, D., Ketchum, D., Maneta, M.P., Colligan, T., Brinkerhoff, D., Ketchum, D., Maneta, M.P., Mapping Irrigation with Fully Convolutional Neural Networks. *AGUFM*, 2019, B31L–2473, 2019.
25. Adnan, M., Ahsan Latif, M., Nazir, M., Estimating Evapotranspiration using Machine Learning Techniques. *Int. J. Adv. Comput. Sci. Appl.*, 8, 9, 108–113, 2017.
26. Maione, C., Batista, B.L., Campiglia, A.D., Barbosa, F., Barbosa, R.M., Classification of geographic origin of rice by data mining and inductively coupled plasma mass spectrometry. *Comput. Electron. Agric.*, 121, 101–107, 2016.
27. Tripathi, M.K. and Maktedar, D.D., Recent machine learning based approaches for disease detection and classification of agricultural products. *Proc.—2nd Int. Conf. Comput. Commun. Control Autom. ICCUBEA 2016*, 2017.
28. Sambasivam, G. and Opiyo, G.D., A predictive machine learning application in agriculture: Cassava disease detection and classification with imbalanced dataset using convolutional neural networks. *Egypt. Inform. J.*, 2020, https://doi.org/10.1016/j.eij.2020.02.007
29. Zhong, Y. and Zhao, M., Research on deep learning in apple leaf disease recognition. *Comput. Electron. Agric.*, 168, 105146, 2020.
30. Ullah, M.R., Dola, N.A., Sattar, A., Hasnat, A., Plant Diseases Recognition Using Machine Learning. *2019 8th Int. Conf. Syst. Model. Adv. Res. Trends*, pp. 67–73, 2019.
31. Mwebaze, E., and Owomugisha, G. Machine Learning for Plant Disease Incidence and Severity Measurements from Leaf Images. *2016 15th IEEE Int. Conf. Mach. Learn. Appl.*, 158–163, 2016.
32. dos Santos Ferreira, A., Matte Freitas, D., Gonçalves da Silva, G., Pistori, H., Theophilo Folhes, M., Weed detection in soybean crops using ConvNets. *Comput. Electron. Agric.*, 143, 314–324, 2017.
33. Forero, M.G., Herrera-Rivera, S., Ávila-Navarro, J., Franco, C.A., Rasmussen, J., Nielsen, J., Color classification methods for perennial weed detection in cereal crops. *Lect. Notes Comput. Sci. (including Subser. Lect. Notes Artif. Intell. Lect. Notes Bioinformatics)*, 11401 LNCS, 117–123, 2019.
34. Yu, J., Sharpe, S.M., Schumann, A.W., Boyd, N.S., Deep learning for image-based weed detection in turfgrass. *Eur. J. Agron.*, 104, 78–84, 2019.
35. Pantazi, X.E., Moshou, D., Alexandridis, T., Whetton, R.L., Mouazen, A.M., Wheat yield prediction using machine learning and advanced sensing techniques. *Comput. Electron. Agric.*, 121, 57–65, 2016.

36. Maimaitijiang, M., Sagan, V., Sidike, P., Hartling, S., Esposito, F., Fritschi, F.B., Soybean yield prediction from UAV using multimodal data fusion and deep learning. *Remote Sens. Environ.*, 237, 111599, 2020.
37. Gómez, D., Salvador, P., Sanz, J., Casanova, J.L., Potato yield prediction using machine learning techniques and Sentinel 2 data. *Remote Sens.*, 11, 15, 1745, 2019.
38. Cai, Y., Guan, K., Lobell, D., Potgieter, A.B., Wang, S., Peng, J., Xu, T., Asseng, S., Zhang, Y., You, L., Peng, B., Integrating satellite and climate data to predict wheat yield in Australia using machine learning approaches. *Agric. For. Meteorol.*, 274, 144–159, 2019.

## 9

An IoT-Based Multi Access Control and Surveillance for Home Security

Yogeshwaran, K.[1]*, Ramesh, C.[1], Udayakumar, E.[1], Srihari, K.[2] and Sachi Nandan Mohanty[3]

[1]Dept. of ECE, KIT—Kalaignarkarunanidhi Institute of Technology, Coimbatore, India
[2]Dept. of CSE, SNS College of Engineering, Coimbatore, India
[3]Dept. of CSE, ICFAI Foundation of Higher Education, Hyderabad, India

Abstract

In the current scenario, our daily tasks are controlled by mobile devices like smart phones and iPads. A home security system integrates multiple sub-systems that are all controlled by a master home automation controller using IoT. To provide home security and monitoring, system mainly concerns about theft & provides evidence against trespassers. Right now, the present structure and usage of a home security framework to identify an unauthorized person who enters into the home when authorized person is not in the home. This home at home security system uses PIR sensors, finger print module, float-sensor, smoke sensor and is controlled by PIC microcontroller. It also indicates excess water level as well as the gas leakage in and around home. This automation system has been interfaced with GSM which sends a message to the authorized person whose mobile number has been programmed with controller. There is an alert system which is also an indicator.

Keywords: Embedded home security system, float sensor, smoke sensor, PIC microcontroller, GSM modem, PIR sensor, IoT

9.1 Introduction

Today security and prosperity is just a tick of the reasonable development away, and with such movements happening, the security of one's home ought to in like manner not be deserted. Current advances in equipment and correspondence developments have provoked the downsizing and improvement of the introduction of PCs, sensors and frameworks organization. These movements have offered rise to the improvement of a couple of home computerization progressions and structures Automated home is the blend of home security and perception system. Observation can be characterized as checking of the conduct, other evolving data, exercises, watching or examining specific region to impact, coordinating, overseeing or ensuring. A home security framework ought to give

Corresponding author: emperoryogi.yogesh@gmail.com

Monika Mangla, Suneeta Satpathy, Bhagirathi Nayak and Sachi Nandan Mohanty (eds.) Integration of Cloud Computing with Internet of Things: Foundations, Analytics, and Applications, (153–164) © 2021 Scrivener Publishing LLC

security and wellbeing highlights to a home from disturbing the occupants from common, unintentional or potentially human perils, for example, fire, flooding, burglary, creatures attacking, and so on. Home robotization structures using Bluetooth and Zigbee similarly go under this class. These have obstacles of confined access run. Remotely controlled structures use an Internet affiliation or blend in with a present. Accomplice mobile phones, for instance, PDAs and Smart phones with the automation structure get less difficult in remote frameworks. There are different issues included when arranging a home robotization system. Cloud frameworks organization and data system empower individuals to screen, direct, and control their own data centers through the IoT [5]. This executes the subtleties of home security framework utilizing GSM when nobody is available inside the home. PIR and unique mark module are used to report a gatecrasher present inside the home. A caution framework is used to demonstrate the overabundance water level in indoor condition. Utilizing this strategy robbery, fire accident, water spillage can be corrected successfully.

The organization of this chapter is to provide IoT issues of security in home. The web administration is an ideal blue print for the light-footed business condition because of its free coupling in nature, adaptability, re-convenience, straightforwardness, receptiveness, understandability and so on. Web administration is the up and coming wave for tomorrow's business needs and right now is the one of the major provoking segment for the engineers to ensure the secrecy, validation, trustworthiness, approval and non-revocation of machine to machine collaboration. So security isn't debatable to foresee a protected ancient rarity for web administration. Web administrations depend on framework and henceforth the experienced in organization is experienced in web benefits too.

Classification determines that the substance of the message ought to be received between just by the sender and beneficiary. This is accomplished by proper encryption and unscrambling calculations. Here an automatic surveillance system is implemented with the help of IoT sensors and IoT cameras, Pic microcontrollers. The hardware used is Approved assets and administrations accessible consistently are implied by accessibility. Forswearing of Service (DoS) is the generally experienced issue identified with accessibility. So as to keep up the prominence and notoriety of a site, the nature of administration seen by clients; particularly the administration accessibility is a triumph factor. A help that is as often as possible inaccessible may effectively affect the notoriety of the specialist co-op, or bring about loss of business openings. From the client's viewpoint, a help that displays low quality is for all intents and purposes proportionate to an inaccessible assistance [9].

The difference in message content during travel prompts loss of uprightness. It is a chief worry for the WSDL document. Web administration security alone doesn't give programming security. Building secure programming implies applying the product security contact focuses during plan and execution and it isn't just hauling a specific security innovation into an endeavor actualizing it [16]. It is to be fused at different degrees of administration arranged undertaking application improvement, for example, examination, structure and execution. The proposed work is detailed in order to understand the security issues at prior degrees of advancement cycle and not at later during usage level. The proposed work deals with expanding the accessibility of the administrations without overpowering the safety efforts [34].

9.2   Related Work

A focal controller-based home security framework might want to improve the security of the homes in a domain by joining different homes into a security partner with a control place devoted for each area relying on the measure of clients. These control places are obliged by a few focal or director control that focuses with incredibly high managing power. The security structure portrayed, called Home Security System on Intelligent Network (HSSIN) uses such a focal controller-based procedure. The proposed framework needs present day security parameters. The structure proposes a constant home computerization and watching framework. The structure cautions the home credit holder by cell phone utilizing GPRS and the [20] client can continuously see the home utilizing live camera. The structure utilizes a Rabbit Core Module to relate an electrical gadget in the home to the home framework, commonly a PC. Each home structure is connected with a focal server. Bunny Core has an IP address, so every contraption related with it will as a rule be seen and is worked through cell phones utilizing GPRS [4]. The client sends contraption the authorities heading to a focal server. The proposed model offers centrality to correspondence and system strategy rather than security. It shows impedance affirmation, at any rate no solid parameters perceiving obstructions are referenced. Sharp Eye utilizes camcorders for security using IoT. Its security issues are talked about underneath. Likewise, similar to all combined home security frameworks, the proposed structure is not perfect for checking single homes, yet best suits a social event at homes and the producer's occurrences of "increment in outline rate prompts increment in security" is far from being obviously substantial and misleading. If all else fails, a focal controller-based security framework is hard to finish and raises some unprecedented protection concerns [11].

People will all in all be unusual or extraordinary on occasion. Rather than PCs, they improvise, and will when all is said and done choose incautious decisions about their interesting circumstance. Setting careful enrolling raises a significant issue of customer security. With setting careful enrolling, the system [20] has impressively dynamically close to home information about the customer. In order to execute setting careful enrolling, the structure should share this information. In any situation, the system will have self-learning technique to control the situation by ts own. By day's end, the evacuating power of what is essential is still the initiative of home tenants regardless of careful setting and configuring done [12].

Sensor-based home computerization and security system [13] has the standard game plan of home security structures and regularly screens just the property and prerequisite physical control segments of the house itself. Moreover, the term security isn't all around depicted considering the path that there is a period delay between the prepared structure going on and certifiable showing up of the safety crew. Structure and use subtleties of the home control and security framework dependent on field programmable gate array (FPGA) is all around expensive. Existing strategy of home security utilizes FPGA. They are not interfaced in one single security frameworks [30]. There are different sensors which have not been interfaced into a lone controller. Utilizing a FPGA pack, we can process a significant number of entries. A constrained application has been utilized for this structure using IoT issues.

9.3 Hardware Description

A PSO-based improvement of AES and Blowfish encryption. The recommendation given by this chapter is the key that will be created through the ECDH calculation and encoded by both AES and Blowfish strategies. The molecule swarm streamlining is utilized for the choice of figure content. The test works are not completed and just the content document is considered for the preparation. Because of the two-encryption calculations, the remaining burden will be increment. Gupta *et al.* [16] proposed a staggered encryption for the information security in the cloud. Right now, level of encryption happens on the information 1. Blow fish encryption and 2. AES encryption. Also, the unscrambling procedure is opposite of it. The technique will improve the security yet the blowfish calculation works on a 64-bit premise, which isn't appropriate for enormous information. Just as the client needs to remind the three keys to unscramble the information. The computational time will increment for bigger dataset and multifaceted nature likewise increment [16].

The security of the cloud is improved by utilizing AES calculation for the encryption of information in the cloud. Right now, encryption standard is utilized for the information safeguarding and the outcomes were best as far as execution when contrasted with different calculations like DES, Triple DES and RC2. The execution of AES on pictures rather than content requires less time contrasted with RC4, blowfish and RC6. It clarified about the administration models and the security issues in that administration, the security issues in SaaS information related issues, security in the web application, and so on. In PaaS the supplier must be solid as far as information spillage when the interruption happens between the host and application. In IaaS the information is gone through different outsider foundations along these lines, the information must be sent with acceptable encryption approaches and steering convention to arrive at the beneficiary. Here the overview of security cloud is portrayed with different related works. Ref. [9] proposed a four-level structure for improving the web application security. Open network gathering gives guidelines about the framework subtleties for the distributed storage [33].

Already, get to control strategies were composed by hard coding legitimately into the program by the software engineer. Later on, as the strategies turned out to be progressively confused, separate strategy determination dialects were created [31]. There are numerous strategy detail dialects and they can be either nonexclusive or explicit to applications of IoT issues. Conventional arrangement determination dialects are intended for upholding access control in wide areas like circulated approach the executives, ensuring the security of ventures, and so forth. They proposed an intelligent language for get to control that permits the detail of various access control approaches. It has been comprehensively received to determine get to control arrangements for different applications, particularly Web administrations [4].

XACML approaches are formalized utilizing a math-based procedure variable known as Communicating Sequential Processes (CSP). This work uses a model checker to officially confirm properties of approaches, and to contrast get to control arrangements with one another. Introduced a formalization of XACML utilizing Answer Set Programming (ASP), which is an ongoing type of revelatory [15] programming, and utilized existing ASP reasoners to lead arrangement confirmation. Nonetheless, inadequacy with regards to a comprehensive elicitation of properties, the fulfillment of the examination consequences of strategy check can't be ensured.

Verification is the foundation of evidence of characters among elements associated with the framework. Username and secret word are utilized for verifying of the client. In web administrations, get to control instruments are given in XML type. Approved assets and administrations accessible consistently are implied by accessibility. Disavowal of Service (DoS) is the ordinarily experienced issue identified with accessibility. So as to keep up the prominence and notoriety of a site, the nature of administration seen by clients; particularly the administration accessibility is a triumph factor. An assistance that is much of the time inaccessible may effectively affect the notoriety of the specialist co-op, or bring about loss of business openings. From the client's point of view, a help that displays low quality is for all intents and purposes proportionate to an inaccessible assistance [29].

The difference in message content during travel prompts loss of honesty. It is principally a worry for the WSDL record. On altering and changing this record, planned assistance may not get tie to the requestor and even issues may emerge if there should arise an occurrence of structure. Legitimate hashing calculation or XML mark may beat this issue [10].

Web administration security alone doesn't give programming security. Building secure programming implies applying the product security contact focuses during plan and execution and it isn't just hauling a specific security innovation into an undertaking and actualizing it. It is to be joined at different degrees of administration with arranged venture application improvement, for example, investigation, plan and execution of IoT issues. The proposed work [9] is defined in order to explain the security issues at prior degrees of advancement cycle and not at later during usage level. The proposed work deals with expanding the accessibility of the administrations without overpowering the safety efforts [31].

The proposed runtime check has during the most recent decade seen a huge number of frameworks for observing occasion arrangements (follows) discharged by a running framework. The goal is to guarantee rightness of a framework by checking its execution follows against formal details speaking to necessities. An exceptional test is information parameterized occasions, where screens need to monitor the blend of control states just as information limitations, relating occasions and the information they convey across time focuses. This represents a test regarding productivity of screens, just as expressiveness of rationales. An information robot is a type of automata where states are parameterized with information [14], supporting checking of information parameterized occasions. They portrayed the full subtleties of a basic API in the SCALA programming language, an inside DSL (Domain Specific Language), executing information automata.

They proposed arrangement of disseminated forms, where accuracy can be guaranteed by (statically) checking whether their piece fulfills properties of intrigue. Conversely, web administrations are being structured with the goal that each accomplice finds properties of others progressively, through a distributed interface. Since the general framework may not be accessible statically and since every business procedure should be moderately basic, they propose to utilize runtime observing of discussions between accomplices as a method for checking conduct rightness of the whole web administration framework. In particular, they distinguish a subset of UML 2.0 arrangement outlines as a property detail language and show that it is adequately expressive for catching security and exuberance properties. By changing these outlines to automata, they empower conformance checking of limited execution follows against the particular [5].

A standard based system for characterizing and executing limited follow observing rationales, including future and past time fleeting rationale, expanded normal articulations, ongoing rationales, interim rationales, types of evaluated worldly rationales, etc. The rationale, EAGLE, is actualized as a java library and includes novel methods for rule definition, control and execution. Checking is done on a state-by-state premise, without putting away the execution follow.

The thought of causality for interface contracts communicated in a first-request expansion of Linear Temporal Logic (LTL). He introduced CTL-FO+, an expansion over Computation Tree Logic that remembers first-request measurement for message content notwithstanding fleeting administrators and furthermore proposed how CTL-FO+ is satisfactory for communicating information mindful limitations, give a sound and complete model checking calculation for CTL-FO+, and build up its intricacy to be PSPACE-finished.

9.3.1   Float Sensor

Fluid level buoy switches drift in fluids and are utilized to gauge the degree of a fluid inside a compartment. These buoys can basically show the degree of the fluid, or they can hold different capacities like turning siphons on or off when they arrive at a specific level in the compartment. How they are made and introduced demonstrate what they will do and how they will function. Fluid level sensors primary capacity is to glide on the fluid they are in. A few fluids might be acidic to plastic, which is the reason treated steel glides are in some cases utilized. Buoys are commonly made out of materials that are less thick than the fluid they are intended to skim in. In some cases they are given their own window with the goal that you can see them. They can likewise drive a winding shaft with a pointer on it, similar to a gas tank marker on ranch hardware or little vehicles, similar to bikes. Different sorts of fluid level sensors can really open and close circuits. These circuits are called reed switches [17]. This chapter executes the nuances of home security system using GSM when no one is accessible inside the home. Figure 9.1 shows the square outline of home security structure PIR and one of a kind finger impression module used to report an intruder present inside the home. A ready structure used to show the bounty water level in indoor condition. Using this methodology burglary, fire accident, water spillage can be revised effectively [36].

A reed switch has two wires housed in glass packaging and epoxy and is mounted at a fixed situation in its holder. The two wires sit by one another inside the glass packaging yet don't contact. A magnet is set in a buoy, and when the magnet comes into scope of the two wires, they are charged and met up, shutting the circuit. At the point when the magnet is moved out of range, the two wires are demagnetized and subsequently open the circuit. This can be rearranged, with the goal that the wires are continually shutting the circuit except if the magnet is available, in which case, they open. Everything relies upon what they are being utilized for realizing how a fluid level buoy switch functions can assist you with choosing if you need one in the gear that you use all the time. It additionally encourages you choose which kind will have the option to best serve your necessities, and help you realize what you truly need in a fluid level sensor [8].

9.3.2   Map Matching

For certain administrations, such as directing [36], it is important to coordinate the gathered information to a diagram portrayal of the street organize, taking into account preparing and relationship of information per road. We map each area's information obtained

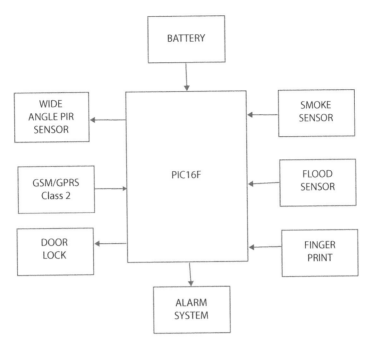

Figure 9.1 Block diagram of home security system using IoT.

from the street system given by the communitarian Open Street Map venture. For schedule follows, e.g., gathered by SMC members and Bus-Net transports, we utilize an outside administration that improves precision of the coordinated street positions by coordinating and approving the entire follow and not point-by-point [15].

9.3.3 USART Cable

This applet is the first of a progression of related applets that exhibit the USART 8251 or all inclusive synchronous and nonconcurrent collector and transmitter. The USART chip incorporates both a transmitter and a beneficiary [16] for sequential information correspondence dependent on the RS-232 convention. It permits interfacing a microcomputer framework to an assortment of outside gadgets, for example mouse or trackball, sequential consoles and terminals, printers and plotters with RS-232 interface, microcontroller advancement frameworks, streak developers, and so on [36].

The RS-232 protocol for sequential information correspondence is fairly straightforward. For a careful clarification, see the RS-232 link. The transmitter is associated with the beneficiary through only two wires (sign and ground) for unidirectional correspondence, for bidirectional correspondence between two gadgets, two separate unidirectional channels are consolidated, with the transmitter of one gadget associated with the recipient of the other gadget. For this situation, two sign wires and a shared view association are required. A few variations of the convention are being used, which vary in the genuine image encoding by means of voltage levels or flows. The first current-circle encoding utilized an enduring state current of 20 to show an uninvolved line and zero amps to demonstrate a functioning state. Along these lines, a messed up association between the transmitter and collector could be distinguished right away. In chip frameworks, it is regularly progressively advantageous to encode the images with voltages. Here, an abnormal state ('1') is utilized to demonstrate a latent line, while a low level ('0') shows the dynamic condition of the line. Regularly, additional converter chips like the prominent max-232 driver are utilized to enhance the yield sign of a feeble transmitter chip and to shield a microchip framework from glitches on the outside correspondence line [3].

To demonstrate the start of an information transmission, the transmitter first drives the sign line to the low state for one time of the transmitter clock. This is known as the begin bit. During the following times of the transmitter clock, the chose number of information bits are transmitted beginning with the least huge piece. Whenever empowered, an equality bit is embedded after the most noteworthy information bit. At last, the sign line is kept high for at any rate one transmitter clock period, this is known as the stopbit [10]. Regularly, two-stop bits are utilized. After the stop bit, the sign line is kept in the inert state until the begin bit of the following information is to be transmitted clearly, the beneficiary must be designed to utilize a similar number of information bits, equality, and stop-bits as the transmitter. Additionally, the bit clock of the recipient must match the transmitter's clock inside a couple of percent for effective information gathering [4].

The reenactment model utilized in this applet depends on the Intel 8251 chip, which was initially produced for frameworks dependent on the 8080/8085 arrangement 8-piece microchips, yet can likewise be joined to the framework transports of other microchip frameworks. Be that as it may, the Hades reproduction model so far just underpins [25] the more typical non concurrent mode, where the sequential correspondence line is kept inactive between transmissions [35]. The activity of the chip and its few working modes will be clarified underneath and in the accompanying applets. The schematics demonstrates the 8251 chip in the middle, with the transport interface flag on the left and the sign of the sequential correspondence interface on the right. At the top are the transmitter yield and two transmitter status yields, the transmitter prepared sign and the transmitter [13] void sign. An outer clock generator is required to drive the clock contribution to create the reference bit clock for the transmitter. Additionally, the base gathering of sign has a place with the recipient with the information input and a different piece clock input. The status yield flag that the beneficiary has gotten an approaching character, which should then be perused by the status sign demonstrate that information has been gotten or transmitted, they can likewise be utilized to produce interfere with solicitations to the host chip; some extra rationale may be required for this. The center gathering of sign is the standard stream control or modem-control lines, to be specific [26] clear-to-send, prepared to-send, informational index prepared, and information terminal-prepared. The sign likewise straightforwardly controls the transmitter square; characters are just transmitted while is held low using IoT issues.

Before the 8251 chip can be utilized for real correspondence, its working mode should initially be chosen by means of composing the comparing mode and order registers. To dodge the many mouse-snaps of the info switches for the introduction succession, this applet incorporates a boosts generator that consequently produces the information arrangement to empower the 8251 chip for standard RS-232 non concurrent information transmission with the accompanying parameters, 8 information bits, no equality, and 2 stop-bits. After the introduction succession has finished, you can utilize mouse-clicks or the bind keys to intelligently control the information transport and control sign of the USART to transmit characters through the transmitter yield or to peruse [28] the status register. The transmitter clock is set to an exceptionally moderate pace of 0.5 Hz, which permits viewing the sequential correspondence bit for bit during the intuitive recreation. A short presentation about the registers and order set of the 8251 chip is given toward the part of the arrangement; for a full clarification of all highlights please download and counsel the datasheet. The predefined information arrangement utilized by this applet takes around 90 s, intentionally backed off to permit observing every single sign change during the liveliness. In the event that you like to think about the sign wave forms after a speedy instatement of the 8251 using IoT [22].

9.4   Software Design

Figure 9.2 shows the complete schematic diagram of the proposed home security system. Right now UART0 pins (T × D and R × D) are associated with R × D and T × D pins of GSM module individually. Bell is associated with P0.15 pin of PIC. PIR sensors are associated with P0.25 and P0.28 sticks individually.

Attacks on essential national structure for essentialness, for instance, the reported ambush comprise the PIC microcontroller board, unique mark module and PIR sensor, GSM modem, power supply and ringer. At the point when an interruption is recognized, the client gets an alarm message on his cell phone. With this, he can make suitable move to recognize interruption in his home. Figure 9.3 shows the model usage of the home security framework subsequent to situating the segments properly. A variety of PIR sensors might

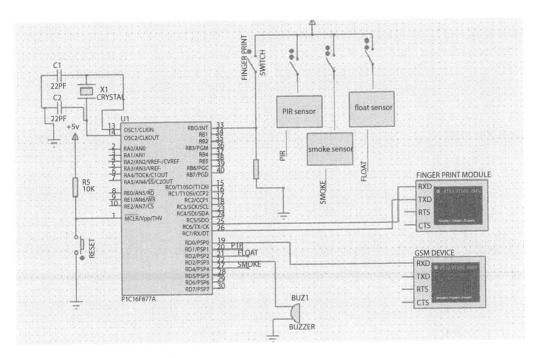

Figure 9.2 Schematic diagram of home security system.

Figure 9.3 Block diagram of proposed system.

be utilized in genuine home condition to build the adequacy of interruption identification utilizing IoT issues.

9.5 Conclusion

In this chapter, we have structured and actualized a savvy PIC microcontroller-based home security framework. The proposed framework gives home security and reconnaissance utilizing IoT, sending sensors, utilizing GSM to distinguish, report and screen interruption occasions to clients diminishing harms brought about by robbery. Various PIR sensors might be utilized to get more extensive inclusion. By incorporating multi contact versatile framework, remote correspondence, and caution framework, a completely utilitarian home mechanization can be planned and constructed.

Future scope: In future, the IoT-based 5G communication is implemented for controlling the home security for controlling all the applications of the daily used appliances.

References

1. Arora, A., Kaur, A., Bhushan, B., Saini, H., Security Concerns and Future Trends of Internet of Things. *2nd International Conference on Intelligent Computing, Instrumentation and Control Technologies (ICICICT)*, Kannur, Kerala, India, pp. 891–896, 2019.
2. Malik, A., Gautam, S., Abidin, S., Bhushan, B., Blockchain Technology-Future Of IoT: Including Structure, Limitations And Various Possible Attacks. *2019 2nd International Conference on Intelligent Computing, Instrumentation and Control Technologies (ICICICT)*, Kannur, Kerala, India, pp. 1100–1104, 2019.
3. Maple, C., Security and privacy in the internet of things. *J. Cyber Policy*, 2, 2, 155–184, 2017.
4. Chowdhury, Z.I., Imtiaz, M.H., Azam, M.M., Sumi, M.R.A., Nur, N.S., Design and implementation of Pyroelectric Infrared sensor based security system using microcontroller. *Proc. of IEEE Students*.

5. Shin, D., Yun, K., Kim, J., Astillo, P.V., Kim, J., You, I., A Security Protocol for Route Optimization in DMM-Based Smart Home IoT Networks. *IEEE Access*, 7, 142531–142550, 2019.

6. Sunehra, D. and Bano, A., An intelligent surveillance with cloud storage for home security. *2014 Annual IEEE India Conference (INDICON)*, Pune, pp. 1–6, 2014.

7. Das, S.R. *et al.*, Home automation and security for mobile devices. *IEEE International Conference on Pervasive Computing and Communications Workshops*, Seattle, WA, 21–25 March 2011, pp. 141–146.

8. Dickey, N., Banks, D., Sukittanon, S., Home Automation using Cloud Network and Mobile Devices. *Proc. of IEEE South Eastcon*, pp. 1–4, 15–18, 2012.

9. Sakthivel V., *et al.*, Implementation of Alexa-Based Intelligent Voice Response System for Smart Campus. In: Saini H., Srinivas T., Vinod Kumar D., Chandragupta Mauryan K. (eds) Innovations in Electrical and Electronics Engineering. Lecture Notes in Electrical Engineering, Springer, Singapore, vol. 626, pp. 849–855, 2020.

10. Vetrivelan, P. *et al.*, Design of Smart Surveillance Security System based on Wireless Sensor Network. *Int. J. Res. Stud. Sci. Eng. Technol., Sryahwa Publications*, 4, 5, 23–26, August 2017.

11. Santhi S., *et al.*, SOS Emergency Ad Hoc Wireless Network. In: Anandakumar H., Arulmurugan R., Onn C. (eds) Computational Intelligence and Sustainable Systems. EAI/Springer Innovations in Communication and Computing, Springer, Cham, pp. 227–234, 2019.

12. Abdul-Ghani, H.A. *et al.*, A Comprehensive Study of Security and Privacy Guidelines, Threats, and Countermeasures: An IoT Perspective. *J. Sens. Actuator Netw.*, 8, 22, 2019.

13. Kodali, R. K., Jain, V., Bose, S., and Boppana, L., IoT-based smart security and home automation system,, 2016 International Conference on Computing, Communication and Automation (ICCCA), Noida, pp. 1286-1289, 2016.

14. Maiti, A. and Sivanesan, S., Cloud Controlled Intrusion Detection and Burglary Prevention Stratagems in Home Automation Systems. *2nd Baltic Congress on Future Internet Communications (BCFIC)*, 25–27 April 2012, IEEE, Vilnius, pp. 182b–186.

15. Hoque, M.A. and Davidson, C., Design and Implementation of an IoT-Based Smart Home Security System. *Int. J. Networked Distrib. Comput.*, 7, 2, 85–92, April 2019.

16. Neshenko, N., Bou-Harb, E., Crichigno, J., Kaddoum, G., Ghani, N., Demystifying IoT Security: An Exhaustive Survey on IoT Vulnerabilities and a First Empirical Look on Internet-Scale IoT Exploitations. *IEEE Commun. Surv. Tutor.*, 21, 3, 2702–2733, third quarter 2019.

17. Prakash, N. and Kumareshan, N., Arduino Based traffic congestion control with automatic signal clearance for emergency vehicles and Stolen Vehicle Detection. *2020 International Conference on Computer Communication and Informatics (ICCCI)*, Coimbatore, India, pp. 1–6, 2020.

18. Prakash, N. *et al.*, GSM based design and implementation of women safety device using Internet of Things. *Proceedings of International Conference on Big Data and Cloud Computing (ICBDCC-2019), Advances in Big Data and Cloud Computing, Springer—Advances in Intelligent Systems and Computing (AISC) series*, 2019.

19. Srihari, K., *et al.*, An Innovative Approach for Face Recognition Using Raspberry Pi, Artificial Intelligence Evolution, Universal Wiser publisher, vol. 1, issue 2, pp.103-108, August 2020.

20. Vetrivelan, P., *et al.*, A Neural Network-Based Automatic Crop Monitoring Robot for Agriculture. *The IoT and the Next Revolutions Automating the World*, edited by Dinesh Goyal, *et al.*, IGI Global, pp. 203–212, 2019.

21. Reinisch, C. *et al.*, Wireless Technologies in Home & Building Automation. *Proc. of 5th IEEE Int. Conf on Industrial Informatics*, vol. 1, pp. 9398, 23–27, 2007.

22. Quadri, S.A.I. and Sathish, P., IoT-based home automation and surveillance system. *2017 International Conference on Intelligent Computing and Control Systems (ICICCS)*, Madurai, pp. 861–866, 2017.

23. Tamilselvan, S. *et al.*, A Smart Industrial Pollution Detection and Monitoring using Internet of Things (IoT). *Futuristic Trends in Network and Communication Technologies, Communication in Computer and Information Science (CCIS) series*, vol. 1206, Issue 1, Springer Nature, pp. 233–242, April 2020.

24. Ramesh C., *et.al.*, An Enhanced Face and Iris Recognition-Based New Generation Security System. In: Singh P., Pawłowski W., Tanwar S., Kumar N., Rodrigues J., Obaidat M. (eds) Proceedings of First International Conference on Computing, Communications, and Cyber-Security (IC4S 2019). *Lecture Notes in Networks and Systems*, vol. 121, pp. 845–855, Springer, Singapore, 2020.

25. Srihari, K. *et al.*, Automatic Battery Replacement of Robot. *Adv. Nat. Appl. Sci.*, 9, 33–38, June 2015.

26. Furber, S., ARM System-on-Chip Architecture, 2nd edition, Pearson education, March 2000.

27. Sunehra, D. and Bano, A., An intelligent surveillance with cloud storage for home security. *2014 Annual IEEE India Conference (INDICON)*, 2014.

28. Sharma, T., Satija, S., Bhushan, B., Unifying Blockchian and IoT: Security Requirements, Challenges, Applications and Future Trends. *2019 International Conference on Computing, Communication, and Intelligent Systems (ICCCIS)*, Greater Noida, India, pp. 341–346, 2019.

29. Kanagaraj T., *et al.*, Control of Home Appliances and Projector by Smart Application Using SEAP Protocol. In: Das H., Pattnaik P., Rautaray S., Li KC. (eds) Progress in Computing, Analytics and Networking. Advances in Intelligent Systems and Computing, vol. 1119, pp. 603–610, Springer, Singapore, 2020.

30. Kanagaraj, T. *et al.*, Foot Pressure Measurement by using ATMEGA164 Microcontroller. *Adv. Nat. Appl. Sci., AENSI Journals*, 10, 13, 224–228, September 2016.

31. Hassija, V., Chamola, V., Saxena, V., Jain, D., Goyal, P., Sikdar, B., A Survey on IoT Security: Application Areas, Security Threats, and Solution Architectures. *IEEE Access*, 7, 82721–82743, 2019.

32. Kumar, S., Swetha, S., Kiran, V.T., Johri, P., IoT based Smart Home Surveillance and Automation. *2018 International Conference on Computing, Power and Communication Technologies (GUCON)*, Greater Noida, Uttar Pradesh, India, pp. 786–790, 2018.

33. Priyadharshini, M., A Framework for Securing Web Services by Formulating an Collaborative Security Standard among Prevailing WS-Security Standards. *Commun. Comput. Inf. Sci.*, 193, pp. 269–283, 2011.

34. Sunehra, D. and Bano, A., An intelligent surveillance with cloud storage for home security. *2014 Annual IEEE India Conference (INDICON)*, 2014.

35. Sivaganesan, *et al.*, An Event Based Neural Network Architecture with Content Addressable Memory. *Int. J. Embed. Real-Time Commun. Syst., IGI Global*, 11, 1, pp. 23–40, January 2020.

36. Prakash, N. and Kumareshan, N., Arduino Based traffic congestion control with automatic signal clearance for emergency vehicles and Stolen Vehicle Detection. *2020 International Conference on Computer Communication and Informatics (ICCCI), Coimbatore*, India, pp. 1–6, 2020.

37. Talal, M., Zaidan, A.A., Zaidan, B.B. *et al.*, Smart Home-based IoT for Real-time and Secure Remote Health Monitoring of Triage and Priority System using Body Sensors: Multi-driven Systematic Review. *J. Med. Syst.*, 43, 42, 2019.

38. Pavithra, D. and Balakrishnan, R., IoT based monitoring and control system for home automation. *2015 Global Conference on Communication Technologies (GCCT), Thuckalay*, pp. 169–173, 2015.

## 10

Application of IoT in Industry 4.0 for Predictive Analytics

Ahin Banerjee*, Debanshee Datta and Sanjay K. Gupta

IIT(BHU), Varanasi, India

Abstract

Extensive use of high-end industrial properties is the current paradigm shift as an essence to Industry 4.0. The life cycle assessment in tandem is the prerequisite for such automated systems in order to optimize the return on this significant investment. To achieve results without human intervention Internet of Things (IoT) assists by sharing of data to the network of interconnected devices. Miniaturization in sensors and extensive storage space the data gets collected. Using unmatched computing power and predictive maintenance algorithms the real time data is analysed. The present study and its results reflect an idea of advanced communication and control in an automotive domain by reliably estimating the remaining useful life of equipment within predefined probability limits. One of the prerequisites in order to carryout predictive maintenance is to accurately define the signal. The initial challenge in defining an IoT signal to monitor the machine's current condition is seen to overcome. Further works includes pre-processing the sensor data besides degradation modelling. Performance results show the advantages and benefits of the approach by assessing the extent of the system's degradation from its expected normal operating conditions. In particular, predictive maintenance and industrial IoT discuss the identification of irregularities that can result in high costs due to downtime in production besides assisting in human comfort and higher safety standards.

Keywords: Industrial-IoT, RUL, predictive maintenance, industry 4.0

10.1 Introduction

The progressive shift in industrialization from mechanization (18th century) at the beginning and extending towards the concept of mass production (19th century) happened in almost a century. The later part of the era emerged with a completely new concept by using automated production with the support of electronics and information technology thus leading towards the third industrial revolution (a.k.a., I3.0). The rapid advancement

---

*Corresponding author: ahin49banerjee@gmail.com

Monika Mangla, Suneeta Satpathy, Bhagirathi Nayak and Sachi Nandan Mohanty (eds.) Integration of Cloud Computing with Internet of Things: Foundations, Analytics, and Applications, (165–182) © 2021 Scrivener Publishing LLC

in industrialization gave more impetus to the shift further moving from I3.0 towards I4.0 that demonstrates the exponential profile of our daily life; our work synchronized to the progress of physical systems under cyber domain including security and IoT platform. It could be worth mentioning about the agility in complex manufacturing technologies over near net shape of products which reduces the production costs by nearly a quarter with the use of industrial machinery. In view of this revolutionary technology, an effective prediction of abnormal behaviors by means of data driven approach to automate the maintenance in industrial machinery under the diverse working conditions becomes a necessity. Periodic and continuous monitoring are alternatively defined as predictive maintenance, which is one of the means of achieving such enhanced maintenance of the critical systems. The predictive maintenance of such machines within industries [1] using sensors and human–machine interaction networked together is by far one aspect of IoT (a.k.a., industrial-IoT). With a complex degree of automation via advanced robotics and cloud computing, industrial-IoT is a progress towards all the interconnected systems that permits for optimized process control. The use of predictive maintenance in the domain of I4.0 and RUL as a tool in enhancing different needs during maintenance of complex engineering applications is a progress in implementing industrial-IoT. The continuous monitoring of equipment and the valuable insights to the user community using IoT interface is one such promising approach of I4.0. Figure 10.1 describes the framework of industrial-IoT.

The agility of industries in the domain of manufacturing is an important reason for the application of I4.0 while, industrial-IoT discusses in the view of proactive maintenance. The industrial-IoT acts as a driving force behind the I4.0 movement, with much needed automation, gathering data, and performing analytics. Figure 10.2 explains the different stages of working in the framework of industrial-IoT.

Stage 1 encompasses the use of sensors (accelerometers, piezoelectric types) which establishes a relation with the working environment. The sensors help in capturing signal or data from the device that is under the observation and then converts it to a meaningful information. In stage 2, internet gateways are used to convert the analog signal or data into its digital form. Using data acquisition system (DAS) the conversion of analog data into digital data is made possible. Stage 3 deals with the pre-processing of the data before it is being sent to the actual device. This is done because IoT data is very vast which can hamper the speed of the system. Therefore, it is always first that the data is converted into its digital form and then is fed into the system. Hence, only the required and important data captured by the sensor in the previous stage is allowed. Finally, in stage 4 the preprocessed data is sent to the data centers and cloud based servers for final analysis. Thus, the cloud platform provides a major advantage by reducing the hardware cost.

With the much-appreciated intelligence empowered by IoT, the industrial devices can then be automated to work in tandem to yield outputs on an assembly line. Applications are not only limited to automotive, manufacturing, and oil and gas industries, which promises to elevate the productivity besides enhancing the country's gross domestic product. A promising performance improvement with big data analytics in the context to these data-driven industrial scenarios is foreseen. One of the highest forms of intelligence is cognitive action, which prioritizes learning and decision making from the monitored industrial data via expert system adding to its logic and planning. Figure 10.3 discusses

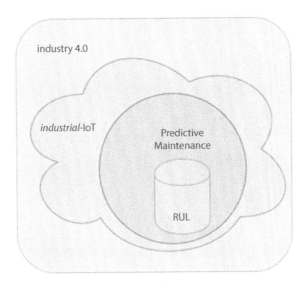

Figure 10.1 Architectural layers of industrial-IoT.

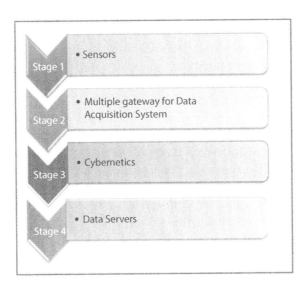

Figure 10.2 Stages of industrial-IoT.

the use of strategic "Assess–Analyze-Act" to estimate the RUL and further extend its role in decision making.

The RUL is a predictive maintenance tool that supports in prior assessment of system's health. In context to decision making, it is compulsory to keep in mind about the various industrial challenges that the manufacturer overcomes. The advantages of predictive maintenance are listed as:

- Increased productivity
- Increased uptime

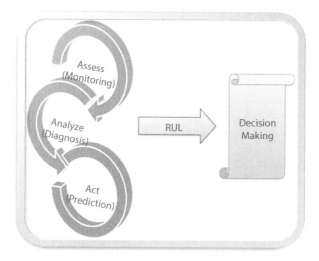

Figure 10.3 RUL as a tool in industrial decision making.

- Increased lifetime of equipment's
- Increased safety standards
- Decreased cost of maintenance
- Decreased equipment failures/rate of failure
- Decreased stock in inventory.

Advantages in predictive maintenance thereby assist in meeting I4.0 standards by enabling the production lines and setting the benchmark of business standards. The disabled human intervention thus assists the machines to instantly make a perfection over multiple production lines anywhere in the world, which is one of the major improvements over traditional operating plants in silos. Incorporating just-in-time capability in manufacturing industry thus helps in reducing idle time and increasing productivity. Such innovative implementation requires an upfront investment in industry, but in the long run also reduces the cost of manufacturing. The various advantages of I4.0 are:

- Flexibility within engineering systems
- Collective workability of machines
- Efficient productivity
- Easier compliance
- Low manufacturing costs
- Good return on investment.

10.2   Past Literary Works

10.2.1   Maintenance-Based Monitoring

The industrial maintenance has been a critical issue in gaining an optimized return-on-investment towards complex engineering systems within an international economic

Table 10.1 Advanced techniques towards industrial maintenance and their measures of accuracy.

Application areas	Techniques		Accuracy measures
Rotor bearing [3], ECG data [4]	Classification	1-class Support Vector Decomposition, Artificial Neural Network, k-Nearest Neighborhood	Mean absolute error, Mean squared error, Root mean squared error, coefficient of determination, Relative accuracy
Wind turbine [5], Lithium-ion battery [6], Aircraft fuselage [7], Milling CNC [8]	Regression	Logistic regression, Proportional hazards model, Support vector regression, Random forest, Particle filter, Relevance vector machine, Extreme learning machine, Neural networks	

and business environment. The involvement of human lives in areas of defence, space exploration and almost all sectors likewise, manufacturing and automobile has proven its importance and has set a new benchmark to the safety standards. The increased attention towards ageing machinery in the past five decades and the need to assess the service life with the help of condition monitoring has gained utmost importance. The significant change in the performance observed for any working system needs to be sought. Such observable change in performance from its normal operating standards is defined as the useful life of the system. Various well-known efficient approaches in finding the useful life can be found cited in the literature. The model based approach and the data driven approach are the two methods to estimate RUL [2]. Markov chain model, hidden Markov model, filtering based models such as Kalman filter and regression models have also been highlighted under the data driven prognostics approaches. Table 10.1 provides a list of few advanced techniques, practiced as a tool in modern engineering industry.

The above well-known approaches are classified on two-fold basis. These techniques help in obtaining accurate results using much lesser time, thus adding to computational benefits. It is well recognized that constructing precise classifiers for classification problems requires large amount of labeled data and such labeled s are often difficult to obtain. The subsequent section below lists few research works in context to the data driven approach to RUL estimation.

10.2.2   Data Driven Approach to RUL Finding in Industry

Prognostics and structural health management [9] has been one of the most common tasks in the estimation of remaining useful life (RUL). Data repositories were targeted for exploring some of the data driven methods in the initial stages. One such case study was provided using data from the International Conference on Prognostics and Health Management (2008) challenge problem, which was meant for RUL estimation. Algorithms used for the estimation were centralized data processing, decentralize data processing and hierarchical data pre-processing. Additionally, methods like wavelets denoise and similarity search were some other data processing techniques. Centralized data processing method used the principal component analysis (PCA) based correlation matrix in the estimation of RUL. The decentralized processing makes use of the individual sensor measurement; each considered as one feature, for the RUL estimation. Clustering approach has been adopted in case of hierarchical data pre-processing. The linear combination of these clusters resulted in the final RUL estimation. The PCA algorithm has been the basis of the entire process. All the above-mentioned RUL estimation methods depend heavily on the similarity search algorithm. A comprehensive review [10] on the available historical data and statistical models were proposed for the estimation of the RUL. The availability of the asset information were classified for a directly observed state processes and in the absence of such data. Brief taxonomy of statistical data driven approaches are narrated in the purview of future needs. The two types of data namely, the event based and condition monitored data was used. Further, Bayesian updating and expectation maximization algorithm presented the novel approach in developing the data driven [11] degradation model. Exponential degradation approach for modeling the degradation process and Bayesian process to update the stochastic parameters was observed during point estimation of RUL. A practical case study for global positioning system receiver was conducted in order to achieve RUL estimation in which mean squared error (MSE) metric was the measure of effective accuracy. The use of fusion algorithm [12] that contains the collaborative characteristics of Bayesian updating and ECM algorithm [13] was identified for the RUL estimation of a real time sensor data of a single system without a prior knowledge. Exponential degradation model and error fluctuations have been used to support the modeling. The stochastic parameters of the exponential degradation model have been assumed to be normally distributed. The prime objective of the prognostics was the computation of the failure time until the degradation signal reached the set threshold. The extended Kalman filter or the Kalman filter algorithm for the RUL [14] estimation of lithium ion battery was another evidence in the selection of empirical degradation model. The extended Kalman filter algorithm was used for prediction using historical data and mean absolute error (MAE) index was the metric for the evaluation of the proposed approach in terms of battery capacity trend prediction. Figure 10.4 schematically explains the idea of RUL i.e., the point until state of failure.

A review work on prognostic health management (PHM) focussing on the data driven [15] approach was presented for different engineering applications. A workflow of PHM system was established and three aspects of maintenance were proposed namely, fault diagnostics, prognostics and the condition-based maintenance. The commonly used time-domain features were presented and fast Fourier transform as a means of feature extraction in frequency domain was described. Three stochastic processes were categorised as a means of modeling for data driven prognostics namely, the Weiner, Gamma and the inverse Gaussian process. Finally, the RUL of the gear tooth for a rotating machinery was predicted by modeling the degradation signal and calculating the failure threshold.

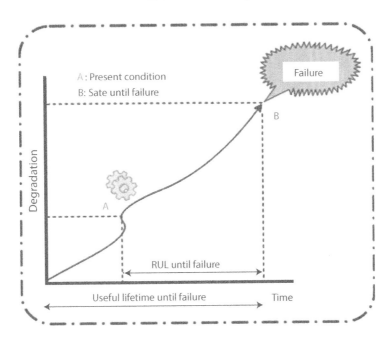

Figure 10.4 Schematic of RUL prediction.

Tool condition monitoring by means of data-driven [16] framework was another application in estimating RUL. The analysis encompasses pre-processing with a proposed adaptive Bayesian change point detection for programmed data arrangement, time window process, feature extraction, feature selection and a multi-layer neural network, thus, formulating the machine learning algorithm. The feature extraction process in both time and frequency domain has been explained. Feature selection process includes Pearson's correlation coefficient and PCA. Root mean squared error (RMSE) and R-sq score have been used for assessing the performance. A nonlinear data driven [8] prognostics model was proposed to overcome the industrial challenges for a milling CNC tools' life estimation. The proposed study made use of wavelet packet transform and extreme learning machine for tool wear condition monitoring. Wavelet packet transform assisted in feature selection stage whereas extreme learning machine made use of the extracted features for nonlinear regression in a high dimensional feature space for mapping, in order to build the prognostic model.

Comparison between three data driven [17] prognostics techniques namely relevance vector machine, neural network and Gaussian process regression was seen to be proposed for a sufficient test data. Relevance vector machine and Gaussian process regression along with prognostics also helped in providing uncertainty estimates. The former enables to detect the underlying trends in the noisy data whereas the later yields the variance around the mean prediction. The disadvantage of all of these methods is about the low signal to noise ratio present in the data along with a small number of training data set. Innumerable research works in the automotive domain for PHM of commercial and passenger vehicles was carried out for different applications such as, batteries, bearings, automobile tyre and automobile engines. The RUL [18] of commercial and passenger vehicle was evaluated using the mathematical model of wear for a given mileage. Data was retrieved from the onboard sensors of the vehicles and simulink model based results were generated that proposed a finite visualization of the outcome for prognostics. The surge in the use of neural network laid the foundation of many significant findings. Apparent idea of different prognostic methods [19] namely, physics based, data-driven and the hybrid approach along with their advantages and disadvantages were proposed in one of the condition monitoring based work. The data-driven approaches are further divided into two categories: the artificial intelligence approach that includes the application of neural network and fuzzy logic while another category is the statistical approach which uses the gamma process (favored generally for sensored data), the hidden Markov model (mostly used for state estimation) and regression-based model, such as Gaussian process regression, relevance vector machine, and least square regression. Initial difficulties in using neural networks were identified under the network model definition i.e., the number of nodes and layers that needs to be defined. Second issue was finding optimal parameters i.e., weights and biases. Performance of the model was seen to deteriorate under non-optimal parameters. Finally, uncertainty in data i.e., noise in the data and the associated bias in training the model. Defining the covariance function, the scale parameters to the covariance function and the uncertainty in the number of data was another major setback of using Gaussian process regression.

In the process of RUL estimation, fundamental progress in health indicator (HI) extraction has emerged. Simulation data of Lithium-ion battery and turbofan engine degradation from NASA repository have been used for the estimation of RUL [20] for an offline and online data driven method. Offline phase locates variables containing information regarding degradation behaviour using unsupervised learning and in online phase k-nearest neighbour classifier has been used to trace the most similar offline HI to the online HI. Finally, Bayesian filter was applied to estimate the degradation state. PCA and instance learning using turbofan engine data was performed to find RUL [21]. Training and testing were the two approaches used during the analysis. Training process incorporates the PCA for reducing dimensions and weighted Euclidean distance for estimating the HI while testing phase uses instance learning. Development of a prognostics approach for RUL [22] estimation of Lithium-ion battery was seen by unifying the two types of HI's. To trace the non-linear patterns of the battery degradation, a data driven monotonic echo state network algorithm was developed. Both direct (based on the battery capacity) and indirect (based on the time interval of identical discharging voltage difference) data were used for RUL estimation.

Finally, with the use of HI, efficient model parameter estimation for stochastic decision making and its accuracy need to be found. One such parameter estimation was seen in the works using electric vehicles [23] lithium ion battery degradation data for a data-driven RUL prediction method boosted by the identified mechanism degradation model. Additionally, the Frisch scheme for bias compensating recursive least squares algorithm was developed to identify the model parameters. Generated data and limited measurement data have been used in order to train the support vector regression model. Root mean squared error (RMSE) has been used as the performance indicator for model prediction. On-line data driven [24] dynamic RUL prediction of lithium-ion battery based on support vector regression was proposed for battery health monitoring. Authors have found the demerits of model based approach in prognostics as it requires prior knowledge and information about model parameters. Online dynamic learning kernel algorithm was implemented for battery RUL estimation. A two-stage data driven [25] modeling was carried out in order to predict the health status of a degraded bearing for a rotating machinery. Mahalanobis distance was used in estimating the degradation point in the bearing. For the estimation of RUL, enhanced Kalman filter and expectation- maximization algorithm was used. The model parameters were estimated using expectation maximization algorithm and Bayesian updating method. The appropriateness and effectiveness of the work was tested using Gebraeels's model and Si's model. RUL was predicted for turbofan engine data [26] by combining the time window and extreme learning algorithm. Extreme learning machine which helps in tracking the state of change from normal trend on the basis of change point was used to model the relation between time series data and RUL. The need for RUL is addressed in the subsequent section where an elaborative discussion is provided in context to industrial-IoT systems.

10.2.3   Philosophy of Industrial-IoT Systems and its Advantages in Different Domain

The following section relates to the IoT-philosophy [27], applications and advantages in different engineering domains. The link between smart objects and living being by IoT has added innovative dimensions. Owing to its wide applicability in various domains an exponential upsurge in the interconnected devices is expected to hit 34 billion by the end of this decade [28]. Aiding to the communications, this value-added technology is a boon to the industrial experts and consumers, thus growing the inherent quality of services to retain the prolonged life. The applications [29] are IoT smart cities, IoT health care, IoT smart homes, IoT platform, the industrial-IoT and energy-IoT. The above applications use network of sensors to accumulate the data on a communicating device for computing, apart from the components to perform the desired operations. Secured interlink between the two operating devices can ease the data transfer other than providing safe communication within the networks. Evidences reflect the use of near field communication and radio frequency identification for short range low power communication protocols. Frequently used wireless fidelity and Bluetooth communication are some of the most popular medium range services in the industrial-IoT system for building personal area networks. The network developed thereby offers the privilege of special networking protocols for interoperability of communicating devices to the IoT environment. The present work shown in Figure 10.5 outlines the detailed structure of IoT platform with the use of three communicating layers, namely, the hardware, the midlevel a.k.a., IoT platform and the application level.

The hardware level indicates the user for the automobile component which needs to be monitored by retrieving the data to the application level for further processing over the IoT platform. The processed data is then modeled to quantify the useful life displaying it to the user's dashboard. Connecting embedded electronics to exchange data without human intervention and its practice in the industry has been defined as one of the aspects of industrial-IoT. It is to be kept in mind that the agility of I4.0 and the innovations has

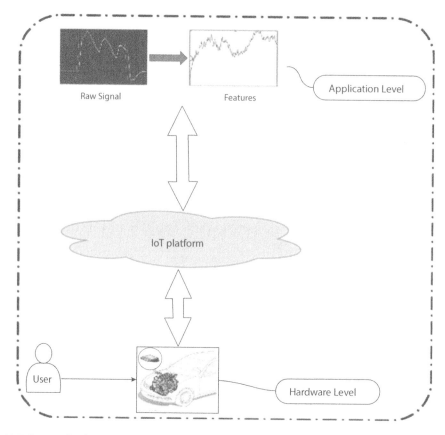

Figure 10.5 Layers of industrial-IoT platform showing the hardware level to the application level.

permitted the use of IoT into the mainstream. In contrary to better decision-making capabilities, it is also ensured that IoT will have a radical effect on waste management. The concept of smart cities with improved traffic management thereby helps in informing the users about the less congested routes over the cellular services is an example of improved decision making. The use of autonomous vehicles in roads will further ease the things with this intelligent management of traffic. Above all, IoT healthcare will be the most supervised issue by the government to help critical patients with improved diagnostics. IoT platform is a multi-layer technology in addition to an essential component of a large ecosystem that connects all components within the system of connected devices. The connectivity of the hardware to the cloud by using robust connectivity options with improved data processing powers enhances the efficiency. Core aim of IoT platform is to function as a mediator between the application and hardware layers. Performing data collection from the devices and transferring them over various protocols and network thus helps in remote device configuration and control. Connecting critical machines and sensors in mega/giga factories involves higher investment like important industries such as manufacturing, healthcare, and industrial control. The platform of IoT basically relies on the built-in infrastructure of industrial-IoT for any further application. The use of intelligent cyber-physical systems to interpret and analyze the critical data from components and making decisions without human intervention is one of the major breakthroughs. The use of automated manual transmission in vehicles is one of the early innovations in the car industry. Monitoring sick person using heart rate signals to the use of robots in hazardous industrial sites are amongst the few applications of industrial IoT systems. Of the few domains where industrial-IoT is gaining use are IoT in parking, energy efficient buildings by adjusting the window panes to retain the room heat for additional comfort. In remote areas, electric pole surveillance is adopted that becomes an added advantage in reducing the hectic travel. IoT in crop management and agriculture is also found to be remarkable.

Structural health monitoring (SHM), has facilitated the prognosis of forthcoming hazard and assessment of the remaining life span [30] of a structure. Under the existing challenge in tracking the data from any location, pre-processing the data is core of structural health monitoring. Thrust in information technology has provided the possibility to track data anytime from anywhere. Sensor data is used for the detection of size and damage of the structure. Implementation was done on raspberry-pi module which then exported the data over internet for remote use. The insistence for SHM has also expanded because of the rise in the necessity to assure the safe health of the structures. It has thereby concurrently affected the human lives associated to it. The ongoing challenging task in the health assessment of structures is to cope-up with the upcoming rise in the advancement and growth of structures. The age of IoT has new encounters in the community of structural engineering as a trade-off to achieve low cost benefits with gifted solutions. This is widely associated to the improvement of the IoT based systems which administers a promising solution for fast, precise and cheaper SHM systems. Again, the combination of IoT with SHM and cloud computing has empowered global facilities. The extensive use of global services enhances powerful data processing beyond traditional systems in health monitoring. Such use of smart monitoring motivates much easier collection of SHM data on a cloud platform thus making way for exhaustive SHM platform along with IoT. In the process of implementation, the proposed SHM enabled IoT make use of tons of sensors and expensive hardware for a much better pre-processing. Authors have tried to classify the damage detection of structures under two areas i.e., local-based and global-based damage detection. The former aids in screening of structures while the later detects vibrations within the system. In account to detect the safe or unsafe health of the structure, methodology of cross correlation has been executed. The method compares the similarity relationship between input and the retrieved signal. The methodology described the benefits in terms of computational processing capabilities, which has been best directed using the mathematical model. From the above contributions by the researchers few advantages regarding industrial-IoT can be pointed out:

- Predictive maintenance
- Rapid informed decisions
- Remote access to real time operational data
- Improved safety.

The increasing use of electronics in complex engineering systems for enhanced control in the areas of manufacturing, automobiles and infrastructure led to the increasing research in the area of intelligent maintenance. The observable shift from the initial value of the changing parameter to the point of threshold is defined as the RUL of a component. The measure of the shift is the probable measure of degradation in the system besides improving the operational reliability. This progress of degradation can be prevented with advanced analytics and modeling.

10.3 Methodology and Results

The two major steps involved in prognostics are: (i) processing of the data in finding the health indicator, and (ii) prediction of RUL using degradation modeling. Estimation of health is the initial step towards quantifying the degradation in the system or the degree of performance which can be expressed in the form of a major indicator that will be used for degradation modeling. The cumulative damage or shift in the system health is actually represented by the health indicator. The next step is the degradation modeling using the health indicator to estimate the progression on the basis of the state and actual operating conditions. The present era of industrial-IoT helps by offering the underlying scheme of work in a network, without human intervention. A data driven approach to modeling is established. The prediction step, evaluates the failure using regression approach by assimilating the physics of modeling with familiarity of future operating conditions and up-to-date estimates of health indicator. Figure 10.6 interprets the sequence of steps in data driven RUL computation.

The computation is basically a three-step approach:

    a. Data preparation
    b. Model fitting, and
    c. Prediction.

The data preparation is one of the major steps in the data driven RUL estimation, as the amount and the quality of data both determines the accuracy in the results obtained. The raw sensor data is collected during experimentation using a highly calibrated lab setup with sensors and data loggers. The collected data consists of noise. The real time data is attenuated to higher harmonics which can largely hamper the dynamic system. The noisy data needs to be taken care in order to extract the much-needed information regarding the system in the present study. In addition, the features from the raw the signal is extracted. These features are basically of three different types: time domain, time-frequency, and the frequency domain approach. The selection amongst the three such approaches is completely based on the expertise and knowledge regarding the domain. The raw features extracted are then passed through filtering approach to obtain the smoothened features that can help in characterizing the trend [31] of a particular feature. The significant amount of data from the smoothened feature set is used for calculating the appropriate health indicator. It is known that no single health indicator can stand sensitive to components failure mode [22], therefore computing a health indicator becomes a must for further analysis.

Of the total time devoted in computation of RUL of a system, the data pre-processing consumes almost two-third of the time. Observing the patterns in a raw signal and

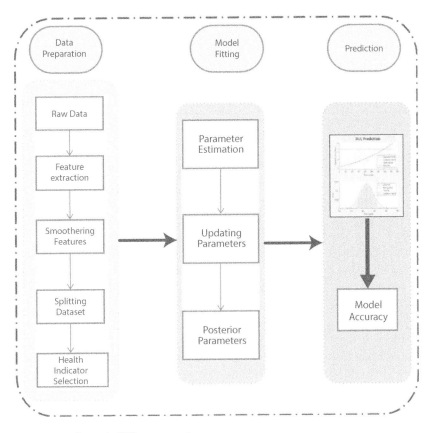

Figure 10.6 Sequence of steps in RUL computation.

identifying it correctly is a major task of prognostics. One such challenge faced by the industry experts is in selecting the appropriate IoT signal for carrying out predictive maintenance of a system. Failure mode effect and criticality analysis (FMECA) need to be carried out for any such industrial system under maintenance. The knowledge of system behavior is critical prior to the failure mode analysis. The present work considers one such application of predictive maintenance in an automobile industry. The component under observation is a motor which helps in automated manual transmission of a vehicle. The motivation around the study is to reduce the maintenance schedule downtime using an industrial-IoT platform. Current (*I*) as an IoT signal was finalized after experimentation in a laboratory setup, by observing the dissimilar patterns for the different sensor data collected. The redundant signals are then omitted prior to prognostic analysis. The intrinsic property of a system can only be known if sufficient knowledge of physics is involved. Proposed approach overcomes the limitations of such knowledge with the application of data driven [5] approach. For a limited class of systems, the application of data driven maintenance model seems to be more meaningful. Summary of the type of data and the RUL estimation approaches can be found in Table 10.2 provided below. The proposed tabular data for three different classes of models will help a user from prognostics community to make decision during experimentation to

Table 10.2 Three data-driven modeling techniques for finding RUL.

Similarity model	Survival model	Degenerate model
• Uses historical data • Compares trend of test data from similar system	• Uses lifetime data • Probability distribution of component failures are use	• Uses known threshold • Infers past behavior to predict future

collect the type of data that motivates in the computation of RUL. The same idea was used to carry out in the present study while conducting the experimentation. The subsequent section describes the model fitting approach in the RUL estimation.

Exponential degradation model [13] is used to fit the industrial IoT signal (see Figure 10.7) thus obtained in the form of health indicator.

The upward increasing trend in the signal gives a clear indication to a progressive failure of the motor. Fitting such nonlinear data into the model is the challenge towards model fitting. Few assumptions along with some conclusive approach are carried out for further modeling. Error is defined to be a continuous time stochastic parameter to compensate the complexity in the data. Prior estimation of parameters is a must for modeling. The use of estimation theory is in mapping the measured data using an empirically developed model to the estimated state/parameters. Bayesian updating criterion is used for updating the model parameters as soon as new data is encountered. For an unobserved variable, '*state*' provides an idea of the system dynamics. Objective function provides the accuracy to the estimator. The true value thus obtained is used to generate the observed data which fulfils the purpose of prediction. Finally, prognosis is carried out with the estimation of the model parameters. The RUL is then calculated using such estimated model parameters. The approximated value of the RUL for the stochastic process always has some inherent

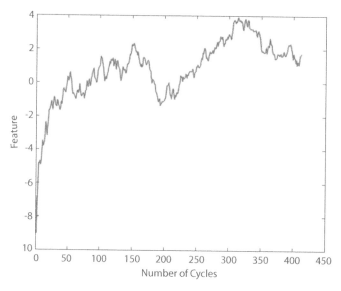

Figure 10.7 Plot of smoothened feature health indicator.

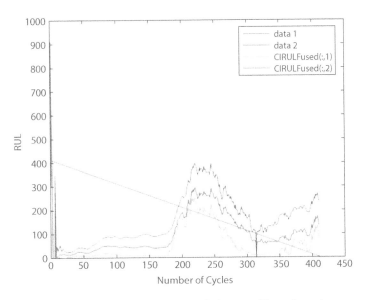

Figure 10.8 Plot of estimated RUL with true RUL along with their confidence bounds.

Table 10.3 Prognostic accuracy results.

Tests	Percentage
error_PR	0.6741
error_MSE	7.1352

uncertainty. The uncertainty in RUL value is the region of confidence for the estimated RUL (see below Figure 10.8).

The developed model needs to be sufficiently accurate while estimating the RUL. Subsequently, two broadly known measures of accuracy have been favored: the mean squared error (*error_MSE*) and the prognostic accuracy (*error_PR*) to quantify the results obtained (see Table 10.3). The MSE is an extensively used performance metric, while the PR is the well-known Pearson's coefficient. PR determines the closeness to the true value in determining the accuracy of the RUL. The higher the value of PR i.e., closer to unity, the better is the result.

10.4   Conclusion

The concept of Industry 4.0 has led to some challenging results in the predictive maintenance technique. With the advent of industrial-IoT and the changing standards in the quality and quantity of data from different technological background, it provided a breakthrough in the use of information processing for estimating the state of the health of the system. The use of prognostic analytics and machine learning to pre-process the information from the data and thereby triggering a useful signal to the user needs an unbiased RUL estimation which was the intended viewpoint of the present study.

Present study depicts the use of sensor data for life estimation of a motor under actual loading conditions. The use of feature-based signal processing technique is recommended for the particular dataset. For a dynamic model the use of parameter estimation followed by modeling and updating of parameters is an attempt towards reducing the uncertainty in the proposed approach that increases the efficiency in the test results. Results may vary, as seen in the initial part of the data prediction, which may be due to the large noise in the data. The later part of the data is seen to be well fitted within the bounds which explain the accuracy in results of the model that can be embedded to a controller of the vehicle. Prior parameter selection, estimation of noise, model fitting, ranging towards the most difficult ones unlike, selection of threshold or a health indicator are few of the challenges that needs continuous review to serve the purpose of health monitoring. The selection of appropriate IoT signal (I) thus assists in proper estimation of health.

RUL results obtained from the study therefore helps in making a robust benchmark indicator for industry in maintenance decision making in addition to implementing IoT standards. A much-appreciated organizational change, new management approaches with stakeholders for implementing predictive maintenance techniques with advance information technologies will provide a breakthrough to the major obstacle faced in the industry in the implementation stages.

References

1. Parpala, R.C. and Iacob, R., Application of IoT concept on predictive maintenance of industrial equipment. *MATEC Web of Conferences*, vol. 121, pp. 1–8, 2017, https://doi.org/10.1051/matecconf/201712102008.

2. Banerjee, A., Gupta, S.K., Datta, D., Chap-4, in: *Remaining Useful Life as a Cognitive Tool in the Domain of Manufacturing, Emotion and Information processing: A practicle Approach*, 1st ed, Springer, Cham., 2020, https://doi.org/10.1007/978-3-030-48849-9_11.

3. Jiang, Z., Feng, X., Feng, X., Li, L., A Study of SVDD-based Algorithm to the Fault Diagnosis of Mechanical Equipment System. *Phys. Procedia*, 33, 1068–1073, 2012, https://doi.org/10.1016/j.phpro.2012.05.175.

4. Wei, L. and Keogh, E., Semi-supervised time series classification. *Proceedings of the ACM SIGKDD International Conference on Knowledge Discovery and Data Mining*, 2006, pp. 748–753, 2006, https://doi.org/10.1145/1150402.1150498.

5. Kramti, S.E. and Ali, J.B., Particle Filter Based Approach for Wind Turbine High-Speed Shaft Bearing Health Prognosis, *International Conference on Signal, Control and Communication (SCC)*, Hammamet, Tunisia, pp. 46–50, 2019.

6. An, D., Choi, J.H., Kim, N.H., Prognostics 101: A tutorial for particle filter-based prognostics algorithm using Matlab. *Reliab. Eng. Syst. Safe.*, 115, 161–169, 2013, https://doi.org/10.1016/j.ress.2013.02.019.

7. An, D., Choi, J.H., Kim, N.H., Prediction of remaining useful life under different conditions using accelerated life testing data. *J. Mech. Sci. Technol.*, 32, 6, 2497–2507, 2018, https://doi.org/10.1007/s12206-018-0507-z.

8. Laddada, S., Benkedjouh, T., Si-Chaib, M.O.S., Drai, R., A data-driven prognostic approach based on wavelet transform and extreme learning machine. *2017 5th International Conference on Electrical Engineering - Boumerdes, ICEE-B 2017*, 2017-Janua, pp. 1–4, 2017, https://doi.org/10.1109/ICEE-B.2017.8192142.

9. Nguyen, H.D., A data-driven framework for remaining useful life estimation. *Vietnam J. Sci. Technol.*, 55, 5, 557, 2017, https://doi.org/10.15625/2525-2518/55/5/8582.

10. Si, X.S., Wang, W., Hu, C.H., Zhou, D.H., Remaining useful life estimation—A review on the statistical data driven approaches. *Eur. J. Oper. Res.*, 213, 1, 1–14, 2011, https://doi.org/10.1016/j.ejor.2010.11.018.

11. Fan, Z., Liu, G., Si, X., Zhang, Q., Zhang, Q., Degradation data-driven approach for remaining useful life estimation. *J. Syst. Eng. Electron.*, 24, 1, 173–182, 2013, https://doi.org/10.1109/JSEE.2013.00022.

12. Yu, Y., Hu, C., Si, X., Zhang, J., Degradation Data-Driven Remaining Useful Life Estimation in the Absence of Prior Degradation Knowledge. *J. Control Sci. Eng.*, 2017, 1–11, 2017, https://doi.org/10.1155/2017/4375690.

13. Gebraeel, N.Z., Lawley, M.A., Li, R., Ryan, J.K., Residual-life distributions from component degradation signals: A Bayesian approach. *IIE Trans. (Institute of Industrial Engineers)*, 37, 6, 543–557, 2005, https://doi.org/10.1080/07408170590929018.

14. Lei, Y., Remaining useful life prediction, in: *Intelligent Fault Diagnosis and Remaining Useful Life Prediction of Rotating Machinery*, pp. 281–358, 2017, https://doi.org/10.1016/b978-0-12-811534-3.00006-8.

15. Tsui, K.L., Chen, N., Zhou, Q., Hai, Y., Wang, W., Prognostics and health management: A review on data driven approaches. *Math. Prob. Eng.*, 2015, 1–17, 2015, https://doi.org/10.1155/2015/793161.

16. Zhang, C., Hong, G.S., Xu, H., Tan, K.C., Zhou, J.H., Chan, H.L., Li, H., A data-driven prognostics framework for tool remaining useful life estimation in tool condition monitoring. *IEEE International Conference on Emerging Technologies and Factory Automation, ETFA*, pp. 1–8, 2017, https://doi.org/10.1109/ETFA.2017.8247659.

17. Goebel, K., Saha, B., Saxena, A., A comparison of three data-driven techniques for prognostics. 1–13, 2008.

18. Kalmakov, V.A., Andreev, A.A., Martyanov, A.S., Remaining Vehicles Useful Lifetime Estimation Based on Operation Conditions Measurement. *Procedia Eng.*, 206, 1716–1721, 2017, https://doi.org/10.1016/j.proeng.2017.10.703.

19. An, D., Kim, N.H., Choi, J.H., Options for prognostics methods: A review of data-driven and physics-based prognostics. *PHM 2013—Proceedings of the Annual Conference of the Prognostics and Health Management Society 2013*, pp. 642–655, 2013.

20. Mosallam, A., Medjaher, K., Zerhouni, N., Data-driven prognostic method based on Bayesian approaches for direct remaining useful life prediction. *J. Intell. Manuf.*, 27, 5, 1037–1048, 2016, https://doi.org/10.1007/s10845-014-0933-4.

21. Yongxiang, L., Jianming, S., Gong, W., Xiaodong, L., A data-driven prognostics approach for RUL based on principle component and instance learning. *2016 IEEE International Conference on Prognostics and Health Management, ICPHM 2016*, 2016, https://doi.org/10.1109/ICPHM.2016.7542815.

22. Liu, D., Xie, W., Liao, H., Peng, Y., An integrated probabilistic approach to lithium-ion battery remaining useful life estimation. *IEEE Trans. Instrum. Meas.*, 64, 3, 660–670, 2015, https://doi.org/10.1109/TIM.2014.2348613.

23. Peng, J., Wu, M., Gao, D., Zhang, X., Cheng, Y., Zheng, Z., Huang, Z., A Data-driven RUL Prediction Method Enhanced by Identified Degradation Model for Lithium-ion Battery of EVs. *2019 IEEE Energy Conversion Congress and Exposition, ECCE 2019*, pp. 2946–2952, 2019, https://doi.org/10.1109/ECCE.2019.8912614.

24. Zhou, J., Liu, D., Peng, Y., Peng, X., Dynamic battery remaining useful life estimation: An on-line data-driven approach. *2012 IEEE I2MTC—International Instrumentation and*

Measurement Technology Conference, Proceedings, pp. 2196–2199, 2012, https://doi.org/10.1109/ I2MTC.2012.6229280.

25. Wang, Y., Peng, Y., Zi, Y., Jin, X., Tsui, K., *A Two-stage Data-driven Based Prognostic Approach for Bearing Degradation Problem. 3203*(c), 1–9, 2016, https://doi.org/10.1109/TII.2016.2535368.

26. Zheng, C., Liu, W., Chen, B., Gao, D., Cheng, Y., Yang, Y., Peng, J., A Data-driven Approach for Remaining Useful Life Prediction of Aircraft Engines. *IEEE Conference on Intelligent Transportation Systems, Proceedings, ITSC,* 2018-Novem, pp. 184–189, 2018, https://doi.org/ 10.1109/ITSC.2018.8569915.

27. Kalmeshwar, M., K.S., A.P.D.N.P., Internet Of Things: Architecture, Issues and Applications. *Int. J. Eng. Res. Appl.*, 07, 06, 85–88, 2017, https://doi.org/10.9790/9622-0706048588.

28. Perwej, Y., Haq, K., Parwej, F., M.M., The Internet of Things (IoT) and its Application Domains. *Int. J. Comput. Appl.*, 182, 49, 36–49, 2019, https://doi.org/10.5120/ijca2019918763.

29. Alani, A. and Rao, K.P., IoT Based Smart Healthcare System. *2018 International Conference on Advances in Computing, Communications and Informatics (ICACCI)*, 05, 01, pp. 1214–1221, 2018.

30. Abdelgawad, A. and Yelamarthi, K., Internet of things (IoT) platform for structure health monitoring. *Wireless Commun. Mobile Comput.*, 2017, 1–10, 2017, https://doi.org/ 10.1155/2017/6560797.

31. An, D., Choi, J.H., Kim, N.H., Identification of correlated damage parameters under noise and bias using bayesian inference. *Proceedings of the Annual Conference of the Prognostics and Health Management Society 2011*, PHM 2011, pp. 300–309, 2014.

## 11

IoT and Its Role in Performance Enhancement in Business Organizations

Seema Sahai[1]*, Richa Goel[1], **Parul Bajaj**[2] and Gurinder Singh[1]

[1]*Amity International Business School, NOIDA, Uttar Pradesh, India*
[2]*Aligarh Muslim University, Aligarh, Uttar Pradesh, India*

Abstract

Nowadays, technology is helping the company enterprise to allow further harvests at low cost and produce targeted performance. However, in order to cut costs and improve efficiency, automation accelerates market ability by leveraging autonomous system systems to substitute human activity through Robot technology. In order to recognize developments in the structure of jobs, efficiency and employment require gaining perspectives into the interrelationship between technologies with Artificial Intelligence, Big Data and the Web. This chapter will first discuss about the concept of IoT and its usages and it will concentrate on how the organization renders itself capable of lowering expenses and evaluating improvements in the job and expertise or abilities of workers using technology. It will also focus on how technology impacts the performance of the employee and help to pursue their creative goal into new work/life balance technology environment.

Keywords: IoT, employee performance, productivity, work environment, employment

11.1 Introduction

IoT is a way to empower the interlinking and fuse of the corporal world what's more, the web. It addresses the example of future frameworks of organizations, and leads the third surge of the IT business agitate [1]. The arrangement and execution of new sorts of frameworks have been the central asked about subjects subsequently the start of this era. For this case, the National Science Foundation (NSF) of the USA had started two research ventures concerning the Internet: one is Global Environment for System Innovations (GENI) and the other is Future Internet Design (FIND). Being a frameworks organization test condition, the drive of GENI is to progress the designing and organizations without Web limits, to boost investigators to recommend progressive thoughts and strategies for the upcoming Internet [2]. FIND is a whole deal venture under the Networking Innovation and Systems (NETS) investigation program of NSF. FIND booster fabricates a spic and traverse sort out start because of the blueprint of drafts keeping the true objective to fulfill the rations for the approaching 15-year time period. The Internet of Things primary thought was proposed

---

Corresponding author: ssahai@amity.edu

Monika Mangla, Suneeta Satpathy, Bhagirathi Nayak and Sachi Nandan Mohanty (eds.) Integration of Cloud Computing with Internet of Things: Foundations, Analytics, and Applications, (183–196) © 2021 Scrivener Publishing LLC

by MIT Auto-ID Labs toward the finish of which started from the necessity of coordination. ITU Internet demonstrated that we are heading towards one in which arranged and organized gadgets are inescapable. Far along from wearies to toothbrushes will be in communication run, proclaiming the beginning of another time, one in which the present Web (of information and individuals) offers route to tomorrow's Web of Things. The "idea of Things" in IoT has been summed up to conventional protests at show, and the interconnection innovation is likewise stretched out to all organizing innovations, including RFID (Radio Frequency Identification).

IoT systems allow users to get profounder computerization, examination and incorporation into a program. They are increasing the coverage and precision of these zones. Internet of things makes use of current and emerging technologies like sensing, networking and robotics.

IoT is taking advantage of recent technological developments, declining hardware prices and new approaches to engineering. The new and advanced components bring essential improvements in most of the product distribution covering all aspects from political to economic.

There are certain advantages of IoT in business as well as at a personal level:

Technology optimization: Costumer experience is enhanced by the same technology and data with certain enhancement with better use of equipment. Technology cracks a critical ecosphere of purposeful and ground information.

Enhanced client engagement: IoT transforms into a richer and more effective public engagement.

Improvement in gathering of data: Conventional gathering of data is suffering from constraints and limitations.

Reduced Waste: IoT clearly indicates areas for development. Existing research provide us with shallow understanding nonetheless Internet of Things delivers factual evidence, which makes it more efficient in administration of power.

11.1.1 Scientific Issues in IoT

Hurdle 1. Data interchange between heterogeneous large-scale network components.

The fundamental new features associated with the broad use of IoT are access to enormous heterogeneous frameworks and immense data exchange between them. From one perspective, IoT comprehends the interconnection and framework converging by using Internet, media transmission frameworks and other framework stages, and gives information sharing and helpful organization [3]. In any close-knit locale, however, IoT has a clear critical complex self-control. With an ultimate objective to execute a particular arrange errand, distinctive framework segments in each area district self-deal with capably, comprehend the interconnection and interoperability, as needs be to upgrade the framework advantage proficiency by using the information in the nearby self-control territory. In this respect, IoT will face up to a crucial issue: how do we agree on a reasonable compromise between a wide variety of extraordinary components of IoT and complexity, and the need for extraordinarily qualified data sharing. The main goal is therefore to figure out the incredibly successful interconnection between wide-scale, heterogeneous components.

Hurdle 2. Executive incorporation and modification of information unclear.

The IoT seriously supports the real world with numerous intelligent instruments and a substantial degree of weakness simply defines the observed data. The vulnerability needs

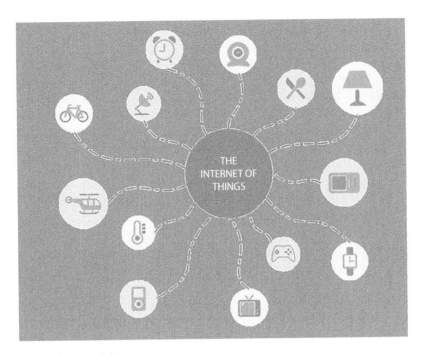

Figure 11.1 Data exchange in IoT.

certain portrayal after some in arrange handling methods, for example, rearrangement, purification and combination, and the outcome will be further provided to administrations. The mixture of information between organization components will exchange data between components in compliance with the criteria of anytime and anywhere with a particular goal to consider very effective knowledge sharing, leading to an additional core question of research: how to analyze, revamp and use the identified data and address connectivity problems.

Hurdle 3. Adaptation of operation to the complex machine climate.

In IoT dynamics, we need to treat intuitive material objects' vulnerabilities, unpredictable interplay of state and runtime constraints that satisfy the shifting demands. We should also consider new planning to develop speculation and support advances, to give the IoT programming framework a clear and dynamic understanding of IoT administrations' environmental versatility [4].

In addition, we need to assemble developing devices, motivate the responsive IoT software to evolve itself, understand the population between three times the demands of our clients, data area and physical space, and allow IoT programming to flexibly adapt to the complex world to provide expert management expertise. They will also tackle modern technology that illustrates IoT environment-friendly speculations, instruments and techniques. The measure of self-adjustment is thus elevated as the third major scientific question, namely, the modification of benefits in the complex system situation (Figure 11.1).

11.1.2   IoT in Organizations

Adoption and successful usage of IT in the performance of the enterprise will tend to improve the efficiency of the company. In order to improve efficiency in the organization, the presence of technology itself is not just accountable for the Age of IT. In an organization, workers need to change their abilities to more analytical and computational abilities. In order to grow the company concept, Artificial Intelligence, Machine & Internet help the organization to create the programs and set the skills. In a modern and diverse environment, technology has become the pillar of industry. Artificial intelligence, IoT and Robotics are making workers perform easier and quicker, while requiring improvements in their abilities or methods of performing their job in an enterprise [9]. Technology often helps to generate interest and describe the way to function and interact inside the enterprise. Figure 11.2 displays the advantages that IOT provides to SCM.

The ground shaking latest technologies cannot be unveiled immediately. Technology implementation involved some more technical growth, and it took decades to see the effect of technology on function and organization. The organization has to consider the usage of financial, physical and other capitals to grow a company.

Advances in technology are moving jobs towards automation and make it easier for an individual or worker to automate their expertise and achieve certain things that they considered difficult and impractical. Technology advances may make it easier to do something on a wide scale instead of performing them on a limited scale. To put forth fresh and different ideas in a way that evolves for the future. The collision of innovation and technology towards industrial revolution, business organization knows how they can transform their business through adopting the technology. Figure 11.3 shows use of IOT in various fields.

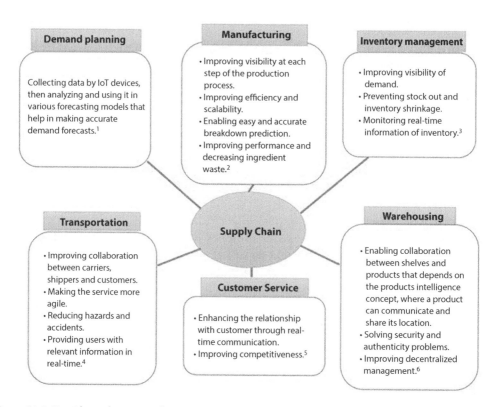

Figure 11.2 Providing advantages of IoT in roles such as SCM [5–8].

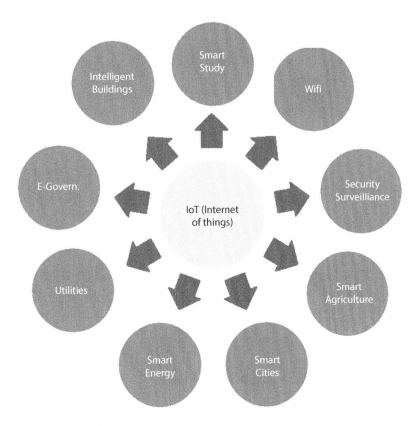

Figure 11.3 IoT and service adaption.

11.1.3   Technology and Business

Technology has a positive effect on market organization because it has made it more convenient. This plays a significant part in recognizing the desires of the client, changing the market method by predicting dynamic resources, maximizing the usage of records for function,
adapting to shifts in the climate. It gives ample benefit that is not linked to the replacement
of labor. Thus elicitation of the output from the technology demands alteration in the entire
process instead of changes in single process. It is required that business organization must
focus on competitor strategy to ensure no troublemaking goes into existing business model.

Technology has emerged with enormous growth in business organization. It helps business organization to reform the existing business process and work. Technology has fig-
ured out the new business process and way to do the business in more effective manner. It
has given an effortless way to perform work more efficiently, faster and more conveniently.
According to Ford, Automation will reduce cost, can perform work faster than human, but
human needs to learn about the skills too to learn about the automation [10].

11.1.4   Rewards of Technology in Business

- It is helping the business organization to be more competitive into market
- It helps to increasing the productivity.
- It collaborates with people.

- It helps to store the data and information accessible anytime by anyone in the organization.
- It enables new learning and skill set for the growth and sustainability.
- It saves time, money and cost.
- It helps business to identify the problem and take the corrective action on time.
- It required privacy concern as data or information can be manipulated by hacker. Therefore, organization needs to be relying on expert.
- It completes the task faster and on time.
- It helps to create the potential of the employee.

A few of the successes in IOT have been shown in Figure 11.4.

11.1.5　Shortcomings of Technology in Business

- It replaces the personal or face-to-face interaction.
- The lack of information about how to use technology can ruin the work.
- The training, software and maintenance become quite expensive for the organization.
- It enables the unemployment and differentiates wage payment.
- It develops a sense of insecurity about losing the job.

11.1.6　Effect of IoT on Work and Organization

Technology has modified the operating environment and state of the enterprise. It has continually modified the working climate and is creating a modern way of doing a

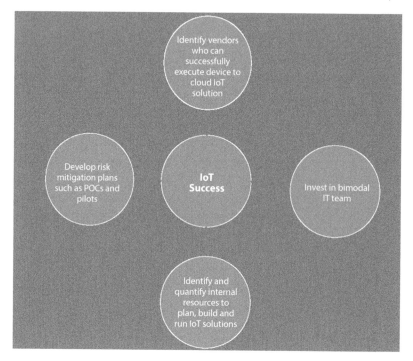

Figure 11.4 Success of IoT.

function or a career. The job cycle has been enhanced by streamlining the waste method and rising.

Speed and Efficiency
Technology also helped to improve the efficiency of workers in all forms of companies, i.e. production and networking. The pace of employment, output and speed outbreak has risen with the company taking place. Today, thanks to technology, work taken an hour ago can be done in only a few minutes. Timely contact and knowledge is essential to carry out the work.

Working Together Made Easier
Technology also made it easy for workers to communicate via electronic networking platforms such as video conferencing. Workers can communicate with other workers at various sites, and the Google Drive app can be utilized for employees to connect their job on the other network. As a consequence, organizations are utilizing work place monitoring techniques to evaluate the output of workers in certain defined fields. In the marketing organization, Technology like AI messaging tools is used to follow up the whole conversation that happened between the employee and customer.

Technology is Changing Office Culture
To create a strong organization culture to tempt in importunity technology has enabled the stereotype change in work place by introducing open office space with video game and beer on tap. Besides opening office space, organization is also offering freelancer and telecommuter jobs by giving them an opportunity to work from home.

No More Need to Live Where You Work
Employees who are searching for a job in every business that choose to operate remotely will easily use the internet as freelancers. It's a tool that makes it easy to connect and function together as a team when you're operating remotely. This allows both the career applicant to work remotely and the recruit boss to get creative from everywhere.

Technology has also led to societal change and to the progress of legal, cultural and organizational growth. Technology has three main infrastructures: the Agricultural Age, the Manufacturing Era and the Digital Period. In the agricultural period, citizens relied on natural resources. In the industrial age, citizens concentrated on the utilization of agricultural capital by the purchase of raw material from other business organization, producing maximum output with minimum utilization of the physical utilization at low cost. The aim of the company was to improve productivity by generating an extra device. In the modern age, people depend on digital content and skills to create the product and service and to describe the business cycle. This age is focused on the architecture of information and communication technology. This age allows a corporate enterprise to operate quickly by cooperation, and coordinating the task. This era is also called the development of computer and IT & communication Era [11].

To support the business and organizational activities, organization linking technology and work process (such as enterprise resource planning, customer relationship management, supply chain management, material requirement planning, human resource management, and enterprise-form automation systems) together.

Figure 11.5–11.7 show some of the advantages and benefits of IOT.

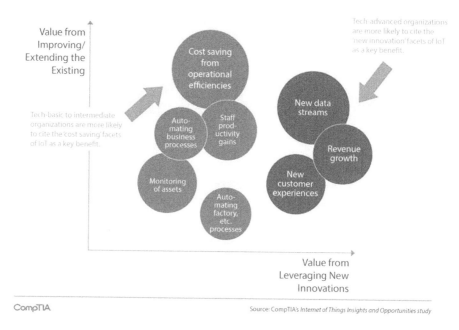

Figure 11.5 IoT benefits. Source: CompTIA's Internet of Things insights and Opportunities study.

Figure 11.6 Disadvantages of IoT. Source: Cyfuture.com.

11.2   Technology and Productivity

Technology has been very important to the company in today's market setting. Technology may help to maximize profitability, performance, enhance coordination and communicate with the workforce. However, it is important to choose the right technology, so let us understand how a company can choose the right technology for its business;

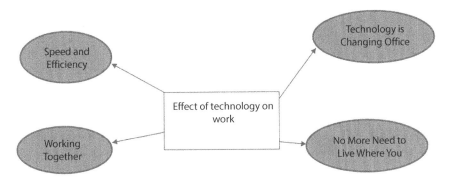

Figure 11.7 Technology change benefits to work.

1. Identify the need of the company.
2. Enabling technology required proper training and education.
3. Communication improvement through communication
4. Improving efficiency through technology.

Productivity tends to raise the quality of life of workers. It doesn't matter how long you're employed and how much money you're utilizing in your company. Technology also allows it possible to improve efficiency and to establish new manufacturing techniques. Productivity is calculated by GDP, by product or output [12].

However, without increasing the output the technology progress can be increased. For example, if Wikipedia and free GPS mapping app are replaced by paper encyclopedia and stand along GPS, the people will be more advantageous even if there is any change in output.

According to the U.S. policy departments that the U.S. is generating IT as well as the IT manufacturing industry, but that efficiency has declined in the past 10 years. Figures have shown that the weak focus on IT output and retail utilization continues to lower efficiency. In order to maximize efficiency, the company will concentrate on technological growth and progression.

Connect Remote Workforce:
Thanks to the need for temporary or home-based job options, the company enterprise is creating virtual offices to operate collaboratively, growing the expense of setting up and managing broad workspaces. It is important for brilliant workers to have access to all details, data and to be able to receive job status from their workers without meeting them. E.g., make a WhatsApp community of the employee helping to employers to communication, delegating task and ask the status of work.

Enable the Communal Tools:
There are several tools that are connecting the employee so that collectively they can work for the organization. For instance, Google's cloud-based application is used in most of organizations to share the data and integrate the employees.

Get Organized:
ERP is a system where information about leaves, salary, work, purchasing and so on are stored in a software by any employee of any department and this could be accessed by any employer without physically meeting with the employee.

Be Reachable:
Technology makes it easier for a company to link its workers by offering up-to-date cell apps and service services as though any missed call might result in a loss of revenue. Therefore, to ensure the continuity of the Integrity Business, technologies such as voice mail, soft phones and job caller ID are used.

Know Productivity Challenge:
Companies are concentrating more to make an evaluation of their productivity challenges so that they can evolve changes in technology tools causing the slowdown of the productivity of an employee. Figure 11.8 shows how IOT helps in increasing productivity.

Explore Virtualization:
Virtualization helps the organization to increase business sacking. It extends the lifespan of older computer desktops. It also helps to reduce the cost of the business.

Trust the Experts:
Organization must distribute the work among the employees and must not be rigid to having an expertise for those tasks which can't be automated.

This is recommended that the study of the level of work and the organisation's efficiency should not be focused on cloud infrastructure, because it relies on the evaluation of the technical climate. This will require a transition in the traditional company environment and the staff. The company has to be more effective when discovering how to utilize technologies instead of relying on the development and creation of the new innovations.

Figure 11.8 IoT and increase in Productivity.

11.3   Technology and Future of Human Work

Today, companies want to utilize time clock technologies to assess the performance of workers. In the past, workers worked on the basis of what they were making, but in the technological age, employment was split into different roles. It is mentioned that, from a learning viewpoint, technology allows the workforce to be more agile and growth-oriented. It is discussed about the global labor market, gig economy and how technology is defining more possibilities in career and job opportunities making employees free from repetitive and monotonous task [13]. Technology is neither good nor bad, no matter how we use it. There are several reasons why organizations are investing on work technology:

- Inhuman task can be possibly performed by technology. For example, in manufacturing companies where work has to be performed in an extremely hot place, it is impossible for the employee to perform task. Therefore, technology helps employee to perform that difficult or impossible task.
- Technology helps to reduce the cost of employing the staff which covers almost 50% of operating cost. It demands lowering the price and investing more on new technology that would create the new task for the employee or increase the job opportunity.
- It enables to increase the potential of the employee, helps them to communicate with others, inbuilt the new skills and new process to perform the task.

In fact, Technology impacts on work as it depends on how much organization is spending to adopt the new technology to increase the potential of an employee. There are two visions considered by an organization:

The fanciful future: imagine if there is no way of recruitment, layoff, retirement, no organization hierarchy and employee not having any sense of stability and employment but employees are collaborating and are productive in technological era as they acquired the required skills.

The stipendiary future: imagine that employees are categorized as skilled and unskilled employees and skilled employees are enjoying the job as they are in demand because they have knowledge about the new technology. This world will be referred to as never ending competition era.

Out of technology, both the fanciful future and the stipendial future have been developed. In a fanciful age, companies are utilizing technology to offer instruction and build employees' ability on how to utilize technology. Yet we do see a stipendial outlook with a pay deficit and work separation and unemployment. Companies are spending further in emerging technologies to make their employees potential.

Technology is also creating the future where employees are not worried about to getting jobs for their survival as the country is also replacing the employee work. To change the world of work technology is more fanciful.

11.4   Technology and Employment

It has described developments in the technology in workers' abilities, jobs and earnings. Several experiments have been undertaken which have indicated that there would not be an improvement in jobs if modern technology is implemented in the organization. Although some have suggested that the reforms would have an effect on jobs. However, the longevity of the work over a long period of time depends on the skills needed [14]. In fact, productivity and technology changes lead to growth in the earning. There are several factors are responsible to affects the level of employment due to change in the technology:

1. The time at what organisation products and services are demanding into market.
2. The survival of new product in domestic and international market.
3. Redefining the process to produce maximum output with low labor requirement.
4. Effect of technology change on wages.

According to the Cambridge Research, Inc., 1986, technology tends to develop the skills needed by the employee that will be ideal for work. Normally, each employee will have two forms of qualifications; technical skills and job skills. Basic abilities are learned by the school program rather than by the organisation. This includes knowledge of the area of research, logic, problem solving, and communication. Job-related skills are one which is acquired by the organisation needed to perform task. Basic skills help to workers to understand what they need to perform in their present and future employment. However, some study stated that job related skills can be acquired through on the job training.

Technology also has an effect on workers' earnings. According to the U.S. study, the shift of technologies has slowly eroded the amount of earnings and controlled the restructuring of the distribution of earnings. This reflects on shifts in the rates of incomes and describes the connection between income inequality and technical transition.

It is found that in the service sectors income distribution is based on the occupational structure. Thus there could be no arising changes in the distribution of income and no change in earning level as the spending structure has been changed in household people.

It has been suggested that modern technologies will render workers redundant. It could be fictional, however. In the 19th century, British cloth employees were worried that they might be displaced when modern technologies became part of the company. Thanks to the assumption of emerging technology for jobs, employees demolished the machines and flamed out John Kay's home, created the "Flying Shuttle."

It is believed that the introduction of modern technologies will eliminate jobs, but would also generate considerable wealth. However, it is also reported that the weekly working hours will be shortened by 15 h and the reporting condition will also improve. The latest technologies would also build a competitive sector, raise competition, increase profits and generate new job prospects, and result in a new service opportunity.

It is almost likely that any profession will be annihilated. It is clear that automation decreases the role of the employee, but it allows the employee flexibility to worry about developing their abilities and getting them more informed in order to become more attractive. It is going to happen in the future of technical transition relies largely on corporate planning and plan as a technology will also create some new job opportunity and these would be depend more on thinking, specialized and analytical skills.

According to the Bureau of Labour statistics, employment opportunity will be increased by 30% by 2020 in the computer field. In the human race we will enter into fourth industrial revolution i.e. 4.0 Industry is defining the collaborating the physical, digital and biological components.

11.5   Conclusion

Methods, jobs and development departments are used to handle the function of workers. A company utilizes technology not just to do business and fulfill the functions of working with remote workers but by embracing a modern definition of freelancer and contract worker. If the company employs robotics, the need for a new professional worker will be present, as the system will allow.

Technology has divided the work in the task and all tasks can't be performed by the technology alone. Therefore, there is an employment for those employees who possess different skills set and acquired the training to perform the specific task. Technology has brought new fanciful future to the business organization where they can set their vision to complete into the competitive environment. Besides reducing the job opportunity or task of the employees it also helps in upgrading their skills. The demand and supply of the products and services will be increased by using automated technology. It has good or bad impact on business organization. The impact of new technology on business is completely dependent on how to use it and the investment on the technology.

References

1. Lee, S.K., Bae, M., Kim, H., Future of IoT networks: A survey. *Appl. Sci. (Switzerland)*, 7, 10, 1072, 2017, https://doi.org/10.3390/app7101072.
2. Elliott, C., GENI—Global Environment for Network Innovations, *Conference: LCN 2008, The 33rd IEEE Conference on Local Computer Networks, The Conference on Leading Edge and Practical Computer Networking, Hyatt Regency Montreal, Montreal, Quebec, Canada, 14–17 October 2008, Proceedings,* October 2008, https://doi.org/10.1109/lcn.2008.4664143.
3. Anderson, N., Potočnik, K., Zhou, J., Innovation and Creativity in Organizations: A State-of-the-Science Review, Prospective Commentary, and Guiding Framework. *J. Manage.*, 40, 1297–1333, 2014, https://doi.org/10.1177/0149206314527128.
4. Angelini, L., Internet of Tangible Things (IoTT): Challenges and Opportunities for Tangible Interaction with IoT. *Informatics*, 5, 1, 1–34, 2018, https://doi.org/10.3390/informatics5010007.
5. Yerpude, S. and Singhal, T.K., Impact of Internet of Things (IoT) Data on Demand Forecasting. *Indian J. Sci. Technol.*, 10, 1–5, 2017.
6. Anita, R., and Bodla Abhinav. Internet of Things (IoT)—Its Impact on Manufacturing Process. *IJETSR*, 4, 889–95, 2017.
7. Qin, W., Zhong, R.Y., Dai, H., Zhuang, Z.L., An assessment model for RFID impacts on prevention and visibility of inventory inaccuracy presence. *Adv. Eng. Inform.*, 34, 70–79, 2017.
8. Schoen, Q., Lauras, M., Truptil, S., Fontanili, F., Anquetil, A.-G., Towards a Hyperconnected Transportation Management System: Application to Blood Logistics, *International Federation for Information Processing*. Cham: Springer International Publishing, pp. 3–12, 2016.

9. Verma, N., Sangwan, S., Sangwan, S., Parsad, D., IoT Security Challenges and Counters Measures. *IJRTE*, 8, 3, 32277–3878, 2019. https://doi.org/10.35940/ijrte.C4212.098319.

10. Acemoglu, D. and Restrepo, P., *Artificial Intelligence, Automation and Work*, 2018, Retrieved from http://www.nber.org/papers/w24196.

11. Cardullo, M.W. and Ansal, H., Impact of technology on employment. *Innovation in Technology Management—The Key to Global Leadership, PICMET 1997: Portland International Conference on Management and Technology*, 45–48, 1997, https://doi.org/10.1109/PICMET.1997.653243.

12. Ghorbanzad, Y. and Beig, M., The impact of information technology on productivity using structural equations technique in Iran Behnoush Company. *Manag. Sci. Lett.*, 2, 4, 1195–1202, 2012, https://doi.org/10.5267/j.msl.2012.03.001.

13. Agbozo, E., Masih, A., Turygina, V.F., Ranuk, S.V., The Effects of Technology on Employment (What The Future Holds). *Социологические Науки Agbozo*, (April), 32–34, 2016.

14. Matuzeviciute, K., Butkus, M., Karaliute, A., Do technological innovations affect unemployment? Some empirical evidence from European countries. *Economies*, 5, 4, 1–19, 2017, https://doi.org/10.3390/economies5040048.

## 12

An Analysis of Cloud Computing Based on Internet of Things

Farhana Ajaz[1], Mohd Naseem[1]*, Ghulfam Ahamad[1], Sparsh Sharma[2] and Ehtesham Abbasi[3,4]

[1]Department of Computer Sciences, Baba Ghulam Shah Badshah University, Rajouri, India
[2]Department of Computer Engineering, Baba Ghulam Shah Badshah University, Rajouri, India
[3]Green Economics Institute, Reading, UK
[4]Kellogg College University of Oxford, Oxfordshire, UK

Abstract

In today's world, the communication system architecture requires human-to-human or human-to-device type of interactions. Currently, lots of researchers are working in the area of Internet of Things (IoT), which promises machine-to-machine interaction. Internet is evolving continuously. IoT is a future interpretation of internet that recognizes machine-to-machine learning. There is an enormous hike in the volume of devices, such as PCs, mobile phones, PDAs, etc, that are associated with each other through Internet and Intranet. Although, the IoT is extremely powerful, it still has various challenges that cloud computing will overcome. The mix of cloud with IoT will bring revolution in this era of computing. In this paper we will discuss evolution of IoT, Architecture of IoT (Generic, Three layers and Six layers), challenges in IoT, and Technology used in IoT. We will also elaborate emergence of cloud computing, models of deployment for cloud computing, service models, cloud computing characteristics, Applications of cloud computing. Further, we will explain Cloud IoT, the necessity for fusion of cloud computing and the IoT. Finally, we will give details of currently existing Cloud-based IoT Architecture and we will also explain the probable Cloud-based IoT applications.

Keywords: IoT, architecture, SAAS, PAAS, IAAS, cloud computing

12.1 Introduction

In 1999, the terminology IoT was coined by Kevin Ashton, with the fast growing technology, IoT came into picture. It is flourishing as a world-wide network where each and every single thing is linked to networks [1]. IoT generally involves objects and internet connectivity. It is the collection of interrelated devices which are connected in such a way that they should be able to collaborate with one other without the need of human mediation. IoT gives us the idea of connecting physical objects to internet that are of use in everyday life. Here, all objects in whole world are embedded with small devices such as sensors, smart objects, RFID, etc. that are connected to a network they can communicate with one another

*Corresponding author: mohdnaseemshakeel@gmail.com

Monika Mangla, Suneeta Satpathy, Bhagirathi Nayak and Sachi Nandan Mohanty (eds.) Integration of Cloud Computing with Internet of Things: Foundations, Analytics, and Applications, (197–210) © 2021 Scrivener Publishing LLC

with the help of some specific protocols. The major goal of IoT is to give easy access to the devices like cameras, actuators, vehicles, etc. It infiltrates the benefits of wireless sensors and the actuator networks (WSAN) and computing domains.

In recent years, large growth in smart devices, wireless technologies and sensors have been observed. So, it's assumed that trillions of smart devices will get connected to network in the upcoming years. In order to hold such huge number of devices, some flexible, scalable and secure network architectures are required. Here, heterogeneous devices interact with one another without any intervention of humans, thus improving the living standard of people. IoT often works neck to neck with cloud. For processing huge amount of data and serving large number of persons cloud computing is essential. IoT allows objects to think, hear and see to make own decisions and to share information. In IoT, "things" can be classified into three categories: people, machine, and information. In Figure 12.1, we have make one of the possible scenarios of IoT-based applications like smart health, smart house, and smart security, etc. [2].

With the exponential growth of IoT, a need of combining IoT with cloud computing is also felt by researchers. Cloud computing, held as long time goal about computing, can

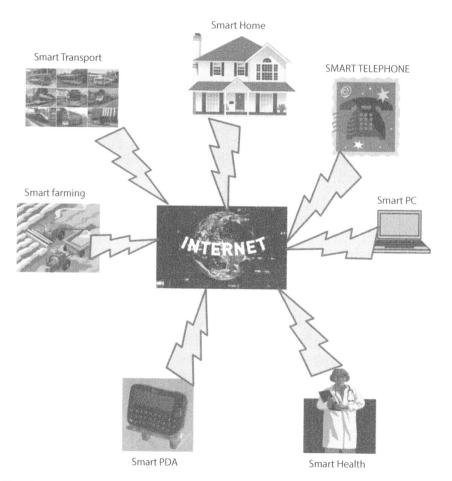

Figure 12.1 Generic scenario of IoT.

possibly change an enormous part of IT businesses, making the software considerably appealing and reshaping the manner in which IT hardware is purchased and designed. Developers with creative thoughts for modern Internet services do not anymore require the huge capital expenses in hardware for deployment of their services or human cost for operating it. They do not need to get worried about over provisioning for service which doesn't meet their expectations. Hence, squandering expensive resources, or under provisioning the ones that become fiercely popular, and thus loosing possible customers and income. In addition, organizations with enormous group tasks could get results as fast as their programs could scale up, for example utilizing 100 servers for an hour costs almost same as utilizing one server for 100 hours. This flexibility of resources, without paying a premium for enormous scope, is exceptional throughout its entire history of IT existence.

The rest of the paper is organized as follows: In Section 12.1 we describe the architecture of IoT. Section 12.2 discuss the challenges of IoT whereas Section 12.3 explains the technologies used in IoT. In Section 12.4, we have analyzed the emergence of cloud computing in details. Cloud computing characteristics are explained in Section 12.5 whereas, Applications of cloud computing in Section 12.6. Cloud IoT has been explained in Section 12.7 whereas necessity for fusing IoT and cloud in Section 12.8. Cloud-based IoT Architecture in Section 12.9 and lastly we have discussed Applications of cloud IoT in Section 12.10. Finally, conclusion is drawn in Section 12.11.

12.1.1   Generic Architecture

The IoT connects trillions of heterogeneous devices by using Internet, so there is a basic requirement for an adaptable layered architecture. Due to the regular increase in the architecture layers, the researchers have not yet proposed a converged reference model. The nonexistence for a single consensus on architecture of the IoT, is accepted globally. Various architectures are presented by different researchers and these are presented in the following section:

a. The generic architecture of IoT

As explain in Figure 12.2, it comprises the following three layers:

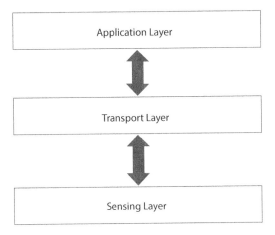

Figure 12.2 Layer defied by generic architecture of IoT.

- Application layer: Application layer makes use of the intelligent computing technologies in order to squeeze out some useful information. It also acts as an interface between user and IoT [2].
- Transport layer: This layer performs the networks operations.
- Sensing layer: It is accountable for assembling information from different sources.

b. Three-layer architecture of IoT

This architecture is put forward by IoT working committee in China. As explained in Figure 12.3, it can classify architecture into three following layers:

- Application and Service Layer: The first layer is accountable for recognizing the objects [3]. There are some identification equipment's that are used for identification of objects. This layer is actually the combination of social division and industry demand [4]. The features of objects are recognized by this identifying equipment's and convert them to digital signals.
- Ubiquitous Network Layer: This layer is accountable for transporting the data into information center [4]. The network layer is like the brain of IoT that transfers and processes the data.
- Perception Extension System Layer: It is this layer that has the responsibility for intelligent processing of the information [4]. The perception layer is like the skin of face and the five sense organs whose major function is to recognize the objects and gather the information. It mainly includes GPS, RFID tags and reader writer camera, etc.

c. Six-Layer Architecture

After 2020, beyond 25 billion objects would be connected to internet, which is gigantic number. So, existing internet architecture cannot handle this network. As already discussed in Section 12.1.1 (b), the triple-layer architecture does not express all features of the IoT.

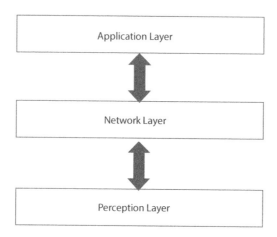

Figure 12.3 Three layer architecture of IoT.

Hence, need for advanced architecture aroused that could address QOS and security issues. Number of multilayer architectures was proposed. Based on the workflow, the three-layer architecture is extended up to six layer architecture that is enumerated in Figure 12.4, explained as follows:

- Coding layer: It is this layer which grants identification to objects that are of our interest. A unique ID is assigned to each and every object thus we can easily identify the objects by their unique IDs.
- Perception layer: 'Device Layer' is another name for perception layer. This layer contains the physical entities and the sensor devices. It gives physical interpretations to each and every object. It's actually the device layer that comprise of several types of sensors like RFID tags, IR sensors or other sensors. This layer acquires all information from sensors, depending upon the sensor's type. This information may be GPS based location, motion, temperature etc. It converts this information into digital signals and passes that digital signal to the network layer. This layer actually perceives the physical properties of the things using various sensors and converts them to digital signals [5].
- Network layer: Another name for this layer is 'transmission layer'. It sends the data from the sensor based nodes to the information processing system. Transmitting medium could be wireless or wired. It receives digital signals with the help of perception layer and transfers that signal to processing system in the middleware through Bluetooth, Wi-Fi, Wi-max, etc.

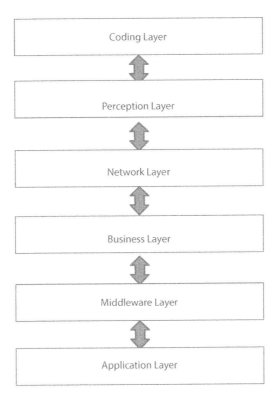

Figure 12.4 Six-layer architecture of IoT.

- Middleware layer: This layer helps in managing the services and it has direct link with the database. Here, the information that is accepted from the sensors is processed. Here, the latest technologies such as cloud computing, ubiquitous computing are used which allows the uninterrupted database accessibility for storing the crucial information. Different smart equipment are used for processing the information and some automated action is taken based on the processed results.
- Application Layer: This layer clearly explains the possible application of IoT in various industries such as smart transport, smart health, smart farming, etc. It is one of the most important layers which is responsible for pushing IoT towards large scale development [5].
- Business Layer: This layer controls the whole system and it behaves like a manager of IoT. This layer is responsible for managing applications, services relevant to IoT, etc. This layer also includes the various business models which are specifically designed for different types of business planning strategies [5].

12.2 Challenges in IoT

In spite of the huge number advantages as well as characteristics of IoT, it still suffers from some shortcomings which should be dealt by researchers in the near future. Some of the challenges are discussed below:

- Device capacity: IoT suffers from a lot of device constraints such as device size, buffer size, available memory size, processing capability, etc.
- Storage: IoT requires huge storage capacity to store its exponentially generating data. However, providing such a huge storage capacity is another big challenge [1].
- Network Capacity: In IoT, devices have to communicate with each other through wireless medium. However, wireless medium itself suffers from a number of constraints such as limited bandwidth, collision of data, hidden terminal and exposed terminal problems, etc.
- Scalability: IoT has millions and billions of connected devices through a wireless network. It is expected that the total number of objects connected to the network would exceed total magnitude of the Internet. Hence, IoT must be scalable so that all applications must work in a robust manner when number of users would be increased exponentially in the network [6].
- Route break: As we have already discussed in the network capacity challenges, IoT devices are connected through wireless medium. Hence, if any device move from its current position or it may become dead due to the complete depletion of device's energy, then route break may occurs. Hence, to start communication once again, source devices have to search the route towards destination devices by transferring the route request packet for route rediscovery process.
- Data Redundancy: In IoT, the receiver node receives information from large number of sensors. Due to this, there is higher probability that some of the

information would be redundant. Hence, transmitting redundant data will waste large portion of bandwidth which will ultimately downgrade the QoS.

- Security: In IoT, one of the biggest challenges is that there is not sufficient security on the objects that are connected to the network. Most of the time, data communicated through IoT devices are extremely important as well as confidential. Hence, security of data must be provided. In IoT, devices are randomly placed in unknown terrain. Hence, in addition to data security, physical security of devices is also necessary due to the theft, weather condition, terrain types, etc. [7].

12.3   Technologies Used in IoT

Some of the useful technologies that are useful in IoT, are explained as follows:

Radio-Frequency Identification (RFID): In IoT, the most useful technologies are RFID. It uses radio waves for transmitting information from electronic bag known as label/RFID Tag which is fixed to the object by reader for uniquely recognizing an object. It has three main parts: RFID Reader, RFID Tag and central computer system. RFID is used for reducing the size, weight, energy utilization of radio. Every object is integrated with radios. RFID has one or more readers and many RFID Tags. RFID allows mapping real world into virtual world. It monitors objects in real time [8]. RFID tag stores the standard information about the objects. These tags are transmitted to central computer system through wireless network. In order to maintain the object transparency, these tags can be shared on the internet [9].

Sensors: To increase the efficiency of IoT, sensors are embedded in the devices. These sensors can be used at any place with any device. Sensors come up with different sizes and shapes. It collects analyses and then responds to the changes, it has collected from outside environment [10]. IoT sensor market is estimated to reach approximately USD 27.7 billion by 2023. The most frequently used types of IoT sensors are as follows:

- *Temperature Sensor:* It is used to check the temperature of the devices. If it is embedded in smart phones, it can check the temperature of the battery.
- *Proximity Sensor:* These sensors are used to monitor and measure the flow of liquids and gases.
- *Pressure Sensor:* It is a device to measure pressure of gases or liquids.
- *Quality Water Sensor:* These sensors check the PH level of water and monitor the ions.
- *IR Sensor:* The mostly used IoT sensors in health are IR sensors. They are used for laparoscopic surgeries.

12.4   Cloud Computing

Cloud Computing is a progressing technology where it can be used as a medium of storage and processing of applications and data. Every authorized user can access the services by using any device [11]. Cloud Computing is the only solution for the resource constrained devices having limited storage and processing capabilities [12]. The processing of data is

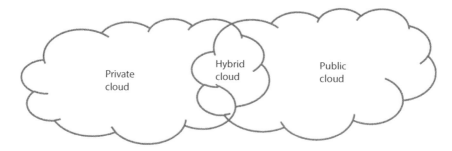

Figure 12.5 Deployment models for cloud computing.

done in the cloud. It provides paradigm which grants all resources that are required for computation like processing, storage facilities from the remote locations, etc. The service providers hold and maintain resources and the clients can access these services from the Internet.

Deployment Models of Cloud Computing

It is commonly categorized into three groups: Public Cloud, Private Cloud and Hybrid Cloud. Using Figure 12.5, each of them is explained as follows:

Public cloud: It is the most dominant deployment model in the cloud computing. Public cloud, as the name reveals, is available to general public for use i.e. open for all types of users. Public cloud is deployed globally and it is also less secure than other types of deployment models. Some of the leading service providers for public clouds are Amazon Web Services (AWS), Microsoft Azure, IBM Cloud and Google Cloud Platform.

Private Cloud: While public cloud offers limited resources and less security, researchers move towards the more resourceful, customized and more secure alternative deployment model in the form of private cloud. This type of deployment model is used by the authorized organization. It is not available for general public and deployed locally. The organization resources can be used only by the authorized users. The private cloud's infrastructure is regulated by a single third party organization. Organization with the prerequisite of maximizing the utilization of resources, security as well as data privacy, private cloud is the only option best suited for such organizations.

Hybrid cloud: It is an amalgam of public and private cloud. It includes the benefits of both. For example, public cloud is cost effective and private cloud is highly secure. Hence, organization, with the prerequisite of getting efficiency, scalability and flexibility at low cost, would prefer hybrid cloud.

12.4.1   Service Models of Cloud Computing

Generally three types of service models are used and these extensively used models are explained using Figure 12.6 in the following section:

Software as a Service (SaaS): Here, only the software or interface is made available to the end users. Clients access various applications, under the category of SaaS, through the network which are released by the cloud consumers. These types of services are generally used by naïve users who can use only services of the software. SaaS is a platform independent service which prerequisite is just a high speed Internet. The end user has no control over

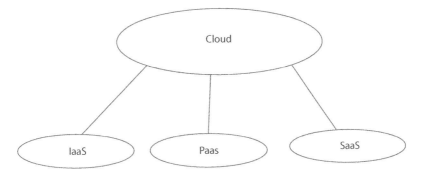

Figure 12.6 Basic service models.

the underlying resources such as storage, operating system, virtual storage, middleware, etc. some of the examples of SaaS are online shopping, Online food delivery, Google Mails, Google Docs, etc. [11].

Platform as a Service (PaaS): Here, the services are provided to the developers to help them in the development of an application. The developers are given access to the users interface in run time environment. Additionally, developers don't have any control on middleware, operating system, data storage, virtual storage, etc. The developing tools, required for developing an application, are provided by cloud vendors. The programming language used is also provided by cloud vendors. In addition to this, all the hardware and software that is used for designing, developing, and deploying the application are provided by the cloud vendors, too. AWS Elastic Beanstalk, Windows Azure, Apache Stratos, etc. are the examples of PaaS [11].

Infrastructure as a Service (IaaS): The cloud vendors provide infrastructure to the client and they can use it as per their needs. They have control over the operating system, middleware, data storage, virtual storage, hardware, etc. It is generally used by administrators. The maintenance and security are provided by cloud vendors. This service model has prime feature of enhancing the flexibility and scalability which is the pre requisite for cloud computing. Virtualization is largely used in IaaS cloud for integrating (decomposing the resources which are in impromptu manner in order to meet the contracting and expanding demands of the cloud consumers.

Some other service models: In addition to service models of cloud computing as already discussed above in Section 12.4.1, there are some other service model already proposed in literature. Some of them are as follows:

- *EaaS:* Its aim is to provide connection to the remote devices.
- *DBaaS:* The main purpose of DBaaS is to provide management of the database.
- *DaaS:* The aim of DaaS is to provide access to all forms of data.
- *SenaaS:* This model manages the remote sensors.

12.5   Cloud Computing Characteristics

IoT applications require the cloud computing technology for storage of its data. Cloud computing has lot of characteristics, some the popular cloud computing characteristics are as follows:

a. *Reliable:* It is one of the important characteristic of the cloud computing. Without reliability, authenticity of data may be questioned. Data may be modified in response to misbehaving devices such as dead node, storage failure, limitation of processing capacity, etc. Hence, reliability is strengthened by modular architecture of clouds. Here, data storage is more secure from accidental damage of servers, other devices and resources.

b. *Secure:* For IoT applications, authentication is one of the challenging issues which catch the attention of researchers. Hence, they come up with new and alternate technology i.e. Cloud computing which offers more security as compare to conventional authentication technologies. One of the deployment models for cloud computing is private cloud which is highly secure. Another deployment model is Public cloud which offers less security as compared to private cloud.

c. *Cost Effective:* Cloud computing is budget friendly because those organizations, which are using it, do not need to buy any resources like hardware or software. The deployment cost is reduced and the cost of maintenance is also cut down as cloud vendors itself maintain software as well as hardware.

d. *Device and the Location Independence:* In IoT, heterogeneous types of devices have to communicate with each other. These devices may be located at different locations. Hence, device and location independence are one of the prerequisite which are most important for IoT applications. Therefore, IoT applications uses the cloud computing technology, using which it can access any device like pc, tablet, and laptop. IoT applications can avail the services of cloud computing anywhere and at any time in the whole world. The only essential requirement is high speed Internet connection.

e. *Maintenance:* It is another concern of IoT application based devices. Maintenance is often costly and time consuming affair. Cloud computing technology offers very low maintenance cost on almost real-time manner. The maintenance services of cloud computing can be availed through cloud vendors on the hire basis.

12.6   Applications of Cloud Computing

Cloud Computing is applicable in various fields like storage purposes, maps, services, etc. Some of the well-known applications of cloud computing are as follows:

- *Storage:* Cloud Computing provides online storage. Any form of data can be stored online without the need for buying any SSD's or hard disks. Any type of data such as audio, video, text, images, etc. can be stored on cloud environment.
- *Maps:* Finding ways using maps is an important function of cloud computing. Google maps is an example of the application of cloud computing.
- *Presentation Software:* Cloud computing possesses presentation software. So, we can get our presentation ready with the enhanced features in cloud computing. We can get our presentations ready without using Microsoft word.

Cloud computing offers other stand-in presentation software which is an alternate of Microsoft word. One of the well-known cloud based presentation software is Slide Rocket.

12.7   Cloud IoT

Cloud IoT has reshaped the entire IoT. Researchers suppose that cloud will remodel the entire IT industry in the future. Cloud computing model allows easy, on demand access of network to the shared resources like servers, storage, services, etc. These resources can be released and provisioned with less efforts of management and interaction of service provider [13]. Today, the research focuses on linking up cloud with the Internet of Things as cloud holds some unique characteristics that are useful for IoT applications. Cloud computing facilitates IoT for utilization of virtual resources that integrates visualization platforms, monitoring of resources, storage devices, analytical tools and delivery of product to the client.

12.8   Necessity for Fusing IoT and Cloud Computing

IoT connects the real word entities with the network that means it connects all the objects (things) to the Internet. But, IoT comes with a snag that it has finite memory, storage and computing capability. This problem comes with the consequential issues like performance, scalability, privacy, etc. Cloud computing on the other hand has boundless computing capability and is able to provide huge memory for storage [14]. It also offers extended service of on demand access to diverse resources such as servers, application services, storage, etc. There are various advantages of mingling IoT and cloud computing that are explained as follows:

- Computational Resources: On-site processing of the data is not possible because of the limited computational capability of IoT devices [13]. Hence, Cloud computing is very useful for remote processing of data using IaaS service model which is already explained in Section 12.6.
- Scalability: IoT has millions and billions of devices connected through a wireless network. In near future, the number of objects that is coupled with the network may exceed the total number of computing devices available on the Internet. To cope with this, researchers can use the services of cloud computing to deal scalability issues as already discussed in Section 12.6.
- Communication: For communication with other objects (Things), IoT has IP enabled based hardware which is expensive. Cloud computing makes use of applications and customized portals, using that communication become easy as compared to IP address-based communication [14].
- Heterogeneity: The things that are associated with the network are of varying nature. Different types of objects (such as computer, sensors, vehicles, door, AC, Refrigerator, etc.) are connected. So, it is very difficult to maintain security, scalability, efficiency, and availability among such types of divergent things [15].

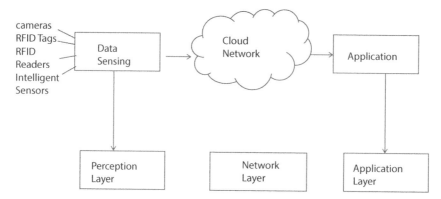

Figure 12.7 Architecture of cloud-based IoT.

12.9 Cloud-Based IoT Architecture

The cloud-based IoT follows three-layer based architecture which are Perception layer, Network layer and Application layer. Using Figure 12.7, working of each layer is explained as follows:

- Perception Layer: This layer has the authority of accumulating information from outside environment and using various sensors and brings the light on various events [16].
- Network Layer: This layer transmits the gathered information to the cloud servers and vice versa.
- Application Layer: This layer supplies the smart services to end users. It provides an easy and user-friendlier interface.

12.10 Applications of Cloud-Based IoT

Cloud-based IoT can be applied in various fields such as smart homes, healthcare, logistics, etc. Some of the applications of cloud computing are explained as follows:

- Smart Homes: The large number of home activities is automated because of Cloud-based IoT. Here, sensors are embedded and cloud computing has facilitated automation in the house hold activities [17]. Example of smart homes applications are energy saver, smart metering, Automatic garage, etc.
- Cloud IoT in Health care: Cloud IoT has accomplished tremendous benefits in healthcare. It can ameliorate the various services of healthcare [18]. Examples of cloud IoT in healthcare include intelligent drug system, pathology, hospital management system, etc. Prabal *et al.* in Ref. [19] presented cloud centric IoT based on the student health care monitoring. It predicts the disease that a student is going through, predicts the level and the severity of disease. The students with waterborne disease were analyzed carefully.

Testing of data is done by K-cross validation. The results are compared with other algorithms like KNN, Decision trees, etc.

- Cloud IoT in Logistics: Nowadays, there is a buzz of logistics service providers because of tremendous growth of online shopping websites. There are number of problems faced by logistics service providers. Hence, this sector also catches the attention of researchers. Researchers have proposed the application of Cloud IoT in logistics which allows smooth movement of goods from producers to consumers and also helps them in tracking of shipments.

- Monitoring Environment: In today's environment, there are number of areas in which, heavy number of sensors are deployed. The main task of these sensor nodes is to gather the information from the environment so as to monitor environmental pollution, quality of water and traffic management, etc. [20, 21].

12.11   Conclusion

In this paper, we have analyzed IoT in detail with its architecture, challenges and its related technologies. We have also discussed cloud computing, service and deployment models of the cloud, its characteristics and applications. In addition to this, we have discussed in detail, the necessity of fusing IoT and cloud computing, cloud IoT architecture and its applications. After complete discussion on this hot topic, we come to the conclusion that there are various challenges in IoT and these challenges cannot be defeated without the assistance of cloud computing. There is a sense of little urgency regarding consideration of merging of cloud and IoT. Researchers need to take into account all the support and services that can be provided by cloud computing to IoT in an inclusive way.

References

1. Hussain, Md I., Internet of Things: Challenges and research opportunities. *CSI Trans. ICT*, 5, 1, 87–95, 2017.
2. Khan, R., Khan, S.U., Zaheer, R., Khan, S., Future internet: the internet of things architecture, possible applications and key challenges, in: *2012 10th International Conference on Frontiers of Information Technology*, IEEE, pp. 257–260, 2012.
3. Wu, M., Lu, T.-J., Ling, F.-Y., Sun, J., Du, H.-Y., Research on the architecture of Internet of Things, in: *2010 3rd International Conference on Advanced Computer Theory and Engineering (ICACTE)*, vol. 5, IEEE, pp. V5–484, 2010.
4. Zhang, M., Sun, F., Cheng, X., Architecture of internet of things and its key technology integration based-on RFID, in: *2012 Fifth International Symposium on Computational Intelligence and Design*, vol. 1, IEEE, pp. 294–297, 2012.
5. Kaiwartya, O., Abdullah, A.H., Cao, Y., Altameem, A., Prasad, M., Lin, C.-T., Liu, X., Internet of vehicles: Motivation, layered architecture, network model, challenges, and future aspects. *IEEE Access*, 4, 5356–5373, 2016.
6. Van Kranenburg, R. and Bassi, A., IoT challenges. *Commun. Mob. Comput.*, 1, 1, 9, 2012.
7. Xu, T., Wendt, J.B., Potkonjak, M., Security of IoT systems: Design challenges and opportunities, in: *2014 IEEE/ACM International Conference on Computer-Aided Design (ICCAD)*, IEEE, pp. 417–423, 2014.

8. Liu, P. and Wang, F., Temporal management of RFID data, in: *Proceedings of the 31st international conference on Very large data bases*, pp. 1128–1139, 2005.

9. Al-Fuqaha, A., Guizani, M., Mohammadi, M., Aledhari, M., Ayyash, M., Internet of things: A survey on enabling technologies, protocols, and applications. *IEEE Commun. Surv. Tutor.*, 17, 4, 2347–2376, 2015.

10. Porkodi, R. and Bhuvaneswari, V., The internet of things (IOT) applications and communication enabling technology standards: An overview, in: *2014 International Conference on Intelligent Computing Applications*, IEEE, pp. 324–329, 2014.

11. **Gibson, J., Rondeau, R., Eveleigh, D., Tan, Q., Benefits and challenges of three cloud computing service models, in: *2012 Fourth International Conference on Computational Aspects of Social Networks (CASoN)*, IEEE, pp. 198–205, 2012.**

12. Dhaliwal, J.K., Naseem, M., Lawaye, A.A., Abbasi, E.H., Fibonacci Series based Virtual Machine Selection for Load Balancing in Cloud Computing. *Int. J. Eng. Technol.*, 7, 3, 12, 1071–1077, 2018.

13. Aazam, M., Khan, I., Alsaffar, A.A., Huh, E.-N., Cloud of Things: Integrating Internet of Things and cloud computing and the issues involved, in: *Proceedings of 2014 11th International Bhurban Conference on Applied Sciences & Technology (IBCAST) Islamabad, Pakistan*, IEEE, pp. 414–419, 2014.

14. Stergiou, C., Psannis, K.E., Kim, B.-G., Gupta, B., Secure integration of IoT and cloud computing. *Future Gener. Comput. Syst.*, 78, 964–975, 2018.

15. Botta, A., De Donato, W., Persico, V., Pescapé, A., Integration of cloud computing and internet of things: a survey. *Future Gener. Comput. Syst.*, 56, 684–700, 2016.

16. **Sharma, S. and Kaul, A., VANETs Cloud: Architecture, Applications, Challenges, and Issues. *Arch. Comput. Methods Eng.*, 1–22, 2020.**

17. Baker, T., Asim, M., Tawfik, H., Aldawsari, B., Buyya, R., An energy-aware service composition algorithm for multiple cloud-based IoT applications. *J. Netw. Comput. Appl.*, 89, 96–108, 2017.

18. Islam, S.M.R., Kwak, D., Kabir, Md H., Hossain, M., Kwak, K.-S., The internet of things for health care: A comprehensive survey. *IEEE Access*, 3, 678–708, 2015.

19. Verma, P. and Sood, S.K., A comprehensive framework for student stress monitoring in fog-cloud IoT environment: m-health perspective. *Med. Biol. Eng. Comput.*, 57, 1, 231–244, 2019.

20. Naseem, M. and Kumar, C., Queue-based multiple path load balancing routing protocol for MANETs. *Int. J. Commun. Syst.*, 30, 6, e3141, 2017.

21. Naseem, M. and Kumar, C., QSLB: queue size based single path load balancing routing protocol for MANETs. *Int. J. Ad Hoc Ubiquitous Comput.*, 24, 1–2, 90–100, 2017.

## 13

Importance of Fog Computing in Emerging Technologies-IoT

Aarti Sahitya

K.J. Somaiya Institute of Engineering and Information Technology, Mumbai, India

Abstract

Emerging technologies like IoT and Big data connect things, people, application, and data through the internet. In terms of capability in handling more than one smart device simultaneously, research-studies show that the number of mobile devices will exceed the number of people i.e. (7.6 billion on earth). Predictions also made by researcher state that 50 billion things will be connected to the internet by 2020. These devices will generate raw data that need to processed more accurately and in real time. So there is need of such platform which handles this task more accurately, and cloud computing paradigm is utilized to handle this type of real time task. Studies have proven that cloud computing fails in giving the performance throughput in terms of bandwidth, latency, data transfer speed, etc. These measures are required by emerging technologies like IoT and Big data to give results accurately in real time. So to gear this there is a layer added between cloud and devices which is nothing but fog or edge computing which handles the massive traffic generated by connected devices in IoT. This study further extends the concepts of utilization of Fog in IoT-based smart enterprise, smart manufacturing factory and smart healthcare systems.

Keywords: IoT, fog, edge, smart, intelligence

13.1 Introduction

As IoT connects things, people, applications and data, to connect these items together, there is a requirement of wide spectrum IoT networking. Right now in the market people are using smart devices like smart phone, smart watch, smart tablet or smart pad, but think about the future when people will be using smart glasses that support augmented reality and various virtual reality interactive services, smart wearable devices such as shoes, belt, necktie, etc. To transfer data from these devices to cloud technology again there is a requirement of power intensive IoT networking [1]. These smart intelligence devices generated are connected with sensors which generate massive amount of raw data in various forms of unstructured, semi-structured and structured data. To process such types of data there is an additional requirement of big data intelligence engines which extract important data from this raw data. Companies like Atmel

Email: aarti.sahitya@somaiya.edu

Monika Mangla, Suneeta Satpathy, Bhagirathi Nayak and Sachi Nandan Mohanty (eds.) Integration of Cloud Computing with Internet of Things: Foundations, Analytics, and Applications, (211–232) © 2021 Scrivener Publishing LLC

Corporation, Android Things, Samsara, Zingbox and Uber are continuously making an effort to provide IoT services. These companies are using technologies like Wireless Sensor Network, Wifi, Bluetooth, Zigbee, Cloud computing technologies to make services possible [2–14].

13.2   IoT Core

Let us understand each core in detail:

1. IoT Architecture
    IoT architecture is comprised of four layers as shown Figure 13.1:

    Bottom layer—Sensor connectivity & Network
    Layer above bottom layer—Gateway and Network
    Layer above Gateway and Network layer—Management Service
    Top Most layer—Application layer.

    Description of each layer is as follows:

    1. Sensor Layer—The sensor layer is made up of sensors and smart devices, where the sensors are used to collect and process real time information from these devices. The sensors use low power and low data rate connectivity. Sensors are grouped together according to the purpose and data type. E.g. in a fire alarm system, heat measuring sensors, temparature measuring sensor, humidity measuring sensor are grouped together to detect smoke. Now the question is if we are saying that sensors are grouped together according to the purpose then how is overall sensor data collected, monitored and networked together, different sensors like environmental sensors, military sensors, body sensors, home sensors, survelliance sensors since they all have their own domain and network connectivity format. Sensors are aggregating data through gateways. Gateways comprise the following things like LAN (Local area network), WLAN (Wireless LAN) Wi-Fi, Bluetooth, Zigbee and 6LowPAN. Sensors that do not require connectivity to a LAN gateway can be directly connected to the Internet through a WAN (Wide Area Network) interface as depict in Figures 13.2 and 13.3 [16, 23, 24].

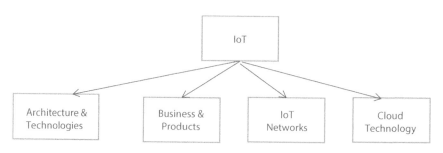

Figure 13.1 Different IoT Cores.

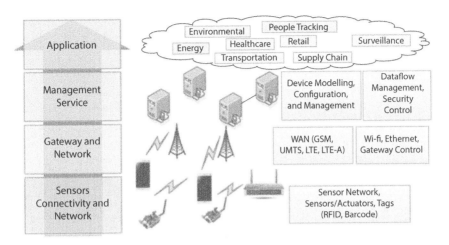

Figure 13.2 IoT architecture.

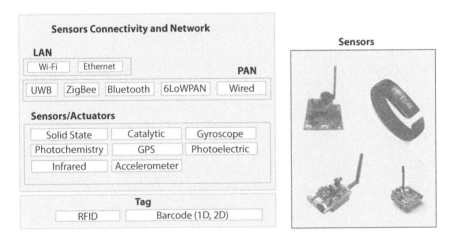

Figure 13.3 Sensor layer architecture.

2. Gateway & Network Layer—This layer collects massive amount of data produced by sensors after collecting from smart intelligence devices. This layer requires a robust and reliable platform to maintain performance and also supports private, public, hybrid network models. This layer's Qos requirements consist of the following properties: low latency & Error probability, high throughput & energy efficiency, high levels of security & scalability. IoT networks need to be scalable to efficiently serve a wide range of services and applications over large scale networks as depict in Figure 13.4.

3. Management Service Layer–This layer is in charge of information analytics, security control, process modeling, device management. Some sensor data require filtering, whereas some data may require immediate delivery and response for e.g. patient medical emergency sensor data as depict in Figure 13.5.

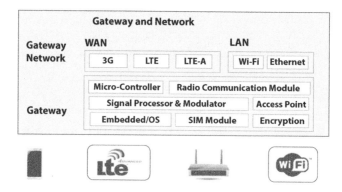

Figure 13.4 Gateway and network layer architecture.

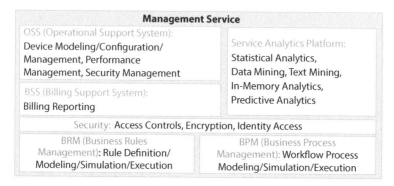

Figure 13.5 Management service layer architecture.

4. Application Layer—Various applications from industry sectors can use IoT for service enhancement. Applications are classified in to business model, type of network they are using, size, availability, heterogeneity, coverage and real-time or non-real time as depict in Figure 13.6.

2. IoT Technologies
   In making IoT networking and services possible, technologies play an important role. Various technologies used in IoT are shown in Table 13.1.

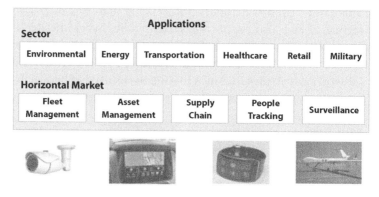

Figure 13.6 Application layer architecture.

Table 13.1 IoT technologies.

Sr. no.	Name of technology	Description
1	Wireless Sensor Network	1. Efficient, low cost, low power devices for use in remote sensing applications, low power integrated circuits and wireless comunications. 2. A large number of intelligent sensors collect raw data and create valuable services by processing, analyzing and spreading data. 3. Challenges are related to limited processing capability and sensor data sharing for multiple device/system coorporation [15].
2	Cloud Computing Support	1. For advanced IoT services, IoT networks may need to collect, analyze and process segments of raw data and turn it in to operational control information. 2. Advanced IoT services will need support of cloud computing. IoT applications will need support from a reliable, fast and agile computing platform. 3. IoT devices can overcome lack of software, firmware, memory storage, hardware, data processing capability through cloud computing [28].
3	Identification Technology	1. IoT devices produce their own contents. Contents are shared by an authorized user. 2. Identification and authentication technologies need to be converged and interoperated at a global scale. 3. Management of unique identities for 'things'. Handling of multiple identifiers for people and locations [6–8].
Hardware Technologies		
1	Sensors	1. In eco system of IoT, IoT hardware platform takes charge of collecting, storing and processing data based on the connection of the Internet [5–7]. 2. Detect events or changes in its near physical environment. Types of sensors are temperature/humidity sensor which detect actual temperature and humidity, pressure sensor which detect pressure with respect to atmospheric pressure. Flow sensor which detect rate of fluid flow. Imaging sensor which detect conversion of variable attenuation of image in to signal. Ultrasonic sensor detect presence of an object by ultrasonic wave [9–11].
2	Actuators	1. Motor that is responsible for controlling or taking action in a system. 2. Electrical actuator converts energy to mechanical torque, mechanical linear actuator converts rotary motion to linear motion. Hydraulic/Pneumatic actuator converts fluidal (liguid/gas) compression to a mechanical motion.

(Continued)

Table 13.1 IoT technologies. (*Continued*)

Sr. no.	Name of technology	Description
3	RFID (Radio Frequency Identification) Antenna coil Chip	1. Transmit pre-embedded 'information' directly to the RFID reader. 2. RFID chip (tag) holds information about a 'thing'. Antenna is used to receive energy from the reader tat is used to operate the RFID device. 3. RFID tag transmits its information back to the reader. 4. Low frequency RFID has a working frequency of 125–134.3 KHZ and a rea range of 10–30 cm, High frequency RFID has a working frequency of 13.56 MHZ, Ultra-high frequency rfid has a working frequency of 860–960 MHZ.
4	Processor and Microcontroller	1. Connect sensor and actuator to the internet. 2. Operates corresponding instructions. 3. Processor and microcontroller consist of technologies like Arduino, Raspberry Pi and Beagle board. 4. Arduino-Open-source microcontroller & hardware which comprises of single board microcontroller and kits for easy sensing and controlling objects. 5. User-specific program can be developed and uploaded using the IDE uses USB connection to an arduino board. 6. Arduino product type-1Arduino Uno R3 (for entry and General purpose) Arduino Yun (IoT)

(*Continued*)

Table 13.1 IoT technologies. (*Continued*)

Sr. no.	Name of technology	Description
		Arduino Lilypad (Wearable) 7. Raspberry pi-developed by raspberry pi foundation in the UK. Developed as a low cost single-board computer to promote basic computer science skills in schools. Supports general computations and basic web serve functions. Hardware specifications required are broadcom Soc, ARM CPU, On-chip GPU, Software required as raspbian os. Product series like mainline raspberry pi 3 model B has a working frequency of 1.2 GHZ ARM cortex cpu based micro computer for general IoT functionality. Subline raspberry Pi zero is smaller in size and rstricted I/O, GPIO capabilities 8. Beagle Board –open-source single-board computer produced by Texas instruments, fully functional basic computer, supports various OS like linux and android, little more expensive than other single-board computers. Key features of this board is that it is very low power consuming up to 2 W, it has programmable real-time unit (PRU) which is used for deterministic latency up to 5 ns per instruction. It is enchanced with 3D graphics Image processing.

IoT Business & Products

1. Mobile device and things become more valuable, for eg the application like changing the color of light according to the brightness of color through switch, to handle these type of application, IoT is one way solution. Just consider the case of North America IoT market and industry, there are 2,888 companies and products had emerged, in addition to $125 billion finding is generated from these companies as shown in figure given below.

2. North America IoT market research studies indicate that there are large number of consumer iof IoT than business domain, as shown in Figure 13.7 below.

3. Three domains of IoT market & Industry as first—Connected apps and process, which have smart consumers and users as well as smart

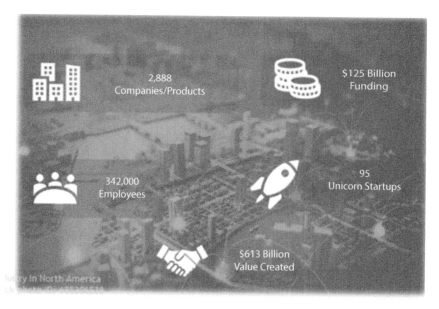

Figure 13.7 North America IoT market & industry.

enterprise inside of its domain, second—Connected intelligence which has smart data and smart cloud technology, talking about big data engines which process raw data collected from sensors, third— Connected and autonomous things. This means that we are having new objects, new things, new entities that are connected to the mainframe infrastructure that are receiving intelligent information and guidance, and they are also operating automatically based upon what they were told to do, where small decisions and immediate things that they need to do are pre-programmed so that they are safe and stably and reliably operated as shown in Figures 13.8–13.13.

IoT Products & Services (IoT Companies)
Iot companies like Atmel Corporation, android things, Samsara, Zingbox and Uber are continuously making an effort to provide flawless IoT services to the market. Description for each company is provided below according to type of products and services they are developing along with their diagrams shown in Figures 13.14 and 13.15.

1. To develop a Iot application one must require a good quality of hardware, so Atmel is one of the companies which manufactures arduino board, radio frequency devices, flash memory, application-specific products, etc. The revenue of company is $3.84 billion by the end of fiscal year 2019.

2. Next thing required to develop a IoT application is a requirement of android-based embedded OS. In the market, Android Things is developing an android OS which supports Raspberry Pi 3, Intel Edison for

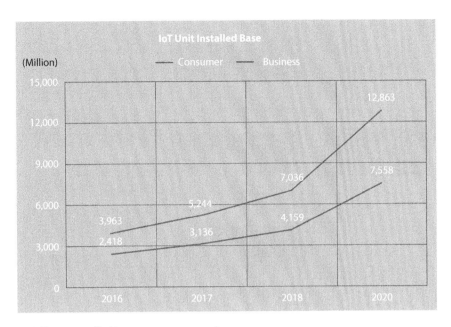

Figure 13.8 IoT unit installed base on consumer unit.

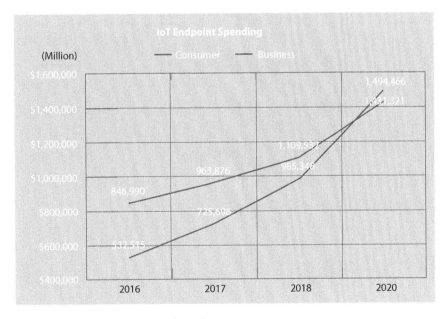

Figure 13.9 IoT endpoint spending on product of IoT.

initial prototyping of Android Thing products. To put IoT application upon android OS, the company has added a feature in the architecture as Thing Support Library where one can place IoT applications.

3. Now once the application is developed using Android Things, the next is requirement is a high quality network, so for that Samsara is connecting hardware and software to the network. The company

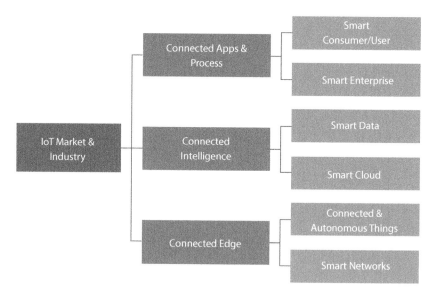

Figure 13.10 IoT market & industry.

Figure 13.11 Connected apps & process of IoT.

Figure 13.12 Connected intelligence.

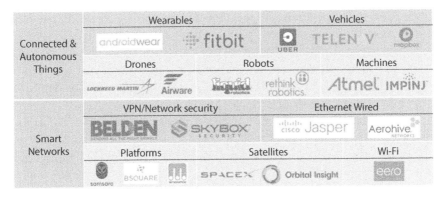

Figure 13.13 Connected edge (connected & autonomous things).

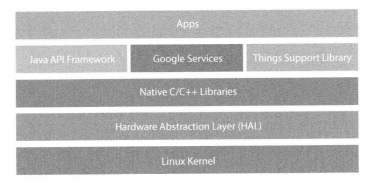

Figure 13.14 Architecture of android things.

IoT Gateway for Vehicles

Wireless
Environmental Monitor

Software Solution
(Driver App, Dashboard)

Figure 13.15 Products manufactured by Samsara company.

was founded in 2015 by Forbes and Fortune as a future leading IoT company in 2015. It provides IoT-integrated platforms such as IoT gateway, camera & Sensor modules and also it provides software for mobile apps and cloud-based dashboard. It also supports under 15 minutes of intuitive installation by adopting plug-and-play technology.

4. After connecting application to networking, next requirement is how to add a security to application, so for that there is one company named Zingbox that develops enterprise-based IoT security solutions. It discovers & protects connected IoT equipment. To provide security to the network, they are using IoT Guardian which is claiming to be the first deep-learning algorithm based industry security solution [19–21].

5. Now we have studied that to develop Iot applications, one has to use products manufactured by different Iot companies. Here we represent which applications of Iot have used products produced by companies like Samsara, Zingbox, etc. Uber is one of them which connects car (things) to a server (internet) and users. Location sensor data of the drivers and passengers mobile device is transmitted to the Uber system. Uber 'back end' cloud system provides analytics for the optimized driver/passenger pair. In 2018, Uber supports services in 84 countries and over 760 cities. Uber owns a 77% share of the ride hailing market in the United States.
6. Iot Economic impact—predictions have been made that Iot has the potential to increase global corporate profits by 21% by the end of 2022. Machine-to-Machine (M2M) connections are increasingly important. Person-to-Person (P2P), Person-to-Machine (P2M) and Machine-to-Person (M2P) still represent the majority of IoT's economic value as shown in Figures 13.16 and 13.17 [6, 7, 25–27].

3. IoT Networking
IoT networking technology comprises of following things shown in figure below. Let us study explanation for each technology along with diagram depicted in Figure 13.18.

1. The very first technology is Wi-Fi which is coming under wireless local area network or wireless personal area network. Wi-Fi is a technology

Segment	Description	Companies/Organizations
Services	BSP (Business Service Providers/Business Solution Providers)	Jasper wireless, ECHELON, KORE, Axeda, e3
	System integrators and IoT solution providers for enterprises	hp, QUALCOMM, Deloitte, IBM, accenture, CSC
Network	Network operators, communications service providers, and transport infrastructure providers	verizon, Sprint, at&t, cisco, vodafone

Figure 13.16 M2M ecosystem.

Segment	Description	Companies/Organizations
Software	Software manufacturers, middleware and application infrastructure vendors, IoT OS providers	ORACLE, Google, Honeywell, SAMSUNG, SAP, QUALCOMM, vmware, GE
Hardware	Manufacturers of GPS chips, wireless sensors, wearable devices, actuators, and embedded hardware devices	QUALCOMM, Sixnet, SIERRA WIRELESS, SONY, SAMSUNG, MOTOROLA, LG, TEXAS INSTRUMENTS

Figure 13.17 M2M ecosystem.

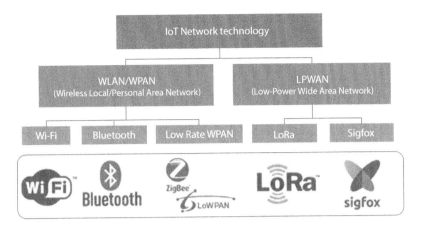

Figure 13.18 Networking Technologies—IoT.

based on the IEEE 802.11 standards. Devices like smart phones, smart devices, laptop computers, pcs, etc. are connected to Wi-Fi. So applications like Home, school, computer laboratory, office building, etc. are a part of Wi-Fi. Wi-Fi devices and APs (Access points) have a wireless communication range of about 30 m indoors. Comparison is shown in Table 13.2.

2. Second technology under WPAN protocol is designed by the Bluetooth SIG (special interest group). It replaces cables connecting many different types of devices such as mobile phones & Headsets, Heart monitors & medical equipment. Bluetooth's standard PAN range is usually 10 m (50 m in Bluetooth 4.0). Bluetooth 4.0 provides [12] reduced power consumption and cost while maintaining a similar communication range. Different Bluetooth types is shown in Table 13.3.

3. IEEE 802.15.4 standard is a low-cost, low-speed, low-power WPAN. Applications under this are Zigbee, 6LoWpan (IPV6 over low power WPAN), WirelessHART (Highway Addressable Remote Transuder), MiWi (Microchip Wireless Protocol), RFACE [22] (Radio Frequency for Consumer Electronics, ISA100.11a [18, 19]. Different Wi-Fi data rates is shown in Table 13.4.

4. Next technology coming under network technology of IoT is LPWAN (Low-power wide area network), which is a wireless telecommunication

Table 13.2 Comparing previous security solution with Zingbox.

	Previous solution	**Zingbox**
Purpose	Detecting malware and data protection	Defending deviation from IoT devices non-standard behavior
Method	Rule-based detection & Database update	Unsupervised deep learning & enforcing trusted behavior
Operation	End-point installment of products	Clientless (no install and management of software agent)

Table 13.3 Bluetooth protocol types data rates.

Sr. no.	Bluetooth protocol types	Data rates
1	Bluetooth 2.0 + EDR	2.1 Mbps
2	Bluetooth 3.0 + HS	24 Mbps
3	Bluetooth 4.0	25 Mbps
4	Bluetooth 5	50 Mbps

Table 13.4 Wi-Fi data rates are based on protocol type.

Sr. no.	IEEE Standard	Data rates
1	802.11a	54 mbps
2	802.11b	11 mbps
3	802.11g	54 mbps
4	802.11n	150 mbps
5	802.11ac	866.7 mbps
6	802.11ad	7 Gbps

network designed for long range communication at low power and low bit rates. LPWAN types are comprised of LoRa-based networks and Ultra Narrow Band) networks like Sigfox, NB-IoT(3GPP) as shown in Figure 13.19, etc.

4.1 LoRa is a wireless modulation technology that can support long range communication links. Single gateway or base station can cover an entire city (hundreds of square kilometers). LoRa defines the network communication protocol (MAC) and system architecture. It can cover more than 10 km range with high link budget and has a 10–20 year battery lifetime. Cisco, IBM, Semtech, Swisscom, Kerlink, etc. are LoRa alliance-based standardization.

4.2 Sigfox is an LPWAN technology that uses UNB modulation and is suitable for low data rate, lightweight device-based IoT services. It uses the license free ISM (industrial, scientific & Medical) RF (Radio Frequency) bands as a) 868–869 MHZ in Europe and b) 902–928 MHZ in USA.

5. IoT & Mobile communication networks—3GPP (The 3rd generation partnership Project) which refers to 7 telecommunication standarization groups to produce 3GPP standard releases for cellular networks services like radio access, QoS, core transport network, security, etc. [17].

4. IoT Cloud Computing Technology
   Top cloud provider companies such as Amazon Web service, microsoft, IBM and Google [31, 32]. As shown in Table 13.5.

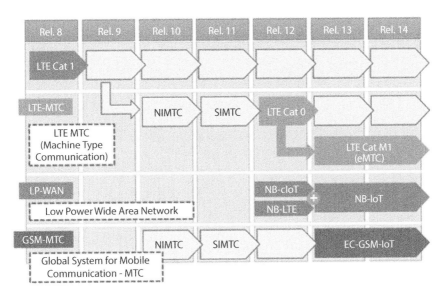

Figure 13.19 3GPP & IoT.

Table 13.5 Cloud companies and the services the provide.

Sr. no.	Cloud companies	Services/Features
1	Amazon Web Service	1. AWS global cloud based products are comprises of computing, storage, databases, analytics, networking, mobile, IoT, management, security developer and management tools and enterprise apps. 2. Amazon EC2 (Amazon Elastic Compute Cloud) webservices provide cloud computations in a very secure manner. 3. Amazon S3 (Simple Storage Service) provides services like security through secure connections using Virtual private cloud and Access management for easy accessibility of data on cloud. It provides storage through web service interfaces. 4. Amazon Cloud Drive was released in March 2011 for connecting multiple mobile devices and different computers together. It allows user to browse and play music from any computer or android device based on song titles, albums, artists and playlist. It provides unlimited storage for photos and raw data files [33].
2	Microsoft	1. It launched in 1975, but from year 2014, the company started to focus more on cloud technology. 2. Microsoft Office 365 which provides cloud-based services like One Drive and Microsoft teams for meeting puprose, to enable users to create and share anywhere on any device. 3. It provides hybrid cloud technology which helps users to develop data-driven intelligent apps [35].

(Continued)

Table 13.5 Cloud companies and the services the provide. (*Continued*)

Sr. no.	Cloud companies	Services/Features
3	IBM (International Business Machines) corporation	1. It supports public, private and hybrid clouds. 2. It offers more than 130 unique services such as IAAS (Infrastructure as a service), PAAS (platform as a service), SAAS (Software as a service). 3. IBM cloud object storage provides direct application connection to object storage and integration to IBM cloud services. 4. It Supports self-service portals & REST (Representational State Transfer) APIs. 5. IBM cloud streaming video provides solutions that simplify workflow management and video streaming.
4	Google	1. Google Search is the most dominant search engine in the united states market, with a market share of 65.6%. 2. In 2011, Google started the Google cloud platform. 3. Google Compute Engine provides Iaas based VMs that run in Google's data centers. 4. Enables Scalable global services based on advanced load-balancing cloud technology. 5. Google App Engine released as a preview in April 2008 and provides a platform as a service for web applications [30].
		6. Google BigQuery is a data analysis tool that users SQL like queries to process big datasets in seconds. 7. Google Compute engine provides Iaas support to enable on demand launching of VMs. 8. Google Cloud Endpoints released in November 2013 is a tool to create services inside App engine. 9. Google cloud data store which data storage of NoSQL (No Structured Query Language).
5	Apple's iCloud	1. Developed by Apple Inc., for storage and cloud computing. 2. It uses operating system 10.7 Lion or later). 3. It provides features like backup & restore, find my iphone-enables a user to track the location of an iOS device or Mac. 4. It provides facilities like back to My Mac- enables remote log in to other computers that have back to my Mac installed (using the same Apple ID), iwork for icloud provides Apple's iWork suite on a web interface. 5. It provides also iCloud Drive which save photos, videos, documents and apps, also provides icloud keychain which secures database for website, Wi-Fi password, credit card [34] and debit card details for quick access and auto fill [29].

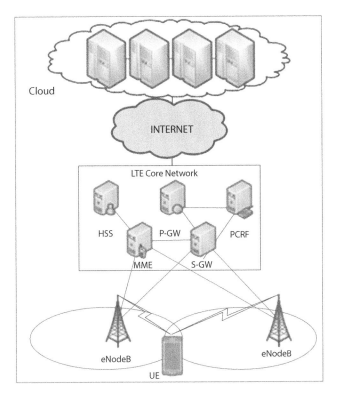

Figure 13.20 MCC over LTE networks.

Other cloud computing paradigms

1. Mobile cloud computing allows cloud computing to mobile and IoT users. UE (User equipment) and IoT systems can use power computing and storage resources of a distant centralized cloud through a core network of a mobile operator and the internet as shown in Figure 13.20.

13.3   Need of Fog Computing

As in market applications like smart traffic light systems, smart windmill farms, smart health care systems, smart enterprises, smart manufacturing factories, all are rigourously generating massive amount of raw data through sensors. So to compute that amount of data and to transport meaningful data properly to destination without delay in real time. So to do this now a days an additional layer is attached between the cloud layer and application layer, that is nothing but a connected edge or fog layer which solves the problem of computation and also maintain the network Quality of services factors like low consumption of bandwidth, low latency, etc. Fog computing architecture is represented below it depicts that fog computing services are a part of management service layer of IoT architecture. An explanation of each layer follows as shown in Figure 13.21 [13, 44].

1. Bottom layer—Sensors & endpoints—Here sensors used to collect raw data from environment depend upon the application for which they are used.

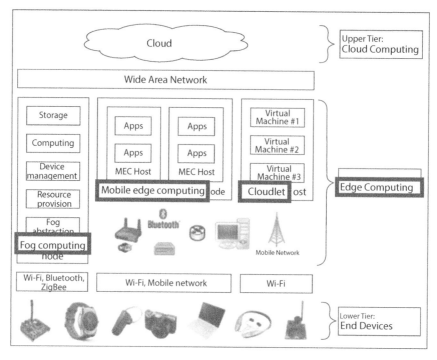

Figure 13.21 IoT & Mobile cloud technology.

2. Layer above bottom Gateway & Network—In this layer Iot devices or applications are connected to the network through WLAN/WPAN, blueetooth, Zigbee, 6Lowpan, Lora, Sigbox, etc. [18].

3. Third layer from bottom side Operating system & Fog services—Here application developed in android operating systems, embedded OS can use fog services for faster computation of raw data [39, 40].

4. Application layer—application like smart cab booking system or other be part of this IoT and Fog computing [41–43]. Refer to Table 13.6 for comparison between MCC and Edge Computing.

Table 13.6 Comparing MCC & Edge computing.

Technical aspect	MCC	Edge computing
Deployment	Centralized	Distributed
Distance to the UE	Far	Close
Latency	Long	Short
Jitter	High	Low
Computational Power	Abundant	Limited
Storage Capacity	Abundant	Limited

Now next we covered about usecases of applications as Smart health care syastem, smart enterprise system, and smart manufacturing factory as shown in Figure 13.22.

1. Smart Health Care system

   Above figure depicts the architecture of Smart Health care system in which a patient record is stored over the cloud and data is given to health care professional to prescribe the medicines based on diagnosis. Now here fog interplay with cloud is used if patient has to be treated in near real time so how to prescribe medicine instantly that too with low bandwidth for that purpose immediate event is kept in fog layer. Now one can think how sensors are useful in this as there are types of sensors like pressure sensors, pulse oximeter sensor they read current patient situation data and transmit to cloud for storing of database as shown in Figure 13.23.

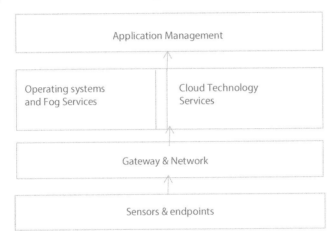

Figure 13.22 Fog computing architecture.

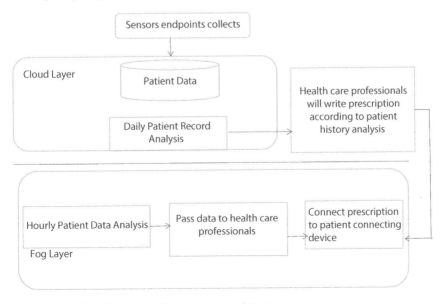

Figure 13.23 IoT & Fog based smart healthcare system architecture.

Figure 13.24 IoT and Fog based smart manufacturer factory baseline architecture.

2. Smart Manufacturing Factory (e.g. Loreal + IBM cloud services makeover with industry 4.0).

Here the architecture Loreal + IBM cloud services is depicted whre loreal company uses IBM cloud services to store the cosmetic. They used this Iot and Fog based architectecture which uses agile methodology to manufacture customized cosmetic according to the customer choice, this create a lot revenue for the company as shown in Figure 13.24 [36–38].

References

1. Bradley, J., Barbier, J., Handler, D., Embracing the Internet of Everything To Capture Your Share of $14.4 Trillion, Cisco India, White Paper, 2013.
2. Bradley, J., Reberger, C., Dixit, A., Gupta, V., Internet of Everything: A $4.6 Trillion Public-Sector Opportunity, Cisco India, White Paper, 2013.
3. Evans, D., The Internet of Everything, Cisco India IBSG, White Paper, 2012.
4. Mitchell, S., Villa, N., Stewart-Weeks, M., Lange, A., The Internet of Everything for Cities, Cisco India, White Paper, 2013.
5. Hersent, O., Boswarthick, D., Elloumi, O., *The Internet of Things: Key Applications and Protocols*, John Wiley & Sons, England, Dec. 2011.
6. Machine 2 Machine Perspective on Industry Status (Key Challenges and Opportunities), Frost & Sullivan, Research Paper, Dubai UAE, Nov. 2011.
7. M2M Sector Map, Beecham Research, Sep. 2011, USA, [Online] Available from: http://www.beechamresearch.com/download.aspx?id=18 [Accessed June 1, 2015].
8. Behmann, F. and Wu, K., *Collaborative Internet of Things (C-IoT)*, John Wiley & Sons, USA, 2015.

9. Gubbia, J., Buyyab, R., Marusica, S., Palaniswamia, M., Internet of Things (IoT): A vision, architectural elements, and future directions. *Future Gener. Comput. Syst.*, 29, 7, 1645–1660, Sep. 2013.

10. Atzori, L., Iera, A., Morabito, G., The Internet of Things: A survey. *Comput. Networks*, 54, 15, 2787–2805, Oct. 2010.

11. Li, S., Xu, L.D., Zhao, S., The Internet of Things: A Survey. *Inf. Syst. Front.*, 17, 2, 243–259, Apr. 2015.

12. Jara, A.J., Ladid, L., Skarmeta, A., The Internet of Everything through IPv6: An Analysis of Challenges, Solutions and Opportunities. *J. Wirel. Mob. Netw. Ubiquitous Comput. Dependable Appl.*, 4, 3, 97–118, 2013.

13. Vermesan, O. and Friess, P., *Internet of Things—Global Technological and Societal Trends From Smart Environments and Spaces to Green ICT*, River Publishers, USA, 2011.

14. Vermesan, O., Friess, P., Guillemin, P., Gusmeroli, S., Sundmaeker, H., Bassi, A., Jubert, I.S., Mazura, M., Harrison, M., Eisenhauer, M., Doody, P., Internet of Things Strategic Research Roadmap, in: *European Research Cluster on the Internet of Things*, Sep. 2011.

15. IEEE Std. 802.15.4-2006, Part 15.4: Wireless Medium Access Control (MAC) and Physical Layer (PHY) Specifications for Low-Rate Wireless Personal Area Networks (LR-WPANs), IEEE, USA, Sep. 2006.

16. Kushalnagar, N., Montenegro, G., Schumacher, C., IPv6 over Low-Power Wireless Personal Area Networks (6LoWPANs): Overview, Assumptions, Problem Statement, and Goals, *IETF RFC 4919*, Aug. 2007.

17. Montenegro, G., Kushalnagar, N., Hui, J., Culler, D., Transmission of IPv6 Packets over IEEE 802.15.4 Networks, *IETF RFC 4944*, Sep. 2007.

18. ZigBee Alliance, ZigBee specification: ZigBee document 053474r13 Version 1.1, ZigBee Alliance, USA, www.zigbee.org, Dec. 2006.

19. Behmann, F. and Wu, K., *Collaborative Internet of Things (C-IoT)*, John Wiley & Sons, 2015.

20. Gubbia, J., Buyyab, R., Marusica, S., and Palaniswamia, M., Internet of Things (IoT): A vision, architectural elements, and future directions. *Future Gener. Comput. Syst.*, 29, 7, 1645–1660, Sep. 2013.

21. Atzori, L., Iera, A., Morabito, G., The Internet of Things: A survey. *Comput. Networks*, 54, 15, 2787–2805, ct. 2010. Li, S, L. D. Xu, and Zhao, S., The Internet of Things: A Survey. *Inf. Syst. Front.*, 17, 2, 243–259, Apr. 2015.

22. Jara, A.J., Ladid, L., Skarmeta, A., The Internet of Everything through IPv6: An Analysis of Challenges, Solutions and Opportunities. *J. Wirel. Mob. Netw. Ubiquitous Comput. Dependable Appl.*, 4, 3, 97–118, 2013.

23. Koetsier, J., IoT In The USA: 3,000 Companies, $125B In Funding, $613B In Valuation, 342,000 Employees, Forbes, NY, July 10, 2017, [Online] Available from:https://www.forbes.com/sites/johnkoetsier/2017/07/10/iot-in-the-usa-3000-companies-125b-in-funding-613b-in-valuation-342000-employees/67c322d33ef5 [Accessed Feb. 20, 2018].

24. van der Meulen, R. and Gartner, Gartner Says 8.4 Billion Connected "Things" Will Be in Use in 2017, Up 31 Percent From 2016, Gartner, NY, Feb. 7, 2017, [Online] Available from: https://www.gartner.com/newsroom/id/3598917 [Accessed Feb. 20, 2018].

25. Android Things Overview, Google Android, USA, [Online] Available from: https://developer.android.com/things/get-started/index.html [Accessed Feb. 20, 2018].

26. Holodny, E., Uber and Lyft are demolishing New York City taxi drivers, NY, Oct. 12, 2016, [Online] Available from: http://www.businessinsider.com/nyc-yellow-cab-medallion-prices-falling-further-2016-10, [Accessed Feb. 20, 2018].

27. Kumar, K. and Lu, Y.H., Cloud Computing for Mobile Users: Can Offloading Computation Save Energy? *Computer*, 43, 4, 51–56, Apr. 2010.

28. Wikipedia, http://www.wikipedia.org.

29. Apple, iCloud, https://www.icloud.com.
30. Google, Google Cloud, https://cloud.google.com/products [Accessed June 1, 2015].
31. Virtualization, Cisco's IaaS cloud, http://www.virtualization.co.kr/data/file/01_2/1889266503_6f489654_1.jpg [Accessed June 1, 2015].
32. Tutorialspoint, Cloud computing, http://www.tutorialspoint.com/cloud_computing/cloud_computing_tutorial.pdf [Accessed June 1, 2015].
33. WS Simple Icons Storage Amazon S3 Bucket with Objects, Amazon Web Services LLC, [CC BY-SA 3.0 (http://creativecommons.org/licenses/by-sa/3.0)], *via* Wikimedia Commons.
34. iCloud Logo, By EEIM (Own work) [Public domain], via Wikimedia Commons, NY, 2016.
35. MobileMe Logo, By Apple Inc. [Public domain], via Wikimedia Commons, NY, 2019.
36. Bar-Magen Numhauser, J., *Fog Computing introduction to a New Cloud Evolution. Escriturassilenciadas: paisaje como historiografía*, pp. 111–126, University of Alcala, Spain, 2012, https://www.wikipedia.org/.
37. IoT, from Cloud to Fog Computing, blogs@Cisco - Cisco Blogs, India, Retrieved 2017-04-07. (https://blogs.cisco.com/perspectives/iot-from-cloud-to-fog-computing).
38. What Is Fog Computing? Webopedia Definition, www.webopedia.com. Retrieved 2017-04-07. (https://www.webopedia.com/TERM/F/fog-computing.html), Mach, P. and Becvar, Z., Mobile Edge Computing: A Survey on Architecture and Computation Offloading. *IEEE Commun. Surv. Tuts.*, 19, 3, 1628–1656, 3rd Quart. 2017.
39. Dinh, H.T., Lee, C., Niyato, D., Wang, P., A survey of mobile cloud computing: Architecture, applications, and approaches. *Wirel. Commun. Mob. Comput.*, 13, 18, 1587–1611, 2013.
40. Barbarossa, S., Sardellitti, S., Di Lorenzo, P., Communicating while computing: Distributed mobile cloud computing over 5G heterogeneous networks. *IEEE Signal Process. Mag.*, 31, 6, 45–55, Nov. 2014.
41. Khan, A.R., Othman, M., Madani, S.A., Khan, S.U., A survey of mobile cloud computing application models. *IEEE Commun. Surv. Tuts.*, 16, 1, 393–413, 1st Quart. 2014.
42. Mobile Edge Computing: a building block for 5G, Telecompaper (subscription), Jul 14, 2015, (https://www.telecompaper.com/background/mobile-edge-computing-a-building-block-for-5g-1092281).
43. Ahmed, A. and Ahmed, E., A Survey on Mobile Edge Computing, in: *Proc. 10th International Conference on Intelligent Systems and Control (ISCO)*, Jan. 2016, pp. 1–8.
44. Satyanarayanan, M., Bahl, P., Caceres, R., Davies, N., The case for VM-based Cloudlets in Mobile Computing. *IEEE Pervasive Comput.*, 8, 4, 14–23, Oct.–Dec. 2009.

## 14

Convergence of Big Data and Cloud Computing Environment

Ranjan Ganguli

All India Institute of Local Self Government, Deoghar, India

Abstract

Big Data is created every day from various heterogeneous sources over the internet and is a challenging task in processing, handling and storing for major organization. To be dealt with, convergence of Cloud computing with Big data has played a vital role as a solution of cost effective, better flexibility with data security at a higher level. This creates an edge over traditional computing methods and delivered at a cheaper rate. This Chapter introduces Big data and its challenges in respect of traditional databases. In various other parts, we will discuss how convergence activities played a major role with Big data in finding a solution in Cloud computing platform for handling large volume, fast moving and ever increasing data in the internet along with its pros and cons of the system. Finally, future aspects of Big data with Cloud computing will be discussed.

Keywords: Big data, Cloud computing, Hadoop, Cassandra

14.1 Introduction

The term big data is common to IT industry or business companies nowadays which collects data from hundreds of heterogeneous sources, including social media, email correspondence, video posts or tweets and credit card data. So, data is becoming huge and need special attention to analyze and analytic engine for greater efficiency and at reduced cost. Organizations need to have special value chain system to coordinate effective activities. This can only be achieved through integrated systems that can manage smooth data flow from devices to data center [1]. In various small to large scale enterprises, organizations are moving rapidly towards cloud-based solutions for taking advantages of scalability, QoS (Quality-of-Service) management, privacy and security. This type of closed services in the market reduces infrastructure and operational cost.

Like SQL-based relational data model generated a platform for expressing various requirements options and cooperate customers to choose from several vendors and in converse, it increases the competition rate of selection process. The main problem is to handle and integrate the present challenges faced by the existing feature and in big data

Email: ganguliranjan1979@gmail.com

Monika Mangla, Suneeta Satpathy, Bhagirathi Nayak and Sachi Nandan Mohanty (eds.) Integration of Cloud Computing with Internet of Things: Foundations, Analytics, and Applications, (233–250) © 2021 Scrivener Publishing LLC

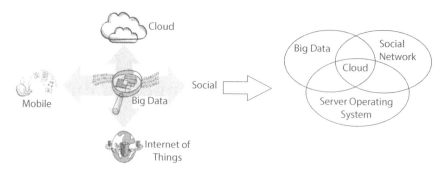

Figure 14.1 Next generation convergence technologies.

area. As was discussed in previous stage of cloud-based services, network technology was considered as a separate thing with data center and the associated client. But Lamport's [2] theory on distributed computing are widely accepted and recognized as a vital step for problem solving of consistency and persistency with fault-tolerance mechanism. Thus an integrated platform shown in Figure 14.1 must be available to increase the potential of investment with decrease in overall application development cost for more effective data handling and management from device to the data center directly. Several organizations are busy creating a model of leveraging several application development processes in respect of mobility awareness solutions to deliver and create sophisticated end-to-end secure user experiences. Only specific group members can access the private clouds that exist for a certain group of organizations.

Cloud technologies use different APIs to process Big Data in a simpler way, just like Amazon EC2 virtual machine's capacity is 1 to 20 processors, with up to 15 GB of memory and 160 TB of storage and uses Web.

Service (WS) portal. Presently, Cloud-based toolkits manage virtual machines directly because of per flexible requirement of consumers. So, to look ahead, a need of re-structuring of internet service environment is required with people preferring more personalized services.

14.2   Big Data: Historical View

The general historical view of big data started 5,000 years back to Mesopotamia, when they keep track of their accounting information and business activities like crop growth and herding in a specified manner. The principles continued to grow until in 1663, when John Graunt, was able to record and analyze the mortality rate of the bubonic plague that happened during that time in London. He did this effort to raise a concern and awareness among the people. This was the first statistical analysis of data ever recorded in the world. With this revolution of taking care of data until 1889 (also starting point of modern era), Herman Hollerth made an attempt to organize census data using a computing system. After his great effort, the various other next noteworthy data development continued until 1937, when US government contracted with IBM (International Business Machine) to develop a punch card reading system to keep track of millions of Americans. Also, the first data processing machine was developed in 1943 and named 'Colossus' was used to decipher Nazi codes and to identify or search for patterns to appear in intercepting regular messages during Second World War. But with the development of first data center in US in 1965, which had stored millions of tax returns and fingerprint sets has made a significant impact in conversion of paradigm from data to information, when first introduced the term 'Big Data' by Roger Mougalas in 2005. In 2010, Eric Schmidt, executive chairman of Google, told a conference in Lake Tahoe that the volume of data is being generated every two days is same as was created from the beginning of time up to the year 2003 and created a new leap of information era. Later on in 2012, the definition of big data included 3Vs as Volume, Velocity and Variety to understand the characteristics of big data. There are many other interesting changes that will appear in Big Data revolution in the next few years. International Data Corporation (IDC) which defined big data as "a new generation of technology and architecture that is designed to collect or extract meaning or value from a large volume set of wide variety of data, by enabling the high velocity capture, discovery or analysis," pointed out that the 3Vs of big data can be extended to 4Vs by adding 'Value' namely as 'Volume', 'Variety', 'Velocity' & 'Value' and creates a new definition of big data that is widely recognized because of its highlighting the necessity of data.

14.2.1   Big Data: Definition

Based on several observations and various aspects in respect of big data, it can be generally defined as "a new form of data integration to uncover hidden patterns from large datasets that are diverse (structured, semi & unstructured), complex and massive in scale" as shown in Figures 14.2 and 14.3.

    (i)   Volume: It refers to varieties (heterogeneous form) and different sizes of data that is continuously generated from various sources for finding patterns from information through analysis. Nokia motivated, mobile data challenge initiative collects longitudinal data (that requires efforts and investments)

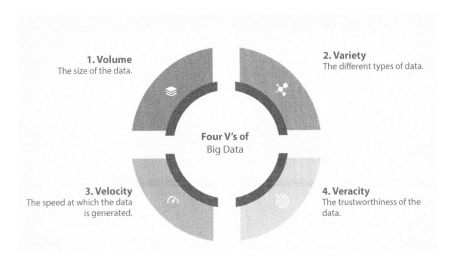

Figure 14.2 Four vs of Big data: Data scientist view.

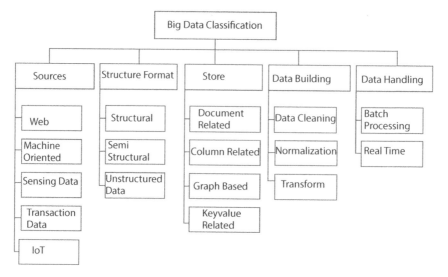

Figure 14.3 Big data classification.

from various smart phones and made this available for research in community [3]. This challenge produced an interesting result similar to the predictability of human behaviour patterns for complex data.

(ii) Variety: When data is collected via various sources like phones, sensors, social networks-data appears in various heterogeneous format or data types like structured, semi structured and unstructured. Like, most of the mobile data and sensors collected data is unstructured in format along with internet users that generate randomly, all set of structured, semi & unstructured data [4].

(iii) Velocity: It describes the speed of incoming and outgoing data with the time taken to process and analyze as streamed data are collected across time in multiple sources, legacy collections, predefined achieved data.

(iv) Veracity: It is not only the measure of the quality of data but also the trustworthiness (types, source and analysis) of data.

14.2.2   Big Data Classification

For better understanding of characteristics, Big data is classified in different categories: i) Sources, ii) Structure format, iii) Stores, iv) Data Building, and iv) Data Handling.

The complexities of each category have been mentioned in Figure 14.3. Various data sources like internet data, sensing data, transactional data and others are shifted from unstructured to structured form and stored in various formats like the relational database which comes in many varieties.

14.2.3   Big Data Analytics

We know that big data deals with data set of higher dimension in terms of volume, diverse contents including structured, semi-structured and unstructured data (as variety), arriving and processing at a faster rate (as velocity) than any small to large scale organization had to deal or face with such as oceanic volume of data produced through several devices connected across any network like PCs, smart phones to sensors including traffic cameras that arrive under various formats. The significance of big data comes when this is analyzed—discovered or finding hidden patterns, helping decision makers with broader sense of adaptability and ability to handle and respond to the world in a more challenging situation with uses of more intelligence-based algorithm or through recent approaches like machine learning, artificial neural network, computational mathematics, etc. to move through data for discovering interrelationship among data. So, for Analytics:

(i)   Data is more important than ever—like what can be done with the data? – medium to large enterprises looking to unlock data's competitive advantage
(ii) Moving Data analytics from batch to real time systems
(iii) Predictive analytics under real time basis
(iv) Scope of big data analytics increases.

Thus, data processing and analytics can be applied to cloud-based solutions, IT support infrastructure with high end computation and capacity solutions.

14.3   Big Data Challenges

(i)   Data Collection
      The important thing about big data is its increasing data collection phase with increase in velocity all the time and brings sometimes a major issue in delivering the data into cloud for further processing. Existing internet standard would create a bottleneck for cloud to perform services in the cloud and need next level of supporting standard or techniques to deal with present scenario for higher efficiency and smooth data traversal across or to the cloud system.
(ii) Storage
      Today's legacy database systems are not able to find a way to grab possible advantages of scalability, present in cloud's environment for optimal state or use. Thus, a scalable model is required in new systems under consideration.
(iii) Analysis
      Data analysis helps to find value from big data. Modern Techniques and methods must be researched and available to process rising data sets. Also, simplification must be a goal of consideration during the analysis phase of big data.
(iv) Security
      Two main challenges need to focus in securing big data in large systems: a) Limited expenses to be carried out without effecting the performance. b) Extensive experimentation or testing is required on data

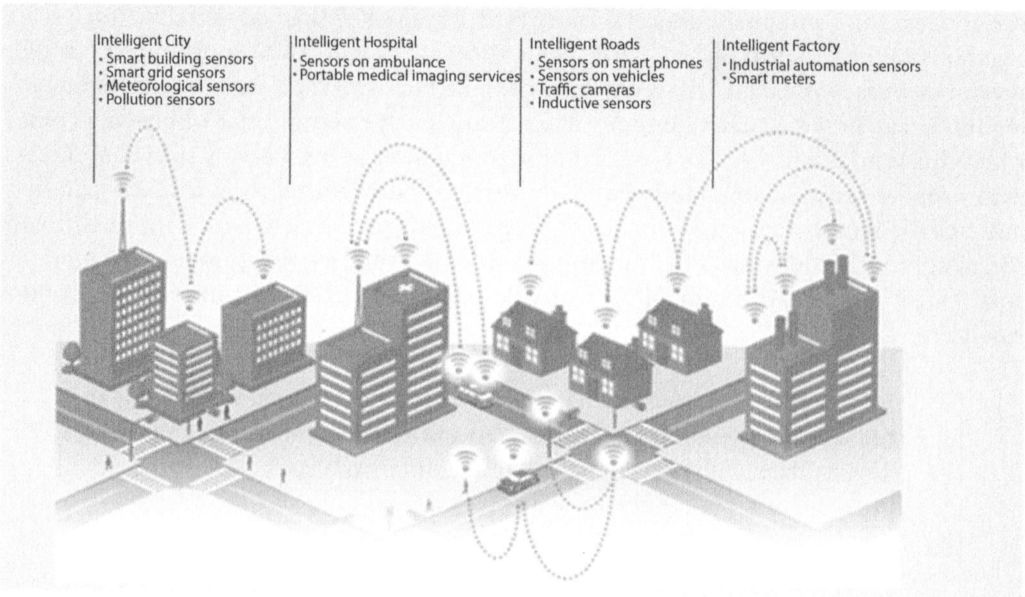

Figure 14.4 A big data view on smart city formation.

analysis process to identify possible attacks on mostly used RDBMS, NoSQL.

(v) Lack of skilled professionals
Big data analytics requires extensive knowledge about data and portion of statistics to understand the problems and providing a better business decision. Skilled data scientist and analyst with in-depth knowledge about analytics tools are less in the market and the demand will grow with adoption of large scale integration (Figure 14.4).

In 2015, a survey conducted to address the problems faced in big data working environment is shown in Figure 14.5.

14.4 The Architecture

The Big data architecture is a multilayer processing system which consists of various components that includes data sources & storage, batch processing, real-time messaging sources, data streaming, analytical storage with reporting and orchestration. But the abstract view of the whole thing can be categorized as three independent layers as i) storing—that generally holds the data, ii) Handling—done as the mid-level layer, and iii) Processing—at the upper level that support various tools that meet the end user. Below Figure 14.6 shows the convergence abstract view.

The platform used is No SQL or Parallel DBMS. Map Reduce supports a parallel processing of large volume of data after dividing the user query and sent it to different nodes in cloud. A prioritized ranking system of result with reduced phase is done and integration is maintained using DBMS technology.

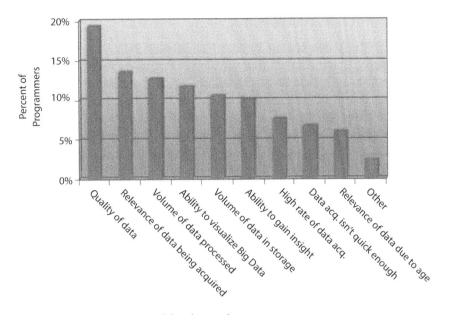

Figure 14.5 Programmers challenges with big data analytics.

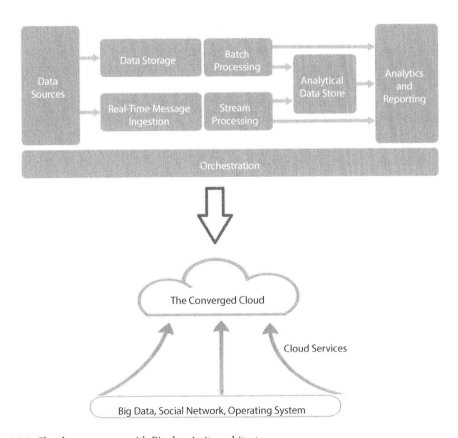

Figure 14.6 Cloud convergence with Big data in its architecture.

14.4.1 Storage or Collection System

There is a remarkable improvement in capacity technologies in dealing with Big data to deal with data rehydration. The meta data management requires high end storing capacity and bandwidth. Sometimes, a single centrally handled file is responsible to deal with millions of files and meta data records. Distributed storage share between processors in the system is a big challenge for a storage management. So, data that can be stored and measured either it is customer information, service log or call record generated by telecom industries, sensor data, user created data (social data), blogs, various mails, etc., everything. Multicore processors have additional cycles to combine that meet with storage systems. Presently, cloud based storage systems that supports distributed file division exist like HDFS (Hadoop Distributed File Systems), Amazon S3 or OpenStack Swift and Google File System (GFS or GoogleFS) (Table 14.1) for storing huge data in network along with storage area network and network attached storage.

14.4.2 Data Care

With latest Map and Reduce technology to handle and processed in parallel a large set of data in a cluster basis, it acts as a framework in Apache Hadoop—that contributes scheduling with distribution and configuration that constitute the two-step process of map and reduce. Different computers are tied up with a weak correlation mechanism and expanded up to thousands of different computers. So, with no exception, a possibility of system errors is in common. Thus, Map and Reduce-based simplified operations are helpful in solving complicated problems without knowing programmer a deep understanding of parallel programming of handling. Several computers connected in the system supports maximum throughput. Finally, data that is stored in HDFS and is divided to worker and that can be further expressed to a value type with result collected in local hardware (disk). It is then assembled and produced in a separate file.

14.4.3 Analysis

KDD (Knowledge Discovery in Databases) is the process of finding meaningful information in data. It is actually to store the data, process it and analyze it for discovering hidden facts that are unknown so far and converted in knowledge for decision making.

Table 14.1 Distributed file system: On cloud services.

Examples	Descriptions
Google FS (GFS)	A scalable distributed or give out file system that use cluster based commodity hardware for huge data intensive applications with fault handling mechanism.
Hadoop File System	An open source distributed system for huge data computation and operated under MapReduce model with low cost usage.
Amazon Simple Storage Service (S3)	An online public storage web services offered by Amazon.

14.5   Cloud Computing: History in a Nutshell

The timeline of cloud computing showed that the history began in early 60s when computers were considered to be used by more than two people and tried to fill up empty space between user and various service provider. But, later in early 2000s when Amazon introduced their web-based retail services that incorporated cloud computing model and enhanced the computer capacity with more efficiently. The term "Cloud Computing" in the conference was described as—a modern trend where people can access the power of software and hardware applications over any web in replace of their personal desktop computers [5]. Soon after that, large organizations like Google, IBM have started developing cloud supported services and by 2012, Oracle introduced 'Oracle Cloud' with a well-defined architecture that offered three basics of business as IaaS (Infrastructure-as-a-Service), PaaS (Platform-as-a-Service) and SaaS (Software-as-a-Service).

14.5.1   View on Cloud Computing and Big Data

National Institute of Standards and Technology (NIST) defines cloud in respect of its characteristics as "Cloud computing is a model for convenient on shared pool of configurable computing resources (like: networks, servers, storage, services, etc.) that released services with minimal management effort."

Cloud models help organizations to evaluate best business strategy and user requirements. Like an organization can use or add analytics to their own private cloud environment to protect sensitive information with extends to hybrid cloud systems and can take benefits of other data sources come up in public clouds. As per IDC prediction, by the year 2020, 40% of the world data will be in cloud as big cloud-operated companies like Amazon, IBM and Microsoft have already deployed their big data based activities using Hadoop clusters. The relationship between big data and cloud based operations [6] is shown in Figure 14.7.

The Cloud comes up with analytics a high capacity and more processing power with use of large datasets to return more useful information.

14.6   Insight of Big Data and Cloud Computing

User needs can be addressed with full range of data analytics on data that includes Analytics-as-a-Service (AaaS) that support business intelligence to go through an alternative way to deal with software and internal hardware solutions with wide range in delivery to usage of data. In Enterprise-based solutions, data can be optimized with AaaS supporting capabilities as:

- Extract semi, structured and unstructured forms of data from several sources.
- Maintaining all data supported guidelines and policies for control activities
- Performing activities to integrate data, performing analysis, transformation with visualization.

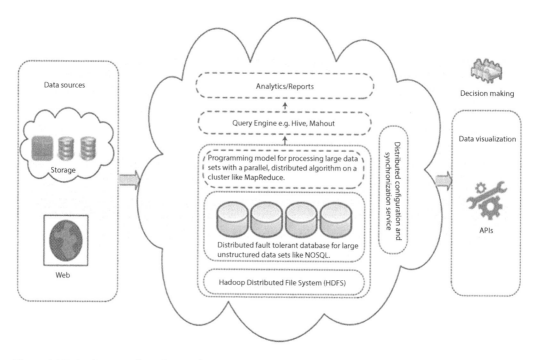

Figure 14.7 Application of Big data in cloud services.

14.6.1 Cloud-Based Services

The basic cloud-based services [7] as described in Figures 14.8 and 14.9 are:

  a) Infrastructure-as-a-service or IaaS
  b) Platform-as-a-Service or PaaS
  c) Software-as-a-Service or SaaS.

  a) Deployment of IaaS (also called Hardware-as-a-Service) is done through a cloud provider that helps to allocate time shared server resources that

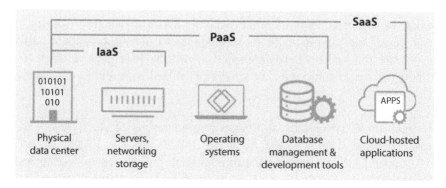

Figure 14.8 Utility model of cloud based computing.

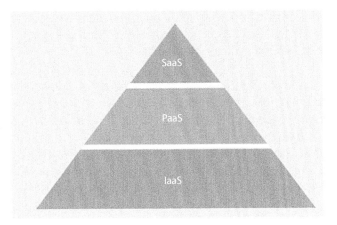

Figure 14.9 Three layered of cloud as a service model.

normally fulfils the required performance or computational and storage needs for all kinds of analytical purposes. Basically, cloud-based operating systems take care of all kinds of networks performance and storage issues. It is a foundation for many companies' cloud-related services with strong involvement of investment and IT support services to implement big data analytics. Organizations install their own software in their platform either like Hadoop framework, or NoSQL database, Apache Cassandra, etc. Resources are managed with automated tools and can be made easier for resource orchestration. List of IaaS service providers in the market technology are:

- Web Services-Amazon
- OpenStack Software
- VMware vCloud Suite
- Windows Azure.

b) Tools and libraries are available for developers for deployment, testing, building and run several applications on cloud supported infrastructure. This puts down various management workloads that Hadoop requires to scale and configure process and served as a development platform for various analytics applications. List of PaaS supported services in cloud related technologies are:

- Open Shift-Red Hat
- Azure-Windows
- Google Compute Engine (GCE)
- Magento Commerce Cloud.

The development environment of PaaS is not hosted locally and opens a window for developers to access it from anywhere in the world. It can be accessed over any internet platform and can create an application in a web browser. So, there are no geographic restrictions for any team to collaborate in the process and produces less control over the development process. The core services offered by PaaS are as follows:

- Development tools—that are necessary for software development which includes a code editor, a debugger, a compiler and other supported tools which may offer by other vendors sometimes; but it creates a framework to perform all activities.
- Middle-layer—as every architecture contains a middle layer that supports all kinds of intermediate activities such that other developers don't have to create it and can work independently. This lies between user applications and machine's operating system; like it supports software to take input from keyboard and mouse. It is required to run applications but end user don't interact it ever.
- Operating system—All kinds of applications are able to run and develop here through specified vendor.
  PaaS providers maintain a database with administer in control. They provide a developer with a Database Management System (DBMS).
- Infrastructure setup—PaaS layer stays above the IaaS layer in cloud service model and contains all the things that is included in IaaS. A PaaS provider either manages storage, servers and data centers.

c) SaaS is a third party hosted software distribution model available to customers over the internet. It is similar to application service provider (ASP) and acts as demand computing software delivery models where the service provider delivers to end user of customer's software. Since SaaS is a software based on demand model, there is single copy of an application that allows customer to access network based activities. The service provider created the software specifically for SaaS distribution. In the network, the source code is same for all customers and any of features are carried out, it is broadcast to all the customers in the network. Depending upon service level agreement (SLA), the data will be stored either locally or in cloud. Application Programming Interfaces (APIs) help to integrate various softwares with SaaS applications.

For example, any business organization can write its own software tools that can integrate with SaaS providers for offering or receiving services.

Basically, the use of SaaS comes when any organization or company wants to launch any new kinds of readymade software quickly of any short term collaboration is required. Sometimes, applications to be used on a short term basis or applications need both web and mobile access.

14.6.2   At a Glance: Cloud Services

Table 14.2 shows comparison of IaaS, PaaS and SaaS where Platform as a Service (PaaS and Infrastructure as a Service (IaaS) give more control to the user segment. SaaS does not require additional efforts to utilize the readymade products.

Table 14.2 Differences between cloud services.

	IaaS	PaaS	SaaS
Who is the User?	System Administrator	Software Developers	End User
What user get?	A logical data store to deploy and create platforms for apps and testing opportunities	A logical platform and supported tools to create, deploy and test apps	Web software to complete business related task
Controllers	Servers, Storage and network virtualization	Same as IaaS with OS, Middleware Runtime	Same as PaaS with Applications Data
User Controls	OS, Middleware Runtime, Applications, Data	Applications Data	–

14.7 Cloud Framework

In the context of exponential growth of data, traditional relational systems fail to meet the present day requirements when dealing with big data. So, a large big data analytics platform like Hadoop, Cassandra, and Voldemort come into the picture.

14.7.1 Hadoop

Hadoop, written in Java and is an open source software that supports all kinds of popular services in cloud environment which consists of two parts or components: i) Map & Reduce (Map Reduce) engine & ii) Hadoop Distributed file systems where Map converts one set of data converted into another set by breaking individual elements into key pairs or tuples. The output moves into Reduce segment to combine tuples to form a smaller set of tuples. It follows a mapping between Map and Reduce segment and scale distributing computing on various nodes. On writing applications with Map Reduce, scaled up even up to thousands of nodes in cluster forms is just a configuration change. It works on top of Hadoop to handle such issues. Different Hadoop segments that work on the commodity level hardware makes it easier to collect, stores, process and analyze large amount of data. Figure 14.10 is the Hadoop ecosystem or platform with various modules [8].

Hive is an Apache open source data warehousing system used for querying and analyzing large volumes of datasets stored in Hadoop files where it uses Hive query language (HQL/HiveQL) that is similar to normal SQL but HQL converts SQL queries into Map Reduce executes on Hadoop. The organization of data is done in tables (consists of rows and columns), partitions and as buckets.

Apache uses a high level language (also known as Pig Latin) that works in between declarative and procedural part of SQL and Java to speed up parallel processing and analysis on large volume of information stored in Hadoop platform. Data sets are compiled into Map Reduce for better performance in Hadoop framework or platform.

HBase is a fault tolerant and works better for structured data and data analyst perform well using HBase. It works on the top of Hadoop distributed system and is highly scalable

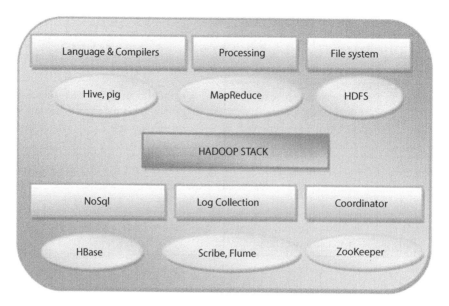

Figure 14.10 Hadoop ecosystem modules.

and provides a distributed data store with consistent read and write options. HBase is a full pledged NoSQL database.

The Zookeeper works on to avoid any single point failure through cluster of servers. It runs a special set of rules (protocol) that determines the leader node in a particular time. ZooKeeper distributed servers holds the information that would retrieve the client's applications.

14.7.2 Cassandra

It is a distributed column-oriented database systems developed by Facebook but built on Google's Big Table and Amazon's Dynamo platform which is responsible to handle mission critical data with no compromise in performance and scalability. It works with lower fault handling mechanism at the cloud infrastructure or commodity hardware. It works with various data centers to provide lower latency for users of all kinds of regional outages. It is a right choice for no compromising options when we need scalability and high availability. For all kinds of mission critical data, linear scalability with fault-tolerance mechanism makes it possible for cloud commodity hardware or infrastructure a perfect platform. It supports lower latency by replicating across many data centers and provides a peace of mind to users knowing to exist in regional outages [9]. Cassandra holds the columns (which is not pre-defined as was in a relational table) in a single row. Thus, it is a database with multiple rows in the form of a key-value.

14.7.2.1 Features of Cassandra

Fault Tolerant: Data is copied to various nodes for fault tolerance and replicated to many data centers. A node in failure stage is replaced easily with no time gap.

Performant: Apache Cassandra is a variant of NoSQL that uses partition algorithm to decide the node to organize the data. The performance gets improved through streaming process.

Decentralized: Each node in the cluster acts identically with no network overhead.

Proven: Various companies, organizations like CERN, eBay, GitHub, Go Daddy, Instagram and many others use Cassandra that have large volume of active data sets.

Scalable: With this, big companies like Apple's; deployed 75,000 nodes storing over 10PB data, Netflix (with 2,500 nodes, 420 TB data and handling 1 trillion requests every day), eBay (over 100 nodes and 250, TB data) are supported easily.

Elastic: Improved throughput (read and write operations) with no time consuming in adding and removal of nodes without any interruption in applications executions.

Durable: Very less chance of data loss even when entire data canter goes down.

Control Mechanism: Option to choose between synchronous and asynchronous copies of data for update and asynchronous operations are can be optimized for cluster consistency with features like Read Repair and Hinted Handoff.

Support: Cassandra supports third party contract and services.

14.7.3   Voldemort

Voldemort is designed in such a way that data are stored across various nodes which works on multiple storage engines in the same framework. This also integrates fast moving, online storage system with large volume of offline data running on Hadoop system. The main features it includes that data is copied on many servers and each server holds only a copy or subset of the portion of total data. Failure of any server is handled transparently with a support of pluggable serialization that allows rich keys and values. There is no single common point of node failure and works independently with each other [10]. To maximize data integrity, data items are versioned without compromising the availability of the system. To measure performance efficiency on a single node, up to 20k operations per second can be expected depending on various factors like machines, network, disk system and replication factor. When using key-value access, read and write access is restricted.

14.7.3.1   A Comparison With Relational Databases and Benefits

Voldemort does not satisfy the general rules of relational database nor does it support object form of database that maps various object based reference graphs nor does it follow any new abstraction like document-orientation. It is a huge, persistent hash table that supports distribution of data across independent nodes. It provides a number of advantages:

- There is no need of separate caching tier as it combines in memory caching with the storage system and acts just as fast.
- Do not require any rebalancing of data as portioning is transparent with cluster expansion.
- Use of simple API can integrate wide range of applications with scope of replicating and placement of data.
- Support unit testing against a throw-away in memory storage system without need of a real time cluster.

14.8   Conclusions

In this chapter, we have discussed a systematic flow of big data role in achieving the cloud computing environment to manage, storage and process the data. Here, historical view of big data has been shown with its definition and classification and opened a new window for data analytics. Big data is merged with cloud computing and becomes a leading part of the digital world nowadays with its several challenges. The architectural part discussed with cloud services, created a foundation for all kinds of convergence activities. Also, history of cloud computing with its insight in big data showed a general view of service model. Finally, various cloud-based services with some of its features and framework like Hadoop, Cassandra, Voldemort have been discussed.

14.9   Future Perspective

Big data combined with cloud computing platform has created a vast distributed system called the telecom industry that has opened a new window of significant advantage in the transition towards distributed cloud computing. Large companies are in the process to deliver the best in class application performance to their customers with fully leveraging heterogeneous computing and storage capabilities.

Data centers are becoming an emerging part of networks and hardware accelerators and play a vital component of formerly specified as software-only services. As the importance and use of hardware accelerators will only continue to increase, a significant challenge exists for certain exposures. To counter this in the future, companies in turn are suggesting a virtualization technique for any domain specific accelerators (heterogeneous form of chipsets) for multi-tenant use of specific hardware. Also, using zero touch orchestration for any hardware accelerators to design and assign service instances based on the map of resources and accelerators capabilities with the use of artificial and cognitive technologies to optimize business standards and reduce complexities.

Optimizing cloud services to go against homogenization and centralization is not an easy task. Another future trend would be use of quantum level services at the cloud to speed up analytics with maximum optimization of resources available in the network with no failure options and to stabilize the quantum level fluctuation.

References

1. Tsuchiya, S., Sakumoto, Y., Tsuchimoto, Y., Lee, V., Big Data Processing in Cloud Environments. *Sci. Tech. J., Fujitsu*, 48, 2, 159–168 2012.
2. Hwang, K., Fox, G., Dongarra, J., *Distributed and Cloud Computing*, University of Southern California, Elsevier Inc., USA, 2011.
3. Laurila, J.K., Gatica-Perez, D., Aad, I., Blom, J., Bornet, O., Dousse, T.-M.-T.O., Eberle, J., Miettinen, M., The mobile data challenge: Big data for mobile computing research, Workshop on the Nokia Mobile Data Challenge, in: *Proceedings of the Conjunction with the 10th International Conferenceon Pervasive Computing*, pp. 1–8, 2012.
4. O'Leary, D.E., Artificial intelligence and big data. *IEEE Intell. Syst.*, 28, 96–99, 2013.

5. Antonio, R., MIT Technology Review, 31 October, pp. 1, 2011.

6. Hashem, I.A.T. and Yaqoob, I., The rise of big data on cloud computing: Review and open research issue. *Inf. Syst.,* Elsevier Publications, 47, 98–115, 2015.

7. Platform-as-a-service. cloudflare, January 30, 2020.

8. Ashish, S., Technocents, 24 March, pp. 1, 2014

9. Apache Cassandra, Retrieved from https://cassandra.apache.org/, 2016.

10. Project Voldemort, A distributed database, Retrived from http://www.project-voldemort.com/voldemort/, 2017.

## 15

Data Analytics Framework Based on Cloud Environment

K. Kanagaraj* and S. Geetha

Department of Computer Applications, Mepco Schlenk Engineering College, Sivakasi, India

Abstract

This chapter discusses the various data analytics frameworks available based on a cloud environment that facilitates the user to make an appropriate choice for their application. Data Analytics become very common in Business Organizations. Usually, the data analytics getting performed using R, Python, or other Machine Learning Tools available in the local computer itself. Now a day, data is growing fast which leads to big data. In the case of big data analytics, the resources required for processing, analyzing, and storing big data are inadequate and also more complex. For existence, the Business Organizations have to invest more finance on infrastructure, software to store and analyze their data to get inference out of it. A lot is happening recently on the subject of data analytics with a cloud environment. The ability of a Cloud environment is already proven in many areas like software, infrastructure, and platform as a service. As the data volumes are growing exponentially, the cost to store and analyze that data cannot be allowed to grow at those same rates. Cloud uses several intelligent mechanisms like auto-scaling to reduce the usage cost. There are a variety of big data applications such as log analysis, optimization solutions, supply chain analytics, and big data analytics with different requirements at the hardware and software level. There exist several cloud service providers and still many are emerging in the market. They are offering data analytics services at a small, medium, and large scale. Though the competition is between big players like Amazon, Google, Microsoft, IBM, etc. there is a large number of service providers offering similar services at a different cost. This offers the freedom to select a cloud service provider of own choice by the users, at the same time, it makes it difficult to decide a suitable service provider for their application. Hence, this chapter will provide better insight into data analytics options in the cloud environment is discussed in brief.

Keywords: Cloud computing, data analytics, virtualization, data center, big data analytics, predictive analytics, streaming analytics, cloud framework for data analytics

15.1 Introduction

Cloud is a technology that supports sharing IT resources that includes server, software (both application and system software), network, storage, etc. All the resources are centralized and

---

Corresponding author: kanagaraj@mepcoeng.ac.in; sgeetha@mepcoeng.ac.in

Monika Mangla, Suneeta Satpathy, Bhagirathi Nayak and Sachi Nandan Mohanty (eds.) Integration of Cloud Computing with Internet of Things: Foundations, Analytics, and Applications, (251–276) © 2021 Scrivener Publishing LLC

made available as a service through the internet. The resources are shared on the demand by the organization. Cloud Computing refers to:

    i.   Software as a Service (SaaS)
    ii.   Infrastructure as a Service (IaaS)
    iii. Platform as a Service (PaaS)

and extending to:

    i.   Business Process as a Service (BPaaS)
    ii.   Desktop as a Service (DaaS)
    iii. Analytics as a Service (AaaS)
    iv. Artificial Intelligence as a Service (AIaaS)
    v.   Continuous Analytics as a Service (CAaaS) [1, 2].

Analytics as a Service (AaaS) presents the capability to consumers that, they can analyze their data with the data analytics tools available in the cloud. Data Analytics [3–5] involves many automated techniques and algorithms. Data Analytics models are essential for extracting required insights out of data generated from various sources. Data Analytics is involved in various domains such as Healthcare, Finance, Government, Energy, Business which includes Retail, Media, etc.

Major reasons to move towards Cloud Computing are cost and operational efficiency, scalability, reliability, and mobility. In the same way, major reasons to move towards Data Analytics are cost efficiency, scalability, easy maintenance, and monitoring of business [6–8]. While looking up the relationship between Cloud Computing and Data Analytics, both are used for their benefits such as efficiency, scalability, and reliability. Cloud Computing provides resources based on demand. Data analytics providing better insight into data. Corresponding to the recent growth of data in the world, the resources required for data analytics become costlier and unable to scale up. To overcome these problems, Cloud Computing Service providers enable their services to offer Analytics also as a Service.

15.2   Focus Areas of the Chapter

The main focus areas of this chapter are Data Analytics based on Cloud Environment which includes various types of Cloud Computing Service Models and various kinds of Data Analytics. Also, it covers the framework of how data analytics can be offered as a service by cloud computing.

15.3   Cloud Computing

Cloud Computing [9–11] is defined as "a model to support the users by providing the services online based on demand." Cloud computing becomes a great support to the organizations to store, process, and retrieve their data without having to own any licensed software.

Organizations that are even having minimum usage can get greater advantage of utilizing software, platform, and infra as a service.

15.3.1 Cloud Service Models

Cloud service parties are given that services in various models [12–14]. They are listed below.

- i. Software as a Service (SaaS)
- ii. Infrastructure as a Service (IaaS)
- iii. Platform as a Service (PaaS)
- iv. Business Process as a Service (BPaaS)
- v. Desktop as a Service (DaaS)
- vi. Analytics as a Service (AaaS)
- vii. Artificial Intelligence as a Service (AIaaS)
- viii. Continuous Analytics as a Service (CAaaS).

All the service models are providing more support to users like business organizations, industries, individuals, etc. Figure 15.1 shows the outline of the various service models.

15.3.1.1 Software as a Service (SaaS)

The software licenses can be shared based on subscription. The cloud service providers have purchased the license for the software and made it available on the internet. The consumers, who want to utilize that software without purchasing it, can take up the cloud services for the required duration. Software as a Service offered by few organizations are Google Apps, Salesforce, etc. The Cloud Applications such as Social Networks, Customer Relationship Management Software, Office Management Suites, etc., are provided as a Service by the cloud service organizations. Figure 15.2 shows the overview of Software as a Service. The characteristics of SaaS are:

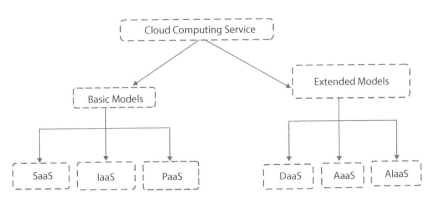

Figure 15.1 Overview of Cloud Computing Service Models.

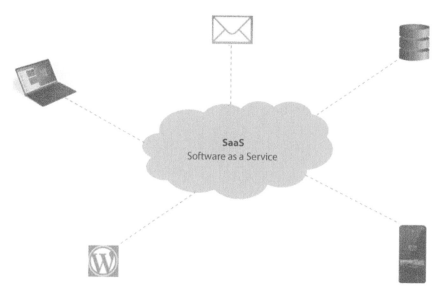

Figure 15.2 Software as a service.

Commercial: The software is commercialized as pay for use. No need of purchasing the software at a high cost. Based on the usage the payment can be done. It is more useful where the customers are using the software for only limited time and purpose.

Centralized: The software is centralized and allowed to access through the internet. The software will be installed in the centralized server, not in the client system.

Third-Party Maintenance: The cloud service providers will take the responsibility of maintaining the software. Usually, maintenance costs will be 60% out of the total cost spent on that software. Hence, there are huge savings for the organizations that are utilizing the software as a service.

Upgraded Version: Software will be upgraded by the cloud service providers as on when new releases are coming.

15.3.1.2 Platform as a Service (PaaS)

The end user developed projects or products can be implemented into the cloud-based infra. This capability is offered by the cloud service organization. The cloud service organization will administer all the essential cloud features, but the consumers have the complete management of the applications and other configurations that are deployed by them. Platform as Service is offered by many Cloud Service organizations which are: Amazon Web Services Elastic Beanstalk, Windows Azure, etc. Figure 15.3 shows the overview of Platform as a Service. The characteristics of Platform as a Service are described below.

Integrated Development Environment: Cloud service providing the facility to do all the basic processes of applications in this environment.

Web-Based UI Tools: User Interface development tools are available through web browsers. It helps to design, test, and deploy the user screen.

Multi-tenant Architecture: PaaS follows the "one to many" model for its service. Multiple users can use the same application concurrently.

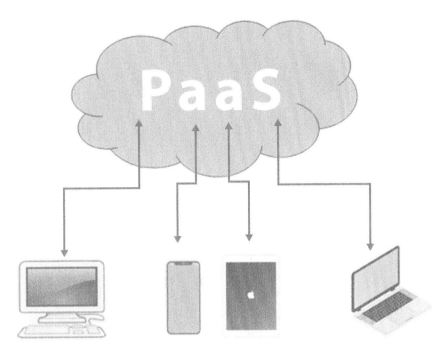

Figure 15.3 Platform as a service.

Scalable Deployment: By default, scalable deployment of software is offered by the Cloud Organizations. It helps to overcome problems like load balancing, failover, etc.

Web Services: Common standards are followed to integrate with web services and standard databases. Web services are available with specific standards to integrate into the development environment.

Collaboration Support: Provides collaboration support for Communication among the team and planning of the project, billing for project resources, etc. Many supporting tools are coming with services for managing the team and project.

15.3.1.3 Infrastructure as a Service (IaaS)

Basic requirements for the creation of any IT applications are offered as a service is called Infrastructure as a Service. Few Infrastructure as a Service offered by Cloud Service organizations are Amazon Web Services EC2, Google Compute Engine, etc. Figure 15.4 shows the overview of Infrastructure as a Service. The characteristics of infrastructure are discussed below.

Distributed Service: Resources to the customers are provided as the distributed service which supports the customer to make use of the resources without any dependency. It also supports the maintenance of resource usage.

Dynamic Scaling: IaaS is mainly providing the facility of dynamic scaling. Based on the usage rate, the resources can be accessed dynamically. Customers have the facility of dynamically configuring the CPU, storage, etc.

Variable Cost Model: It follows the variable cost model and utility pricing model. This provides the most efficient and flexible cost benefits to the customers.

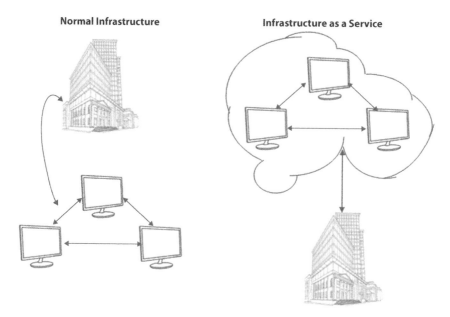

Figure 15.4 Infrastructure as a service.

Multi-User Option: Single hardware can accommodate multiple users which results in a one-many model. Users can access the resources easily.

Automated Administration: The complete infrastructure resource renting is managed automatically.

Wide Services: A surfeit of services can be availed by users. The services include CPU cores, RAM, network, storage space, etc.

Reliability: As the servers are distributed over various locations, the service can be accessed without any interruption in case of server ceases. Users have enormous reliability over resources through Infrastructure as a Service.

15.3.1.4 Desktop as a Service (DaaS)

Desktop as a Service is not a new feature. This kind of service was already there in a different name such as VDI (Virtual Desktop Interface). In the VDI model, the Organization will provide the computers to its employees whereas third-parties will supply the virtual infrastructure and maintain it. In the DaaS model, the cloud service providers will manage the compute, storage, and network infrastructure. Citrix and VMware are the initial virtual desktop providers with conventional architecture. After the cloud computing establishment, Microsoft Azure, Amazon Workspaces, Google Desktop are providing the VDI through the cloud. Now a day, Citrix Virtual Desktops and VMware Horizon Cloud are also offering the VDI as service through the cloud. Figure 15.5 shows the overview of Desktop as a Service. The features of Desktop as a Service are described below.

Agility: Rapid implementation of Desktops through DaaS provisioning the quick access to the desktops. It is very fit for the organizations which look for pushing new applications and desktops in a shorter duration.

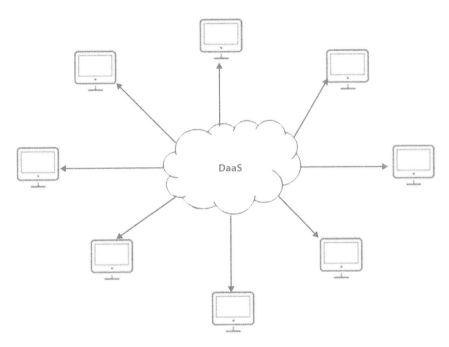

Figure 15.5 Desktop as a service.

Scalability: Provides scalable VDI deployment with significant speed based on the demand. Scaling is not only for increasing the access but also for unused. The User doesn't need to pay for unused desktops.

Zero Code: DaaS allows remodeling the legacy applications with zero code refactoring. It is a very big advantage to the organizations that already have invested much money for their legacy applications.

High-Quality: DaaS provides both on-premises and cloud-hosted options, so that, the user can experience the high quality service.

Reliability: Cloud service providers typically quoting 99.99% uptime levels. Hence, users can relay highly on the services.

Value Propositions: As agile VDIs are offered, users are availing unique value propositions and also a speedy transition of the standard desktop computing environment.

15.3.1.5   Analytics as a Service (AaaS)

In business, analytics is a significant work. Usually, onsite computing devices and analytics software have been used for analyzing business data. But the analysis work becomes a more intensive process. Hence, analytics as a service becomes more valuable to the businesses who are all dealing with the huge amount of data for analytics. Analytics as a Service defines the analytics software that will be offered through web technologies. The AaaS offers customizable analytics [15–18] solutions with collecting, storing, organizing, analyzing, and presenting the results. No need of having owned software by the organization to do any analytics work which is not going to happen frequently. Figure 15.6 shows the overview of Analytics as a Service. The features of analytics as a service are discussed below.

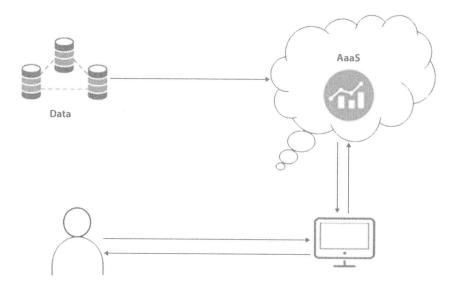

Figure 15.6 Analytics as a service.

Easy Accessible Analytics: Users can work with analytics very easily. When the data is available in the centralized server, any user, it is not necessary to have the expert for data analysis, can access the analytical tools, and perform the analysis of data. It is a kind of self-service model.

Artificial Intelligence: The data analytics solutions have arrived with the support of artificial intelligence. AI-driven analytics uses dozens of advanced algorithms to uncover trends, anomalies, and causal relationships from deep within data.

Simple & Fast: AaaS is very simple and fast access to data and applying analysis. It supports the organization to get speedy inference out of data.

15.3.1.6   *Artificial Intelligence as a Service (AIaaS)*

Artificial Intelligence as a Service offered through cloud technology. Artificial Intelligence means the machine will do the work as the way how humans will do that work. Machine learning, Deep Learning, Natural Language Processing Intelligent documentation, and Robotics automation are the few artificial intelligence services which offered through the cloud. Nowadays, most of the businesses have started applying machine learning algorithms to learn their business data for decision making. Artificial Intelligence providers are Amazon, Google, Microsoft, and IBM in addition to budding companies like Dataiku, BigML, ForecastThis, etc., have also begun to provide AIaaS. Figure 15.7 shows the overview of AIaaS. The main features of AIaaS are discussed below.

Micro Service: Complete software development becomes micro services and APIs. Hence composite of AI micro services is available to serve the dynamic need of the industry.

Integrated Solutions: AIaaS facilitates default AI capabilities that supports businesses to integrate and elect.

Versatile Analytics: AIaaS provides versatile analytics such as healthcare analytics, forecast demand, signal analysis, virtual assistants, and predictive analytics.

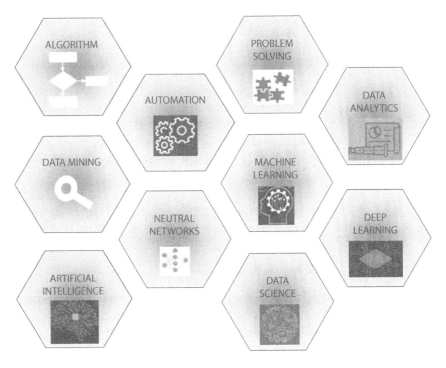

Figure 15.7 Artificial Intelligence as service.

15.3.2   Cloud Deployment Models

Cloud deployment is done in various types commonly called models [19]. The three popular models are public, private, and hybrid. All the services of the cloud can be offered based on these deployment models. Figure 15.8 shows the classification of cloud deployment models.

Public Cloud: A public cloud is the most generic method used provides service for any common individual or an organization. All the services of the public cloud are accessible

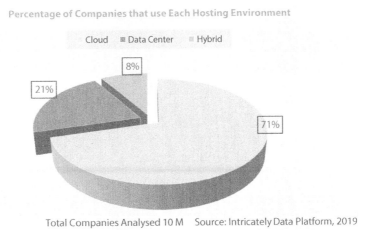

Figure 15.8 Classification of cloud deployment models.

by any paid user with a valid subscription and are accessible using a normal Internet connection.

Private Cloud: A cloud service that designed and accessible only by the employees of a particular organization is called as the private cloud. It usually accessed using a secured intranet or any private network as the organization may exchange confidential information using this cloud environment. Sometimes the services can also be extended for genuine and trusted business partners of the service provider.

Hybrid Cloud: A hybrid cloud can access the public as well as private clouds. Hybrid cloud users use private resources for their normal operation and use public resources during peak and unexpectedly high loads.

Community Cloud: A community-based cloud computing service is a kind of cloud deployment model which allows the organizations to access the infrastructure and resources of others. It is a distributed system developed by integrating the services of different clouds.

15.3.3 Virtualization of Resources

Virtualization [20, 21] is a popular technology used to enable efficient utilization of resources in computing systems such as small desktops, clusters, and large facilities such as cloud data centers. This technology increases the utilization of the underlying hardware with the help of multi-tenancy concept. Moreover, it also isolates different users on the same resource, which is a mechanism for the effective deployment of workloads. Virtualization is a platform to deal with the heterogeneity of resources. Virtualization technology influences the different layers of the computing layer. Rapid improvements in hardware techniques, the need to achieve exascale computing, the use of multiple and decentralized clouds, and the possibilities of decoupling physical and logical networks are paving way for significant innovation in the virtualization arena. Figure 15.9 shows the architecture of virtualization. The emergence of cloud has several advantages including the reduction of cost of operation. The consolidation of servers and providing elasticity for resource provisioning are the unique nature of cloud computing. Though cloud computing is very successful and powerful in providing

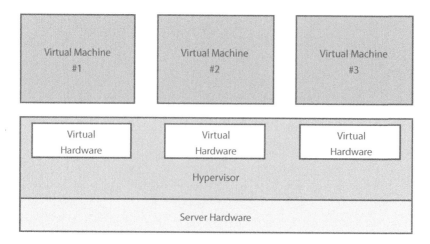

Figure 15.9 Virtualization architecture.

customized resources at a cheaper cost, it requires some improvement to overcome the challenges in some real-time applications. Some other applications like streaming of videos, supporting multiuser games, and managing telecommunication need more sophisticated support from the cloud for hassle-free operation.

Virtualization is used in several domains and for different purposes. The use of virtualization in cloud computing has redefined the way of doing computation. The traditional way of doing computation is replaced using virtualization-based environment. Now users have the freedom to access cloud services from public vendors and from government organizations most of which are provided at free of cost.

15.3.4   Cloud Data Centers

A data center [22] comprises of massive computing resources made up of huge amounts of servers that are connected using a high bandwidth interconnection network. It is a multimillion-dollar investment business. The organization that owns a data center and provides services to its users is called the Cloud Service Provider (CSP). The IT infrastructure that provides these resources is made up of large sets of compute, storage, and networking resources called the resource pool. The concept of multitenancy is an architectural style by which multiple independent clients are serviced using a single set of resources. Metered service takes care of monitoring the utilization of resources and charges them according to the amount and time of usage.

Data centers are envisioned to handle the unpredictable requirement of resources at various times as well as to balance the loads in different servers. A data center is aimed to deliver service round the clock with zero downtime and a hundred percent availability. The data center infrastructure is built by using a shared pool of resources, made up of compute, memory, storage, and network. The data center should also be equipped to monitor, control and optimize resource utilization. A data center has to dedicate resources to each user, business or application, ensure data availability by having a proper backup of the resources. Most of the CSPs have multiple data centers as shown in Table 15.1, distributed in several parts of the globe. The user has the freedom to select a data center of their choice. Mostly selecting a data center nearest to the user's location will be cheaper due to the decrease in data transfer time.

Every cloud service provider needs to qualify the five essential characteristics, self-service, based on demand, elasticity in resource provisioning, pooling of resources, service

Table 15.1 Location of data centers owned by popular CSPs and their performance one month.

Service provider	USA	Asia	Other locations	Total DCs
AWS	19	12	14	45
Azure	31	36	26	93
IBM	29	20	26	75
Google	16	12	16	44

measurement, and broad network access. A user can consume the required services from the cloud whenever required, without human intervention. The advantage of increasing or decreasing the resource to meet the fluctuating demands of the users is called rapid elasticity. Virtualization is a technique that helps the data centers to create multiple virtual machines with different operating systems by multiplexing a single physical machine. The VMs are also replicated in multiple locations called as backup sites to enhance VM recovery. Restoring a virtual machine is a fast and easy task when compared to physical machine recovery. Sometimes VM cloning is also done to create an identical copy of an existing VM. Data center automation is a feature that facilitates the CSPs to schedule and manage the resources effectively.

Popular cloud service providers like Microsoft, Google, and Amazon are investing huge funds in data centers for escalating their businesses. To house the computer servers; the companies have invested nearly $20 billion in the year 2017. This amount is more than the total amount invested by them in the last three years. Most of the recent applications like driverless cars, artificial intelligence based biometrics, and even mobile phones and websites that are becoming essential for day to day activities are supported by the data centers. The cloud also plays a vital role in encouraging new several startups, most of which develop complete applications and services in the cloud. Figure 15.10 shows the cloud applications deployment growth.

Data center automation has opened up new possibilities for research and development in resource provisioning methods. The most common and popular resource provisioning models are demand driven, event driven, popularity driven, and dynamic resource provisioning. Even though cloud data centers have made a significant contribution to the computing industry, it has its own drawbacks. Data center consumes high electric power and generates enormous heat, demanding the need to build green data centers. Figure 15.11 shows the global distribution of data center.

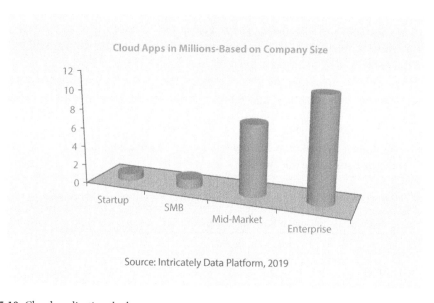

Source: Intricately Data Platform, 2019

Figure 15.10 Cloud application deployment.

Figure 15.11 Data Center—Global Distribution [Source: Internet].

15.4   Data Analytics

Data Analytics involves various steps such as collection, organizing, pre-processing, model-ing, and analyzing [23, 24]. Each process will go with various stages. Finally, useful insights can be taken away from Data Analytics. The first step in Data Analytics is collection of data which involves huge processes like, deciding the group from which the data to be collected, deciding the mode of collection, and deciding the method of storing. The second step is organizing which includes, ordering of data based on numerical or categorical. The third step is pre-processing which plays the major role to get accurate insight out of the analysis. In pre-processing, duplication removal—the duplicate data will be removed, imputation—missing data will be imputed with various imputation techniques, and normalization—data may be normalized. The next step is modeling which includes the mining and visualiza-tion of data. There are various types of Analytics. The basic kinds of Data Analysis are Descriptive Analysis, Diagnostic Analysis, Predictive Analysis, and Prescriptive Analysis. Now, it is getting extended to Augmented Analysis, Cloud Analysis, Big Data Analysis, and Streaming Analytics. Figure 15.12 shows the types of Data Analytics.

15.4.1   Data Analytics Types

15.4.1.1   Descriptive Analytics

Descriptive analytics is a process of bringing inference out of earlier data which can be viewed in the format of easily understandable. As it deals with historical data, it can infer or summarize the past status (for e.g. What was happened?). Descriptive Analytics involves five categories: summary, classification, and clustering.

Summary: Getting an overview of the complete data is called Summary. The sample data is taken from Covid 19 Cases and presented in a column chart to get the summary of Covid 19 cases. Figure 15.13 shows summary of the data.

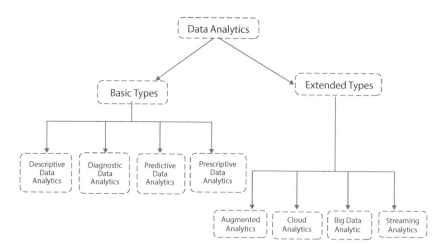

Figure 15.12 Types of data analytics.

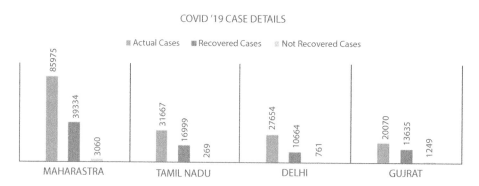

Figure 15.13 Summary of Covid 19 cases (as of 05.06.2020).

Classification: Arranging the data categorically is called Classification. It is shown in Figure 15.14 which depicts Covid 19 cases in gender-wise.

Clustering: Dividing the data into groups is called Clustering. The Covid 19 cases are recorded in different state with gender clustered using k-means clustering and shown in Figure 15.15.

15.4.1.2   Diagnostic Analytics

Diagnostic Analytics refers to find the reason for happening (for e.g. Why it happened?) some event out of data set. It includes pattern-finding then identifying the relationship between the attributes of the dataset. Correlation is a technique that supports majorly for Diagnostic Analytics.

Correlation: It is a statistical measure on each variable how it is associated with other variables. As per Covid 19 data, there is no relationship between the State and the Gender wise affected patients.

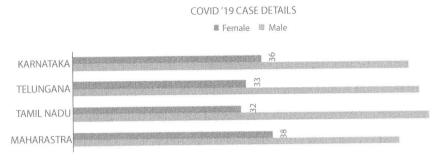

Figure 15.14 Gender wise Covid 19 cases (as of 05.06.2020).

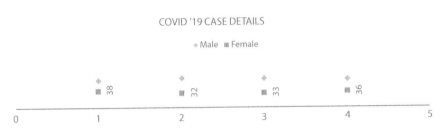

Figure 15.15 Clustering of Covid 19 cases based on gender (as of 05.06.2020).

15.4.1.3   Predictive Analytics

Predictive Analytics refers to discover the future [25]. The inference extracted from the original data will be used to find a future event. Regression is one of the major statistical techniques used casually to forecast the future.

Regression: There are varieties of regression techniques existing to predict the future with the help of historical data.

15.4.1.4   Prescriptive Analytics

After completion of descriptive and predictive analytics on data, what next action will be prescribed through Prescriptive Analytics. It is like a recommendation application. In many cases, the data will be grouped and predicted but what is next will be a big question mark. To overcome this problem, prescriptive analytics provides future decision-making facilities.

15.4.1.5   Big Data Analytics

Big Data Analytics [26, 27] refers to analyze and find trends and patterns on high voluminous, velocity, and variety of data. Data growth has become immense in the entire field. Majorly, in business organizations and all suffering with a huge amount of data. To support such a situation, big data analytics arrived in the information technology field.

15.4.1.6   Augmented Analytics

Augmented analytics defined as the technologies supporting for augmenting the real situation of how the data gets analyzed by a human. Artificial intelligence is used to support for doing all the analytical works on the data. The data collection, preparation, and analysis is taken care of by the AI tools such as Business intelligence tools. It also enhances automation through deep learning models [28].

15.4.1.7   Cloud Analytics

The Data Analytics carried on cloud computing is called Cloud Analytics. Instead of using the own resources for data analytics, now all the resources can be availed from Cloud. All data mining and machine learning modeling can be developed with the help of Cloud Analytics.

15.4.1.8   Streaming Analytics

Streaming analytics [29] refers to analyzing continuous data to infer the required information. The streaming data is a lit bit complex to process than normal data. In recent days, Internet of Things (IoT) becomes very casual. It mainly uses the sensor to automate many works. The sensors will continuously produce a lot of data. Those data can process using streaming analytics tolls to bring out inference [30].

15.4.2   Data Analytics Tools

There are so many tools available in the market for performing data analytics. Out of those, few familiar tools are Excel, R Programming, Weka, Python, Tableau, Infographic, Solver, Hadoop, Spark, etc. Apart from that, so many open source tools are available for each process in the Data analytics.

15.5   Real-Time Data Analytics Support in Cloud

According to Gartner's definition, Real-time analytics is the way to get better inference out of data by applying mathematical and logical formulae. With the help of inference, decision making can be done very fast by the users. The analysis can be performed on the continuous data within seconds after receiving the data from the sources. Continuous data can be sensor data, signal data, social network data, etc. The big data can be processed batch by batch to bring out the inference. But in the case of continuous data, the data have to be stored continuously and analyzed continuously. It is more complex to deal with than big data. In the real-world, the data is growing as big data as well as continuous data. Most of the organizations are facing the issue to get inference out of continuous data as on comes. Hence, the latest research areas are focusing on the techniques for continuous data analysis. Data Process has three stages such as Ingestion (Data Collection), Process (Data into Information), and Analyze (Information into Insight). Cloud techniques are available with various tools to support the organizations which generate and are waiting for inferring the decision out of continuous data.

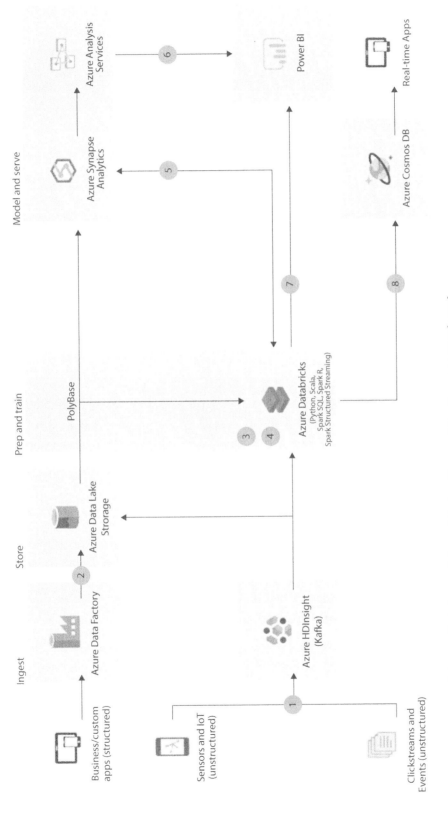

Figure 15.16 Microsoft Azure—Real-time analytics architecture [Sources: https://azure.microsoft.com].

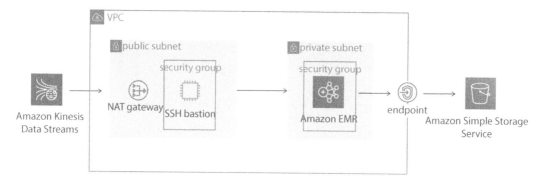

Figure 15.17 Amazon Web Services—Real-time analytics architecture [Sources: http://aws.amazon.com/kinesis/].

Many companies are opting to use cloud services to access data analytical tools instead of building expensive data warehouses themselves. This implies that most of the investment in real-time data will be made from selling hybrid cloud services rather than selling databases. In real-time analytics, the output will be more complex and dynamic. Hence, the implementation of real-time Data Analytics in the Cloud should be hybrid type of deployment. Figure 15.16 shows the real-time analytics architecture of Microsoft Azure [31] and Figure 15.17 shows the real-time analytics architecture of Amazon Web Services [32].

15.6   Framework for Data Analytics in Cloud

The Data Analytics is offered as service through the cloud in different service models. The end-user can access all the services through the cloud for developing, testing, implementing the data analytics applications. The Data Analytics Services through the cloud are shown in Figure 15.18. The framework for Data Analytics in Cloud [33–38] is shown in Figure 15.19. Based on this framework, the implementation of cloud services for data analytics can be achieved. The Data Analytics Service at different service models are provided through the cloud are:

1. Data Analysis Software as a Service (DASaaS)
2. Data Analysis Platform as a Service (DAPaaS)
3. Data Analysis Infrastructure as a Service (DAIaaS)

15.6.1   Data Analysis Software as a Service (DASaaS)

Data Analysis Software as a Service model offers all the data analysis and algorithms over the internet. So many other knowledge discovery applications are also given as a service through the internet to the client. This approach supports the organization to implement the data analysis and mining on their data which brings the inference from the data for decision making.

15.6.2   Data Analysis Platform as a Service (DAPaaS)

Data Analysis Platform as a Service model offers the platform as a service through the web. The developers can use this platform for creating and implementing the data analytics

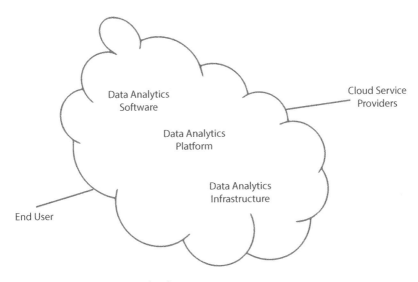

Figure 15.18 Data analytics services in Cloud.

projects without worrying about the architecture requirement. The software platform can be used based on demand.

15.6.3   Data Analysis Infrastructure as a Service (DAIaaS)

Data Analysis Infrastructure as a Service model defines the services through virtualized resources. The whole software and hardware and other resources required for the development of applications, storage of data, executing data analytics applications, and implementation of data mining systems are provided virtually to the end-users. The virtualization of resources is not new, but the implementation of virtual resources required for data analytics applications is very new.

15.7   Data Analytics Work-Flow

The cloud-based data analytics is carried out in a specified work-flow. The work-flow differs based on a variety of facts. The facts are classified into two different groups such as supervised data and unsupervised data. In a general scenario, the data coming with labeled which is called supervised. These data can be handled as little better than unsupervised data. But the unsupervised data doesn't have any label, as it may come in any form that makes the processing step a little complex than supervised data. The supervised data can be analyzed in such a way that Classification, Regression, etc. The unsupervised data can be analyzed in the way of Clustering, Dimensionality reduction, etc. The data can be processed as the batch, micro-batch, or streaming. Figure 15.20 shows the data analytics work-flow in the cloud.

Most of the unlabeled data generated as continuous data which is unsupervised. These data to be handled specifically with cloud tools like Flink, SMAZA, Storm, Kafka, etc. At the same time, the supervised data generated as discrete which can be handled using Spark,

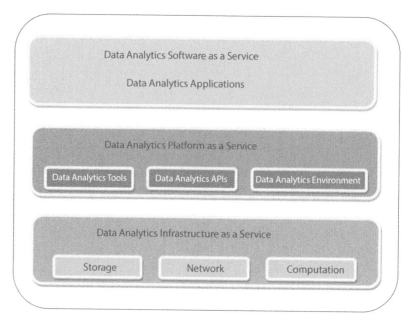

Figure 15.19 Framework for data analytics in Cloud.

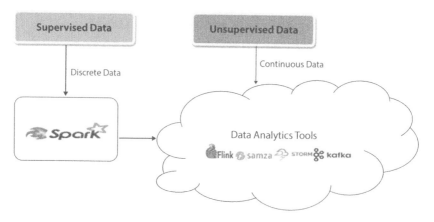

Figure 15.20 Data analytics work flow using Cloud tools.

Hadoop, etc. Many analytical tools are available through the internet to handle continuous data. The organizations can get services from the cloud organizations to handle their continuous data efficiently and quickly.

15.8 Cloud-Based Data Analytics Tools

The lots of cloud service providers are providing Data Analytics tools as service through the cloud. The famous cloud offering organizations like Amazon, Google, and Microsoft are providing various Data Analytics Tools. Those tools are discussed below.

15.8.1   Amazon Kinesis Services

Amazon Kinesis Services provide the facility to-do the collection, processing, and analyzing the continuous data streams and bringing quick and significant inferences out of streaming data. This helps to handle streaming data quickly and supports business organizations in efficient decision making. It offers various services like Data Firehose, Data Streams, Data Analytics, etc. Out of various services provided by Amazon Kinesis Services, the following two services are described here.

1. Amazon Kinesis Data Firehose
2. Amazon Kinesis Data Streams.

15.8.2   Amazon Kinesis Data Firehose

Amazon Kinesis Data Firehose collects, processes and ingests real-time data streams into Amazon S3, Amazon Elasticsearch Service, etc. for enabling analytics on the real-time data and bring out fruitful inference. There is no need of developing any application for analyzing the real-time data as this Amazon Kinesis Data Firehose is supporting through simple configuration steps to take input, convert inputs into required formats, and deliver to Amazon S3.

15.8.3   Amazon Kinesis Data Streams

Amazon Kinesis Data Streams is a service that supports massive and robust streaming data. This service helps to confine continuous data in the size of gigabytes per second from heterogeneous sources such as social media, business transactions, log files, clickstreams, etc. The captured data can be analyzed and resulted very speedily.

15.8.4   Amazon Textract

Amazon Textract is a service which helps to extract data from the text files automatically. Any social media data is coming in text format; this service will support to process it. To work with any sensitive text documents, this service provides a better facility than any other service. It supports processing the documents in real-time and delivers the required information for further decision making. It helps to understand the forms, tables, etc. with machine learning models in the contact intact. Additionally, the better searching, compliance with the document are also reinforced by the Amazon Textract.

15.8.5   Azure Stream Analytics

Azure Stream Analytics is a more or less equivalent tool like Amazon Kinesis Data Streams. It is an engine that supports real-time analytics. Azure Stream Analytics engine is mainly focusing on the analysis of complex and streaming data from heterogeneous data sources. Azure Stream Analytics ingests data from Azure Event Hubs and sends data to the Power BI dashboard for real-time inference. It is more flexible, scalable, and reliable for any type of dataset.

15.9   Experiment Results

Amazon Textract supports extracting the contents from the document as word by word, line by line, the table in the text, and forms in the text. It is done by logging into Amazon Web Services and creates the bucket for Amazon Textract to process with the pdf document and the result is shown below. Any type of document can be used as input for analysis. This tool helps to analyze each word and will bring an understanding of the document. The words of a given document are split into a single word and it will be taken as input to generate a model for understanding. This model will support to learn the context of each word and bring out the inference of that document.

The extracted words will be mined using the analytical tool to bring out an analysis report. The users can make use of this report for their decision making. The analysis of word by word is shown in Figure 15.21.

The text document can be analyzed based on line by line. The document can be of any type such as doc, docx or pdf. This tool supports to split the text into line by line and bring the inference. Figure 15.22 shows the result of analysis based on line by line using Amazon Textract.

The text or pdf document may include the forms also. Amazon Textract tool providing facility to find and analyze the forms involved in the document. Figure 15.23 shows the analysis of forms in the text document.

Most of the text documents will contain the tables to represent significant information. This tool supports to analyze the tables from the text document. Figure 15.24 shows the analysis of tables in the text.

15.10   Conclusion

In Cloud Computing, there are a lot of extensions over the service models. As the need of users are rising significantly, the demand for various services through the internet also increases. Data Analytics as a Service is one of the extended service models which supports

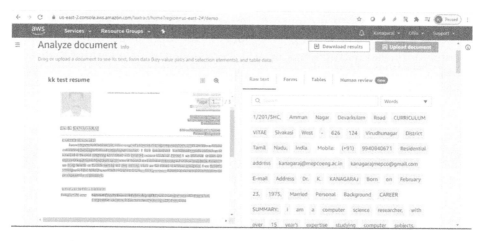

Figure 15.21 Analyzing the text as word by word.

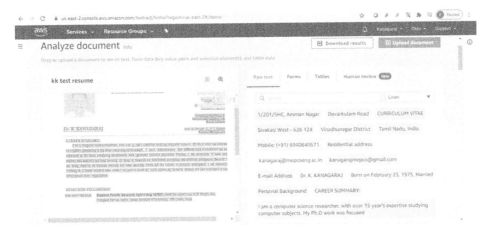

Figure 15.22 Analyzing the text as line by line.

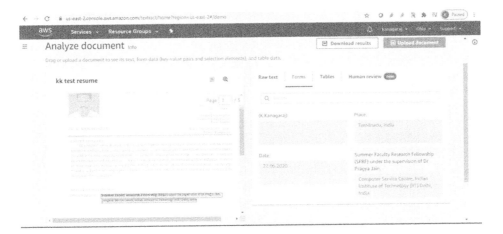

Figure 15.23 Analyzing the forms in the text.

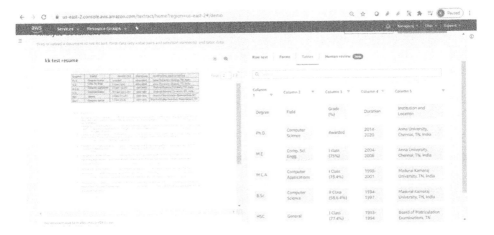

Figure 15.24 Analyzing the tables in the text.

users to analyze the data instantaneously and get rid of inferences and solutions. Various analytical tools are available in the cloud for implementing various analytics such as predictive analytics, video analytics, image analytics, steam analytics, etc. This chapter discusses the framework available for using data analytics in the cloud.

References

1. Chen, Q., Hsu, M., Zeller, H., Experience in Continuous analytics as a Service (CaaaS). *EDBT'2011*, ACM, 2011.
2. Chen, C., Li, D., Li, J., Zhu, K., SVDC: A Highly Scalable Isolation Architecture for Virtualized Layer-2 Data Center Networks. *IEEE Trans. Cloud Comput.*, 6, 4, 1178–1190, 2018.
3. Hilbrich, M., Weber, M., Tschüter, R., Automatic Analysis of Large Data Sets: A Walk-Through on Methods from Different Perspectives. *Int. Conf. on Cloud Comp. and Big Data*, pp. 373–380, 2013.
4. Gui, J., Zheng, Z., Gao, Y., Qin, Z., An Approach for Dynamic Scheduling of Data Analysis Algorithms. *IEEE 4th Int. Conf. on Big Data Anal. (ICBDA)*, pp. 53–57, 2019.
5. Misra, C., Bhattacharya, S., Ghosh, S.K., A fast scalable distributed kriging algorithm using Spark framework. *Int. J. Data Sci. Anal.*, 10, 249–264, 2020.
6. Oneto, L., Buselli, I., Lulli, A., dynamic, A. *et al.*, interpretable, and robust hybrid data analytics system for train movements in large-scale railway networks. *Int. J. Data Sci. Anal.*, 9, 95–111, 2020.
7. Ali, A. and Abdullah, M., A Survey on Vertical and Horizontal Scaling Platforms for Big Data Analytics. *Int. J. Integr. Eng.*, 11, 6, 138–150, 2019.
8. Banda, M. and Ngassam, E.K., A data management and analytic model for business intelligence applications. *IST-Africa Week Conf.*, pp. 1–10, 2017.
9. Zatwarnicki, K., Two-level fuzzy-neural load distribution strategy in cloud-based web system. *J. Cloud Comput.*, 9, 30, 1–11, 2020.
10. Giunta, R., Messina, F., Pappalardo, G., Tramontana, E., Enhancing applications with cloud services by means of aspects. *Int. J. Comput. Appl. Technol.*, 51, 4, 273–282, 2015.
11. Liu, H., He, B., Liao, X., Jin, H., Towards Declarative and Data-Centric Virtual Machine Image Management in IaaS Clouds. *IEEE Trans. Cloud Comput.*, 7, 4, 1124–1138, 2019.
12. Ochei, L.C., Petrovski, A., Bass, J.M., A framework for achieving the required degree of multitenancy isolation for deploying components of a cloud-hosted service. *Int. J. Cloud Comput.*, 7, 3/4, 248–281, 2018.
13. Dong, X., Zhou, X., Zhao, L., Li, K., Cloud Resource Provision of Competitive Content Providers: Models and Analysis. *IEEE Intl. Conf. on Parallel & Distributed Processing with Applications, Big Data & Cloud Computing, Sustainable Computing & Communications, Social Computing & Networking (ISPA/BDCloud/SocialCom/SustainCom)*, pp. 53–60, 2019.
14. Zhang, Y., Yao, J., Guan, H., Intelligent Cloud Resource Management with Deep Reinforcement Learning. *IEEE Cloud Comput.*, 4, 6, 60–69, 2017.
15. Talia, D., A view of programming scalable data analysis: From clouds to exascale. *J. Cloud Comput.*, 8, 4, 2019.
16. Goldin, E., Feldman, D., Georgoulas, G., Castano, M., Nikolakopoulos, G., Cloud computing for big data analytics in the Process Control Industry. *25th Mediterranean Conf. on Control and Automation(MED)*, pp. 1373–1378, 2017.
17. Doyle, J., Giotsas, V., Anam, M.A., Andreopoulos, Y., Dithen: A Computation-as-a-Service Cloud Platform for Large-Scale Multimedia Processing. *IEEE Trans. Cloud Comput.*, 7, 2, 509–523, 2019.

18. Depeige, A. and Doyencourt, D., Actionable Knowledge As A Service (AKAAS): Leveraging big data analytics in cloud computing environments. *J. Big Data*, Springer, 2, 12, 1–16 2015.

19. Bahsoon, R., Ali, N., Heisel, M. *et al.*, Introduction. Software Architecture for Cloud and Big Data: An Open Quest for the Architecturally Significant Requirements, in: *Software Architecture for Big Data and the Cloud*, I. Mistrik (Ed.), Morgan Kaufmann, 1–10, 2017.

20. Alouane, M. and El Bakkali, H., Virtualization in Cloud Computing: NoHype vs HyperWall new approach. *Int. Conf. on Electl. and Inf. Tech.*, pp. 49–54, 2016.

21. Zhu, X., Yang, L.T., Chen, H., Wang, J., Yin, S., Liu, X., Real-Time Tasks Oriented Energy-Aware Scheduling in Virtualized Clouds. *IEEE Trans. Cloud Comput.*, 2, 2, 168–180, 2014.

22. Wu, C. and Buyya, R., *Cloud Data Centers and Cost Modeling A Complete Guide to Planning, Designing and Building a Cloud Data Cente*, Morgan Kaufmann, Elsevier B.V., 2015.

23. Gupta, A.K., Singhal, S., Garg, R.R., Challenges and Issues in Data Analytics. *8th Int. Conf. on Comm. Sys. and Net. Tech. (CSNT)*, Bhopal, India, 2018.

24. Sobati Moghadam, S. and Fayoumi, A., Toward Securing Cloud-Based Data Analytics: A Discussion on Current Solutions and Open Issues. *IEEE Access*, 7, 45632–45650, 2019.

25. Kathidjiotis, Y., Kolomvatsos, K., Anagnostopoulos, C., Predictive intelligence of reliable analytics in distributed computing environments. *Appl. Intell.*, Springer, 50, 3219–3238, 2020.

26. Lu, Q., Li, Z., Kihl, M., Zhu, L., Zhang, W., CF4BDA: A Conceptual Framework for Big Data Analytics Applications in the Cloud. *IEEE Access*, 3, 1944–1952, 2015.

27. Manekar, A.K. and Pradeepini, G., Cloud Based Big Data Analytics: A Review. *Int. Conf. on Comp. Intelli. and Comm. Net.*, pp. 785–788, 2015.

28. https://www.gartner.com/en/information-technology/glossary.

29. https://cloud.google.com/solutions/smart-analytics.

30. https://www.altexsoft.com/blog/real-time-analytics/.

31. https://azure.microsoft.com.

32. http://aws.amazon.com/kinesis/.

33. Lazovik, E., Medema, M., Albers, T., Langius, E., Lazovik, A., Runtime Modifications of Spark Data Processing Pipelines. *Intl. Conf. on Cloud and Autonomic Comp. (ICCAC)*, pp. 34–45, 2017.

34. Adhikari, M., Amgoth, T., Narayana Sriramaa, S., Multi-objective scheduling strategy for scientific workflows in cloud environment: A Firefly-based approach. *Appl. Soft Comput.*, Elsevier, 93, 1–19, 2020.

35. Gupta, S. and Saini, A.K., An artificial intelligence based approach for managing risk of IT systems in adopting cloud. *Int. J. Inf. Tecnol.*, Springer, 1, 9, 1–9, 2018.

36. Maheshwari, P., Singhal, A., Qadeer, M.A., Data analytics using cloud computing. *9th Int. Conf. on Comput. Intell. and Comm. Networks (CICN)*, Girne, 2017.

37. Hammou, B.A., Lahcen, Mouline, S., Towards a real-time processing framework based on improved distributed recurrent neural network variants with fastText for social big data analytics. *Inform. Process. Manag.*, Elsevier, 57, 1, 1–15, 2020.

38. Carlan, V., Huybrechts, T., Hellinckx, P., Vanelslander, T., A universal middleware streaming framework and data analytics: Analysing their economic feasibility in road transport planning. *Res. Transp. Bus. Manag.*, Elsevier, 34, 1–10, 2020.

## 16

Neural Networks for Big Data Analytics

Bithika Bishesh

School of Business Studies, Sharda University, Greater Noida, India

Abstract

Big datasets when properly managed can lead to critical intelligence and thus, incite informed decisions. However, a major challenge with big datasets lies in identifying new and innovative techniques that can solve real-world complex problems better than traditional techniques, which make use of statistics and econometrics. One useful alternative to these traditional techniques is Deep learning. Artificial neural networks are becoming increasingly popular in Big Data analysis because of their efficiency in handling and analyzing large volumes of data. The objective of this chapter is to understand Machine Learning using Deep learning or Artificial Neural Networks. The chapter will start from very simple ideas by illustrating the fundamentals of neural networks and gradually buildup on the working of these networks and discuss the latest innovations, future scope, applications, and problems of using Deep Learning for Big Data analysis. Finally, a practical application using computer codes will be presented to assist the readers in developing a thorough understanding of the mechanisms of training and applying neural networks.

Keywords: Big data, deep learning, machine learning, neural network

16.1 Introduction

Big datasets when properly managed can lead to critical intelligence and thus, incite informed decisions. However, a major challenge with big datasets lies in identifying new and innovative techniques that can solve real-world complex problems better than traditional techniques which makes use of statistics and econometrics. One useful alternative to these traditional techniques is Deep learning.

Deep learning with artificial neural networks (ANN) is a subset of machine learning that plays a vital role in modern computational intelligence and is capable of some truly impressive feats. Artificial neural networks are becoming increasingly popular in Big Data analysis because of their efficiency in handling and analyzing large volumes of data [1, 2].

Real-world applications for neural networks are booming. Neural nets have become the method of choice for different sectors ranging from engineering, manufacturing, automotive, electronics, telecommunications, aerospace, and medicine.

Email: bithika.bishesh@sharda.ac.in

Monika Mangla, Suneeta Satpathy, Bhagirathi Nayak and Sachi Nandan Mohanty (eds.) *Integration of Cloud Computing with Internet of Things: Foundations, Analytics, and Applications,* (277–298) © 2021 Scrivener Publishing LLC

The objective of this chapter is to understand Machine Learning using Neural Networks. The chapter will start from very simple ideas by illustrating the fundamentals of neural networks and gradually build-up on the working of these networks and discuss the latest innovations, future scope, applications, and problems of using Deep Learning for Big Data analysis. Finally, a practical application using computer codes will be presented to assist the readers in developing a thorough understanding of the mechanisms of training and applying neural networks.

16.2 Neural Networks—An Overview

In a traditional approach, conventional computers used an algorithmic approach for solving a particular problem. This pre-requisite of knowing the specific set of instructions restricted the problem-solving capabilities of conventional computers. With the introduction of super-computing, deep learning with neural networks became popular and gained popularity for solving complex problems.

Artificial neural network resembles the working of the animal brain which consists of billions of complex and interconnected neurons.

Figure 16.1 shows the structure of a typical biological neuron. A neuron is a nerve cell that processes and transfers information. A neuron consists of three main parts—the cell body or Soma, extensions of Soma called dendrites, and Axons for signal propagation.

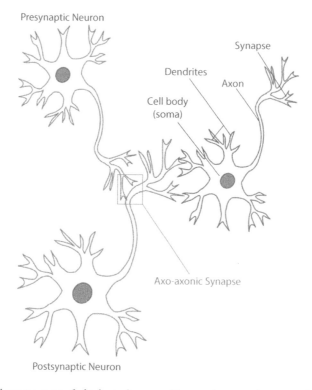

Figure 16.1 Essential components of a biological neuron (Source: Axo-axonic synapse by Shivansh Dave, licensed under CC BY-SA 4.0, https://commons.wikimedia.org/w/index.php?curid=83404696).

Dendrites or dendrons are the branches of a neuron, extending from the Soma, which receive signals from other neurons with the help of receptors. The cell body then performs the computational functions on these sets of inputs, which are then transmitted as signals in the form of the impulse, to other neurons through axons. This impulse is an action potential that triggers the release of neurotransmitters. The processing ability of each neuron depends on the strength of its synaptic connections with other neurons.

Thus, the input signal is received by the dendrites and then passed on to the cell body for integration. Finally, an output signal is released from the synaptic terminal to a target cell, generating a specific response or the desired effect.

Similarly, with the help of software simulation, artificial neural networks are made to emulate the working of this biological neural network. So in a nutshell, artificial neural networks are a network of various interconnected artificial neurons [3].

16.3   Why Study Neural Networks?

Deep learning has a vast scope and its applications can be found in different areas such as science, technology, market forecast, weather forecast, signal processing and, biological applications.

Since a neural network is analogous to a nerve cell; it can simulate many of the characteristics of a biological neuron and hence, finds its applications in diverse fields.

So when some input is provided to this system, an output is generated in response. However, the actual output that we get, may be different from the desired output. Artificial neural networks have self-learning capabilities. Through this learning mechanism, the inputs can be fed and trained in a way to get an output that is almost near to the desired output. This learning ability of neural networks through input–output mapping makes them remarkably different from the conventional computational unit [1, 15]. A neural network can not only generate a response but the response or the output generated by the neural network is substantiated with some degree of confidence. Moreover, just like a brain cell, artificial neural networks can adjust their free parameters to the changes occurring in the external environment and, exploit the non-linearity as it consists of the interconnection of non-linear neurons.

16.4   Working of Artificial Neural Networks

16.4.1   Single-Layer Perceptron

Let us begin by understanding a single artificial neuron called a *perceptron*. The concept of perceptron primarily originates from Rosenblatt's perceptron brain model (1958, 1962). This model uses the McCulloch–Pitts model of a neuron as the fundamental building block of artificial neural networks.

Figure 16.2 shows a prototypical example of artificial neural networks that are analogous to biological neurons.

In Figure 16.2, 'k' represents a neuron receiving a number of inputs from various sources. The inputs are indicated as x_1, x_2,.....,x_n. The synapses or, the strengths of the

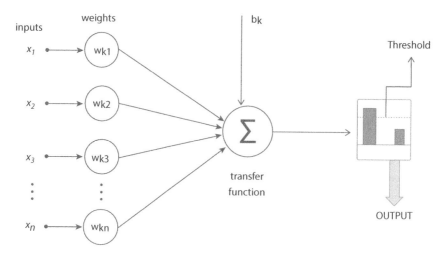

Figure 16.2 Perceptron model (Source: Amended from Rosenblatt perceptron by Perceptron. Mitchell, Machine Learning, p87, licensed under CC BY-SA 3.0, https://commons.wikimedia.org/w/index.php?curid=22329629).

interconnections, existing in the biological neural network are modeled as synaptic weights in artificial neurons. The synaptic weights associated with these inputs are represented as, w_{k1}, w_{k2},....w_{kn}. In other words, we can say that w_{kj} is the strength or connection weight from the neuron 'j' to the neuron 'k'. These weights can have either a positive or a negative value like the excitatory and inhibitory nature of biological synapses and, a large value of weights indicate a strong connection and vice-versa.

A processing element calculates the weighted sum of these various inputs which can be written as:

$$u_k = \sum_{j=1}^{n} x_j w_{kj} \qquad (16.1)$$

An offset or a bias, b_k, can be applied to this system as an input and, the combined output v_k, can then be represented as:

$$v_k = u_k + b_k \qquad (16.2)$$

This will give us some kind of activation value. In order to decide whether a neuron will 'fire' (send message) or 'not fire', the activation value is compared to a threshold value:

Activation value > Threshold value, *'Fire'*
Activation value < Threshold value, *'Don't Fire'*

16.4.2   Multi-Layer Perceptron

In a multi-layer perceptron shown in Figure 16.3, we have multiple neurons present in different layers. It has the same structure as a single-layer perceptron with some additional

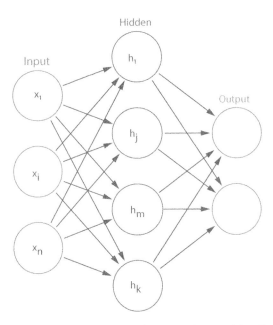

Figure 16.3 Multi-layer perceptron (Source: Amended from neural network by Glosser.ca is licensed under CC BY-SA 3.0, https://commons.wikimedia.org/w/index.php?curid=24913461).

hidden layers. All the inputs are fed into an input layer. Then we have one or more hidden layers that depend on the type of application.

The input layer receives inputs, processes it, and then produces an output. This output is fed as input into the next layer, called the hidden layer. This hidden layer also has various neurons with different activation functions. So, it will perform its own functions on the inputs that it receives from the previous layer. The output from this layer is now transferred to the last layer i.e. the output layer, as an input, and the final output or response is generated.

16.4.3   Training a Neural Network

The most widely used training algorithm for the supervised training of a multi-layer perceptron is called backpropagation. This method is very useful in finding out which node is accountable for how much loss as it can easily learn complex multidimensional mapping and thus, minimize the loss function [4]. It consists of two types of phases or propagation—forward and backward. In forward propagation, the activations are transmitted from the input layer traveling all the way to the output layer. In backward propagation also, the inputs are passed through an activation function and transmitted to the output layer to generate a response or output. However, in the case of backward propagation, the response generated or the actual output is compared to the desired output, and the difference between the two is calculated. This difference is called the error, and the backpropagation technique aims at minimizing this loss or error by propagating backward and adjusting the weights as well as the bias value. Needless to say, this may require a number of iterations.

Backpropagation is thus, the basis of calculating the gradient of the error or loss function.

16.4.4 Gradient Descent Algorithm

Gradient descent is a popular optimization technique that is used in many different types of deep learning models. The objective of this optimization technique is to minimize the loss function so that the model can generate a better or more accurate outcome [14]. Moving in the direction of the steepest descent, the weights are constantly modified using backpropagation, to reach to a point where the error is the least or the global minimum.

To calculate this loss function, let us suppose that, E is the measure of combined error representing the sum total of individual errors E^p, calculated for 'p' number of points.

$$E = \sum_p E^p \tag{16.3}$$

A neural network is going to have a number of outputs or values, however, for one single value, the individual error can be defined as the squared differences between the estimated values, t_0^p and the actual values, y_0^p. This being a squared quantity, the gradient is going to be two times of this value and hence, we can add ½ to this equation for simplicity.

$$E^p = \frac{1}{2} \sum_0 \left(t_0^p - y_0^p \right)^2 \tag{16.4}$$

Now, the gradient of this error in Equation (16.4) is calculated by taking its derivative with respect to the weights in the model. If w_{ij} represents the weight from neuron j to neuron i, then gradient can be written as:

$$G = \frac{\partial E}{\partial w_{ij}} = \frac{\partial}{\partial w_{ij}} \sum_p E^p \tag{16.5}$$

$$= \sum_p \frac{\partial E^p}{\partial w_{ij}} \tag{16.6}$$

By applying the chain rule of differentiation, we get:

$$\frac{\partial E}{\partial w_{oi}} = \frac{\partial E}{\partial y_o} * \frac{\partial y_o}{\partial w_{oi}}$$

Using Equation (16.4), we get

$$\frac{\partial E}{\partial y_o} = -(t_o - y_o) \tag{16.7}$$

And, we know the actual output is the weighted sum of inputs thus,

$$y_o = \sum_j w_{oj} . x_j \qquad (16.8)$$

So,

$$\frac{\partial y_o}{\partial w_{oi}} = \frac{\partial}{\partial w_{oi}} \sum_j w_{oj} . x_j \qquad (16.9)$$

$$= x_i \qquad (16.10)$$

Using Equations (16.7) and (16.10), we get the value of gradient with respect to one particular weight as:

$$\frac{\partial E}{\partial w_{oi}} = -(t_o - y_o) \times x_i \qquad (16.11)$$

If the weight is too small then, the error will be too high and if the weight is too large then the error will be high again. Hence, to find an optimal value for any random weight in the network where the error is the minimum, a step is taken in the direction towards this minimum error [15]. This direction is opposite to the gradient. Thus, we can write:

$$\Delta w_{oi} = (t_0 - y_0)x_i \qquad (16.12)$$

As this is a learning process, we can multiply a learning rate alpha, to Equation (16.12). The learning rate controls the rate of descent and thus, determines the size of each step (epochs) in the gradient descent process.

$$\Delta w_{oi} = \alpha (t_0 - y_0)x_i \qquad (16.13)$$

In modern machine learning and deep learning algorithms, calculating the gradient over the entire data set can be computationally expensive. Thus, the type of gradient descent used mainly depends upon the complexity and the amount of data used. Some of the commonly used types are:

- Batch Gradient Descent: In this type, the complete training data available is used to calculate the gradient [5]. The weights are updated after evaluating all the training examples. This whole process is called a cycle and a training epoch. Since all the data is plugged in, this gives us a better boundary for predicting our data. However, if the training data is large then, using this method can be computationally expensive as it will involve huge matrix computations using tons of memory.
- Stochastic Gradient Descent: This type of descent gives a faster computational result as it uses only one training example. The first step is to randomize

the whole training set and then the parameters are updated for each of the training examples. Since there are frequent updates, it can lead to noisy gradients which instead of decreasing the loss function may actually increase it. In Stochastic Gradient Descent, one might not achieve the best estimate, but since it uses one training example in every iteration, it is faster for larger data sets [6].

- Mini Batch Gradient: This type of gradient descent is very popular for deep-learning problems since; it uses a combination of the previously discussed—Batch and Stochastic descent. Every iteration involves using a set of training examples called batch to compute the gradient. Thus, the training set is separated into small batches and the points in each batch are run through the neural network, calculating the error and its gradient and then, backpropagating to update the weights. This gives us new weights that define a better boundary region and lead to more stable convergence [5].

16.4.5   Activation Functions

Activation functions are used to contain the output between the 'hard limits' and, impart a non-linearity. The logic behind using activation functions is to minimize the error produced in the output and then decide whether the neuron should "fire" or not. This leads to better accuracy in a neural network model.

a. Heaviside function (Step Function)
    Binary step function is very useful in classifiers when the output is to be classified between 0 and 1. Figure 16.4 shows a step function, hard-limited by 0 and 1 thus,
    $f(x) = 0$ if, $0 > x$
    $f(x) = 1$ if, $x \geq 0$.

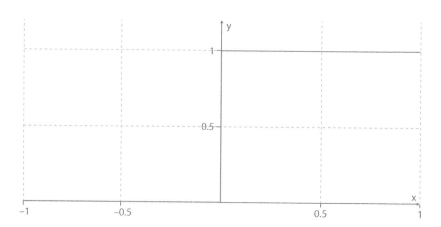

Figure 16.4 Step function (Source: Hard-limit-function by MartinThoma, licensed under CC BY 3.0, https://commons.wikimedia.org/w/index.php?curid=28191475).

b. Identity function

Figure 16.5 depicts an Identity function which is also called the linear function. In this type of activation function, the weighted sum of inputs is converted to output just like a linear regression.

c. Sigmoid Function

Figure 16.6 shows a sigmoid function that is a continuous function gradually varying between the asymptotic values o to 1 (logistic function) or, −1 to +1 (tangential function). The inputs ranging between negative infinity and positive infinity are translated to the range in 0 and 1. The slope parameter is denoted by β, which adjusts the abruptness of the function as it changes between asymptotic values. Thus, a sigmoid function is defined by the formula:

$$f(x) = \frac{1}{1 + e^{-\beta x}} \qquad (16.14)$$

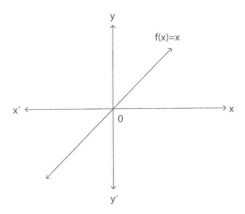

Figure 16.5 Identity function (Source: Amended from—Activation identity by Laughsinthestocks, licensed under CC BY-SA 4.0, https://commons.wikimedia.org/w/index.php?curid=44920411).

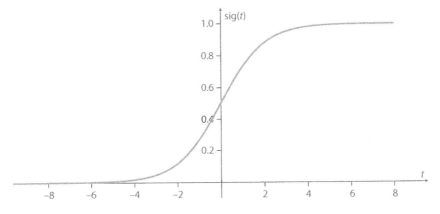

Figure 16.6 Sigmoid function (Source: Amended from Sigmoid-function- by Martin Thoma, licensed under CC0 1.0, https://commons.wikimedia.org/w/index.php?curid=32970804).

However, when dealing with networks containing many layers, training the model becomes lengthy with sigmoid function and it may lead to the 'vanishing gradient problem.'

d. tanh function

Figure 16.7 shows the graphical representation of a tanh function. The value of tanh function ranges from −1 to 1 and it is defined by the formula:

$$tanh(x) = \frac{2}{1+e^{-2x}} - 1 \qquad (16.15)$$

The working of the tanh function is closely related to that of the sigmoid function however, it is always preferred over the latter because of a stronger gradient and better optimization.

e. SoftMax

A widely used function for multiclass classification methods is SoftMax. Similar to the sigmoid function, the output generated by SoftMax ranges between 0 and 1 however, in this case, the output is split in a way that the cumulative total of the final output becomes equal to 1. Thus, the logic behind using SoftMax is to assign probabilities to the output as a vector. The probabilities of different potential outcomes are generated, which is useful for finding out the most probable occurrence or in other words, finding the classification where the probability of a class is maximum.

Considering z, to be a vector of the inputs to the output, the SoftMax function can be represented as:

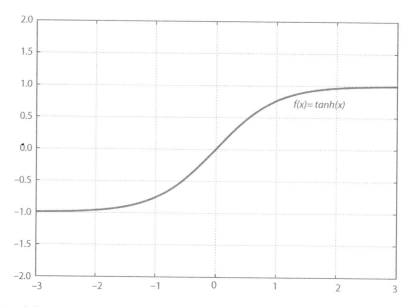

Figure 16.7 tanh function (Source: Amended from tanh function by Geek3, licensed under CC BY 3.0, https://commons.wikimedia.org/w/index.php?curid=32445416).

$$\sigma(z)_j = \frac{e^{zj}}{\sum\limits_{k=1}^{k} e^{zk}} \tag{16.16}$$

for j = 1,....,K

f.   Rectified linear units (ReLU)

ReLU is widely used when it comes to deep learning and even normal neural networks. ReLU works very well for complicated data. If the data has sufficient positive values, the gradient will be positive for all these values. In Sigmoid and tanh functions, values range from zero to one and −1 to +1 respectively. So, as the input values keep on increasing, the output values or the predictions do not change significantly. This leads to a slower learning rate and thus, more time in reaching an accurate prediction. ReLU can learn faster and thus, overcome this vanishing gradient problem. Figure 16.8 shows that,

ReLU(x) = x , if x >0

ReLU(x) = 0 , if x <=0.

This means that ReLU of any input x, is equal to x if is greater than zero, and it is zero if x is less than or equal to zero. Most of the deep networks use ReLU these days but, it's only used for the hidden layers. The output layer generally uses a SoftMax function for classification and, a linear function for regression since, the signal goes through unchanged.

A problem with using ReLU for training neural networks is that some of the neurons may become inactive or 'die'. As a result of this, we get 'dead neurons' which will never be active or recover on any data point again. So the gradients flowing through it will always be zero from that point on. Since all the negative values become zero immediately; it may be difficult to train the data properly.

g.   Leaky ReLU

Leaky ReLU is a good alternative to overcoming the shortcomings of the ReLU function. As shown in Figure 16.9, this variant of the ReLU function

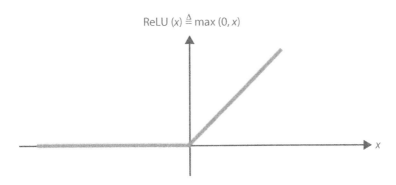

Figure 16.8 ReLU function (Source: ReLU by Renanar2, licensed under CC BY-SA 4.0, https://commons. wikimedia.org/w/index.php?curid=75218611).

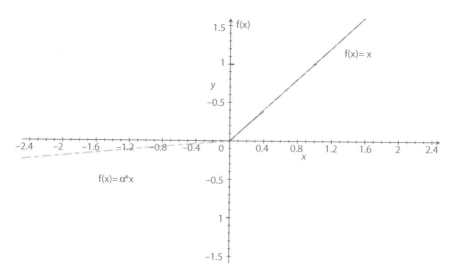

Figure 16.9 Leaky ReLU function (Source: Amended from—Activation Functions by Andreas Maier, licensed under CC BY 4.0, https://commons.wikimedia.org/w/index.php?curid=83106014).

has a small negative slope when the value of x is less than or equal to zero. This solves the dying neuron problem. The negative slope, α is chosen to be a value of the order 0.01.

h. Maxout Activation

This is another popular function which is a generalized form of both ReLU and Leaky ReLU. It takes the maximum value of the pre-activation function (Wx + b) of the hidden unit and converts it into a vector containing only this value. Maxout activation function has all the benefits of ReLU and Leaky ReLU but it needs an extensive number of parameters to be trained.

$$h(x) = \max (W_1.x + b_1, W_2.x + b_2,....., W_n.x + b_n) \qquad (16.17)$$

16.5   Innovations in Neural Networks

16.5.1   Convolutional Neural Network (ConvNet)

Convolutional neural network or CNN simulates the primary cortical region of the brain. Thus, it is mainly used for analyzing visual imagery by using a grid-like topology. Besides, image processing, ConvNets are also popular for signal processing, object detection, and data classification [7]. In the architecture of a classic neural network, a neuron in the layer is connected to all the neurons. But in a convolutional network, a neuron is connected to only a smart portion of the previous layer. So there are fewer amounts of weights to be handled and fewer amount of neurons needed.

This network consists of four different types of layers.

Convolutional layers—These are the hidden layers that form the basis of this network. Just like any other layer, they receive inputs and then transform these inputs to produce an output that acts as input for the next layer. There are filters or kernels present in this layer which assist in pattern detection.

ReLU layer—This layer introduces non-linearity in the ConvNet. They perform an element-wise operation and then, produce a rectified feature map which then goes through the third layer.

Pooling Layer—This layer pools the data together and, reduces the number of parameters while retaining vital information.

Fully-connected layer—Finally, the output is flattened and then fed into one or more fully-connected layers just like a multi-layer perceptron.

16.5.2   Recurrent Neural Network

In a typical feed-forward neural network, there is a flow of information in only one direction. The input layer receives inputs, processes it, and then produces an output which is fed as input into the next layer, called the hidden layer. This hidden layer also has various neurons with different activation functions that receive inputs and then produce an output to be fed as input to the final layer. Thus, the feed-forward network does not have a scope of memory or time, and it cannot handle sequential data. On the other hand, recurrent neural networks create loops by remembering the previous inputs. Figure 16.10 shows a diagram for a one-unit recurrent neural network (RNN). RNN has outputs that are dependent on the previous computations [8]. In other words, they have a 'memory' which remembers the past.

Recurrent neural networks also use backpropagation as the training method but, here the algorithm is applied for every timestamp. This is referred to as 'Backpropagation through Time (BPTT).'

The new state (h_t) at time t, is a function of its old state (h_{t-1}) and input vector (x_t).

$$h_t = f_w (h_{t-1}, x_t)$$ (16.18)

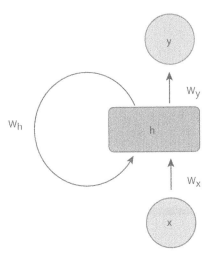

Figure 16.10 Input–output model for recurrent neural network (Source: Amended from- Recurrent neural network unfold by fdeloche, licensed under CC BY-SA 4.0, https://commons.wikimedia.org/w/index. php?curid=60109157).

The recursive function (f_w) is a tanh function.

$$h_t = \tanh(w_h h_{t-1} + w_x x_t) \tag{16.19}$$

Thus, the output y_t can be calculated as:

$$Y_t = w_y s_t \tag{16.20}$$

The weights (w_x, w_h, w_y) are shared across time. Reusing the same weight matrix at every step reduces the number of parameters.

A Vanilla neural network shown in Figure 16.11 is the simplest form of RNN which takes in a sequence of inputs to give one output. To overcome some of the shortcomings of RNNs such as the vanishing gradient problem, several extensions of this network have been introduced over the years.

(i) Deep RNNs—In Deep RNNs, there are multiple layers per time step and, the output calculated serves as input to the new layers.

(ii) Bidirectional RNNs—A standard RNN can only look in the past and, the current state cannot be used to obtain information about the future input since, the input data is fixed. Bidirectional RNN considers that the output is not just dependent upon the previous values, but also on the future values.

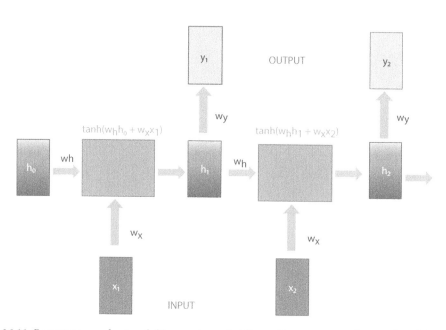

Figure 16.11 Recurrent neural network (Source: Amended from—Recurrent neural network unfold by fdeloche, licensed under CC BY-SA 4.0, https://commons.wikimedia.org/w/index.php?curid=60109157).

16.5.3   LSTM

These networks have a 'memory' since they can learn from the past. Unlike a standard RNN, Long short term memory or LSTMS have four different layers that interact amongst themselves and all the repeating modules have varying structures (refer Figure 16.12).

The core concepts used for remembering past behavior are cell states and gates. Cell states are like conveyor belts that carry the relevant information down the entire chain. Information can flow unchanged along with these cell states. Gates are used to add or delete information from these cell states.

The first step in the LSTM network is to decide which information from the past is to be retained and which is to be removed. This step makes use of the sigmoid function and a forget gate f_t. After analyzing the current input and the past output, the forget gate removes the irrelevant information from the previous time and produces an output in the form of a vector between 0 and 1. An output '0' means the forget gate will get rid of that information whereas; an output '1' is for retaining the information.

$$f_t = \sigma(w_f.[h_{t-1}, x_t] + b_f \qquad (16.21)$$

The second step deals with selectively updating the cell state values. It has two parts—sigmoid and tanh. The sigmoid function is part of the input gate (i_t) which produces an output vector between 0 and 1 to decide which information is to be retained and which is to be removed. The information that is retained is evaluated by the tanh function to assign weights between −1 and +1. This is done by looking at the level of significance of the values that are retained or passed through by the input gate.

$$i_t = \sigma(w_i.[h_{t-1}, x_t] + b_i \qquad (16.22)$$

$$\tilde{C}_t = \tanh(w_C.[h_{t-1}, x_t] + b_C \qquad (16.23)$$

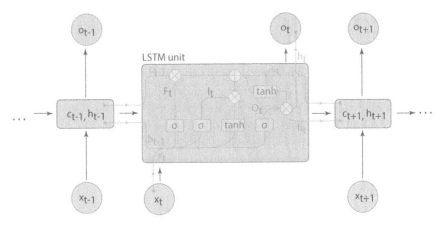

Figure 16.12 LSTM neural network (Source: Long Short-Term Memory by fdeloche, licensed under CC BY-SA 4.0, https://commons.wikimedia.org/w/index.php?curid=60149410).

The third step has an output gate o_t, with sigmoid function to decide which information should go to the hidden state. The output thus generated is multiplied by tanh of cell state (c_t).

$$o_t = \sigma(w_o.[h_{t-1},x_t] + b_o \qquad (16.24)$$

$$h_t = o_t \times \tanh(C_t) \qquad (16.25)$$

16.6 Applications of Deep Learning Neural Networks

Deep learning neural networks have an interdisciplinary approach in their applications. They are revolutionizing business and everyday life. With rapid progression in Big Data Analysis, these networks are widely used in visual art processing, robotics, recommendation systems, and pattern and speech recognition [1]. The application of Machine learning and neural networks has changed the way businesses operate as they have the ability to make the most out of the available information. Recurrent neural networks help businesses in streamlining the workflow by assisting in report generation and text summarization. Banks and insurance companies use RNNs for document generation to make customized forms for each client. RNNs are also widely used for machine translation such as Google Translate and eCommerce platforms to increase the efficiency of search results.

In recent years, researchers have experimented with and developed different types of deep learning networks, to find solutions to key problems in engineering and science. In engineering, neural networks are applied to several fields including automotive control, chemical engineering, flight control and, power plants [10, 15]. In science, these networks have revolutionized healthcare, medicine, chemistry, and food research.

LSTMs are used to advance the state of the art for many difficult problems, for instance, analyzing and forecasting sequential data [9].

In advertising, deep learning has optimized advertising campaigns. Deep learning is also reshaping the healthcare industry by delivering new possibilities to improve people's life. In the healthcare industry, CNNs have proved to be very successful through predictive analytics. Although image classification and facial recognition are the primary fields of CNN, they also find application in the fields of document or handwriting analysis, understanding climate, and for complex purposes such as historic and environmental collections.

Following are some of the major areas, where deep learning is implemented:

a. Speech & Image Processing—Face recognition, face detection, image and speech recognition, image reconstruction, noise removal.
b. Healthcare & Medicine—Computer-aided disease detection, analyzing genomes, discovering new drugs, medical imaging
c. Entertainment Industry—Netflix, Amazon and film making, music generation.
d. Defense—Unmanned aerial vehicle, automated target recognition.
e. Automobile—Self-driving cars, virtual sensors, improved guidance systems.
f. Sales/Marketing—Predicting the price of commodities, chatbots.

16.7   Practical Application of Neural Networks Using Computer Codes

To understand the practical implementation of neural networks, the following section will discuss the algorithm to build a neural network model for predicting stock prices.

A great way to implement RNN specifically the LSTM models is time series forecasting since they have the ability to retain memory for a very long period. LSTM models are powerful in stock price prediction with good accuracy. The model discussed here, is built using Google Colab (Figure 16.13).

The first step is to import several libraries or packages such as—'NumPy' to apply mathematical functions to our multi-dimensional arrays, 'matplotlib' to visualize the data and, 'pandas' to analyze the data and create a data frame. The open-source library called Keras, is used to build and train the model. The sklearn.pre-processing package is used for scaling and transforming the data into vector form [11].

For building this prediction model, the historical data (from Yahoo Finance) for 'Infosys' stock price from 2009–2019 is used. After the data is uploaded, it has to be pre-processed using three main steps—data cleaning to detect any missing values, data discretization to reduce the data and, data transformation to scale the data. For normalization, MinMaxScaler is used to transform features by scaling each of them to the range 0 and 1.

The training data set is created by incorporating 60 timestamps and 1 output at each step and then converted into a three-dimension array.

The most important part of this network is building the model. For this time series forecasting, LSTM model is used since it has the potential to remember long term dependencies. The first step is to initialize the LSTM by using a regression model. This model consists of an input layer called the sequential layer, which groups a linear stack of layers. This layer is followed by three LSTM layers with dropout. Dropout trims down overfitting in the deep learning network, so it drops out units in a neural network [8]. Finally, there is the dense output layer for updating the values in the matrices during backpropagation.

The type of optimization technique used is important to efficiently reach the global minimum. Here, Adam optimizer is used to compile the model.

Next, we fit the model to run on 10 epochs. Epoch is a frame of line in deep learning indicating the number of passes through the entire training dataset. Batch size is selected as 32 to show the number of training examples used in a single iteration.

Finally, we get the model's predicted value and plot it against the actual value.

From the graph in Figure 16.14, we can see that the actual value (top line) is quite close to the predicted value (bottom line). Thus, LSTMs are quite powerful in analyzing time series and sequential data.

16.8   Opportunities and Challenges of Using Neural Networks

Big Data analysis involves collecting a substantial amount of data and making them available across various domains. However, this often involves using data exceeding the capacity of traditional methodologies to process accurately and timely. Thus, managing these

```
# Import the libraries
import math
import pandas_datareader as web
import numpy as np
import pandas as pd
from sklearn.preprocessing import MinMaxScaler
from keras.models import Sequential
from keras.layers import Dense, LSTM, Dropout
import matplotlib.pyplot as plt
# Get the stock quote
df = web.DataReader('INFY.NS', data_source='yahoo', start='2009-01-01', end='2019-12-17')
# data cleaning
df.isna().any()
# create a new dataframe with only the close column
data = df.filter(['Close'])
# convert the data frame to a numpy array
dataset = data.values
#get the number of rows to train the LSTM model on
training_data_len = math.ceil(len(dataset) * .8)
training_data_len
#scale the data
scaler = MinMaxScaler(feature_range=(0,1))
scaled_data = scaler.fit_transform(dataset)
#create the training dataset
train_data = scaled_data[0:training_data_len, :]
 #split the data into x_train and y_train data sets
 x_train= []
 y_train= []
 for i in range(60, len(train_data)):
   x_train.append(train_data[i-60:i, 0])
   y_train.append(train_data[i, 0])
   if i<= 60:
# convert x_train and y_train into numpy array
x_train, y_train = np.array(x_train), np.array(y_train)
#Reshape the data
x_train = np.reshape(x_train, (x_train.shape[0], x_train.shape[1], 1))
#build the LSTM model
regression = Sequential()
regression.add(LSTM(units = 50, activation= 'relu', return_sequences= True, input_shape = (x_train.shape[1], 1)))
regression.add(Dropout(0.2))
regression.add(LSTM(units = 60, activation= 'relu', return_sequences= True))
regression.add(Dropout(0.3))
```

Figure 16.13 Infosys stock price prediction using recurrent neural network (Source: Author's own work using Google Colab). *(Continued)*

voluminous data sets poses certain challenges. Following are some of the challenges for the application of artificial neural networks to Big Data:

- Noisy and poor data—Neural networks can be stymied if the data is not of high quality or even if there is a small variation in the input data.

```
regression.add(LSTM(units = 120, activation= relu))
regression.add(Dropout(0.5))
regression.add(Dense(units=1))
regression.summary()
=compile the model
regression.compile(optimizer = adam, loss=mean_squared_error)
Train the model
regression.fit(x_train, y_train, batch_size=32, epochs=10)
= create the testing dataset
test_data = scaled_data[training_data_len-60: , :]
=Create the data sets x_test and y_test
x_test = []
y_test = dataset[training_data_len:, :]
for i in range(60, len(test_data)):
  x_test.append(test_data[i-60:i, 0])
=convert the data to a numpy array
x_test= np.array(x_test)
=Reshape the data
x_test = np.reshape(x_test, (x_test.shape[0], x_test.shape[1], 1))
= Get the predicted price values (for x_test)
predictions = regression.predict(x_test)
predictions = scaler.inverse_transform(predictions)
=plot the data
train = data[:training_data_len]
valid = data[training_data_len:]
valid[predictions]= predictions
=visualize the model data
plt.figure(figsize=(16,8))
plt.title(Model)
plt.xlabel(Date, fontsize=18)
plt.ylabel(Close Price INR, fontsize=18)
plt.plot(train[Close])
plt.plot(valid[[Close, predictions]])
plt.legend([Train, Val, Predictions], loc=lower right)
plt.show()
```

Figure 16.13 (Continued) Infosys stock price prediction using recurrent neural network (Source: Author's own work using Google Colab).

- Trustworthiness of data analysis—The data needs to be stored and handled securely while developing a neural network algorithm.
- Unlabeled data/noisy labels—A Majority of the dataset may not be labeled or there may be noisy labels that would require a more efficient cost function or a new training strategy.

Artificial neural networks are making inroads into the big data analysis, as they can solve real-world complex problems better than the traditional techniques which makes use of statistics and econometrics. A growing challenge in big data is the storage and retrieval of information. Deep learning aids in providing semantic indexing, particularly useful in natural language processing, which helps in classifying and retrieving data by storing them

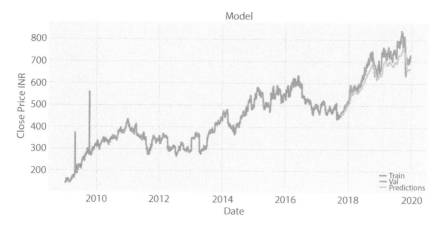

Figure 16.14 Actual stock price vs. forecasted stock price for infosys (Source: Own work using Google Colab).

as data bit strings. This improves the relational understanding of the data. Another challenge in dealing with voluminous data is to develop efficient linear models. Deep learning overcomes this challenge by extracting complicated linear features from the data and performing discriminative tasks on them. Thus, neural networks make discriminative tasks relatively easier in Big Data analysis.

However, apart from managing large quantities of data, there are several other challenges with Big Data Analytics such as, multi-modal data, data parallelism, poor quality of data, security concerns, and dealing with high dimensional data, which can make deep learning computationally expensive [12]. So while there is tremendous potential for neural networks to help derive more value from Big Data analytics, they pose significant challenges as well. There is a need to have action-oriented insights for data analysis. Leading data-driven discoveries require diverse sources of data, and the capability to ask big questions along with advancement in the technical skills [13].

16.9 Conclusion

The application of Machine learning and neural networks has changed the way businesses operate as they have the ability to make the most out of the available information.

Artificial neural networks are becoming increasingly popular in Big Data analysis because of their efficiency in handling and analyzing large volumes of data. Real-world applications for neural networks are booming. But deep learning is still a low-maturity field and thus, it needs to be explored further. Extensive future research is required to adapt the algorithms to the various shortcomings related to Big Data.

References

1. Liu, W., Wang, Z., Liu, X., Zeng, N., Liu, Y., Alsaadi, F.E., A survey of deep neural network architectures and their applications. *Neurocomputing*, 234, 11–26, 2017.

2. Zhang, J., Ma, L., Liu, Y., Passivity analysis for discrete-time neural networks with mixed time-delays and randomly occurring quantization effects. *Neurocomputing*, 216, 657–665, 2016.

3. Walczak, S., Artificial neural networks, in: *Advanced Methodologies and Technologies in Artificial Intelligence, Computer Simulation, and Human–Computer Interaction*, pp. 40–53, IGI Global, Hershey, Pennsylvania, 2019.

4. Hecht-Nielsen, R., Theory of the backpropagation neural network, in: *Neural networks for perception*, pp. 65–93, Academic Press, Cambridge, Massachusetts, 1992.

5. Hinton, G., Srivastava, N., Swersky, K., Neural networks for machine learning lecture 6a overview of mini-batch gradient descent, *COURSERA Neural Networks Mach Learn [Internet]*. 31, 2012. Available from: http://www.cs.toronto.edu/~tijmen/csc321/slides/lecture_slides_lec 6.pdf

6. Bottou, L., Stochastic gradient descent tricks, in: *Neural networks: Tricks of the trade*, pp. 421–436, Springer, Berlin, Heidelberg, 2012.

7. Krizhevsky, A., Sutskever, I., Hinton, G.E., Imagenet classification with deep convolutional neural networks, in: *Advances in Neural Information Processing Systems*, pp. 1097–1105, 2012.

8. Zaremba, W., Sutskever, I., Vinyals, O., Learning simple algorithms from examples. in: *33rd International Conference on Machine Learning, ICML 2016,* Recurrent neural network regularization, *International Machine Learning Society (IMLS)*, M. F. Balcan, & K. Q. Weinberger (eds.), *arXiv preprint arXiv:1409.2329*, vol. 1, pp. 639–647, New York City, United States, 2016.

9. Chen, Y., Cheng, Q., Cheng, Y., Yang, H., Yu, H., Applications of recurrent neural networks in environmental factor forecasting: A review. *Neural Comput.*, 30, 11, 2855–2881, 2018.

10. Schumann, J., Gupta, P., Liu, Y., Application of neural networks in high assurance systems: A survey, in: *Applications of Neural Networks in High Assurance Systems*, pp. 1–19, Springer, Berlin, Heidelberg, 2010.

11. Accessed from https://scikit-learn.org/stable/modules/preprocessing.html.

12. Najafabadi, M.M., Villanustre, F., Khoshgoftaar, T.M., Seliya, N., Wald, R., Muharemagic, E., Deep learning applications and challenges in big data analytics. *J. Big Data*, 2, 1, 1, 2015.

13. Zhou, Z.H., Chawla, N.V., Jin, Y., Williams, G.J., Big data opportunities and challenges: Discussions from data analytics perspectives [discussion forum]. *IEEE Comput. Intell. Mag.*, 9, 4, 62–74, 2014.

14. Villarrubia, G., De Paz, J.F., Chamoso, P., De la Prieta, F., Artificial neural networks used in optimization problems. *Neurocomputing*, 272, 10–16, 2018.

15. Gusmão, A., Horta, N., Lourenço, N., Martins, R., Artificial Neural Network Overview, in: *Analog IC Placement Generation via Neural Networks from Unlabeled Data*, pp. 7–24, Springer, Cham, 2020.

## 17

Meta-Heuristic Algorithms for Best IoT Cloud Service Platform Selection

Sudhansu Shekhar Patra[1]*, Sudarson Jena[2], G.B. Mund[3],
Mahendra Kumar Gourisaria[3] and Jugal Kishor Gupta[4]

[1]School of Computer Applications, KIIT Deemed to be University, Bhubaneswar, India
[2]Computer Science Engineering Department, SUIIT, Sambalpur University, Sambalpur, India
[3]School of Computer Science & Engineering, KIIT Deemed to be University, Bhubaneswar, India
[4]Dept of Computer Sc. & Engineering Vidya College of Engineering Meerut, Meerut, India

Abstract

Due to the rapid growth of the IoT, social media, digitization, wireless communication technology and the use of internet in various sectors the volume of data is increasing very rapidly. To handle the data storage and to facilitate the processing capacity, cloud computing is an emerging solution. Currently many service providers are providing service. In this chapter, a constrained multi-criteria federated cloud provider selection strategy mathematical model is proposed. Three meta-heuristics algorithms (Bird Swarm Algorithm, TLBO, Jaya) were discussed and implemented to solve and verify the validity of the model, and a suppositious case study is used to compare the model performance. For the comparison, robust design method of Taguchi's was used for selecting the algorithm parameters, feasible solution is rendered by analytic hierarchy process (AHP), a widely used technique for solving the problem of cloud provider selection in a federated cloud. Results shows that TLBO, Bird Swam Algorithm, Jaya improved the AHP solution by 58.78, 61.43, and 62.02%, respectively.

Keywords: IoT, cloud provider, broker, multi-criteria selection problem, meta-heuristic algorithms

17.1 Introduction

Internet of Things (IoT) is the rising trend in all the sectors and is going to be the most prominent in the field of technical, financial and social area. There was a major development of wireless communication technology in the recent years. The intention of IoT is to connect all or many devices to the internet or other connected devices [1–3] and in the coming years many devices will join in the list. IoT is the collected network of physical devices, home appliances, vehicular networks plugged with sensors, electronics along with network connectivity that gathers and exchange data and information [4, 5]. The IoT generates massive volume of data sometimes structured and unstructured through the sensors

---

*Corresponding author: sudhanshupatra@gmail.com

Monika Mangla, Suneeta Satpathy, Bhagirathi Nayak and Sachi Nandan Mohanty (eds.) Integration of Cloud Computing with Internet of Things: Foundations, Analytics, and Applications, (299–318) © 2021 Scrivener Publishing LLC

and sends them to the cloud storage where the cloud computing provides a defined path of the data for its destination. Having a complementary relationship between Cloud computing along with IoT both increases efficiency in our daily life. Cloud computing is a epitome which delivers computing resources through the internet through mainly 3 service models: IaaS, SaS, and PaaS. Due of the rapid growth of IoT and Cloud Computing technology many service providers intend to enter into this sector and provide services to customers. The cloud market becomes competitive because of the growth in the number of providers. Because of the large provider base, the customers face the most significant challenge in cloud service provider selection. Price demands and performance commitment of the same types of services offered by different providers are varied, and accordingly, the selection of a suitable provider who will accomplish the QoS requirements with the mentioned budget becomes challenging. For comparing the providers the customers must have pre defined and robust measurement criteria by which the service providers can be compared as well as ranked based on these criteria.

Federated cloud includes the interconnected cloud environment of several cloud service providers in to load balance the traffic and plan for spikes in network as well as compute traffic [6–8]. Due to the flexibility of the federated model in meeting their business and technology requirements the clients can optimize their enterprise IT spend and select their optimal service provider with the help of a cloud broker. The vendor-lock-in is a problem in which a customer has to rely only on a single provider but the federated cloud assists customers to reduce trust on a single cloud provider and make it possible to select its best provider out of the available cloud service providers. The selection of suitable provider with minimum cost and valid SLA increases the value of the model. In this chapter, a constrained multi-criteria federated cloud provider selection [9] mathematical model is proposed. Although bill amount is a main criterion in selecting a cloud provider, because of the growth of number of providers the customers have to consider many other criteria as well as the variety of services offerings. The measurement of the defined measures was not an easy task due to the deficient standard defined by different cloud providers. Because of that the Cloud Service Measurement Index Consortium have designed a standard called service measurement index (SMI), a framework which assists the decision-makers here the brokers for comparing the services provided in a federated cloud by multiple providers. Figure 17.1 shows a customer requests for a different infrastructure services which in contrast sends

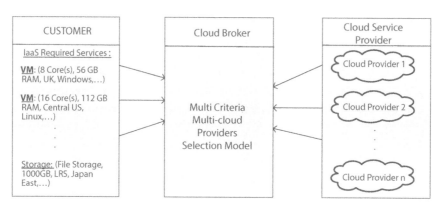

Figure 17.1 A cloud provider selection from a federated cloud, a multi-criteria selection.

the request to a broker and the its responsibility is the selection of multiple cloud providers which satisfies the customer's requirements by minimizing the cost and maximizing the benefits with a mentioned constraint [10].

The cloud service provider selection problem can be articulated as muti-constrained multi-criteria optimization problem. The important points discussed in this article are:

- Need a model which can select a provider for a service in a multi-cloud environment by taking care of the IaaS services.
- Cloud providers evaluation strategy and the cloud services evaluation strategy are taken care of.
- The cloud service consumer acceptable criteria are taken care of.
- Three meta-heuristic algorithms have been suggested the solution of the the multi-criteria multi-cloud provider optimization problem.

The multi-criteria federated cloud provider selection problem can be categorized into two types, static or dynamic approach. In the static approach the requested services and the available services by the service provider are constant and the cloud provider condition doesn't change over the time and is same throughout the life cycle. In the other hand in the dynamic approach the cloud provider condition goes on changing in the whole life cycle. In this chapter we focused only on the static approach [11–13].

The problem is a NP Hard problem and can be formulated as an integer programming problem. In this chapter three meta-heuristic algorithms Bird Swam Algorithm, TLBO, Jaya have been considered and compared. The algorithm's performance have been studied by five different ways: a) through a hypothetical study, b) The algorithm's parameter values have been selected through Taguch's robust design [14] technique, c) AHP being taken to generate the initial feasible solution, d) through the implementation of the algorithms the quality of the AHP solutions have been increased, e) The AHP limitations are avoided by replacing an initial viable answer generated randomly and the performance of the algorithm were examined. The outcomes shows that the suggested algorithms for this multi-criteria selection improves the AHP solution significantly. Following the introduction, Section 17.2 describes the federated cloud selection problem; the problem description as well as the model formulation is done here. Section 17.3 describes the details of the algorithm, Section 17.4 verifies the behavior of the suggested algorithm in the federated cloud environment. Finally, the chapter concludes in Section 17.5.

17.2   Selection of a Cloud Provider in Federated Cloud

An IoT-based federated cloud system has three stakeholders: cloud provider, cloud consumer and a cloud broker. In the federated cloud selection problem the cloud broker has a vital role as it acts as an intermediator between the cloud consumer and the provider. A customer needs different types of infrastructure services. In the context of the federated cloud service selection problem, the broker selects a set of providers that need to be satisfied by the customer needs in conjunction with minimum cost and maximum benefit with a set of constraints. The problem is phrased as an integer programming problem having the following assumptions:

a. The service model is considered to be IaaS.
b. It is considered for the public cloud.
c. There must be pay-as-per-usage pricing model.
d. Each service that requested by the consumer is rented only from a single service provider.

Main characteristics considered for preparation of SMI (Service Measurement Index Consortium) are as follows and they have to determine the basis on which the service providers have to be examined:

a. *Accountability*: Independent of the service being provider to the customer how much accountable is the provider for the services provided by the service provider organization.
b. *Agility*: This attributes measure the impact of a service upon the client's direction, strategy and tactics with minimal disruption.
c. *Assurance*: This attribute assures the client how likely the service is available as assured in the SLA.
d. *Financial*: The amount of money a client has to spend to get the reliable service by the provider.
e. *Performance*: This attribute measures the performance, features and the functionalities of the provided services.
f. *Security and Privacy*: This attribute measures the control on access to services, service data and privacy of the data.
g. *Usability*: The ease or technique with which the user can easily use the services provided by the provider.

SMI incorporates seven main features with more than KPI (key performance indicators) in every characteristics. The presented model is formulated by taking care of the 5 criteria: Performance, Financial, assurance, usability, and accountability. Table 17.1 shows the various notations used in the algorithm.

The formulation for the cloud provider selection problem from federated has been formulated as:

$$\text{Minimize: } \sum_{i=1}^{N}\sum_{j=1}^{M}(Cost_{ij} * a_{ij}) + \sum_{j=1}^{M} I\,Cost_j * b_j \qquad (17.1)$$

$$\text{Maximize: } \sum_{i=1}^{N}\sum_{j=1}^{M} Perf_{ij} * a_{ij} \qquad (17.2)$$

$$\text{Maximize: } \sum_{i=1}^{N}\sum_{j=1}^{M} Assurance_{ij} * a_{ij} \qquad (17.3)$$

Table 17.1 Notations used in the proposed algorithm.

Notation	Description
Index	
i	Denotes which service is requested, $<i = 1,...N>$
j	Denotes the provider giving service, $<j = 1,...,M>$
k	service index offered by the provider, $<k = 1,...K>$
α	Denotes the service index parameter, $<\alpha = 1,....A>$
b	Service parameters index offered by the provider, $<b = 1,....B>$
u	Customer's ID, $<u = 1,...U>$
R	Transaction's ID, $<R = 1,...,TR>$
Quantities	
$Cost_{ij}$	The cost of availing the requested service i by cloud provider j
$I\,Cost_j$	Integrating the cost of provider j
$Perf_{ij}$	Performance of the provider j serving requirement i
$Assurance_{ij}$	Assurance when renting requested service i by the cloud service provider j
$Usability_{ij}$	Usability for renting service i by cloud service provider j
$Accountability_{ij}$	Accountability of renting the service i by cloud service provider j
$Budget$	The budget of the client request for the service
$A\,RespT_{ij}^{(P)}$	The provider j's service response time for serving i requested by consumer
$Timeu_{ij}$	Difference between the time the user ID u has requested service i from cloud provider j and the service really available
$count\_Request_{ij}$	The total number requests from provider j of service type i
$A\,RespT_{ij}^{(R)}$	Maximum acceptable response time by the client
$Suitability_{ij}$	Suitability value for service i rented from cloud service provider j
$Features_{ij}^{(P)}$	No. of features (i.e., essential as well as nonessential) furnished for the requested service i by the cloud provider j
$Features_{ij}^{(R)}$	No. of features (i.e., essential as well as nonessential) needed by the client for service i
$Availability_{ij}^{(P)}$	% of the time a user accessing the requested service i while renting it from cloud provider j

(Continued)

Table 17.1 Notations used in the proposed algorithm. (*Continued*)

Notation	Description
$Availability_i^{(R)}$	The required availability window by client
$ServiceTime_{ij}$	Total served time provider j serving service i
$DownTime_{ij}$	Total time for which provider j was not served service i
$Reliability_{ij}$	Reliability expectation provider j to serve service i
$DownTime_{ij}^{(P)}$	Downtime expectation provider j to serve service i
$UFail_{ij}$	No. of users got failures those who are not able to meet the promised service time from the cloud service provider j for the requested service i
$DownTime_i^{(R)}$	Service downtime of service i accepted by the user
$Transparency_{ij}$	Level of transparency provider j is provided to service i
$Install_{ij}$	Installability of service i offered by cloud provider j
$ChangeTime_{uij}$	The time if there is a change in service i running at cloud provider j for the users application u.
$Count\_Changes_{ij}$	Number of changes occurred in requested service i at cloud provider j
$ElapsedTime_{ij}$	Elapsed time for installing requested service i at cloud provider j
$Reputation\_Value_j$	Reputation-factor of cloud service provider j
$Recommendation_{Rj}$	Recommendation R of cloud service provider j
TR_j	Transactions cloud provider j performed
Decision Variables	
a_{ij}	1 if the requested service i is consumed given by cloud provider j; else it is 0.
b_j	1 if at least an service is consumed offered by service provider j; else, it is 0.

$$\text{Minimize:} \sum_{i=1}^{N}\sum_{j=1}^{M} Usability_{ij} * a_{ij} \tag{17.4}$$

$$\text{Maximize:} \sum_{i=1}^{N}\sum_{j=1}^{M} Accountability_{ij} * a_{ij} \tag{17.5}$$

Such that

$$\sum_{i=1}^{N}\sum_{j=1}^{M} a_{ij} = 1 \tag{17.6}$$

$$\sum_{i=1}^{N}\sum_{j=1}^{M} Cost_{ij} * a_{ij} \leq Budget \tag{17.7}$$

$$A \operatorname{Re} spT_{ij}^{(P)} \leq A \operatorname{Re} spT_{i}^{(R)}, \forall i \in N \tag{17.8}$$

$$Suitability_{ij} > 0, \forall i \in N \tag{17.9}$$

$$Availability_{ij}^{(P)} \geq Availability_{i}^{(R)}, \forall i \in N \tag{17.10}$$

$$DownTime_{ij}^{(P)} \leq DownTime_{i}^{(R)}, \forall i \in N \tag{17.11}$$

$$a_{ij} \in \{0,1\} \tag{17.12}$$

The goal of Equation (17.1) is to minimize the value of the cost the consumer has to pay. The total cost includes the rented service cost and the provider's integration cost. The used coefficient is fixed for most of the services but for some services it leads to a dynamic nature and its value increases if the need of consumption increases. Therefore the cost $Cost_{ij}$ is denoted as,

$$Cost_{ij} = f(service\ parameter\ values\ given\ by\ the\ customer) \tag{17.13}$$

Equation (17.2) is to maximize the performance of the model. The performance attributes for IaaS services includes suitability and the average service response time.

$$Perf_{ij} = w_1^{(r)} * A \operatorname{Re} spT_{ij}^{(P)} + w_2^{(r)} * Suitability_{ij} \tag{17.14}$$

Where $w_1^{(r)}$ is denoted the weightage of the above response time as well as $w_2^{(r)}$ is the weightage of suitability.

$$A \operatorname{Re} spT_{ij}^{(P)} = \sum_{u}^{U_{ij}} Timeu_{ij} / count\_Request_{ij} \tag{17.15}$$

The Suitability is denoted by:

$$Suitability_{ij} = \begin{cases} 1, if\ all\ the\ requested\ features\ have\ fulfilled \\ Features_{ij}^{(P)} / Features_{ij}^{(R)}, if\ all\ requested\ features\ have\ satisfied \\ 0, if\ any\ one\ of\ the\ requested\ features\ have\ not\ satisfied \end{cases} \tag{17.16}$$

Equation (17.3) is necessary for assurance of the service.

$$Assurance_{ij} = w_1^{(r)} * Availability_{ij}^{(P)} + w_2^{(r)} * Reliability_{ij} \tag{17.17}$$

Here $w_1^{(r)}$ is denoted the weightage of availability as well as $w_2^{(r)}$ is the weightage of the reliability. The availability

$$Availability_{ij}^{(P)}\% = \frac{ServiceTime_{ij} - DownTime_{ij}}{ServiceTime_{ij}} * 100 \tag{17.18}$$

The $Reliability_{ij}$ can be defined as follows which measures the time the services are down

$$Reliability_{ij} = \left(1 - \frac{UFail_{ij}}{U_{ij}}\right) DownTime_{ij}^{(P)} \tag{17.19}$$

Equation (17.4) is used for minimizing the usability

$$Usability_{ij} = w_1^{(r)} * Transparency_{ij}^{(P)} + w_2^{(r)} * Install_{ij} \tag{17.20}$$

$$Transparency_{ij} = \sum_{u=1}^{U_{ij}} \frac{\sum \frac{ChangeTime_{uij}}{Count\_Changes_{ij}}}{U_{ij}} \tag{17.21}$$

$$Install_{ij} = \sum_{u=1}^{U_{ij}} \frac{ElapsedTime_{ij}}{U_{ij}} \tag{17.22}$$

Objective function (5) is used for maximizing the accountability. The providers reputation is only considered as the accountability.

$$Accountability_{ij} = Reputation\_Value_j$$

$$Reputation\_Value_j = \frac{\sum_{R=0}^{TR_j} Recommendation_{Rj}}{TR_j} \tag{17.23}$$

$$Reputation\_Value_j = \frac{\sum_{R=0}^{TR_j} Recommendation_{Rj}}{TR_j} \tag{17.24}$$

Every service should be served by only one cloud provider is depicted in constraint (17.6). The add up cost incurred should not be more than the clients budget is described in constraint (17.7). Equation (17.8) shows the clients acceptable response time should be more than the provider's response time. The suitability of the cloud provider must be at least one. Equation (17.10) ensures the cloud provider's availability window for a service must be more than the required window of the customer. Equation (17.11) ensures that the provider's service downtime is smaller than the downtime acceptable of the required service. X_{ij} is a binary variable which is shown in Equation (17.12).

17.3   Algorithmic Solution

Multiple service selection from multiple service providers is a NP-Complete problem and it is a similar problem as the MIVS (Multi-item-Vendor-Selection) problem where multiple items have to be procured from different vendors. Let there are N number of distinct articles to be purchased from M number of suppliers there would be M^N solutions. With the large number of suppliers and large number of articles have to purchase, this will be a very large number and computationally difficult.

In the above mentioned problem, each IaaS request by the client is considered as an item and is going to be rented from any of the single cloud provider from the federated cloud, with no dependency among each other. This problem is a NP-Complete problem and has to solved by any meta-heuristic algorithm a) BSA (Bird Swam Optimization), b) TLBO (Teaching Learning Based Optimization), and c) Jaya algorithm.

All the 3 algorithms have their own benefit and have applicable to several fields of optimization problems such as constrained and problems having unconstrained optimization, problems of combinatorial optimization, nonlinear programming as well as stochastic programming.

All the meta-heuristic algorithms can locate the global optimal values as non of them trapped in a local optimal value as well as able to search a larger space in candidate solutions.

17.3.1   TLBO Algorithm (Teaching-Learning-Based Optimization Algorithm)

This is a stochastic population based algorithm suggested by Rao *et al.* in 2016 [15]. The inspiration of the algorithm is the knowledge transfer in a class room environment. The parameters required is the size of the population and the how many times the iteration to be carried out. The flow chart of the TLBO is presented in Figure 17.2.

This algorithm constitutes two phases and the working principle of the algorithm is shown in Figure 17.3.

- Teacher Phase
  - Newly generated solution is the most beneficial solution and mean of the population.
  - Greedy Selection: Accept newly generated solution if it is better than the present solution.
- Learner Phase
  - Partner solution is used for generating the new solution.
  - Greedy solution: Accept new solution if better than the current solution.

Each solution undergoes teacher phase followed by learner phase.

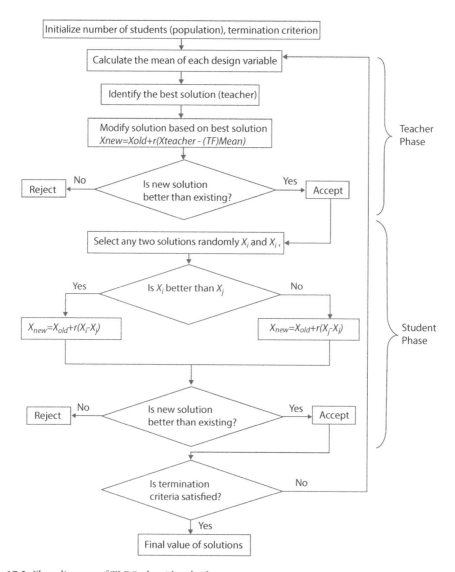

Figure 17.2 Flow diagram of TLBO algorithm [15].

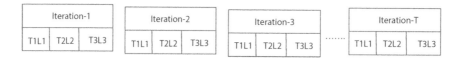

Figure 17.3 Working principle of TLBO algorithm.

17.3.1.1   Teacher Phase: Generation of a New Solution

- New solution is generated with the help of teacher and mean of population.
- Teacher: Solution corresponding to the best fitness value.
- Each variable in a solution (Y) is modified as

$$Y_{new} = Y + r(Y_{best} - T_f Y_{mean})$$

T_f is the same for all variables, r to be selected for each variable.

where Y = current solution

Y_{new} = New solution

Y_{best} = Teacher

Y_{mean} = Mean of the population

T_f = Learning factor (i.e., 1 or 2)

r = Random number between 0 and 1

17.3.1.2   Learner Phase: Generation of New Solution

- New solution is generated with the help of the partner solution.
- Partner Solution: Randomly selected solution from the population.
- Each variable in a solution (X) is modified as

$$Y_{new} = Y + r(Y - Y_p) \quad if \quad f < f_p$$

$$Y_{new} = Y - r(Y - Y_p) \quad if \quad f \geq f_p$$

where Y = current solution

Y_{new} = New solution

Y_p = Partner Solution

f = fitness of current solution

f_{new} = fitness of parameter solution

r = Random number between 0 and 1.

17.3.1.3   Representation of the Solution

In the vector form the solution is represented having two rows shown in Figure 17.4. The customer requesting the services are represented in the first row, where as the provider ID providing the service is represented in second row. For an instance the required service by the client $S_1^{(R)}$ is provided by provider 3, $S_2^{(R)}$ by provider 21 and so on.

17.3.2   JAYA Algorithm

Instead of taking two phases as in TLBO, Jaya algorithm [16] has a single phase along with simpler to apply. Assume $f(y)$ be an objective function needs to minimize or maximize. At the ith, iteration let there may be 'm' intent variables i.e., j = [1,m] and having a population size of 'n' i.e., the number of candidate solutions k = [1,n]. Assume that from the whole candidate solutions *best* and f(Y_{best}) is the candidate value and the optimized solution and similarly *worst* and f(Y_{worst}). Let the jth variable has value $Y_{j,k,i}$ for kth population in the iteration i, then the modified value is is represented in Equation (17.25).

$$Y'_{j,k,i} = Y_{j,k,i} + \alpha_{1,j,i}(Y_{j,best,i} - |Y_{j,k,i}|) - \alpha_{2,j,i}(Y_{j,worst,i} - |Y_{j,k,i}|) \tag{17.25}$$

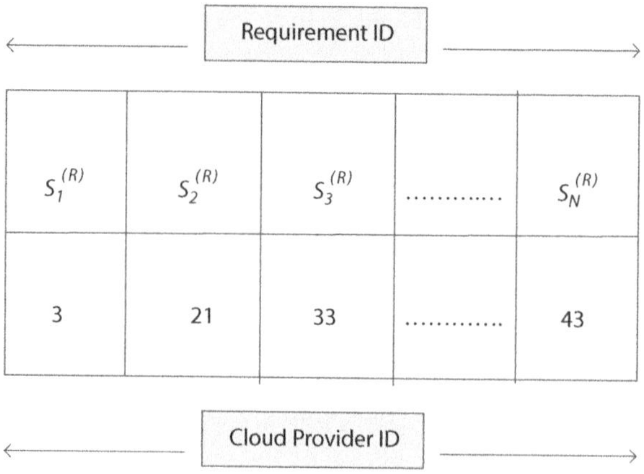

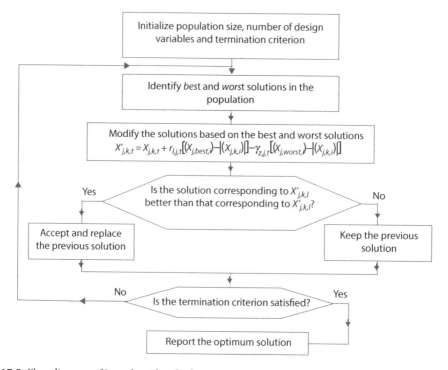

Requirement ID				
$S_1^{(R)}$	$S_2^{(R)}$	$S_3^{(R)}$	....	$S_N^{(R)}$
3	21	33	....	43

Figure 17.4 TLBO solution representation.

where, $Y_{j,best,i}$ and $Y_{j,wosrt,i}$ are the values of the variable j for the best and the worst candidate. The modified value of $Y_{j,k,i}$ is $Y'_{j,k,i}$ is and the random numbers are $\alpha_{1,j,i}$ and $\alpha_{2,j,i}$ for the jth variable in the range [0, 1] in the ith iteration. The terms "$\alpha_{1,j,i}(Y_{j,best,i} - |Y_{j,k,i}|)$" and the term "$-\alpha_{2,j,i}(Y_{j,worst,i} - |Y_{j,k,i}|)$" shows the trend of the solutions to proceed nearer to the best solution as well as avoids the worst solution. $Y'_{j,k,i}$ will be admitted in case it generates the better function value. Each function values those which are accepted at the end of the iteration are kept and used as the input for the next iteration. The flow diagram of Jaya algorithm is shown in Figure 17.5.

Figure 17.5 Flow diagram of Jaya algorithm [16].

$S_1^{(R)}$	$S_2^{(R)}$	$S_3^{(R)}$	....	$S_N^{(R)}$
3	21	33	....	43
31	43	10	....	9
⋮	⋮	⋮	⋮	⋮
1	19	25	....	39

Requirement ID ⟵ ⟶

Cloud Provider ID ⟵ ⟶

Figure 17.6 Jaya Algorithm solution representation.

17.3.2.1   *Representation of the Solution*

The Population is shown in the form of a matrix depicted in Figure 17.6. Every row is assigned with a solution, gives the solution which service to be taken from which provider. The required services are shown in columns. For instance, the first solution shows the services requested $S_1^{(R)}$, $S_2^{(R)}$ and $S_3^{(R)}$ is going to be hired from cloud service providers 3, 21, 33 respectively. The other rows can be similarly described.

17.3.3   Bird Swarm Algorithm

By the inspiring nature of social iterative behavior of birds, Bird Swarm Algorithm (BSA) [17] was evolved as a swarm intelligent with global optimization algorithm. The three major characteristics of birds are vigilance, flight and foraging was proposed by the authors in their BSA algorithm. The idea which describes the algorithm is summarized as follows using five prevails:

- Prevail 1: Every bird is in any one statuses i.e., vigilance or foraging.
- Prevail 2: Foraging condition says every bird tracks and remembers its self best feel and the past best feel from all the food perspectives. This data affects the bird's movement as well as food search path.
- Prevail 3: In the vigilance condition, every bird attempts to proceed towards the center considering the birds having greater reserves nearer to the middle in the flock. Birds placed in the center have less probability to be attacked by different predators.
- Prevail 4: Birds go on moving from one end to the other and they iteratively switches in between producing as well as scrounging. The algorithm considers that birds having maximum holds with producers whereas the minimum

with scroungers. Otherwise, the other birds are randomly considered as scroungers or producers.

- Prevail 5: Raising birds contribute the food search where the scrounging is arbitrarily adopt single raising bird.

The flow chart of Bird Swam Algorithm (BSA) is represented in Figure 17.7.

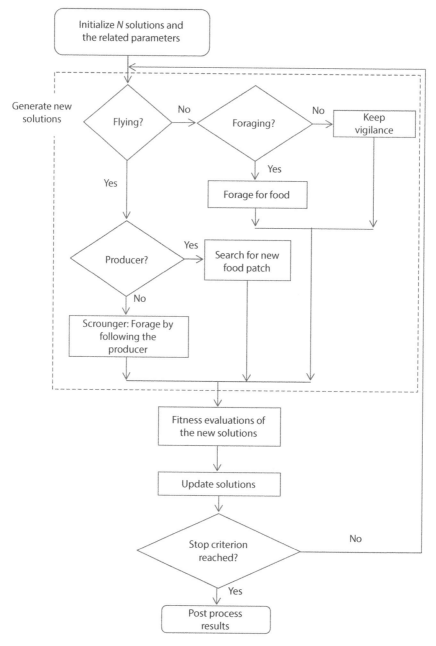

Figure 17.7 Flow diagram of Bird Swarm algorithm [17].

17.3.3.1   Forging Behavior

Every bird searches it's food based on own and swarm's experience. It can be mathematically described as follows:

$$y_{i,j}^{t+1} = y_{i,j}^t + \left(p_{i,j} - y_{i,j}^t\right) * c * random(0,1) + \left(g_j - y_{i,j}^t\right) * s * random(0,1) \quad (17.26)$$

17.3.3.2   Vigilance Behavior

Birds always try to move to the swarm center, and they will necessarily compete with one another. So, each bird will not move directly to the swarm center. These formulations for the motions are as follows:

$$y_{i,j}^{t+1} = y_{i,j}^t + b1\left(mean_j - y_{i,j}^t\right) * random(0,1) + b2\left(p_{k,j} - y_{i,j}^t\right) * random(-1,1)$$
$$(17.27)$$

$$b1 = a * exponent\left(\frac{-pFit_i}{sumFit + \varepsilon} * N\right) \quad (17.28)$$

$$b2 = b * exponent\left(\left(\frac{pFit_i - pFit_k}{|pFit_k - pFit_i| + \varepsilon}\right) * \frac{N * pFit_k}{sumFit + \varepsilon}\right) \quad (17.29)$$

17.3.3.3   Flight Behavior

Birds might be flying to other site because of predation threat as well as foraging or any distinct issues. After arriving a new site, birds again forage to find food. Several birds behaving as producers will search to food patches, whereas others try feeding food patch obtained by producers. The producers as well as scroungers are separated from the swarm agrreing to prevail 4. The criteria of the producers as well as scroungers are respectively depicted mathematically as follows:

$$y_{i,j}^{t+1} = y_{i,j}^t + random(0,1) * y_{i,j}^t \quad (17.30)$$

$$y_{i,j}^{t+1} = y_{i,j}^t + random(0,1) * y_{i,j}^t \quad (17.31)$$

17.3.3.4   Representation of the Solution

Each matrix shows a solution having row represents the cloud providers and the columns showing the requested services as depicted in Figure 17.8. The entries keep the binary values only either 0 or 1. The entry which contains 1 describes that the associated service is leased from the defined provider otherwise it is resulting zero. For an instance, during the

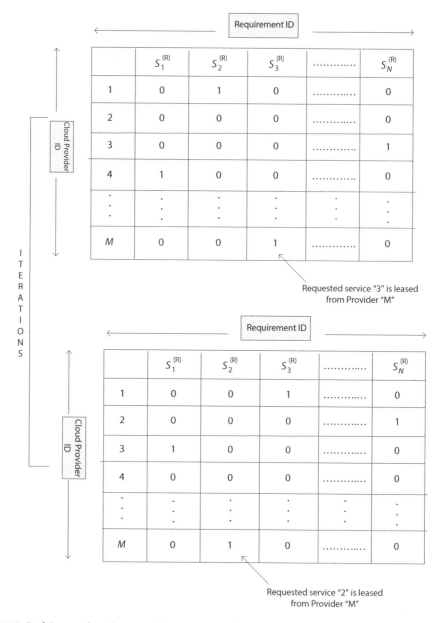

Figure 17.8 Bird Swarm algorithm population representation.

1st solution iteration, the requested service $s_1^{(R)}, s_2^{(R)}, s_3^{(R)}$ will be serviced from cloud service providers with cloud Provider ID-4, ID-1 as well as ID-M respectively.

17.4 Analyzing the Algorithms

Hypothetically a case study was used to study the behavior of the 3 algorithms. Different sources had been used to collect the data as a single source is not gives all the data to study the performance; certain parameters are gathered from cloud provider's websites [18–21] such as availability, price per hour. Some data were gathered from various datasets including response time and usability [22–24]. Certain values are available on websites through experiments which calculates the various metrics used in the cloud industry [25–28] including reliability, usability and some data were took out from several research articles discussed in references. Case study of 8 client's requirements are done. Other than that, data of [29, 31–33] cloud providers were generated. This study answers 2 main questions: (a) What is the improvement in cost of using federated cloud selection in place of single cloud selection? and (b) Is there any robust model to solve the problem? The answer to the first question is the service selection problem in multi cloud environment is better by 25% in comparison to the single cloud service selection problem in terms of the cost parameter. Through 3 phases the performance of the three algorithms was studied. In the first phase, by Taguchi's method [30] the parameters of each algorithm were determined. In the second phase, to yield the candidate value the AHP method [34–37], the most trusted method of cloud service selection was used. The experimental values of the suggested 3 algorithms are represented in Table 17.2. The initial feasible solution was generated with AHP technique for all the customer demands as depicted in Figure 17.9. Figure 17.10 shows the best solution of the 3 algorithms—chosen parameters. TLBO converges after 3,000 evaluations but the other two algorithms Jaya and BSA continued to improve the solution.

Table 17.2 Experimental results of 3 algorithms.

	Performance parameter values		
Experiments	**TLBO**	**Jaya**	**BSA**
1	0.059098	0.043104	0.052332
2	0.054503	0.042373	0.052047
3	0.057573	0.045373	0.053383
4	0.046378	0.041761	0.045262
5	0.052625	0.049622	0.046282
6	0.052355	0.047383	0.046585
7	0.051812	0.045837	0.046289
8	0.045242	0.039373	0.042737
9	0.057237	0.051527	0.047828

$S_1^{(R)}$	$S_2^{(R)}$	$S_3^{(R)}$	$S_4^{(R)}$	$S_5^{(R)}$	$S_6^{(R)}$	$S_7^{(R)}$	$S_8^{(R)}$
33	21	33	43	33	21	33	43

Figure 17.9 The initial solution using the AHP method.

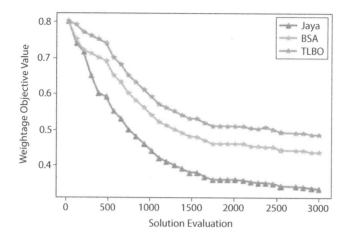

Figure 17.10 Best possible solution of the three suggested algorithms.

17.5 Conclusion

This chapter solved constrained multicriteria federated cloud provider choosing problem. It was defined and solved using integer programming problem and then 3 meta-heuristic algorithms (Jaya, TLBO, BSA) were suggested as well as the performance was analyzed for its solution. For comparing the algorithm performance 4 stages were applied. At 1st step, the algorithm's parameters value was determined by applying Taguchi's method. In the 2nd step we derived a candidate solution with the help of AHP method. Algorithm's behavior has been examined with AHP's candidate value considering the initial result in the 3rd step. The algorithm performance was better comparing the AHP solution; TLBO, BSA and Jaya improved AHP solution by 58.78, 61.43, and 62.02%, respectively. But, Jaya has better properties than TLBO and BSA. Cost evaluation is limited to pay-as-per-usage pricing model.

References

1. Armbrust, M., Fox, A., Griffith, R., *Above the clouds: A Berkeley view of cloud computing*, Technical Report No. UCB/EECS-2009–28, Electrical Engineering and Computer Sciences, University of California at Berkeley, Berkeley, CA, 2019, http://www.eecs.berkeley.edu/Pubs/TechRpts/2009/EECS-2009-28.html.
2. Buyya, R., Yeo, C.S., Venugopal, S., Broberg, J., Brandic, I., Cloud computing and emerging IT platforms: Vision, hype, and reality for delivering computing as the 5th utility. *Future Gener. Comput. Syst.*, 25, 6, 599–616, 2009.
3. Andrikopoulos, V., Strauch, S., Leymann, F., Decision support for application migration to the cloud: challenges and vision. Paper presented at: *Proceedings of the 3rd International Conference on Cloud Computing and Service Science, CLOSER 2013*, Aachen, Germany, May 8–10, 2013.

4. Andrikopoulos, V., Darsow, A., Karastoyanova, D., Leymann, F., CloudDSF—the cloud decision support framework for application migration. Paper presented at: *European Conference on Service-Oriented and Cloud Computing*, Berlin, Heidelberg, September, 2014.

5. Li, S., Da Xu, L., Zhao, S., The internet of things: A survey. *Inf. Syst. Front.*, 17, 2, 243–259, 2015.

6. Pflflanzner, T. and Kertesz, A., A taxonomy and survey of IoT cloud applications. *EAI Endorsed Trans. Internet Things*, 3, 12, 1–14, 2018.

7. Lee, I. and Lee, K., The Internet of things (IoT): Applications, investments, and challenges for enterprises, Elsevier. *Bus. Horiz.*, 58, 431–440, 2015.

8. Uviase, O. and Kotonya, G., IoT architectural framework: connection and integration framework for IoT systems, in: *First workshop on Architectures, Languages and Paradigms for IoT EPTCS*, D. Pianini, G. Salvaneschi (eds.), vol. 264, pp. 1–17, 2018, https://doi.org/10.4204/eptcs.264.1.

9. Menzel, M., Schönherr, M., Tai, S., (MC2) 2: Criteria, requirements and a software prototype for cloud infrastructure decisions. *Softw. Pract. Exp.*, 43, 11, 1283–1297, 2013.

10. Repschlaeger, J., Wind, S., Zarnekow, R., Turowski, K., Decision model for selecting a cloud provider: A study of service model decision priorities. Paper presented at: *Proceedings of the 9th Americas Conference on Information Systems*, 2013.

11. Totiya, S. and Senivongse, T., Framework to support cloud service selection based on service measurement index. Paper presented in: *Proceedings of the World Congress on Engineering and Computer Science*, 2017.

12. Alkhalil, A., Sahandi, R., John, D., Migration to cloud computing: A decision process model. *Central European Conference on Information and Intelligent Systems*, 2014.

13. Repschläger, J., Wind, S., Zarnekow, R., Turowski, K., Developing a cloud provider selection model. *Enterprise Modelling and Information Systems Architectures (EMISA)*, vol. 190, pp. 163–176, 2011.

14. Baranwal, G. and Vidyarthi, D.P., A framework for selection of best cloud service provider using ranked voting method. Paper presented at: *IEEE International Advance Computing Conference*, 2014.

15. Rao, R.V., Teaching-learning-based optimization algorithm, in: *Teaching learning based optimization algorithm*, pp. 9–39, Springer, Cham, 2016.

16. Rao, R., Jaya: A simple and new optimization algorithm for solving constrained and unconstrained optimization problems. *Int. J. Ind. Eng. Comput.*, 7, 1, 19–34, 2016.

17. Meng, X.B., Gao, X.Z., Lu, L., Liu, Y., Zhang, H., A new bio-inspired optimisation algorithm: Bird Swarm Algorithm. *J. Exp. Theor. Artif. Intell.*, 28, 4, 673–687, 2016.

18. Amazon AWS, https://aws.amazon.com/. Accessed June 10, 2018.

19. DigitalOcean, https://www.digitalocean.com/. Accessed June 10, 2018.

20. Microsoft Azure, https://azure.microsoft.com/en-us/. Accessed June 11, 2018.

21. Google Compute Engine, https://cloud.google.com/compute/. Accessed June 11, 2018.

22. Yang, P.C., Wee, H.M., Pai, S., Tseng, Y.F., Solving a stochastic demand multi-product supplier selection model with service level and budget constraints using genetic algorithm. *Expert Syst. Appl.*, 38, 12, 14773–14777, 2011.

23. Kirkpatrick, S., Gelatt, C.D., Vecchi, M.P., Optimization by simulated annealing, *Am. Assoc. Adv. Sci.*, 220, 671–680, 1983.

24. Park, M.W. and Kim, Y.D., A systematic procedure for setting parameters in simulated annealing algorithms. *Comput. Oper. Res.*, 25, 3, 207–217, 1998.

25. Mitchell, M., *An Introduction to Genetic Algorithms*, pp. 6–30, MIT Press, Cambridge, MA, 1998.

26. Kennedy, J. and Eberhart, R.C., Particle swarm optimization. Paper presented in: *Proceedings of the IEEE International Conference on Neural Networks*, 1995.

27. Kennedy, J. and Eberhart, R.C., A discrete binary version of the particle swarm algorithm. Paper presented at: *Proceedings of the 1997 IEEE International Conference on Systems Man and Cybernetics, Computational Cybernetics and Simulation*, 1997.

28. Ezenwoke, A., Daramola, O., Adigun, M., *Simulated cloud service QoS dataset, Mendeley Data, Version 1*, Elsevier, Amsterdam, Netherlands, https://doi.org/10.17632/5vffs75j85.1, 2018.

29. *The Cloud Service Industry's 10 Most Critical Metrics*, https://guidingmetrics.com/content/cloud-services-industrys-10-most-criticalmetrics/, guidingmetrics blog, 2018.

30. Taguchi, G., Taguchi on robust technology development: bringing quality engineering upstream. *J. Electron. Packag.*, 116, 2, 161, 1994.

31. Saaty, T.L., *Decision Making for Leaders: The Analytic Hierarchy Process for Decisions in Complex World*, Third Revised Edition, RWS Publications, Pittsburgh, PA, 2012.

32. Barr, R.S., Golden, B.L., Kelly, J.P., Resende, M.G., Stewart, W.R., Designing and reporting on computational experiments with heuristic methods. *J. Heuristics*, 1, 1, 9–32, 1995.

33. Alhamad, M., Dillon, T., Wu, C., Chang, E., Response time for cloud computing providers. Paper presented at: *Proceedings of the 12th International Conference on Information Integration and Web-based Applications & Services*, 2010, https://doi.org/10.1145/1967486.1967579.

34. R.H. Flores and S.H. Leonard, Inventors, International Business Machines Corp, assignee. Performance monitor for multiple cloud computing environments, US Patent Application 13/570,193, 2014.

35. Ipsilandis, P.G., Spreadsheet modelling for solving combinatorial problems: The vendor selection problem, arXiv preprint arXiv:0809.3574, 95–107, 2008.

36. Patra, S.S., Amodi, S.A., Goswami, V., Barik, R.K., Profit Maximization Strategy with Spot Allocation Quality Guaranteed Service in Cloud Environment, in: *2020 International Conference on Computer Science, Engineering and Applications (ICCSEA)*, IEEE, pp. 1–6, 2020.

37. El-Sawy, A.A., Hussein, M.A., Zaki, E.S.M., Mousa, A.A., An introduction to genetic algorithms: A survey a practical issues. *Int. J. Sci. Eng. Res.*, 5, 1, 252–262, 2014.

## 18

Legal Entanglements of Cloud Computing In India

Sambhabi Patnaik and Lipsa Dash*

KIIT School of Law, KIIT University, Bhubaneswar, India

Abstract

Technology has never failed to surprise us! The legal aspects of cloud computing is integral for us to understand the complexities and challenges that an individual has to deal with under the Indian regime. Data ownership, intellectual property issues, privacy concerns, cyber security issues, intermediary liability, government surveillance powers and interoperability are a few threats involved in cloud computing. Cloud service providers handle sensitive personal information and any breach/leakage could attract legal actions. "Right to Privacy" was recently declared as a Fundamental Right under Constitution of India. The Personal Data Protection Bill, 2019 in India recognizes right of privacy as a natural right and has paved the way for a transformational shift towards safeguarding personal data which is an essential aspect of informational privacy, thus, keeping pace with the rapid digitization the country is experiencing. The worldwide accessibility and usage of cloud computing makes the choice of law and jurisdiction a pertinent concern for the larger perspective of the worldwide legal framework and India's interaction with the same. The authors will also analyze different international laws to curb the problems, bridge the gap and simplify the international issues in cloud computing.

Keywords: Privacy, data protection, cloud computing, Information Technology Act 2000, sensitive personal information, cyber security

18.1 Cloud Computing Technology

Cloud computing is a rapidly growing configured technology which has significant demand and is an effective platform for organizations and individuals to share their resources. The users, service providers and the businesses requiring these IT services are acquainted with the needs to combat the risks associated with it. Every year, billions is spent in the IT sector innovations. The service providers are leveraging the cyberspace and the physical world to achieve their goals which might be for the greater good. Services of the cloud include a stack of layers namely Infrastructure as a service (IaaS), Platform as a service (PaaS) and Software as a service (SaaS) having different functions. The services might be paid or free depending on the service provider's discretion. IaaS is the Information Technology infrastructure which belongs to the cloud provider and this infrastructure is used as a platform. PaaS, is where a developer manages to develop, test and maintain the created software applications and mobile apps without

---

**Corresponding author*: lipsadash1993@gmail.com

Monika Mangla, Suneeta Satpathy, Bhagirathi Nayak and Sachi Nandan Mohanty (eds.) Integration of Cloud Computing with Internet of Things: Foundations, Analytics, and Applications, (319–342) © 2021 Scrivener Publishing LLC

worrying about the storage, network or other requirements. The supply of software applications as per subscriptions by the users are delivered under the SaaS layer. The cloud helps store and recover data in huge quantities. The cloud can be a public, private or hybrid cloud based on architectural model and beneficial for organizational sectors like IT, telecom, healthcare, hospitality, entertainment and educational, etc. It is considered as one of the most impactful economic innovations of this century. Companies rely on cloud services for cost savings, flexibility and its easy accessibility resulting in exponential and potential growth of the technology. They are more centralized, offering stricter privacy policy and quicker responses to cyber security breaches and compromises. A few service providers are highly trusted in the use of sophisticated technical service. The structure of the internet and the constant innovations in the IT field widely impacts the society. The whole architecture of cloud is to prevent breach of the security and provide privacy of stored data with high encryption tools and techniques. The strength of each type of cloud is different depending on its shape and size. It is a virtual space leading to save energy and time thereby assuring a quality service simultaneously.

However, the virtual environment of cyberspace is vulnerable to cyber attacks and monitoring them is expensive [1]. The cyber security threat is increasing rapidly and thus overcoming its impact has become difficult. Cloud computing has an adverse effect on the cyber security as it detaches computers and other devices and stores information on a huge space that is solely dependent on the internet. The vendors and stakeholders pay a hefty price for high security firewalls to protect data of clients from cyber attacks.

The social benefit derived from resource pooling includes facilitating innovations which are agile, scalable and cost reducing. The cloud enables convenient working model and on-demand network access to a shared pool of configurable computing resource networks (servers, storage, applications and services). The cyberspace fundamentally shapes the nature of cyber threats and the widespread nature of the internet is one of the main reasons of cyber insecurity. The dilemma of stronger encryption is highly required as they have proved to be the best protection mechanism for all the sensitive personal information in the information networks and systems. However the probability of creating a rift between law enforcement bodies, technology companies and other government organizations is relatively high. The extensive implementation of the strong encryption technologies limits a few law enforcement bodies access to the cloud's data [3]. The cryptographic standards and their implementation in the cloud increase the safety standard. Easy access to data because of the indefinable structure of cloud contributes to cyber threats. In the cloud the actual data exists giving exposure to high risk of sensitive data loss even with strong encrypted virtual systems. Those who get access are capable of misusing, causing real damage and targeting the exact vulnerabilities putting the users in highly compromising circumstances. The controls of the infrastructure are kept transparent in terms of security, though both the concepts of sharing and security are slightly contradictory of each other. These resources can be rapidly provisioned and released by service provider interactions and minimal management efforts. The elastic nature of cloud computing gives rise to different service models for their working. Firstly, the acquisition model is based on purchasing of these services. Secondly, the technical model is scalable, elastic, multi-tenant and sharable. Thirdly, the access model brings data over the network to any device. And lastly, the business model is based on pay for use [4]. The Figure 18.1 below depicts the system of cloud computing, its types and model. The picture represents the different types of cloud on basis of their location and services and their working including the advantages and disadvantages of the same.

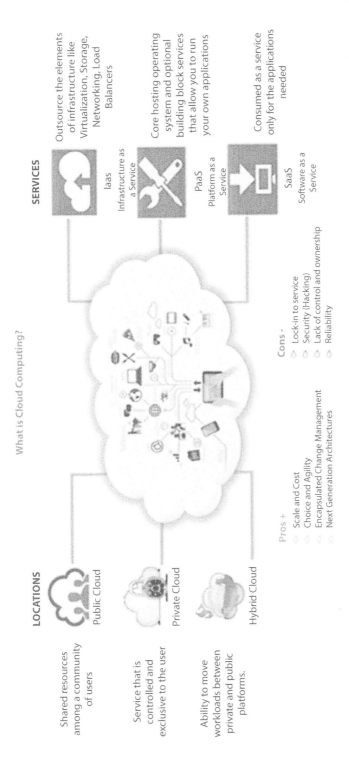

Figure 18.1 Which depicts the system of cloud computing, its types and model [2]. The picture represents the different types of cloud on basis of their location and services and their working including the advantages and disadvantages of the same.

The belief of this generation is that computing is the backbone of advanced technology for the upcoming decade. The agreement or standards to use the cloud exists but it lacks in successful implementation both by people and legislations to end the dichotomy of trust and control. A virtual access layer in the cloud can be protected by a security service layer. However, the security network layers are obviously kept a secret as no one would go public with their security infrastructure, keeping the weak links undisclosed to prevent breaches. In March 2020, during the pandemic of Covid 19 it was declared that few service providers would provide free cloud computing platform to researchers to save data collected for accelerated research, innovation and development using cloud computing. The workflow of cases becomes smoother as it removes cost limitations and other barriers. There is an internal team working on deployment of the resources around the world. Many artificial intelligence bots are created using the cloud and a natural conservation of data is experienced [5]. Cloud helps in task management by integrating huge amount of data and organizes it in the cloud for the users. Racks of servers are disintegrated in accordance to required resources and virtual servers are created individually as cloud. The economic aspect for the cloud providers is also definitely one of the cost beneficiary roads to be considered. The returns of their investments by an effective monetization strategy is very important which leads to resource bundling options, licensing and making different priced models affordable. A range of applications are cloud hosted like Microsoft Suite, ERP applications, CRM applications, etc. The most established players expand their IT infrastructure and create lasting impressions.

18.2   Cyber Security in Cloud Computing

When we store any kind of data on our individual smart phones, we would like to believe that we have secured these data with a security lock (pattern lock, biometric security features, etc.) on our devices. But, the question arises, is it absolutely safe in the real sense? Moreover, what about those data which we upload on our Google drive, iPhone cloud or any other cloud services offered by mobile operating systems? Are there chances of hacking of these data and unauthorized dissemination of the same? Cyber criminals are on the rise and use various available platforms to level up their game. They are no longer stuck to age old desktops but are expanding their wings to other available resources be it, mobile phones, tablets, smart devices and Voice over Internet Protocol technology (VoIP). It can be seen that VoIP has become a preferable medium for cyber criminals to carry out data theft, financial frauds and other crimes. One would be surprised to see the extent that cyber criminals would go to carry out malware attacks via social engineering. For example, it is very common to see how an attacker tricks any naive user over the internet and gains their confidence which later helps them to execute malicious code on the user's system. Cloud services also come under the radar for such kinds of attacks because the attacker wants to take advantage of the massive amount of sensitive data available over cloud.

Cloud security can be achieved with a system that includes government policies, procedures, various control mechanisms and its related technologies that cooperate as a single entity to ensure protection of data stored and available in the cloud's infrastructure. The service providers have security measures to protect data/information in the cloud and protect each client's privacy. These security features can help in compliance with mandatory regulatory framework as well as can help in establishing authentication regulation for individual users and their devices [6]. Users have come across various cyber security threats which make the cloud a high risk premise. With each passing day, the natures of threats are constantly changing. Their sophisticated features makes it even more pertinent for any individual or business enterprise to use cloud providing customized security features for the protection of the user's most valuable possession, i.e. data. The implementation of cloud security is not an individual entity's job but a joint responsibility of the business owner and the solution provider.

18.3   Security Threats in Cloud Computing

A cloud involves ample collection of processors, memory, computer applications and other resources, connected together to the World Wide Web. Cyber attackers are always on the prowl to find the security lapses and cloud vulnerabilities with mala fide intentions. Protection and security of software and data will top the list of concerns when there is an involvement of a third party outsourcing the services making it further inaccessible for the organization's firewall (security) system. It is of utmost importance to be aware as to where exactly one's system could be at risk, and what one can do about fixing the loopholes and system vulnerabilities. Some of the major cybersecurity threats that could affect one's cloud computing services are discussed below.

18.3.1   Data Breaches

This is the easiest and the most recurring threat in cloud computing. Hackers majorly get attracted towards cloud service providers because of the availability of huge amount of data stored on the clouds. Data breaches can majorly lead to unauthorized access to one's cloud accounts by cyber criminals which further can cause loss/leakage of data. These breaches can expose financial information, personal information; if related to health, intellectual property of an organization, etc. resulting in severe damage. Data breach attracts legal liabilities as they result in violation of various legal compliance and contractual obligations.

18.3.2   Denial of Service (DoS)

The DoS attack is one of the common destructive threats against cloud computing. Stopping the DoS attacks, are mostly impossible so one might not be able to mitigate its effects only. DoS attacks usually subdue resources of a cloud service making users unable to access data or resources. This kind of attack is capable of making the cloud services shut down by sending massive amount of web traffic, which further affects the servers. Servers are backbone of any business and the DoS attack will directly hit them by making it inaccessible for any kind of buffering and processing. If any business is entirely dependent on cloud services, then it will be doomed by such deadly DoS attack.

18.3.3   Botnets

These robots are malware programs that slyly get installed on a system helping an unauthorized person to remotely access and control the system for carrying out any malicious activity. Botnets are considered dangerous for cloud security as compared to other malware, because they have a distributed platform which can provide a hot bed for all cyber criminal activities over the cloud. For example, a botnet can be used to spam any operation system by blasting out millions of messages. Botnets are useful for an attacker who wants to crack open password-protected or encrypted information.

18.3.4   Crypto Jacking

It is a fairly recent form of cyber attack which indulges in mining for cryptocurrencies like bitcoin. The attackers can easily access computing systems/resources from one's cloud system which can make one's operation slow while the program still runs. Therefore, detection of this attack is complicated and can easily go under the radar. Many just believe that there is either processing issue or slow internet issue while their system is being crypto-jacked.

18.3.5   Insider Threats

It is a common belief that cyber criminals/hackers are major cyber security threats for cloud services. However, it is surprising to know that security issues can not only originate from outside but inside as well because of their unique position and access to networks and systems. As the name suggests, threats which can occur from the organization itself. Insiders (staff, employees and administrators) of the organization or cloud service providers might abuse their authorized access or because of their negligence and error can become the threat. Sometimes, a malicious insider can cause more harm than an outside attacker. The malicious insider might be a revenge seeking previous employee or a present member of the organization, or an accessory with the credentials intentionally gaining access and misusing the secured information. Therefore, organizations have to be alert and keep a tab on any cyber criminal activity caused by their employees and make full proof off-boarding process, which will make sure that the access of employees is deactivated after they leave the organization.

18.3.6   Hijacking Accounts

This is one of the most explored cyber crimes to date. Hijacking can easily be done by employing various techniques like phishing, password cracking which becomes easy for cyber criminals to access numerous accounts, including cloud services. Hackers once having secured access to accounts can create havoc easily while the users are unaware of the occurrence of a crime. Proper training, permission management and end user agreements can be some basic techniques to minimize the risks associated with such attacks. Organizations and celebrity cloud accounts are extremely vulnerable to such hijacking.

18.3.7   Insecure Applications

Securing your own applications, systems and network sometimes is not enough as one might get a threat form an external source even though downloaded from authentic app stores. Any third-party service or application has the potential for serious cloud security risks, even though the organization's own system is well insulated against most common cyber threats. Therefore, it is highly advisable that proper precautionary measures should be followed while installation of any third party applications as to its viability and security to the organization's own network. It is usually discouraged to download an external unauthorized file by a member of organization without proper approval of the IT team of the organization, whose primary business involves securing client data.

18.3.8 Inadequate Training

A few instances of cyber attacks can be seen to have been caused by employees due to their negligence in their conduct. This can sometimes be due to lack of seriousness of threat of a cyber crime or mishandling of a threat. Therefore, it is advised by the experts that each and every member should be trained from time to time, which will equip them with updated and adequate information and can help in early detection resulting in timely handling of any kind of cyber threat, specially to cloud services [7].

18.3.9 General Vulnerabilities

Users of cloud services use different web browsers to navigate and maximize various services offered by cloud service providers. Web browsers also have their own share of cyber security vulnerabilities via which different malicious code gets executed and perform malicious activities on the user's computer, without the knowledge of users. For instance, Cross-Site Scripting (XSS) is a threat that can affect the user system as it can install malicious script into web pages, while a user is using the web browser.

18.4 Cloud Security Probable Solutions

18.4.1 Appropriate Cloud Model for Business

It is advisable for organization to opt for private cloud service model over public cloud service for their businesses. Public clouds are cost effective than private clouds, which makes it popular. Private clouds have been proved to be more secure than the public clouds as these are used by only one single entity. Business involves financial transactions, confidential information and trade secrets, which makes private clouds the safer option over public clouds. Therefore, choosing the appropriate cloud model for any business is the very first step against any cyber security issues.

18.4.2 Dedicated Security Policies Plan

Strategies always make it easier in shaping the future of a system and prepare one to handle all kinds of risks, which makes security strategies even more crucial. Therefore, service providers of the cloud have explicit security policies which guarantee data security. Users or organizations, being more aware these days, will not trust any service provider with their client information, which does not have a formalized security policy.

18.4.3 Multifactor Authentication

This kind of authentication is common today for anyone using net-banking or making a digital payment. This simple method can be effective for any service provider against any kind of threat. For instance, the cloud providers provides the multilayered authentication system to secure its data with the help of one time passwords, captchas, image identification, user behavior authentication and mobile codes. Even if a hacker tries to access by unlocking through password, he will not succeed. The data owner has exclusive access on his device to the one time password required for authentication, making the hacker's attempt futile to login and access the data. Multifactor authentication is a good arrangement to make the level of protection of data more stringent [8].

18.4.4 Data Accessibility

This is one of the most basic and crucial step towards protecting data over cloud against any misuse. The access to data should be very limited and must be given to administrators only. This restricted access will be instrumental in providing the much required security to the data over the cloud with enhanced protection. A large number of cloud applications provide unpaid programming trials and openings in administration to probable attackers, having client collaborations. These attackers might take advantage by downloading or signing in Denial of Service attacks, through spammed emails, or a system to extort through computerized clicks. The cloud service supplier has to be equipped with a strong team and IT experts who being in charge of controlling the quality of the structure can come up with unique solutions by observing their own cloud condition in such situations.

18.4.5 Secure Data Destruction

The lifecycle of data also includes destruction of the data which needs to be done securely. Data not destroyed under careful supervision can be retrieved anytime and misused. The risks of data leakage and misappropriation of the same will always be lurking, in case of unsecure data destruction. One has to be careful and be aware of the information annihilation process of the cloud services. All sensitive and classified information will be at risk, if the service provider does not appropriately pulverize information which is no longer required.

18.4.6 Encryption of Backups

Data, being the primary subject of cloud service, needs to be backed up in regular intervals to prevent loss of data. Whenever data over cloud is being backed up, it needs to be secured. Encryption of cloud backups of data is necessary to avoid data compromise. A hacker can easily get access to these data which will no longer be secured, if data backups are not protected with appropriate encryption methods. Data, at all times, during its entire lifecycle should be protected from all kinds of intrusion.

18.4.7 Regulatory Compliance

Compliance is a crucial aspect for any organization and these entities must ensure that effective governance, risk and compliance, regular audit processes exist for achieving required security standards to their cloud services. The chapter in the later part deals with it in details.

18.4.8   External Third-Party Contracts and Agreements

Security standards have to be spelled out with specific onus of liabilities in cloud service agreement, as it might involve more than a single entity. Whenever, the cloud service provider is subcontracting, there is involvement of a cloud merchant who has access to massive amount of classified data that might be manhandled by another supplier while storing. The general security of the data chain must be maintained at all times, otherwise the guarantee of complete security against any cyber attack as provided by the seller might be compromised [9].

18.5   Cloud Security Standards

The Cloud Standards Customer Council (CSCC) has been established as "an end user advocacy group which is devoted to accelerate cloud's successful adoption, lying down the standards, catering to security and interoperability issues which usually surround the transition to the cloud". It is reported that majority of leading organizations from around the world having similar interests have joined the CSCC [10]. The Council has prescribed ten steps that each cloud service customer must consider to implement for managing the security of their cloud environment which can help them to handle the cloud security risks. Each step has its own cloud specific security standards and certifications which can be utilized for a safe and secured cloud environment. Following are those ten steps:

1. Ensure effective governance, risk and compliance processes exist
2. Audit operational and business processes
3. Manage people, roles and identities
4. Ensure proper protection of data and information
5. Enforce privacy policies
6. Assess the security provisions for cloud applications
7. Ensure cloud networks and connections are secure
8. Evaluate security controls on physical infrastructure and facilities
9. Manage security terms in the cloud service agreement
10. Understand the security requirements of the exit process [10].

18.6   Cyber Security Legal Framework in India

India at present does not have an exclusive cyber security law per se; instead what we have is a National Cyber Security Policy, 2013. The policy was framed by the Ministry of Communication and Information Technology aiming at encouraging all organizations to implement best international practices by developing security policies coordinated with their business model and strategies. The policy has laid down certain recommendations for creating a secure cyber ecosystem which can strengthen existing legislations and create methods for detection of security threats on time and managing corresponding responses to avoid such threats. The National Cyber Security Policy, 2013 is expected to be updated in 2020.

Currently, India regulates cyber security issues, with the aid of the IT Act 2000, IT rules and regulations framed there under. The provisions of the IT Act 2000 can be made applicable to cloud services in India as it uses digital medium and is rendered over the internet. The Act also has provisions for the constitution of Computer Emergency Response Team (CERT-In) read with the Information Technology (The Indian Computer Emergency Response Team and Manner of Performing Functions and Duties) Rules 2013 (the CERT Rules). CERT is the nodal agency that is bestowed with the responsibility of collecting, analyzing and disseminating information of any incident in the cyber world and also assists in providing emergency mechanisms to control cyber incidents. The protected system of various organizations, identified under the IT Act 2000, must adhere to the information security measures as laid down under the "Information Technology (Information Security Practices and Procedures for Protected System) Rules 2018 (the Protected System Rules)" to mitigate any security threats.

Legislation other than IT Act 2000, such as the Indian Penal Code 1860, The Companies Act, 2013 read with the Companies (Management and Administration) Rules, 2014 contain laws dealing with cyber security issues. The above mentioned rules under the Companies Act 2013 make sure that companies adhere to measures that can ensure security of electronic records and security systems from any kind of unauthorized access and tampering. In addition to these legislations and rules there are sector specific regulators such as the Department of Telecommunication (DoT), the Securities Exchange Board of India (SEBI), the Reserve Bank of India (RBI), the Insurance Regulatory and Development Authority of India (IRDA). These various regulators regulate entities (banks, telecom service providers and others) by mandating certain cybersecurity standards to be maintained by them. For instance, SEBI requires ISO/IEC 27001, ISO/IEC 27002 and COBIT 5 standards to be followed by stock exchanges, depositories and clearing corporations. The RBI regulates for ensuring protection to sensitive information by mandating banks to adhere to the ISO/IEC 27001 and ISO/IEC 27002 standards. If a situation arises where parties involved have not agreed upon any fixed security practices and procedures under a contract, the organization which is in possession of sensitive personal information would be required to follow a minimum standard provided under IS/ISO/IEC/27001 for safeguarding the same information [11].

The Government of India has come up with various initiatives and beneficial measures for improving cyber security standards in India for different organization for both public and private. The Ministry of Electronics and Information Technology (MeitY) has set up the Cyber Swachhta Kendra (Botnet Cleaning and Malware Analysis Centre) under the very ambitious Digital India initiative. This center will be handled by CERT-In, delegated with the power of tackling issues with internet service providers, product or antivirus companies and will help users to tackle botnet and malware threats. The government in order to create awareness for India's cybersecurity preparedness and relevant stakeholders in this field has launched online repository on cyber tech called 'Techsagar'. This repository is the brain child of the National Cyber Security Coordinator and the Data Security Council of India which aims at facilitating the businesses and academia in collaboration and exchange on matters of cybersecurity and innovations [12].

Cybersecurity insurance is creating a wave in different sectors of India and can be seen to have gained popularity in the all the major sectors, including banking, information technology, etc. Like any other insurance, it is will prove to be helpful in protecting online users and victims against any loss arising from any cyber attack.

18.7   Privacy in Cloud Computing—Data Protection Standards

The digitization primarily has acted on improving lifestyle of an average citizen. Individuals, organizations and nations are not fully protected and India is among the top nations in field of cyber crime expecting a higher standard of protection. The data in the cloud is stored and the service providers follow strict international and national privacy policy to avoid legal issues. The regulatory framework of law in India with respect to data protection and privacy is incorporated in the IT Act, 2000 and doesn't have a sui generis law. There is a bill pending under review of the legislators, "The Data Protection Privacy Bill, 2019" which aims to take care of the collection, storage and dissemination of sensitive personal data and rights and duties of the data subjects and data fiduciaries respectively. The data protection principles are widely laid down in the General Data Protection Rights Law (EU—GDPR). The cloud attracts the storage limitation principle to the extent that the data subject gives freedom to store. All users are entitled the right to restrict the free movement of their personal data. The standard of the protection is maintained by data fiduciaries and personal data is processed with certain restrictions. The protection of the personal data stored between data subjects and data fiduciaries is harmonized. All companies and business bodies are using the cloud to store their electronic data as it provides huge network storage capabilities with minimum efforts to manage the data, making the service provider interactions smooth. It reduces the IT costs and increases efficiency. The transborder data flow turns out to be a threat. The data in the cloud while transcending national boundaries show potential dangers of loss, being compromised or hacked so it's done within restrictive data privacy and protection laws. Corporations under investigation must make their arguments ready looking into all relevant laws from gathering, reviewing and producing responsive electronic data [13]. Transgression of any law may result in heavy loss to the corporation unless it falls under any exception between legal obligations. Few countries have their own ministries and autonomous decision making bodies to deal with data protection.

Taking the example of Facebook, the data processors use the cloud to archive and analyze the shared information, locations and interests in different posts tracking likes of users and stores it. In 2018, Facebook reported that Cambridge Analytica, a third party application which was also a political consultancy had breached into their system and the data of 87 million people was inappropriately shared [14]. The system wasn't infiltrated rather the system and its working as designed was flawed. Later Facebook brought the changes and declared that it had successfully changed its DNA hinting at its platform with higher security and user focused privacy requirements. There are two folds of privacy, one being collecting less information and limiting the retention of such data, and the other being limiting the access of information to other people. Backup, recovery, segmentation, fragmentation and duplication are all included. The third party application could be compromised or even lost and irretrievable in a later stage as faced by different companies. The cloud might be getting transferred due to fall of an organization putting people in a skeptical situation about the new environment, posing it as an existing or new threat, bounded by a lock-in period. The choice principle incorporated in data protection here might be at stake. Portability of the data, data provenance, anonymization of the data and data placements makes it risk prone. The procedures of security practices and due diligence to be strictly followed by different organizations is the need of the hour. They can also choose to obfuscate information using techniques of encryption, tokenization, conversion of data to a non-readable format and computational derivation of a value for the original data keeping it in a secure lookup table like the vault [15]. The migration of data includes legal issues in copyright, laws of contract, competition law and other liability fixing legislations.

The personal data privacy guidelines were framed looking into European General Data Protection Regulation, Organization of Economic Cooperation and Development (OECD) privacy guidelines of 1981, the Asia-Pacific Economic Cooperation (APEC), Privacy Framework of 2005; the Data Protection Convention of the Council of Europe of 1981; and finally the European Union's data protection Directive of 1995 on privacy and other international laws. Apart from EU GDPR other legislations include The UK Data Protection Law, the Swiss Federal Act on Data Protection, Russian Data Privacy Law, The Canadian Personal Information Protection and Electronic Documents Act.

Principles of OECD have national application in most of the developing countries. The set of principles are henceforth discussed to understand their application. The collection limitation principle provides a limit on the means to collect the data lawfully with the proper consent and knowledge of the user. The security safeguard principles protect the data by reasonably safeguarding security from any kind of threat/data loss/unauthorized access, use, modifications, disclosures of data and any kind of destructions. Due to lack of physical measures like biometrics or locked doors the virtual measures are implemented. Theft, erasure or destruction of the stored data will lead to legal consequences. The individual participation principle enables the data subject to obtain any kind of information from the data controller through communication and requests. This principle is followed by the openness principle which states the practice of collecting the information and storage of the personal data is with prior knowledge of the data subject. The accountability principle obligates the data controller to be responsible for compliance of the standards simultaneously allowing free flow of data with legitimate restrictions. Any transborder data flow should be done with due diligence and reasonable care, and security [16].

In India, The Constitution of India recognizes Right to Privacy as a fundamental right. The Contract Act 1972, The Indian Copyright Act 1957, and Indian Penal Code 1860 are a few statutes dealing with privacy regulation. The Sensitive Personal Data and Information Rules 2011 govern the transfer of data which is not equipped enough to face the privacy battles. The data protection draft bill which has been constantly under revision was last revised on December 2019.

18.8　Recognition of Right to Privacy

A certain level of restriction is required to be imposed on the organizations which get hold of the personal information of the public starting from name, age, sexual orientation, preferences, and friends to prevent them from misappropriating personal data of the public. Collection of the personal information could result in loss of life, image, independence, free flow of movement, speech, etc. of an individual. Article 21 of The Constitution of India ensures the "right to life and personal liberty" of every person and with continuous judicial interpretation over time it has expanded its reach to different corners including right to privacy which was recently declared as sacrosanct to every individual in the case of *Justice KS Puttaswammy v. State of Kerela* (2017) 10 SCC 1. There was however a constant need of making privacy a fundamental part of Article 21 of The Constitution of India. It is now a natural right and not just an elitist construct which is historic for the Indian legal regime decided by the nine judge bench unanimously. Previously, in the case of Govind v. State of Madhya Pradesh [AIR 1975 SC 1378] it was decided that the "right to privacy is not absolute and could be compromised if there is a greater need for public good". A dynamic data protection law is important to ensure individual's informational privacy as the introduction of ADHAAR card was criticized by majority due to the high chances of data leakage. The data stored in the cloud server makes it prone to cyber attacks. Right to privacy was categorized in three aspects in the Puttuswamy judgment, as right to bodily autonomy, informational privacy, and privacy of choice. These aspects were also considered by the committee of the data protection bill which was chaired by Shri Justice BN Srikrishna. It also ensures a restricted power to the government. With the internet growing as a disruptive technology in keeping private matters of our lives secure, any data collected that is sensitive and personal in nature, the data subject has to have a choice of how the data is being stored or processed and its distribution and usage. The data that once stored in the cloud can be erased or modified as per the data subject's choice. The standards of data protection include direction from the data controller to comply with the rules and provide all information to the data subject. Freedom of speech and expression was ensured to protect liberty of citizens and acceptance of criticisms for the welfare of the government and public. To secure a personal life is to include all physical details as well as informational details to set a boundary from interference by the unwanted. As discussed in the chapter later, the liability of intermediaries have undergone a shift from strict to contributory liability.

The Data Protection Bill, 2019 dealing with personal data includes storage in the definition of "processing" under the umbrella of which the cloud can easily be implied to be a part of. The bill defines 'data principal' [Section 2(14) of the Data Protection Bill] as "any natural person to whom the personal data is related to and 'data fiduciary'] Section 2(13) of the Data Protection Bill] as any person (including juristic persons and the State) who is involved in processing of the personal data" [17]. Personal data can include passwords, financial data, biometric data, etc. and all of them require explicit consent of an individual. The bill explicitly mentions and directs the data fiduciaries whose data centers are located in India to keep a 'serving copy' of the personal data in their remote servers. The bill has been on extensive debate from different stakeholders. The data can also be categorized as critical personal data if the central government deems necessary. The Constitution doesn't confer absolute right and it can be infringed and restrictions can be imposed for larger public interest in coherence with the rule of law [18]. This is also known as the doctrine of proportionality.

There is a primary duty to ensure that the individual has an utmost right on its information along with ensuring public security and safeguard of the general masses. In the case of Modern Dental College & Ors. V. State of MP & Ors. [(2016) 7 SCC 353] the doctrine of proportionality is explained. It was held that if fundamental right is infringed, it should be for a legitimate state purpose and the action infringing the right should be proportionate to the necessity to interfere with the right and more importantly such action should be sanctioned by law. This doctrine is in the form of "reasonable restrictions" in our Constitution as discussed in the case of Kharak Singh v. State of Uttar Pradesh (AIR 1963 SC 1295). The Right to Privacy might be violated only by procedures established by/under the laws to the extent of interference which must be consistent with the need to interfere.

This digitally driven age mandates the need and adoption of a data protection law to uphold human dignity. The IT Act 2000 read along with the IT (Reasonable Security Practices and Procedures and sensitive personal data or information) Rules 2011 contain specific provisions regarding collection, usage and transfer of personal data/information. These provisions of law distinguishes between "personal information" and "sensitive personal data or information" as a subset [19]. The information posted or provided online can be accessed anytime considering the vast storage capacity of the internet and easy accessibility. The existing data protection laws recognize the liability for the failure of protecting sensitive personal data by a body corporate.

18.9   Government Surveillance Power vs Privacy of Individuals

"Those who would give up essential Liberty, to purchase a little temporary Safety, deserve neither Liberty nor Safety."—Benjamin Franklin

In a world of digital data transfer, there is a continuous exchange of information internationally, but the security of the information is often compromised. The collection of large quantity information about online user habits has become a vital source of profit. Online footprints of an individual can reveal a lot about the individual. The organizations use this valuable information to target users via online advertisements. The government bodies and political parties have mala fide intentions and are interested to use the data sets for their personal agenda, election campaigning and propaganda.

The Personal Data Protection Bill 2019 highlights on safeguarding data such as a user's biometrics, financial details, religious and caste beliefs, etc. which can be used for identification of a person. This information collected can be instrumental for the purpose of investigation by concerned authorities. On the other hand, the government can access the personal data for appropriate reasons like national security, sovereignty and integrity of the country to intrude in the lives of the citizen's privacy which defeats the very purpose of the bill. This flexibility proves to be contrary to the bill's primary purpose.

Despite being highly secured network service providers, Facebook and Twitter, were using user's information and sending targeted ads which is clearly a breach of trust. If ever these companies get incentives to collect the government IDs, nothing can then prevent them from breaching user's privacy.

The outbreak of a pandemic known as Covid-19 has led different government bodies across the globe to take all possible measures and protect the public. In India, to control the spread of the virus, there is constant tracking, collecting and processing of the information about individual's travel history, symptoms and their contact with affected patients or public in general is recorded by the central government, state government, public health authorities, not-for-profit organizations, corporate and other stakeholders. But the government has failed to provide any sort of guidance or prescribe any boundaries for the data processing activities of aforementioned agencies.

During any government probe or the pendency of a law suit, the organizations might seek access to user's data available in the cloud for the process of investigation. Few of the Indian laws, such as the Indian Telegraph Act 1885, Indian Wireless Telegraphy Act 1933 under the Department of Telecommunications (DoT) and the IT Act 2000, has provisions that throws light on the instrumental part of being an intermediary thus assisting in legal interception, helping the government and regulatory bodies to access the private exchange of information and data. The Telegraph Act authorizes the government to intercept all kinds of messages, subject to prescribed safeguards, under the grounds of interest of national security, prevention of crime, and public safety as provided under the Act [20]. The IT Act 2000 having similar provisions empowers the government and its authorized agencies to intercept messages. Section 69 of the IT Act 2000 provides that "Any person or officer authorized by the government (central or state) can, it is satisfied that it is necessary or expedient to do so in the interest of sovereignty and the integrity of India, the defense of India, the security of the state, friendly relations with foreign states, public order or preventing incitement to the commission of any cognizable offence relating to the above, or for the investigation of any offence, can inter alia, direct any of its agencies to intercept, monitor or decrypt, or cause to be intercepted, monitored or decrypted, any information that is generated, transmitted, received or stored in any computer resource, in the event it is satisfied that it is necessary or expedient to do so in the interest of sovereignty and the integrity of India, the defense of India, the security of the state, friendly relations with foreign states, public order or preventing incitement to the commission of any cognizable offence relating to the above, or for the investigation of any offence". The Government has been also empowered to monitor and collect data traffic or any information for the cyber security through any computer resource under Section 69 B of the IT Act 2000. The Information Technology (Reasonable security practices and procedures and sensitive personal data or information) Rules 2011, authorizes governmental agencies to seek for any information including sensitive personal information from a body corporate or service provider, taking prior consent of the data subject, if such disclosure is required under law. However, the IT Act 2000 has provisions to hold a government official liable who has information under their possession and discloses the same information to a third party without prior consent from the provider; shall be liable to pay damages for any wrongful loss suffered by the aggrieved person under 72 A of the IT Act 2000. These provisions prove fruitful for government agencies whenever there is any contravention or investigation of a cyber crime to intercept data for cyber security incidents.

18.10   Data Ownership and Intellectual Property Rights

The nature of the cloud is multi-jurisdictional and this uncertain nature gives rise to complications in intellectual property rights specifically patent laws causing difficulty in targeting potential infringers. When a technology is innovated and patented which uses a cloud service in some other country that helps in processing the data and few other activities, there arises a chance of infringement and the question of data ownership might shift. Each component of the cloud is operated and managed by different parties and subsequently the issue of sub-contracting within the departments leads to attaching different responsibilities and accordingly provides its service to the users. Further this gives rise to divided infringement issues which is one of the biggest shortcomings in our legislative framework. The service provider of the cloud may be liable for inducing the infringers by not protecting the client's patents in the best interest. According to World Intellectual Property Organization (WIPO), an IP is an asset and in collaboration with different corporations and organizations which accelerates the global economy. The collaboration is easier in the cloud and offers unprecedented advantages in terms of storing and syncing data across multiple devices in the digital world [21]. The cloud enables cross border coordination and smooth access to files in intervals as many organizers sign to stay in the cloud and use the services. These trends definitely have started a concern of protecting Intellectual Property online while identifying trademark/copyright/patent infringements by cybercriminals. The threats that we encounter has already been discussed among the cyber security issues initially in this chapter. Access and privileges of few people makes it riskier and prone to infringements. Most companies restrict users to use their personal phones for work as there are high chances of linking it to the cloud and the loss of a phone will lead to loss of huge amount of data compromising company and its client's. The files need to be encrypted to make it difficult for the infringer to decrypt the files. Clouds can be equipped with firewalls to protect our intellectual property right and information giving an additional layer of protection to their servers. Along with benefit of the cloud, a company can secure its data safely as the in-built mechanism is encryption. The process of effective encryption and decryption of personal data or sensitive content is to ensure high digital protection and any person trying to break it will be liable under the IT Act 2000. In cloud, neither any unauthorized user nor the service provider can access an individual's data ensuring strong security. Rigorous and constant monitoring by the technology prevents data breaches and theft. The standard of encryption differs from country to country, where India allows up to 40 bit according to the telecom licensing condition and Section 84 A of the IT Act 2000 but there are countries who allow beyond 256 bit which furthers strengthens the security of the cloud. The service provider has to maintain minimum regulatory standards of monitoring, interception, encryption, decryption, providing minimum and maximum limits to manage the cloud. There are arrangements between countries like the Wassenar Arrangement [22] established to contribute international and national security of dual use technologies promoting transparency and reliability within member states preventing destabilizing accumulations of these technologies. India being a member of the arrangement participates and understands the risks attached to exchange of information of the sensitive technologies. The data's nature of confidentiality, ideas and expressions, trademarks and brand secrets,

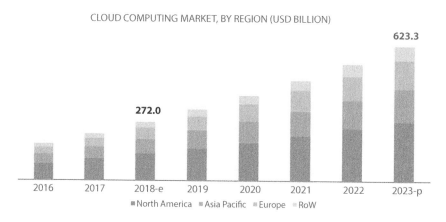

Figure 18.2 The estimated cloud computing market report by the survey of by markets and markets [24]. The comparison is between the regions of North America, Asia Pacific, Europe and rest of the world for the year 2016 to prospective 2023.

designing and software blueprints are attached to the cloud making it targets of potential infringement. The facilitation of exchanging of assents in the cloud is spreading worldwide, whether or not a country signs up for the use. There could be chances of reverse engineering and misuse. The non availability of a definite law to tackle the issue makes the hardware owner, service providers of the cloud, and other parties' accomplice to the infringement. An international consensus along with a flexible tool and its territorial use to avoid any sort of infringement is necessary. The alarming feature of the cloud, whenever there is an attempt of hacking or attacking a particular IP is communicated to the user giving a chance to stop the breach. Revoking access of public and ex-employees are a few steps to prevent misappropriation of data. Each file has a level of protection in the cloud server giving it a myriad of advantage in storing IP, sharing them and managing collaborative projects working together with people and creating a safe work environment [23]. The Figure 18.2 above depicts a chart that estimates cloud computing market report by the survey of by markets and markets. The comparison is between the regions of North America, Asia Pacific, Europe and rest of the world for the year 2016 to prospective 2023.

Technology giants enter into agreements to run these software applications as their assets under the umbrella of intellectual property. The devices and their components are designed as highly sophisticated automation softwares. Due to the technology competition in the market, the tech giants are proving to be the best protector in the market.

18.11 Cloud Service Provider as an Intermediary

Section 2(w) of the Information Technology Act 2000 defines Intermediary means "any person who on behalf of another person receives stores or transmits an electronic record or provides any service with respect to that record and includes telecom service providers, network service providers, internet service providers (ISPs), web-hosting service providers, search engines, online payment sites, online auction sites, online market places and cyber cafes". Almost all cloud service providers, depending on business model, are considered as an intermediary, according to the above mentioned definition. All cloud service providers/ intermediaries will have to adhere to due diligence procedures and compliance under the IT Act 2000 and other relevant laws. Intermediaries being platforms which are gateways that can regulate the sharing and flow of information has always been presumed to have control over content of data being uploaded and shared. In general, data protection laws provide exception from liability to intermediaries in form of safe harbor principles. Intermediaries can only be able to exercise their right of exemption from liabilities if they have exercised due diligence as provided and instructed by the Government timely under different regulations. It is daunting for law makers to make these platforms liable for hosting content that belongs to third parties. The Indian courts have to ascertain the extent of liability and responsibility for intermediaries for facilitating the hosting of any user content. However, the legislature of India has enacted certain provisions specifically for intermediaries:-

- Section 79 of the Information Technology Act 2000 read with the Information Technology (Intermediaries Guidelines) Rules 2011 (which got amended in 2018) mandates intermediaries for implementation of reasonable security practices and procedures for security of their computer resources.

- Cybersecurity incidents are required to be reported to CERT-In by the intermediaries under the Act. Any failure on the part of intermediaries to report such incidents to CERT-In will lead to liability under the Act. The fine will be a sum not exceeding 25,000 rupees. CERT-In may request for information from body corporate, service providers, intermediaries who fail to comply with such request. They are liable to imprisonment up to one year or a fine which may extend to 100,000 rupees, or both.
- The intermediary while discharging his duties under the Intermediary rules 2018 has to take proper due diligence "(1) The intermediary shall have to publish the privacy policy, rules and regulations, and user agreement for access or usage of the intermediary's computer resource by any person. (2) Such rules and regulations, terms and conditions as included in the user agreement shall inform the users of computer resource not to host, upload, display, modify, publish, transmit, update or share any information that, which might affect public health and safety and Critical Information structure [25]".
- According to Clause 3 of Section 79 of the IT Act 2000, an intermediary would not be able to take the advantage of exemption "if it has conspired or abetted or aided or induced whether by threats or promise or otherwise in the commission of the unlawful act; or the intermediary upon receiving actual knowledge, or on being notified by the appropriate Government that any information, or communication link residing in or connected to a computer resource controlled by the intermediary is being used to commit the unlawful act, the intermediary fails to expeditiously remove or disable access to that material on that resource without vitiating the evidence in any manner".

In India, the landmark case for deliberating on the liability of any intermediary by the court is *Avnish Bajaj v. State* [(2005) 3 Comp LJ 364], which involved the upload of a MMS video clip available on a website and Mr. Bajaj was the CEO of the website. This came under the scrutiny of the public as well as the Court because it was believed, that the content should have been removed from the internet as soon as possible. The video rather went on being circulated rapidly which invited criticism and created much havoc. The Court discharged the Managing Director of the concerned website (Baazee.com) from all criminal charges owing to discrepancies in the provision of Section 292 of the Indian Penal Code.

Internet being so vast and having global reach is difficult to be regulated. It was believed that by introducing liability for intermediaries, law makers will be successful in filtering the unlawful content and they could be equated to that of 'Gatekeepers of Information' [26]. India has incorporated the safe-harbor model with respect to the intermediary liability under the cyber law legislation along with other countries which provides for both conditional immunity and complete immunity. The legislation requires these internet intermediaries to exercise due diligence and comply with the regulation requirement to enjoy conditional immunity/ protection against liability. The complete immunity is provided to all these facilitators who merely provide the third parties access to information [27]. Initially, the safe harbor principle was rendered to the intermediaries only. The amendment brought to the IT Act in the year 2008 extended the exemption for intermediaries against liability along with amendments to other laws. The exemption from any liability provided to the intermediaries is subject to the fulfillment of requirements as provided under clauses (2) and (3) of Section 79.

Cloud service involves three main stakeholders: the cloud service provider, the customer and the telecom service provider/internet service provider. India lacks an exclusive law on cloud computing governing these three stakeholders together. Department of Telecommunications (DoT) had sought recommendations from Telecom Regulatory Authority of India which is the regulatory body, on different broad aspects of cloud computing. TRAI had also sought views via consultation paper [28] during October 2019 to check whether the industry is capable of self regulating. According to TRAI, cloud service providers can come under the regulation of TRAI. However, currently, these service providers are being regulated under MeitY [29]. TRAI has recommenced amendments for smooth regulation of cloud, which is yet to be incorporated. The Ministry of Information Technology and other government departments needs to work together to implement any of the proposed changes.

Finding the right balance is difficult, but there is definitely the pressing need for intermediaries to maintain the digital freedom. The balance that is required for these gate keepers is to have the freedom to formulate methods/policies for regulation of illegal content and at the same time ensure that there is no compromise in freedom of online medium.

18.12   Challenges in Cloud Computing

18.12.1   Classification of Data

The emerging clashes between the internet engineering, omnipresence of cloud all over the globe and the legal compliance requirement of different individual jurisdictions is a major international concern. A cloud service provider might require data-centers, users, end clients, a team and their resources to keep up the system running in various geographical areas. The regulatory bodies seek compliance of their jurisdiction specific requirements, such as cyber security, privacy safeguard, national security, regulation of content, etc., which will be an intimidating undertaking for the service providers due to the above concern. The global architecture of cloud services is defeated because of such legal compliance requirements.

It is not possible for cloud service providers to classify available data on any given parameters as there is no advanced technology available for the same. However, most legislation requires these service providers to segregate data—lawful/unlawful as a part of their legal compliance. The provisions of section 79 under the IT (Amendment) Act 2008, which is applicable to all intermediaries, including cloud service providers is a good instance of the requirement of the above mentioned data classification. This provision provides service providers to regulate unlawful data and removes it whenever such data comes to the knowledge of the intermediary. But, the irony is that these service providers (including cloud service provider) usually have confidentiality clause signed with its users, which does not authorize them to be aware of the contents of data [30].

18.12.2   Jurisdictional Issues

The new means of delivering in the cloud as the advancement of technology giving a platform to users, allowing remote access of applications, resource allocation from one place to another, is economic in nature while jurisdictional issues accompany them. The law has to operate beyond territorial limits and the theories and precedents are to be followed to fix the jurisdiction whether it is under Civil Procedure Code 1908 or Criminal Procedure Code 1973; tests are applied in different transborder disputes or other dispute resolution mechanism. Every application we use including social media accounts use cloud services globally.

The traditional notions of private international law makes the individual nation's laws related to jurisdictions applicable to the nationals and any transactions carried out within the customary limits of the country. However, this traditional concept of jurisprudence on jurisdiction is no longer confined within territorial limits, and has evolved to keep pace with the advancement of technology and commerce. The cloud computing system involves an organization in a country, which might be storing data in a cloud located in another country, under control of a different vendor. Therefore, this may give rise to a situation where the laws of all the above jurisdictions are applicable making parties fight for the applicability of law and proper forum of adjudication. Usually to avoid any such situation, organizations decide on the dispute resolution mechanism while drafting and entering into the agreement. Harmonizing the domestic laws to avoid any conflict and determining the appropriate jurisdiction is a difficult task to attain.

Indian legislation grants the parties involved, the right to choose appropriate laws applicable to them, while entering into any contractual obligations. Indian courts also take into account the nexus to the transaction in accordance to the law as agreed in the contract by choice, while deciding any dispute arising out of any such contracts. The Indian Arbitration and Conciliation Act 1996 which is adopted from the UNCITRAL Model Law (as recommended by the U.N. General Assembly) is instrumental in facilitating international commercial arbitration, domestic arbitration and conciliation, taking care of disputes arising from such cloud service vendor agreements. India, being a party to the New York Convention (1960) agreed upon by major countries makes it easier for enforcing foreign decree. The nature of the cloud is dynamic which allows transits, more often leading to jurisdictional claims causing unrest between nations and their citizens. The decision of one country might affect another country as well.

18.12.3   Interoperability of the Cloud

The revolution of technology and the cloud attract the issues of incompatibility, integration and operational complexity. Software portability and interoperability ensures those issues to be mitigated, and the standards of which needs to be widely adopted. It has the ability to exchange information between two or more systems and to mutually use the information. Similarly, cloud interoperability is the ability to interact with the user's systems or other cloud services by method of information exchange and obtain predictable results [31]. There are five stages of Interoperability. Firstly, the transport interoperability where the exchange of data takes place using physical networks like an external internet or broadband connection. Secondly, the syntactic inoperability which deals with the coding and structure of the stored data. The data may be even coded to different characters to hide the plain text. The semantic interoperability is related to the intended meaning of the written language according to the context and finally the behavior of the service provider [32]. Cloud portability is the transferring of data within clouds without the need of re-entering the data and migrating the applications in the cloud between systems. If an user needs to relocate an application from one cloud to another, needs subscribing to more than one cloud and link their services, connect private cloud to public/hybrid and vice versa or is interested in migrating in-house applications within clouds the mechanism of interoperability is applied. The standards under ISO/IEC 19941:2017 and other recommendations are to be kept in mind to avoid complexities. In India, there is a collaborative effort to address inter-cloud issues to continue using the flexibility along with protecting the data.

18.12.4   Vendor Agreements

The Indian Contract Act 1872 regulates and provides basic principles for all contracts in India, including e-contracts. Section 10A of the IT Act 2000 states that "communication, revocation and acceptance of offer shall not be deemed to be unenforceable solely on the ground that electronic form or means were used for expressing such offer, acceptance or revocation", thereby making any e-contract (click wrap contracts) valid and enforceable in court of law. Cloud computing service providers offer service agreements that are often biased and non-negotiable as being a standard form of contract. Usually, these agreements do not account for any indemnity, warranties with respect to the data security, and provisions for consequential damages or clause for breach of privacy obligations from limitations of liability [33]. Courts have also held that any standard form of contract including online contracts cannot be held invalid solely on the ground of being non-negotiable by one party. Cloud service vendors often limit their liability up to a certain fixed amount, irrespective of the actual loss faced by the party. Therefore, one has to be very careful while entering into an agreement with service provider and check the extent of responsibility that a service provider is willing to take. Cloud services will play a major role in transforming any organization's information technology architecture when used appropriately and can even help in cost savings. It is advised that the entity's legal counsel should carefully negotiate and review agreements entered with cloud service providers, creating a favorable situation for both parties.

18.13   Conclusion

Cloud computing is in emerging stages in India and is facing several problems. It demands automatic on time data backups over a network which can prove to be a manual task, needing a self-healing property. The information can be duplicated in multiple servers. Simultaneously, many users can try to use the feature which sometime creates a rift or conflict, also known as multi tenancy feature that poses a major challenge and needs to be tackled. The cloud fails to handle processing beyond a liner proportion along with simultaneously managing, distributing, processing and protecting the data which puts us in a position to think whether our data is truly safe. The need of clarity with respect to location or jurisdiction, the issues related to its operation, contractual obligations on the stakeholders, issues of security which are persistent and the need of risk management should be our priority. The protection authorities need to have a thorough investigation and the controller has to assert restrictions accordingly. Holding the cloud providers liable for hosting or transmitting any form of illegal data is important. Any exception to this rule should definitely have repercussions. The responsibility is to be specified among the service provider/ the board of directors/the company/an individual responsible for any breach or leakage and hold them accountable for the security of user's data and information. The parameters to track the agencies are to be widened beyond the location as these can be difficult to track due to multi-layering and multiple locations of servers. India not being a signatory to the Budapest Convention of cybercrime is in a situation to rethink the necessity of adoption of legal principles of the convention. The free flow of data across the internet is to be controlled and standards of privacy are to be maintained. Indemnifying the providers is a need not to keep the user stranded in a situation of loss. The clause of indemnification is important in an agreement entered by data fiduciary and data subject.

The cloud is in the hands of data fiduciary; however the ownership of any kind of personal information should be exclusively vested on the data principal. The entity involved in storing, processing or retaining of the data should behave like custodians and not owners having rights over the data. The payment for the cloud service should be for custody of the personal data and not for the ownership. Any processing of the data by the cloud service should be consensual. The consent of the data principal should be our utmost priority. Non-consensual data storing or processing will lead to illegitimate interest and liabilities. The Supreme Court in the Puttuswamy judgment commented on non-consensual processing of personal data stating few circumstances where considerations like criminal investigation, prevention strategies, and allocation of resources or need of national security could be required. The data collected by the government should be to the extent of regulatory functions, keeping in mind the data quality principle providing welfare benefits and social service. The creation of the Data Protection Authority under the bill for handling the body should be given independent authority to work consisting of its own committee. Cloud computing comes with its own share of unique hurdles as well as massive opportunities because of its multi-jurisdictional nature. Different regulators from around the world are wrestling to find unique mechanisms exclusively for cloud computing. Cloud computing is a growing business model which will be regulated by the standards as fixed by the big players of the industry. In absence of an international code, we have witnessed that cloud computing is regulated through few bilateral agreements between governments and multinational corporations. A comprehensive robust international policy or treaty has become a vital requirement that can address various aspects of cloud computing across the globe like jurisdictional issues, different regulatory schemes of nations, etc. by setting up a uniform standard for all nations to adhere to while making their own domestic laws. There have also been few alternative suggestions for addressing conflicts between nations stemming from cloud computing issues. Conflicts pertaining to issues like ownership of data, security of data, privacy of an individual, etc. can be resolved via creating of private-public Memorandum of Understanding (MOUs) between large data center operators and different sovereign governments. The legal framework of safe harbor principles of the European Union and the US can be used to establish a multilateral agreement for all nations for addressing issues of cloud computing.

Currently, our nation lacks an all-inclusive legislation for protecting privacy and protection of data which can aid in regulating issues of cloud computing. The IT Act 2000, with its present form does limited justice for regulation of cloud computing services. It can be witnessed that there has been a sharp rise in number of internet users across pan India because of various government initiatives like 'Digital India' promoting public to go digital. National Digital Communications Policy-2018 conceives that India will become a global hub for cloud computing, data communication systems and services, content delivery and hosting, by developing the required regulatory model for the same [28].

One of the challenges that cloud computing in India is facing is the lack of trust for the service providers and the public's comparative unfamiliarity with the working of this technology. These providers can easily be compelled to disclose any information, including sensitive information, by different government agencies which do not even require an order from the Court. Different departments of government also have their share of inhibitions from using cloud services for their work as they are of the opinion that data is not safe when stored over clouds. Indian law makers need to review existing laws and create a comprehensive framework which can mirror the realities of cloud computing [34]. Government should be careful enough while formulating any policy with respect to cloud services that can strike a balance between regulation of interest of the public and freedom for innovation of different technologies. There seems to be light at the end of tunnel as the Indian government is on its way of drafting the much sought after privacy legislation. The Indian entities should maximize benefit from the recent cloud revolution which can further accelerate growth in economy by effectively dodging the risks associated with it [30].

References

1. Robert *et al.*, *The nature of cyber threats, Center for a New American Security*, https://www.cnas.org/search?q=The+nature+of+cyber+threats, 2011.
2. Javed, A., The Lessons of #CloudComputing—What Have We Learned So Far?, 2017. [Online]. Available: http://www.xorlogics.com/2017/07/31/the-lessons-of-cloudcomputing-what-have-we-learned-so-far/.
3. *The Transatlantic Digital Dialogue, Cyber-Security Cooperation and Strong Encryption*, German Marshall Fund of the United States, 2015.
4. Cilluffo, F., Ritchey, R., Tinker, T., *Cloud Computing Risks and National Security Keeping Pace With Expanding Technology*, Center for Cyber and Homeland Security at Auburn University, 2010.
5. Miller, S., COVID researchers can apply for free cloud services, [Online]. Available: https://techagainstcovid.com/.
6. CyberEdu, What is Cloud Security?, [Online]. Available: https://www.forcepoint.com/cyber-edu/cloud-security.
7. Avey, C., 7 Key Cybersecurity Threats to Cloud Computing, 11 September 2019. [Online]. Available: https://cloudacademy.com/blog/key-cybersecurity-threats-to-cloud-computing/.
8. Dinh, H.T., Lee, C., Niyato, D., Wang, P., A survey of mobile cloud computing: architecture, applications, and approaches. *Wireless Commun. Mobile Comput.*, 2011, geo.edu.al/cloud/wp-content/uploads/2013/12/MCC.pdf.
9. Tabassam, S., Security and Privacy Issues in Cloud Computing Environment. *J. Inf. Technol. Software Eng.*, 2017, https://www.researchgate.net/publication/322120849.
10. Needham, M., Cloud Standards Customer Council Announces Version 3.0 of Practical Guide to Cloud Computing, 05 December 2007. [Online]. Available: https://www.businesswire.com/news/home/20171205005186/en/Cloud-Standards-Customer-Council-Announces-Version-3.0. [Accessed 17 June 2020].
11. Nishith Desai Associates, Cloud Computing—Risks/Challenges—Legal & tax Issues, [Online]. Available: http://www.nishithdesai.com/fileadmin/user_upload/pdfs/Cloud_Computing.pdf. [Accessed 23 06 2020].
12. Rana, A. and Bagai, R., Cybersecurity in India, [Online]. Available: https://www.lexology.com/library/detail.aspx?g=4cd0bdb1-da7d-4a04-bd9c-30881dd3eadf. [Accessed 18 june 2020].
13. Eustice, J.C., Flying into the cloud without falling: understanding the intersection between data privacy laws and cloud computing solutions, [Online]. Available: https://legal.thomsonreuters.

com/en/insights/articles/understanding-data-privacy-and-cloud-computing. [Accessed 17 06 2020].

14. Hutchinson, B., 87 million Facebook users to find out if their personal data was breached, [Online]. Available: https://abcnews.go.com/US/87-million-facebook-users-find-personal-data-breached/story?id=54334187. [Accessed 18 06 2020].

15. S.C.W. Headquarters, Data Privacy and Compliance in the cloud, [Online]. Available: https://docs.broadcom.com/doc/data-privacy-and-compliance-in-the-cloud-en. [Accessed 19 06 2020].

16. *OECD's Revised Guidelines on the Protection of Privacy and Transborder Flows of Personal Data, [Online]*, Available: https://www.oecd.org/internet/ieconomy/oecdguidelinesontheprotectionofprivacyandtransborderflowsofpersonaldata.htm.

17. The Data Protection Bill, 2019.

18. Barak, A., Proportionality: Constitutional Rights and their Limitations, in: *Proportionality: Constitutional Rights and their Limitations*, Cambridge University Press, 2012.

19. Duraiswami, D., Privacy and Data Protection in India. *J. Law Cyber Warfare*, 166–186, 2017.

20. The Telegraph Act, 1885, [Online]. Available: https://dot.gov.in/act-rules-content/2442. [Accessed 20 June 2020].

21. Cidon, A., Protecting Intellectual Property in the Cloud, June 2015. [Online]. Available: https://www.wipo.int/wipo_magazine/en/2015/03/article_0004.html. [Accessed 15 June 2020].

22. The Wassenaar arrangement on export controls for conventional arms and dual-use goods and technologies, 05 December 2019. [Online]. Available: https://www.wassenaar.org/. [Accessed 20 06 2020].

23. Cidon, A., Protecting Intellectual Property in the Cloud, June 2015. [Online]. Available: https://www.wipo.int/wipo_magazine/en/2015/03/article_0004.html. [Accessed 18 June 2020].

24. MarketandMarkets, Cloud Computing Market, 2019.

25. Menon, M.G., Regulatory Issues in Cloud Computing—An Indian Perspective. *J. Eng. Comput. Appl. Sci.*, 18–22, 2013.

26. Arun, C., Gatekeeper liability and Article 19(1)(A) of the Constitution of India, *NUJS Law Review*. 73–87, 2014, https://papers.ssrn.com/sol3/papers.cfm?abstract_id=2643278.

27. Article19, Internet intermediaries: Dilemma of Liability, 2013. [Online]. Available: https://www.article19.org/data/files/Intermediaries_ENGLISH.pdf. [Accessed 18 June 2020].

28. Telecom Regulatory Authority of India, Consultation Paper, 2019.

29. Singh, J., TRAI may regulate cloud service companies, [Online]. Available: https://entrackr.com/2020/02/cloud-service-companies-trai-chairman/. [Accessed 21 06 2020].

30. Data Security Council of India, Legal and Policy Issues in Cloud Computing, [Online]. Available: https://www.dsci.in/sites/default/files/documents/resource_centre/Discussion%20Paper%20on%20Policy%20Legal%20Issues%20in%20Cloud.pdf. [Accessed 17 June 2020].

31. ISO/IEC 19941:2017: Information technology—Cloud computing—Interoperability and portability, 2017. [Online]. Available: https://www.iso.org/standard/66639.html.

32. Sheppard, D., Cloud interoperability and portability—Necessary or nice to have?, [Online]. Available: https://insightaas.com/cloud-interoperability-and-portability-necessary-or-nice-to-have/#:~:text=Cloud%20interoperability%20is%20the%20ability,method%20to%20obtain%20predictable%20results. [Accessed 22 06 2020].

33. Chen, D.Y. and Wilson, W.F., Cloud Computing Agreements: Negotiating Privacy Issues with Large Cloud Vendors, 24 06 2016. [Online]. Available: https://www.accdocket.com/articles/cloud-computing-agreements-privacy-issues.cfm. [Accessed 21 06 2020].

34. Menon, M.G., Regulatory issues in cloud computing—An Indian Perspecting. *J. Eng. Comput. Appl. Sci.*, 2013.

## 19

Securing the Pharma Supply Chain Using Blockchain

Pulkit Arora, Chetna Sachdeva and Dolly Sharma*

Department of Computer Science, Amity School of Engineering and Technology,
Amity University, Noida, India

Abstract

Through this chapter we aim to provide a solution to the currently flawed and highly unsecure prevalent model followed in the supply chain of the Pharmaceuticals. In the current scenario the stakeholders in the supply chain take full advantage of this out-dated system to make easy money keeping the health of people at stake. The prevalent system gives the people with such mal intent to manufacture and supply counterfeit drugs, or for example hoard the drugs high in demand to gain profit later. The solution to this should be a cost effective one and must not require a complete change in the model followed instead, the solution should be adaptive in nature such that it can be blended in the current scene. Through this chapter, we propose a solution to this problem by modifying the current system minutely. To achieve the desired results, we shall use the already in use, QR codes and a Unique ID already assigned to the drugs and attach a RFID mechanism on the batch. The information of the transit shall be timestamped, and all the data shall be encrypted and linked to the UID. This information shall contain all the details of the transit such as time, location, temperature, humidity, and pressure. Because the drugs are very sensitive to these physical conditions and any unwanted change in these can render the drugs useless and, in some cases, might also render them harmful. All this information shall be made public and any person with the credentials can check on the authenticity and the details of transit and can decide then if they want to buy the drug or not. This solution not only provides transparency, it also shall provide a trustworthy and reliable solution to falsified, and duplicate drugs as all the drugs' credentials can be verified online and anyone who wishes to fiddle with the data would render the data useless as any tampering with the blockchain's data can be caught.

Keywords: Blockchain, smart contracts, hash functions, QR codes, RFID, cryptography, TripleDES

19.1 Introduction

While the world has seen its fair share of technological advancements, and a lot of ventures have modified their age-old models with the change in technology, the supply chain in industries have not quite well kept up with the progression. It must be noted that with the advancement in technology the threats and risks associated with them also increase.

Corresponding author: dolly.azure@gmail.com

Monika Mangla, Suneeta Satpathy, Bhagirathi Nayak and Sachi Nandan Mohanty (eds.) Integration of Cloud Computing with Internet of Things: Foundations, Analytics, and Applications, (343–360) © 2021 Scrivener Publishing LLC

The drugs industry, for example, must not face any compromises as any trade off within the industry shall mean playing with the lives of the patients. The pharma supply chain for the fact has not quite improved much since its inception.

In the current scenario, the stakeholders in the supply chain take full advantage of the rigid system to make easy money keeping the health of people at stake [1, 2]. The prevalent system gives the people with such mal intent to manufacture and supply counterfeit drugs, or for example hoard the drugs high in demand to gain profit later [3]. Currently, the system that prevails is as follows: First, an order for the required drugs is made after the order is received, the manufacturer manufactures the drugs using the raw materials. After the manufacturing process is done, the drugs are packaged along with a barcode or a QR code. It is followed by the process of drugs being transported to the wholesaler. In the next step, the wholesaler dispatches the drugs to the final destinations (Hospital dispensaries, pharmacists, etc.) and the end consumer buys the drugs from the pharmacists or dispensaries and consumes the drug prescribed by the doctor.

The above steps have a huge margin of error and quite a few big loopholes that are exploited by the current stakeholders. As it is quite well known that neither the customer nor the retailer checks the authenticity or credentials of the drug while buying it by scanning the QR code on the back, the ones with mal intentions take advantage of this trusting nature of them and introduce a lot of counterfeit medications in the supply chain.

Now, it is partly the fault of the consumer and a huge fault of the system, as there is no prevalent app or any other mode through which the customer can scan and know each and every detail of the drug by examining the QR code. As of now if we scan the QR code using the apps on our phones or any other mode we can get the unique id of the medicine. But that is of no use to a common person as he cannot access the database of the manufacturer to check the authenticity of the medicine he is buying. Also, even if he had it would be very tedious and a time-consuming task that most of us would want to avoid.

We need a system in which the consumer can have the details of the medicine through which he can know the authenticity of the medicine on his fingertips without much effort and discomfort. A solution to this can be as simple as adding the whole details of the medicine in the QR code so that on scanning the consumer can get all the details of it.

But this system still has a loophole that hasn't yet been addressed. The selling of counterfeit drugs can still continue despite the consumer being able to examine the QR code and gaining the details of the medicine. A counterfeit drug with a similar packaging and a similar QR code or even if a different QR code (if leads to a similar output) and seems legitimate can still fool the consumer into trusting its source and buying the fake drug.

To rectify this, we must provide a solution that would verify the source of the medicine; this can be done by the help of digital signatures [4] and can be easily applied to the current system. And to eliminate the issue of forging using an exact copy of packaging, and using the same QR code, that is, to eliminate the scope of reusing a QR code we can use the a simple concept of DBMS, that whenever an item is dispatched it's entry be updated in the database and the same for the scenario when it has been sold it must not be shown into the database available for selling rather there must be a separate table for the ones that are sold. This can be achieved using a QR scanner at the billing desk of the pharmacist.

Now to achieve all these and also make this solution transparent a non-centralized solution must be achieved, but with a distributed system, the number of threats and attacks also increase with each increasing node, also a distributed system would not be immutable as per our requirement.

We need a system which would be secure and allow access only to those who are authorized to whilst still being transparent and immutable. But over all this, the solution must not incur a lot of extra cost and must fit-in well using the given resources and be compatible with the current system.

All this can be achieved if we propose a solution to this using blockchain.

19.2   Literature Review

A blockchain is an incorruptible developing rundown of records which is bound together by cryptographic hash values which make it immutable [5]. As shown in Figure 19.1, is a diagrammatic representation of blocks in a blockchain.

The Strength of a blockchain lies in its three pillars i.e. Decentralization, Immutability and Transparency [6]. These features are the main reason for us to choose blockchain as a viable option for this solution. The blockchain is considered very secure as it is widely used in various cryptocurrencies. Blockchain, which is a brainchild of Satoshi Nakamoto, created it to serve as a digital ledger for the cryptocurrency Bitcoin [7, 8]. Since then it has been adopted in other cryptocurrencies as well. The Blockchain then became so popular that now it is no longer limited to just cryptocurrencies it is also making way in different scenarios such as the Power Distribution Industry, Online Voting using Blockchain, etc. One of the most popular use cases is in supply chains. One of the most important features of blockchain is the inclusion of smart contracts, a smart contract is a self-verifiable contract among the parties involved. It enables the contract to validate and verify itself without the involvement of a third party and hence is considered more secure as less people are involved, the chances of errors are reduced too. The smart contracts are majorly used in crowdfunding but can also be used in other areas such as insurance to process claims, banks

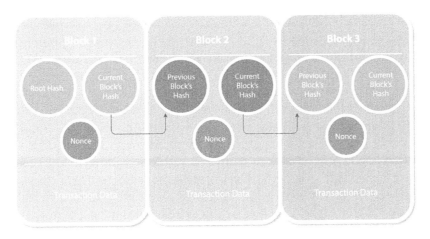

Figure 19.1 Block diagram of a blockchain.

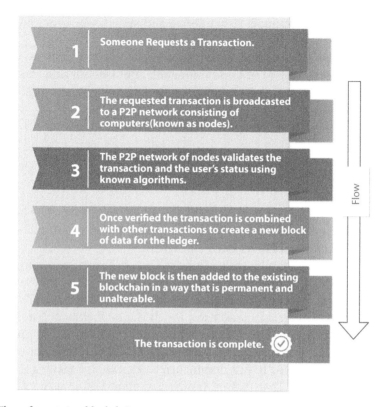

Figure 19.2 Flow of events in a blockchain.

for loans and automatic payments, postal delivery for payments on delivery etc. As shown in Figure 19.2, the Flow of Events in a Blockchain is as follows:

19.2.1   Current Scenario

To explain the current scenario, we would like to start with the following excerpt from a study: "A Fraser Institute Study says that worldwide pharmaceutical sales reached USD 1.1 trillion in the year 2015. The OECD has found that counterfeit-goods accounted for 2.5% of the global pharmaceutical drugs trade" [9]. As shown in Figure 19.3, the number of fraudulent cases in the years 2012 to 2016 can be seen in the form of a line graph.

"Total number of fraudulent pharmaceutical incidents has risen by 56% since 2012. A fraudulent incident is defined as either counterfeiting, illegal diversion or theft" [10].

It is also estimated that the counterfeit drugs are sold at more than twice the rate followed by the actual legal ones. This is a very grave issue and must be entertained as soon as possible as the intake of such drugs can be life threatening, also even if the drugs are legitimate, they might still have been tampered with or might have lost their integrity in the transit thereby still risking the lives of those consuming it. So, the issues in the prevalent system can be summarised as: "Falsified medicines like those which are tampered with it can be in any way such as wrong ingredients, fake packaging, authenticity, low product quality, fake shipment history, error prone paperwork, slow processing, etc." [10, 11].

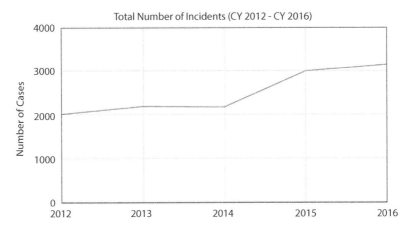

Figure 19.3 Number of fraudulent incidents (from 2012 to 2016).

19.2.2   Proposal

Using a blockchain based system can pose a major boom to the pharmaceuticals' supply network, at each phase, we propose, to use standardized QR codes that would be scanned and be used as a primary key to the records they point to, each transaction shall be recorded on the blockchain and shall be ciphered such that only the ones authorized to view the details can view them this would add a component of privacy and data abstraction to the system whilst also giving it a cent percent transparency [12, 13]. This would create a trail of drug records. Also, sensors which are already available in the vehicles of transit can be used to record real time data such as temperature and humidity which would be recorded into the blockchain if any unwanted change is experienced. Though this is especially for the drugs that require to be kept in cold storage, but it can also be beneficial for tracking any unwanted tampering of the drugs in transit. A temperature sensor can be installed on the inside of a consignment. If it catches any sudden change in temperature it would mean that the consignment has been opened as only that could lead to a sudden change in temperature it can be both sudden rise and sudden dip in temperatures. The sensors must immediately record it on to the blockchain.

The smart contracts would come in handy at this time to verify if the drugs have been opened by someone who was designated to do so or have they been opened by someone who was not supposed to be opening them, this, we propose, can be achieved by using an private and public key combination along with GPS tracking. So that only the authorized personnel handles the drugs at the designated place only, the drugs must never be tampered with in the transit.

Now as there are temperature sensors already installed in the containers in which the drugs are transported and the pharma companies already use the QR codes the blockchain inclusion in the current supply chain wouldn't bear much cost so the solution would reduce the complexity and cost in turn as it would make the drugs easier to be tracked and the centralized system to store the details of the drugs would help in keeping charge of the expiry dates hence would in turn improve the control over the stock. The blockchain solution would also strengthen the security, the smart contracts would also reduce errors, and build trust in the transactions. To maintain immutability, we use cryptographic hash functions.

Now for the transparency to the consumer, using this the consumer would be able to trace the transit of the drug he is buying from the source till the destination that is him. A blockchain based tracking system would enable him to scan the QR code on a drug and verify it immediately by checking the digital signature and the secure transit it has had. If the consumer is satisfied with the drug being legitimate, we propose that the retailers who sell the drug to the consumer must use a digital platform for the checkout it would add a transaction on the blockchain and the product can be removed from the inventory hence duplicate packaging and duplicate QR codes wouldn't be of any use, and anyone using duplicate QR codes can be caught.

Now, as it has been mentioned earlier, the immutability is achieved through the concept of cryptographic hash. In straightforward terms, hashing implies taking an information string of any length and giving out a yield of a fixed length. The hash functions are also called one-way functions, as an output can only be generated using a given input and any other input cannot generate the same output. Nor can the input be generated using the output string; hence it is safe and secure and highly trustworthy. Hence even in the case of bitcoins where information is highly sensitive and very important, the hashing algorithms are used. Therefore, as drugs are a very sensitive concern, we must use hash functions to achieve immutability.

If someone tries to tamper with any one of the blocks of the blockchain, they would end up changing its hash value, now as a blockchain is linked using hashes all the other blocks would fail and the blockchain shall be nullified. As shown in Table 19.1, two different sequences of characters do not have the same hash value and as shown in Table 19.2, even the slightest change would alter the hash value.

Table 19.1 Example of corresponding hash values of random texts.

Input	Corresponding hash value
Hi	3639EFCD08ABB273B1619E82E78C29A7DF02C1051B1820E99FC39 DCAA3326B8
Transaction received	53A53FC9E2A03F9B6E66D84BA701574CD9CFS01FB498C41731881 BCDC68A7C8

Table 19.2 Illustrating the change in hash value just by changing the case of the first letter.

Input	Corresponding hash value
This is a test	C7BE1ED902FB8DD4D48997C6452F5D7E509FBCDBE2808B16BCF4EDCE 4CO7D14E
This is a test	2E99758548972A8E8822AD47FA1017FF72F06F3FF6A016851F4C398732BC 50C

19.3   Methodology

All the stakeholders that can be involved in the production and the distribution of drugs are as follows:

1. Manufacturers
2. Logistic Service Providers
3. Hospital/Pharmacy
4. Patient
5. Supplier
6. Transporter
7. Wholesaler
8. Distributer

Step 1: Manufacturer manufactures the drugs and adds QR code to it

When a manufacturer manufactures the drugs, he shall add a QR code stamp to it and the QR code shall contain all the essential information such as the time, location manufacturing and expiry dates, etc. All this information gets added on to the blockchain and is universally available hence all the stakeholders involved can trace the supply of drugs transparently [14].

Whenever a new info is added to the blockchain a new HASH id is produced which can be used to trace the flow of events in the complete lifespan of the blockchain.

As the drugs will be shipped to the distributors, the trucks used to transport them shall be equipped with temperature sensors to enable cold-chain shipping.

The inclusion of blockchain in this market will also enable the possibility of exchanging and storing the data gathered by temperature sensors on the blockchain. The transparent and immutable distributed ledger can save a lot of time in case of auditing of storage conditions of the drugs that are sensitive to variable temperatures.

The drugs transferred through such IOT vehicles can send real time data such as location, etc. to the blockchain so that those involved and the government can keep a check on the time of the receiving and delivery of the drugs.

Step 2: Distributors send the drugs to hospitals/pharmacists

As the service provider who manages the logistics sends the medicines to the distributer, the origin of the medicines can be verified using the hash ID's corresponding to the QR codes in the blockchain.

In this step the temperature sensors and other sensors such as the humidity and GPS tracker come in handy, they can be used to track all the parameters in the IOT enabled vehicles whilst keeping the drugs safe and under constant surveillance.

The distributors on receiving the medicines provide a digital signature along with the timestamp which is then added to the blockchain.

Step 3: Pharmacists receive the drugs and verify its source

When the retailer pharmacists receive their drug consignments they can trace the drugs back to their origin, they can view all the stoppages that occurred in the transit they can see if the temperatures were maintained and once they accept the consignment it goes on as a contract using the smart contracts and they cannot deny accepting the consignment later on ever in the future as they are bound by the smart contracts.

If and when a distributor attempts to sell counterfeit drugs this can be verified using the hash code on the back of the medicine as the counterfeit drug will not be able to imitate the QR code of the original drug as the QR code is made using the Hash ID of the medicine and no two hashes are ever identical. Even if the QR code has been duplicated out of any other drug that can also be verified as the whole distribution circle would act as a giant inventory once it is "de-centrally" connected using blockchain. Also, the robust nature of blockchain prevents such fraudulent distributors to illegally add a fake transaction in the blockchain as the transaction will immediately be termed as invalid. Moreover, without the private key of the authorized personnel these individuals will not be able to carry out such fraudulent transactions.

Hence pharmacists shall immediately get to know of any anomalies if carried out within the transactions.

Once he approves the received medicines' transaction the new medicines' details are added to the blockchain.

Step 4: Patients buy the drugs and scan the QR code to trace back its source

Patients ought to be assured that the drugs they buy are safe to take. By following a simple procedure of scanning the QR code attached to the drug they are buying they can see on their mobile phones the complete details of the medicine and its journey to the drug store and if it meets the quality standards.

There is a hash ID which is linked to the QR code which can be used to get the information from the blockchain and the patients can see the essential details which are in the blockchain.

Also, the patients can give the feedback for the medicine they bought and it would be linked to the drug's ID that is stored on the chain. The rating they give shall be fruitful for the other consumers and would help them choose wisely amongst a wide range of similar drugs.

To show the above described features are achieved we have designed a prototype model which uses RFID tags in place of QR codes to keep a track of the information and uses a TripleDES cryptographic algorithm to encrypt and decrypt the information to and from the source of its inception. Whenever new information is stored onto the database it is first encrypted and only the authorized personnel can view the encrypted information using the key to show he is authorized to do so.

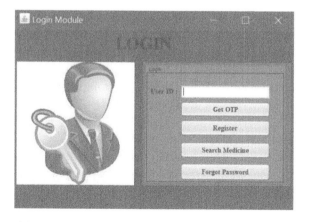

Figure 19.4 Screenshot of the login page.

As shown in Figure 19.4, a screenshot of the login page of our prototype, in this the authorised personnel can login using their credentials, an OTP is generated each time to maintain secure and selective entry.

From this module anyone who has a valid RFID card can search for the medicines, i.e. their whereabouts and other details. As shown in Figure 19.5, the interaction diagram shows the processes involved in the same.

The admin panel, as shown in Figure 19.6, has the various functions that the admin can perform are listed, that is he can add or remove branches, add, update or view cargo details.

All the cargo details are linked to a separate RFID tag.

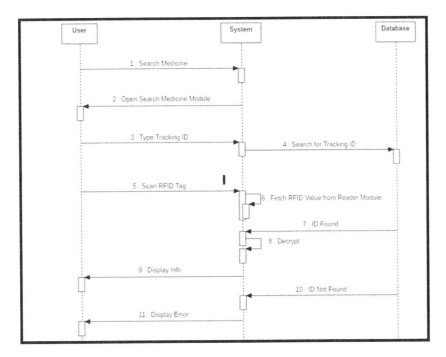

Figure 19.5 Search medicine's interaction diagram.

Figure 19.6 Screenshot of the admin account module.

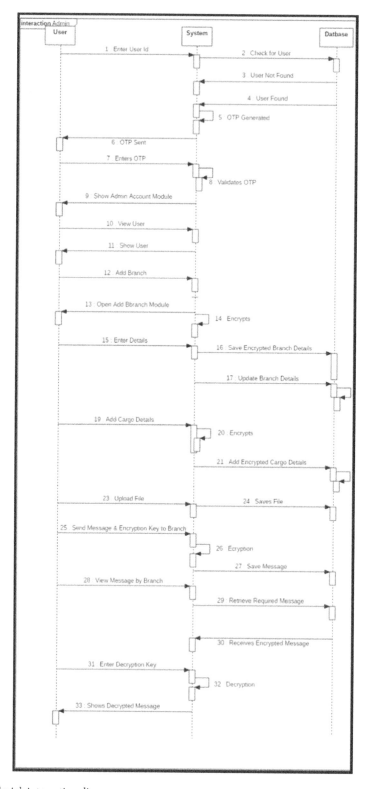

Figure 19.7 Admin's interaction diagram.

To showcase what all can be done using the admin panel the sequence diagram as shown in Figure 19.7, can be referred for all the actions that an admin can perform:

We even tried to create a secure private communication channel for the branch managers and admin, as shown in Figure 19.8, the admin can send a cryptic message to the branch manager and only that manager shall receive the message and can only read the message if he has the key to decipher the message.

As shown in Figure 19.9, the message remains unreadable unless the key is entered.

As shown in Figure 19.10, once the correct key is entered the message gets decrypted, this encryption and decryption process is done using the TripleDES algorithm that we used in this model to encrypt the other data too.

The schematic diagram for hardware-based solution for fetching the details using RFID reader module was drawn, as shown in Figure 19.11.

As shown in Figure 19.12, all the functions that a branch manager can perform in our prototype are depicted in a sequence diagram, almost all the functions of a branch

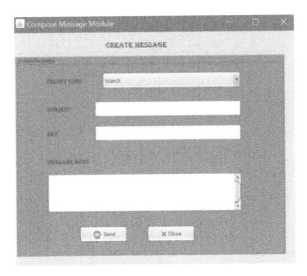

Figure 19.8 Screenshot of the chat module between admin and branch manager.

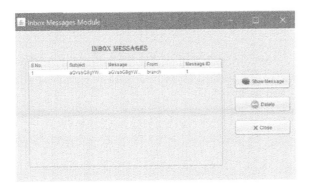

Figure 19.9 Screenshot of the encrypting part of a decrypted received message.

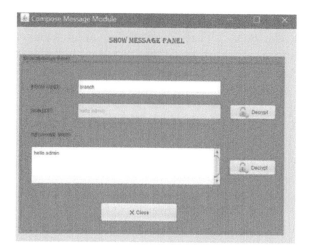

Figure 19.10 Screenshot of the decrypted received message.

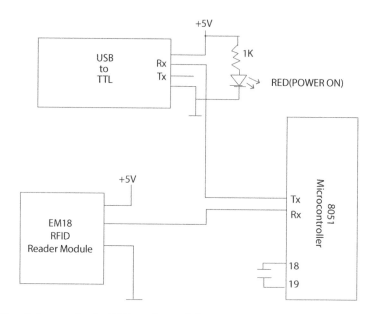

Figure 19.11 Circuit diagram for the RFID reader module.

manager are similar to the admin, but it mainly just deals with the collection and ship-ment of consignments and the admin has much more responsibilities than the branch manager.

19.4   Results

Now, to cope with the various technological advancements in the various fields, and the adaptation of those technical leaps in the industries, we have proposed a model for the

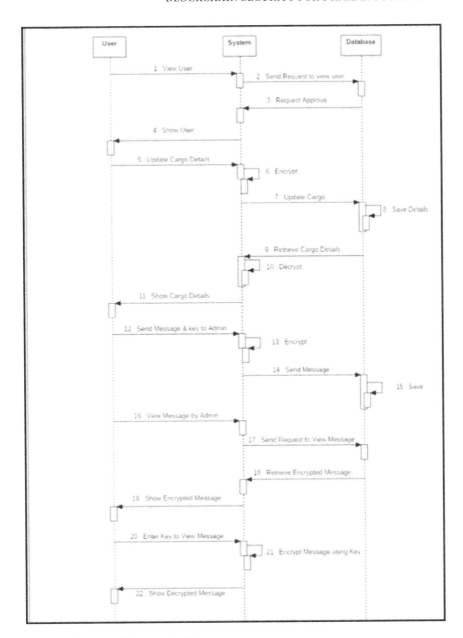

Figure 19.12 Branch manager's interaction diagram.

pharmaceutical supply chain, which would use a series of QR codes, RFID tags, temperature and humidity sensors and GPS trackers, a lot of which are already in use hence not causing a huge financial burden on the industry. We have proposed a model of the supply chain which would integrate all the above used components in a blockchain which would make the system not only efficient but also secure it.

We extensively studied the current pharma supply chain model, and various alternatives that can be put in place of the current model or various improvements that can be done and that step by step approach led us to making this blockchain based model. We then researched on various encryption algorithms and hashing techniques and chose the one which is widely used and accepted because of its efficiency and security.

While moving away from the current system which is prone to various loopholes, our model we believe, is robust and is the solution the current pharma supply chain industry needs at this point.

To move further, in the future we would like to try and expand the horizons of our learnings and conduct more research works to try and find even better alternatives to the current model's modules or the module as a whole, we would like to find methods which would make this model even more secure, reliable and efficient.

As the field of blockchain hasn't been here for long, there are various researches already going on about it, also various industries are learning from those researches and trying to implement this new concept into their architectures. With time the researches, would bring some new advancements in this field also there would be a lot to learn from the various new industries that have already implemented blockchain, their learnings and findings can be used to implement, extend and improve our model.

As shown in Figure 19.13, the number of accounted fraudulent cases from the year 2012 to 2016 has been plotted in a graph along with the subtotal of the total cases in those five years. The contents of the following graph have been discussed in the earlier chapters of this report; the following graph shows the number of cases per year in the duration of 2012 to 2016, from this we can estimate the increasing number of cases per year in the years to follow. It must be noted that the following graph only depicts the number of cases that have been reported. There might be uncountable other cases that may go unnoticed every year.

As per the above graph we need to find the estimate change in percentage per year to estimate the number of cases in the years to come. As shown in Table 19.3, the percentage change in number of cases has been calculated, this would aid us to find the estimate increase in the subsequent years' fraudulent cases.

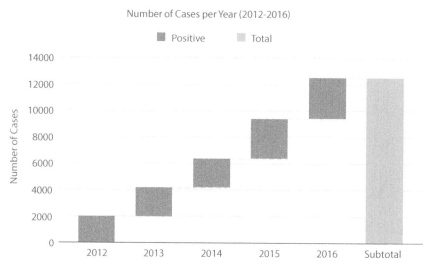

Figure 19.13 Number of cases per year (2012–2016).

Table 19.3 Number of cases vs the percentage increase in cases (2012–2016).

	Number of cases	Percentage change
2012	2018	
2013	2193	8.67
2014	2177	−0.7
2015	3002	37
2016	3147	4.8

Basis this information no concrete value can be chosen to estimate the number of fraudulent cases in the future years.

So, we take the mean of the percentage values which comes out to be 12.4425% increase per annum.

With this we can estimate the number of future cases, at a constant rate of 12.44% growth per annum. As shown in Figure 19.14, we have plotted the estimated number of cases in the years 2017 to 2021 based on the patterns followed in the previous five years.

As can be seen from the chart, the cases get doubled every five to six years if no changes are to be made in the system.

Coming to that, we cannot state exactly how much of a difference our proposed changes to the current supply chain model would make. But the effect would be positive and the decrease in the number of fraudulent cases will drastically increase with each added level of security. Take for example the inclusion of QR codes in our current model that would be a welcome addition.

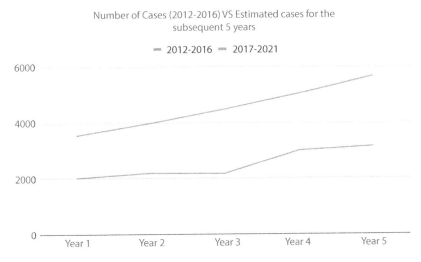

Figure 19.14 Estimated number of cases 2017–2021 basis the previous trends.

19.5 Conclusion and Future Scope

The objectives of this chapter, we believe, were achieved. It was a great learning experience; we got to learn a lot of new technologies, none of which were known to us previously. The chapter's objectives were met, the main objective was to propose a reliable model for the falling pharmaceutical supply chain industry and it was found, proposed, researched and a prototype for the model was made. The main motive of using blockchain was to eliminate all the loopholes the current industry has to offer such as fraudulent drugs, drug hoardings, expired drugs, and health of the drug (using temperature, humidity as the parameters). These aims were achieved while keeping the other aim in mind that is to propose a solution which is also cost effective, now the solution which we proposed doesn't require a lot of new infrastructure only the back-end codes need to be altered as physically the components used are more or less the same, the only financial overhead would be the implementation of QR code scanners and RFID scanners at the billing desks of the retailers, etc.

Blockchain is a new emerging and promising field, which is safe, secure and transparent, which is why it is gaining so much popularity among various industries. During the research phase of this chapter we read lot of literature available on blockchain and we can safely conclude that the future of blockchain is very vast as more and more applications of blockchain are coming into the picture with each passing day. From where we stand today, it would be safe to state that blockchain is the technology of future; it is the framework on which the future models would be based on.

Given a chance to improve our model we would surely like to work upon our proposed model and include cloud storage rather than the physical storage that we have currently used, as blockchain is a decentralized network and for it to work efficiently the data should be stored individually at different nodes. With the inclusion of cloud storage, we would like to study more about SDN and use them too in our model to strengthen the security of our model. Other than SDN and cloud storage, we would like to work with various sensors such as the humidity and temperature sensor and also the location sensors which would give us the exact location and make the system even more trustworthy with the location parameter also included. Also we'd like to include some QR code reader mechanism, we were thinking something cost effective yet efficient and the only thing that strikes our minds is our smartphones but we tried including that aspect even this time, but it wasn't possible as there were many constraints that we couldn't finalize and that was compromising with our security aspect. We would like to use the smartphones in scanning the QR code and giving the customers an easy way to check the drug they are buying in the future.

References

1. How blockchain could strengthen the pharmaceutical supply chain, 171206-163826-JC-OS, pWc 1-5, Report (online report), https://www.pwc.co.uk/healthcare/pdf/health-blockchain-supplychain-report%20v4.pdf, 2017.
2. Enescu, F.M., Bizon, N., Cirstea, A., Stirbu, C., Blockchain Technology Applied in Health, *ECAI 2018—International Conference—10th Edition*.

3. Blockchain: The next frontier for pharmaceutical supply chains, Pharma Logistics, Pharma Logistics IQ, UK, 2018 https://www.pharmalogisticsiq.com/logistics/articles/blockchain-the-next-frontier-for-pharmaceutical-supply-chains.

4. Chaum, Rivert R.L., Sherman, A.K., Blind Signatures For Untraceable Payments, Advance in Cryptology, *Proc. of Crypto 82*, Springer, Boston, pp 199–203, 1983 Back, Hashcash—A Denial of Service Counter-Measure, Http://Www.Hashcash.Org/Papers/Hashcash.Pdf, no. August, pp. 1–10, 2002.

5. Kaid, D. and Eljazzar, M.M., Applying Blockchain to Automate Installments Payment between Supply Chain Parties, *2018 14th International Computer Engineering Conference (ICENCO)*.

6. https://blockchain.wtf/edu/blockchain-101/.

7. Bocek, T., Rodrigues, B.B., Strasser, T., Stiller, B., Blockchains Everywhere—A Use-case of Blockchains in the Pharma Supply-Chain, *2017 IFIP/IEEE Symposium on Integrated Network and Service Management (IM)Florian Tschorsch, "Bitcoin and Beyond: A Technical Survey on Decentralized Digital Currencies*, https://eprint.iacr.org/2015/464.pdf.

8. Dai, W. Nakamoto, S., b-Money, an anonymous, distributed electronic cash system, http://weidai.com/bmoney.txt, 1998.

9. Pharmaceutical Counterfeiting: Endangering Public Health, Society, and the Economy: https://www.fraserinstitute.org/studies/pharmaceutical-counterfeiting-endangering-public-health-society-and-the-economy, Online Report, 1–81, 2018.

10. Blockchain in Pharma Supply Chain—Reducing Counterfeit Drugs, https://www.leewayhertz.com/blockchain-in-pharma-supply-chain/.

11. How Blockchain has Turned out to be a Game Changer in Supply Chain Management, https://www.sofocle.com/blockchain-a-game-changer-in-supply-chain-management/, Online Report [Accessed on: 13/05/2020].

12. BlockChain for Efficient Management of Pharma Supply Chain, sofocle.com, https://www.sofocle.com/how-is-blockchain-contributing-to-the-efficient-management-of-pharma-supply-chain/, Online Report [Accessed on: 13/05/2020].

13. Blockchain in Pharma Supply Chain—Reducing Counterfeit Drugs, *Path Global Health,* 112, 4, 161, 2018, https://www.leewayhertz.com/blockchain-in-pharma-supply-chain/#work.

14. https://www.pharmaceutical-journal.com/news-and-analysis/news/student-proposes-a-blockchain-based-solution-to-counterfeit-medicines/20204676.article?firstPass=false.

Index

Printed and bound by CPI Group (UK) Ltd, Croydon, CR0 4YY